ZODIAC™
STARFORCE

BY THE POWER OF ASTRA

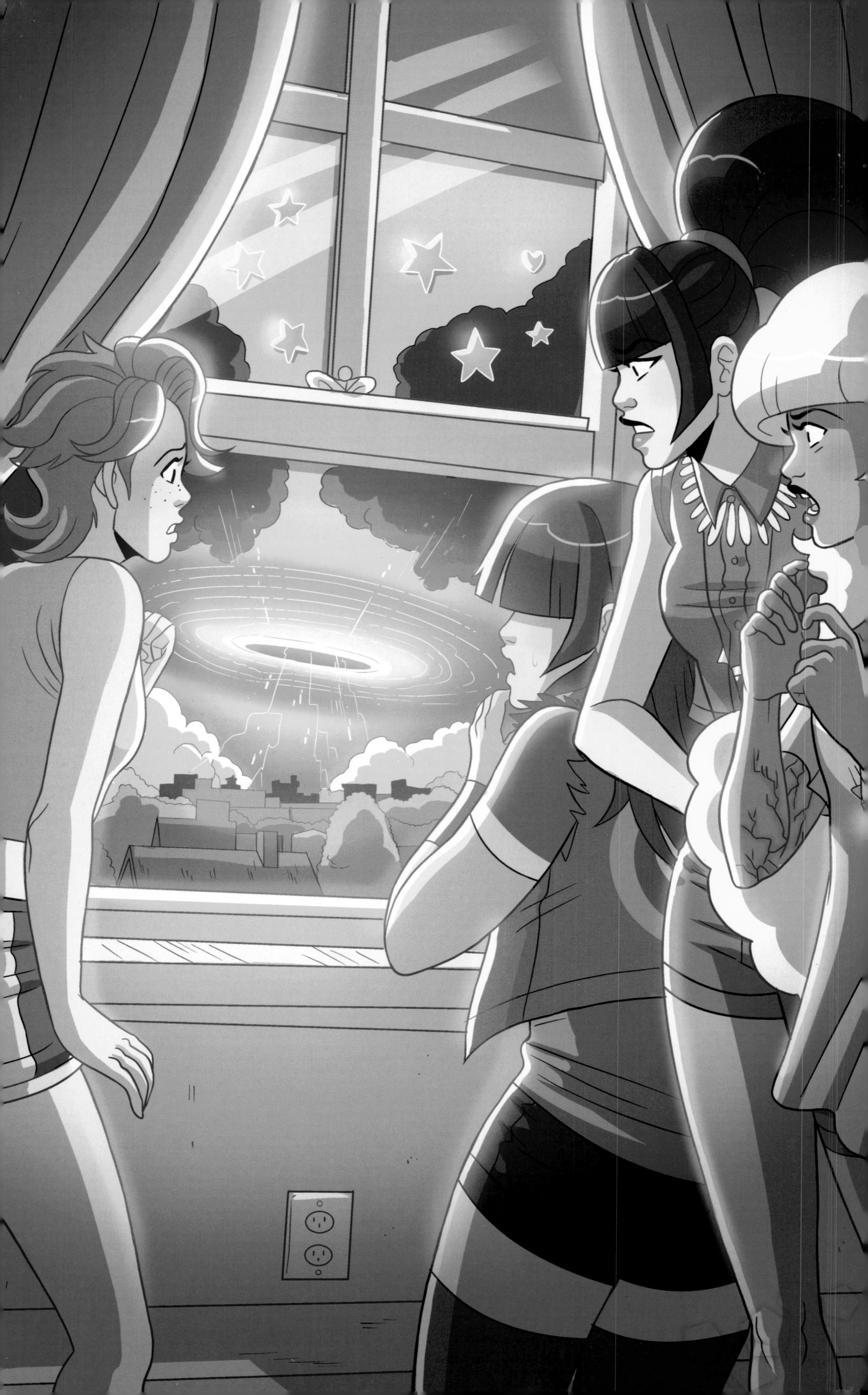

ZODIAC™
STARFORCE

BY THE POWER OF ASTRA

SCRIPT BY
KEVIN PANETTA

ART, COLORS, LETTERING, AND COVER BY
PAULINA GANUCHEAU

COLOR FLATS BY
**SAVANNA GANUCHEAU,
KRISTEN ACAMPORA,**
AND **TABBY FREEMAN**

CHAPTER BREAK ART BY
**MARGUERITE SAUVAGE,
KEVIN WADA, JACOB WYATT,
BABS TARR**

DARK HORSE BOOKS

PRESIDENT AND PUBLISHER
MIKE RICHARDSON

EDITORS
SHANTEL LaROCQUE AND **JIM GIBBONS**

ASSISTANT EDITORS
KATII O'BRIEN AND **SPENCER CUSHING**

COLLECTION DESIGNER
ETHAN KIMBERLING

DIGITAL ART TECHNICIAN
CHRISTIANNE GOUDREAU

Neil Hankerson Executive Vice President **Tom Weddle** Chief Financial Officer **Randy Stradley** Vice President of Publishing **Michael Martens** Vice President of Book Trade Sales **Matt Parkinson** Vice President of Marketing **David Scroggy** Vice President of Product Development **Dale LaFountain** Vice President of Information Technology **Cara Niece** Vice President of Production and Scheduling **Nick McWhorter** Vice President of Media Licensing **Ken Lizzi** General Counsel **Dave Marshall** Editor in Chief **Davey Estrada** Editorial Director **Scott Allie** Executive Senior Editor **Chris Warner** Senior Books Editor **Cary Grazzini** Director of Print and Development **Lia Ribacchi** Art Director **Mark Bernardi** Director of Digital Publishing **Michael Gombos** Director of International Publishing and Licensing

Published by Dark Horse Books
A division of Dark Horse Comics, Inc.
10956 SE Main Street
Milwaukie, OR 97222

First edition: May 2016
ISBN 978-1-61655-913-7

10 9 8 7 6 5 4 3
Printed in China

International Licensing: (503) 905-2377
Comic Shop Locator Service: (888) 266-4226

This volume collects and reprints the comic book series Zodiac Starforce #1–#4.

Library of Congress Cataloging-in-Publication Data

Names: Panetta, Kevin. | Ganucheau, Savanna, illustrator. | Ganucheau, Paulina, illustrator. | Sauvage, Marguerite, illustrator. | Wada, Kevin, illustrator. | Wyatt, Jacob, illustrator. | Tarr, Babs, illustrator.
Title: Zodiac Starforce : by the power of Astra / script by Kevin Panetta ; art and lettering by Paulina Ganucheau ; color assists by Savanna Ganucheau ; cover art by Paulina Ganucheau ; chapter break art by Marguerite Sauvage, Kevin Wada, Jacob Wyatt, Babs Tarr.
Description: First edition. | Milwaukie, OR : Dark Horse Books, 2016.
Identifiers: LCCN 2015039851 | ISBN 9781616559137 (paperback)
Subjects: LCSH: Graphic novels. | CYAC: Superheroes--Fiction. | Astrology--Fiction. | Magic--Fiction. | Friendship--Fiction. | Graphic novels. | BISAC: COMICS & GRAPHIC NOVELS / Fantasy.
Classification: LCC PZ7.7.P22 Zo 2016 | DDC 741.5/973--dc23

CHAPTER ONE

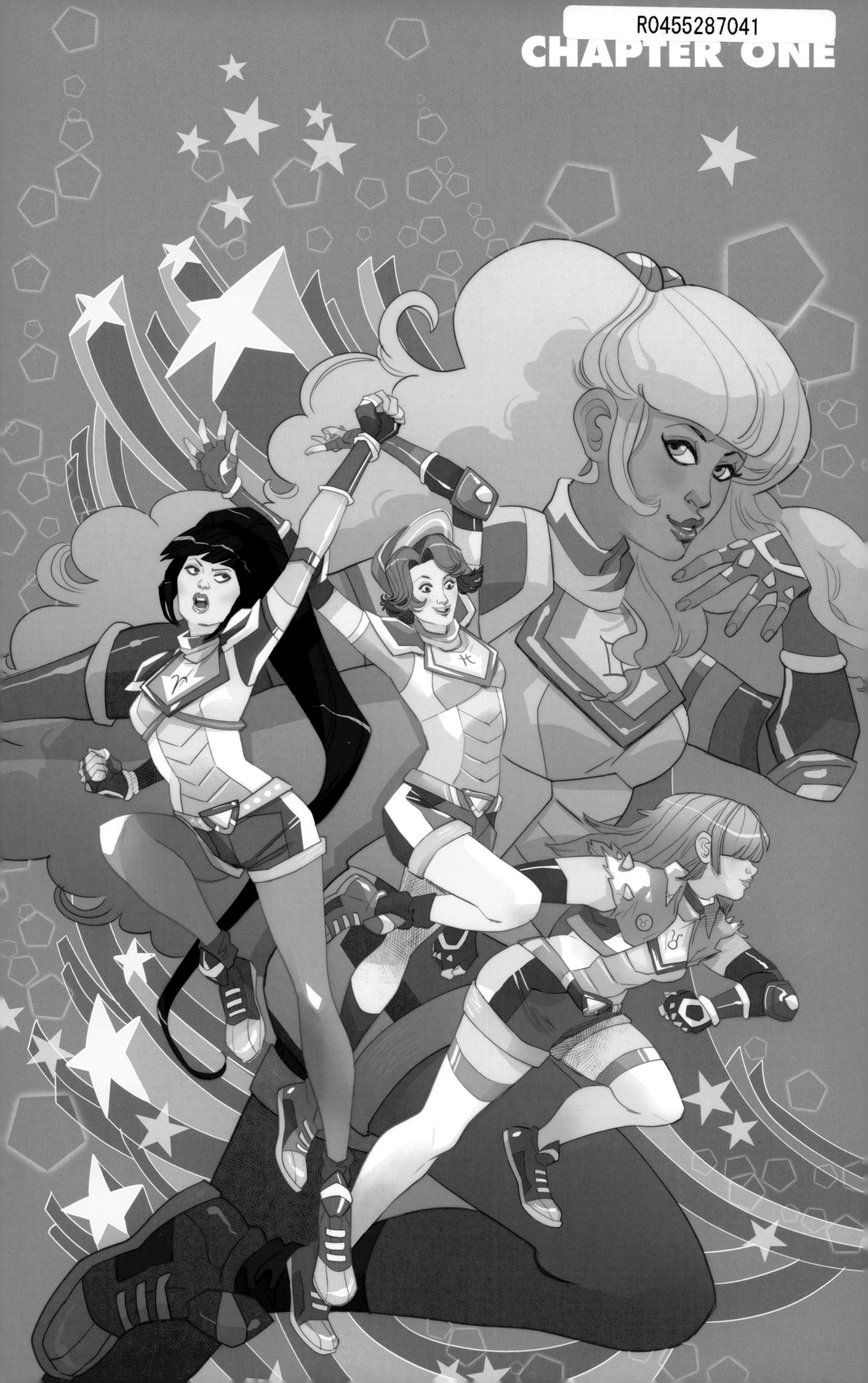

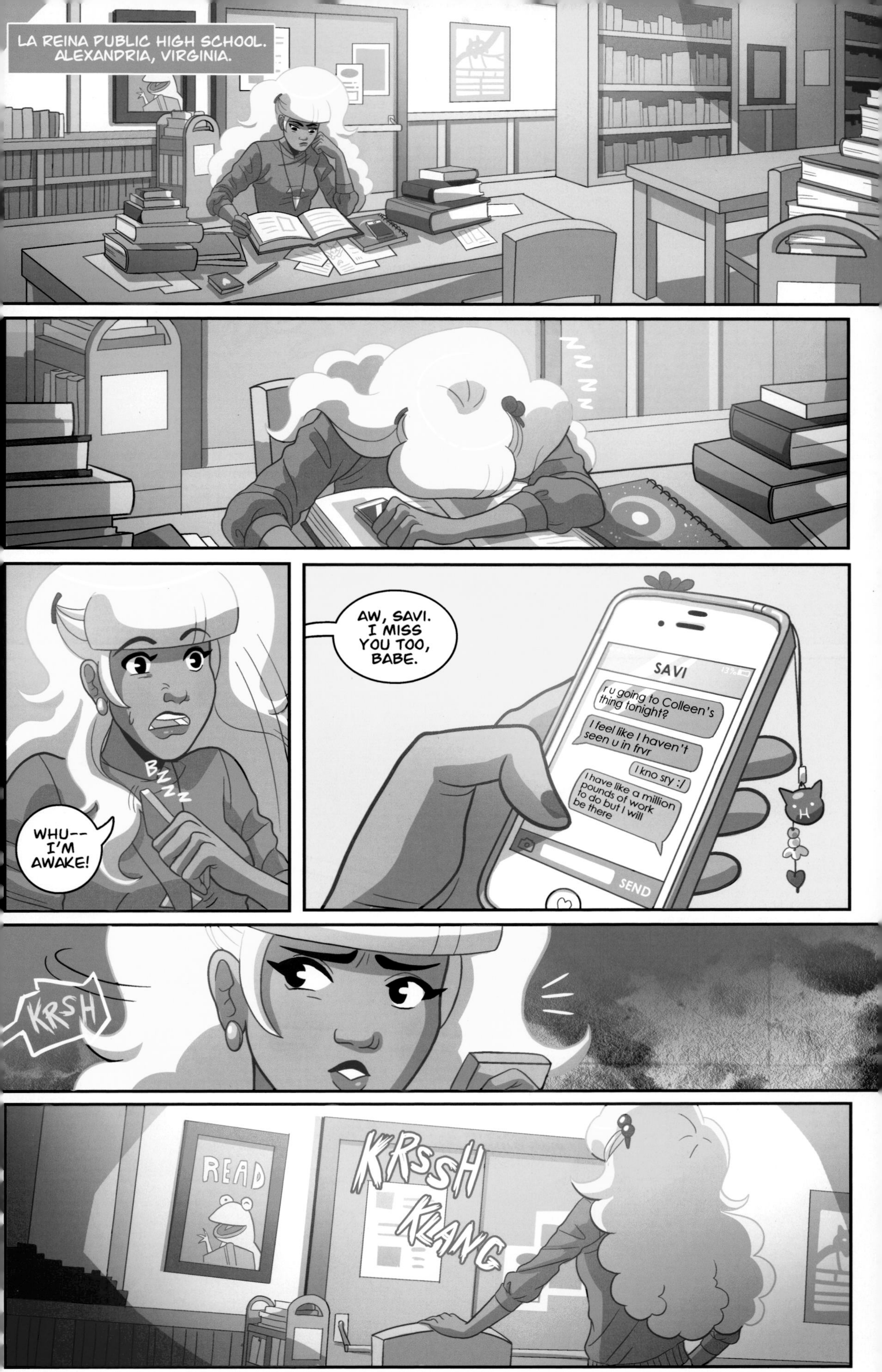

LA REINA PUBLIC HIGH SCHOOL. ALEXANDRIA, VIRGINIA.
Z Z Z Z
BZZZ
WHU-- I'M AWAKE!
AW, SAVI. I MISS YOU TOO, BABE.
SAVI
r u going to Colleen's thing tonight?
I feel like I haven't seen u in frvr
I kno sry :/
I have like a million pounds of work to do but I will be there
SEND
KRSH
READ
KRSSH
KLANG

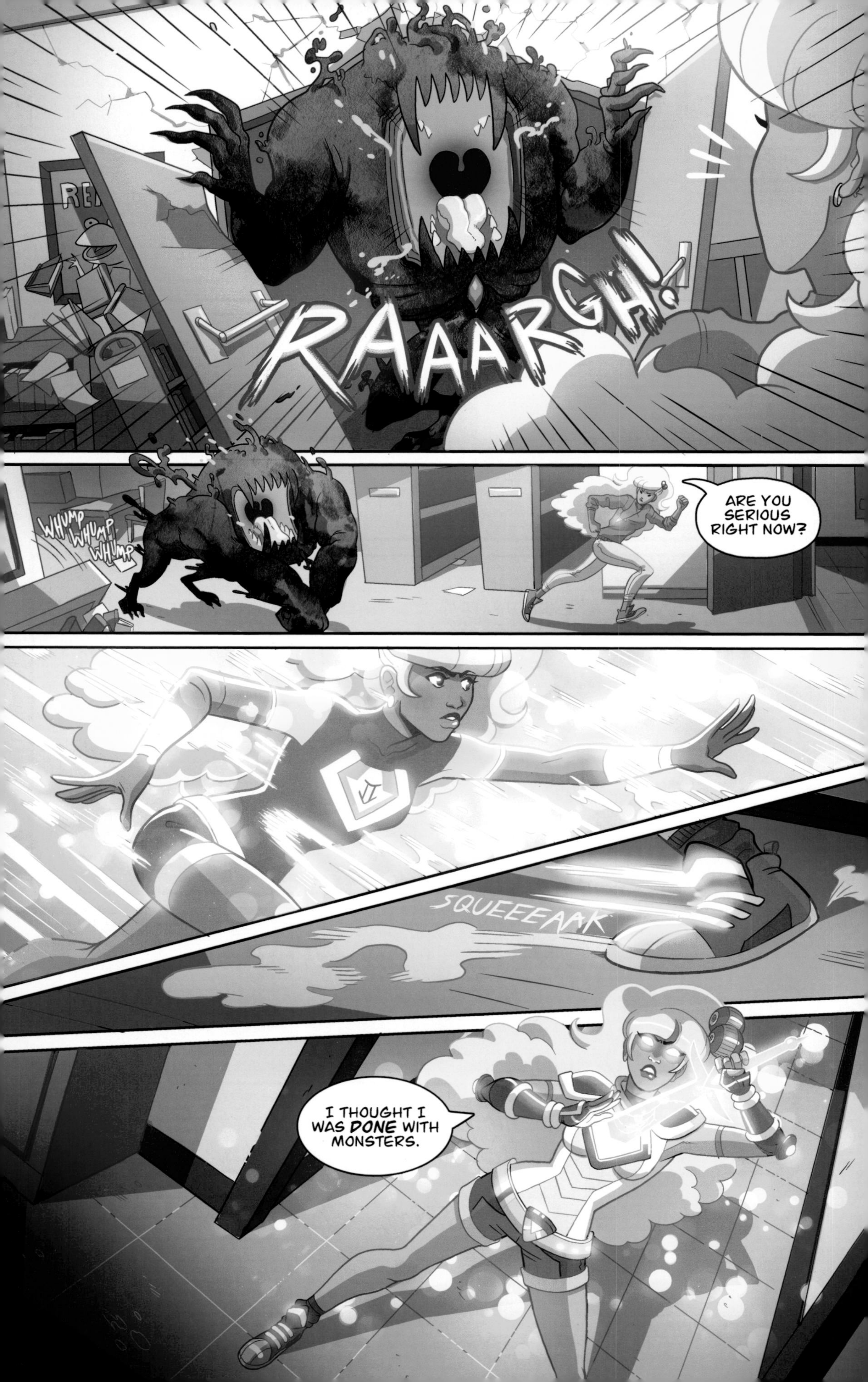
RAAARGH!
WHUMP WHUMP WHUMP
ARE YOU SERIOUS RIGHT NOW?
SQUEEEAAK
I THOUGHT I WAS **DONE** WITH MONSTERS.

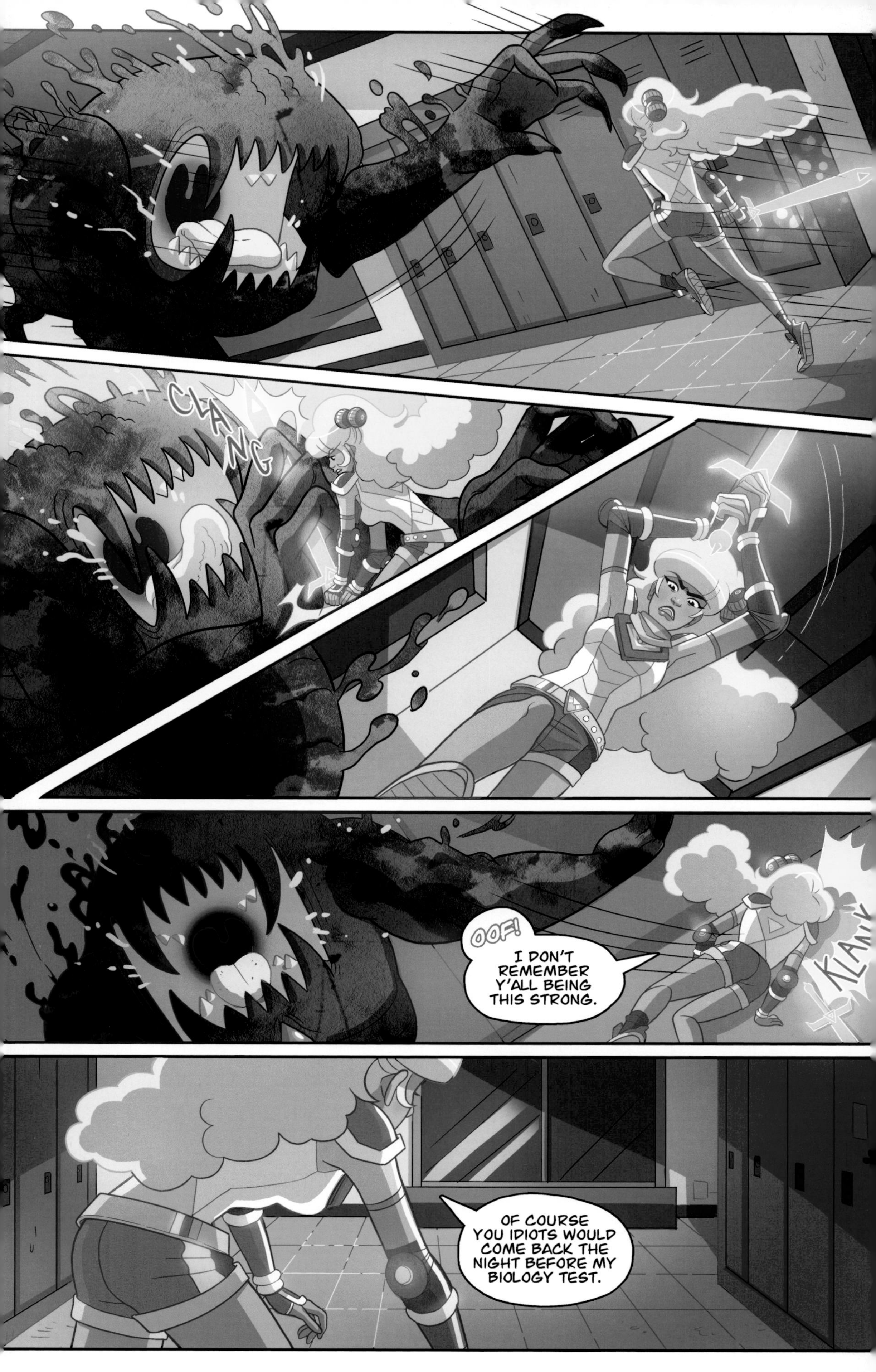
CLANG
OOF!
I DON'T REMEMBER Y'ALL BEING THIS STRONG.
KLANK
OF COURSE YOU IDIOTS WOULD COME BACK THE NIGHT BEFORE MY BIOLOGY TEST.

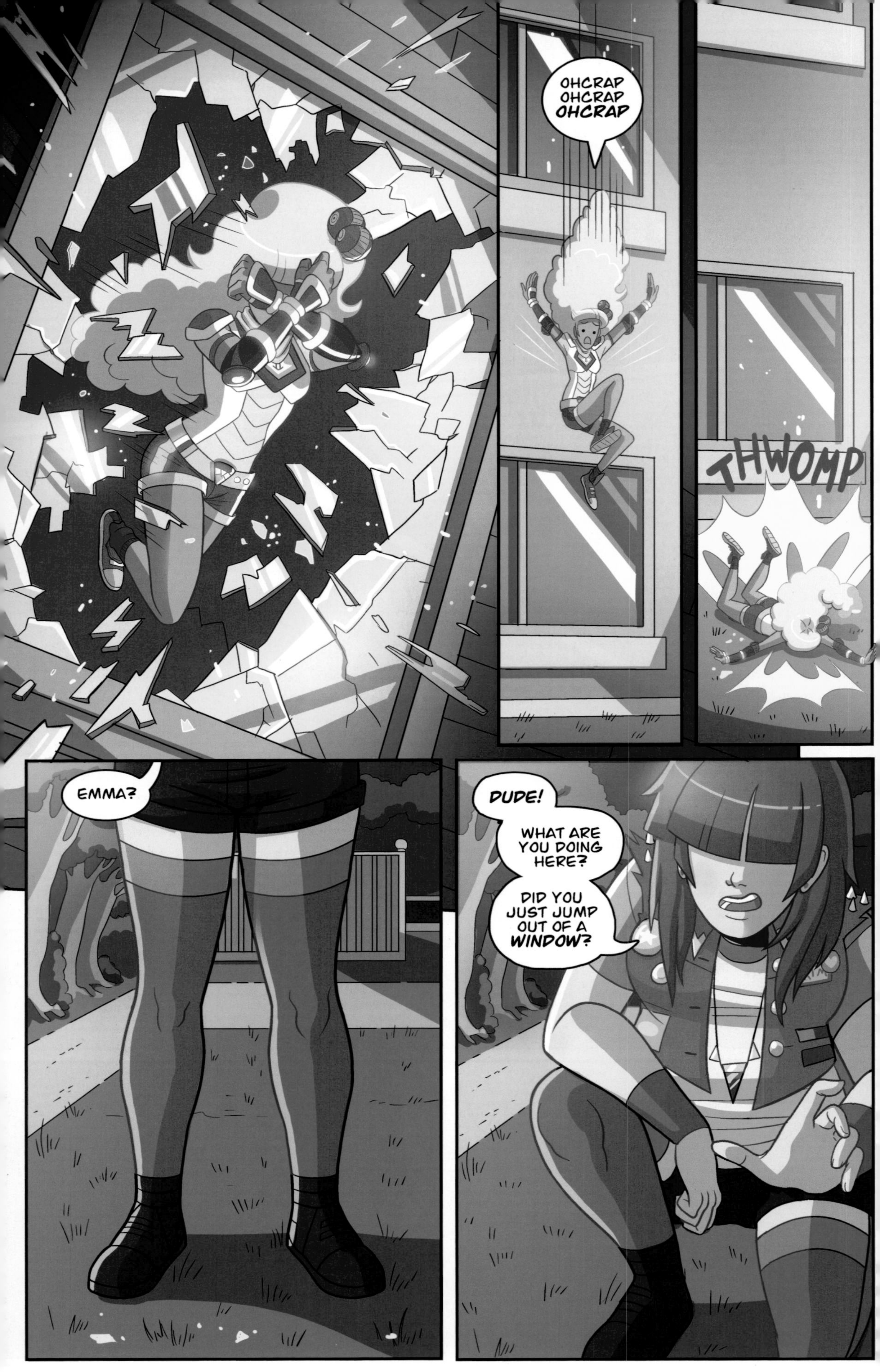
OHCRAP
OHCRAP
OHCRAP
THWOMP
EMMA?
DUDE!
WHAT ARE YOU DOING HERE?
DID YOU JUST JUMP OUT OF A WINDOW?

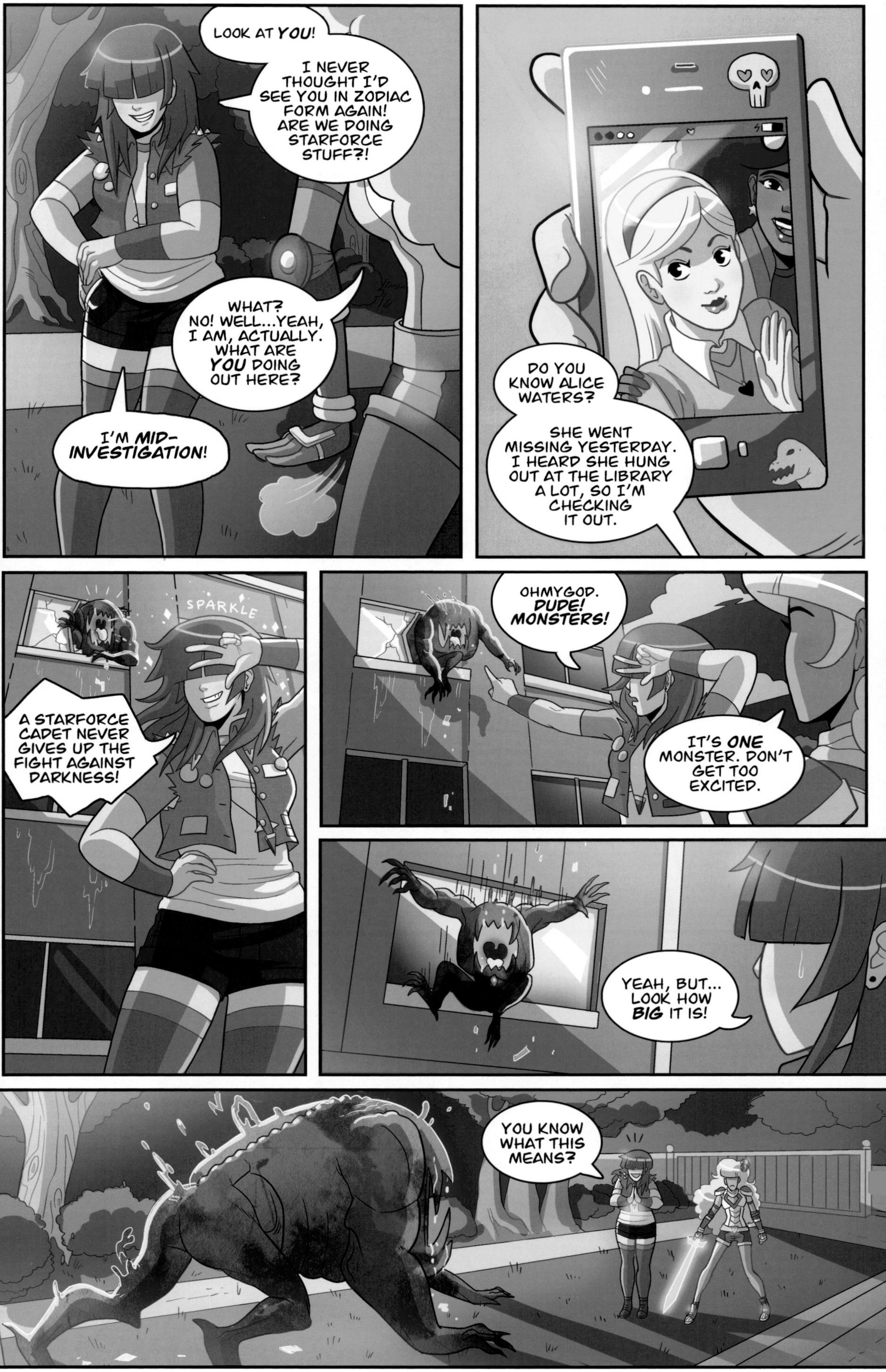
LOOK AT YOU!
I NEVER THOUGHT I'D SEE YOU IN ZODIAC FORM AGAIN! ARE WE DOING STARFORCE STUFF?!
WHAT? NO! WELL...YEAH, I AM, ACTUALLY. WHAT ARE YOU DOING OUT HERE?
I'M MID-INVESTIGATION!
DO YOU KNOW ALICE WATERS?
SHE WENT MISSING YESTERDAY. I HEARD SHE HUNG OUT AT THE LIBRARY A LOT, SO I'M CHECKING IT OUT.
SPARKLE
A STARFORCE CADET NEVER GIVES UP THE FIGHT AGAINST DARKNESS!
OHMYGOD. DUDE! MONSTERS!
IT'S ONE MONSTER. DON'T GET TOO EXCITED.
YEAH, BUT... LOOK HOW BIG IT IS!
YOU KNOW WHAT THIS MEANS?

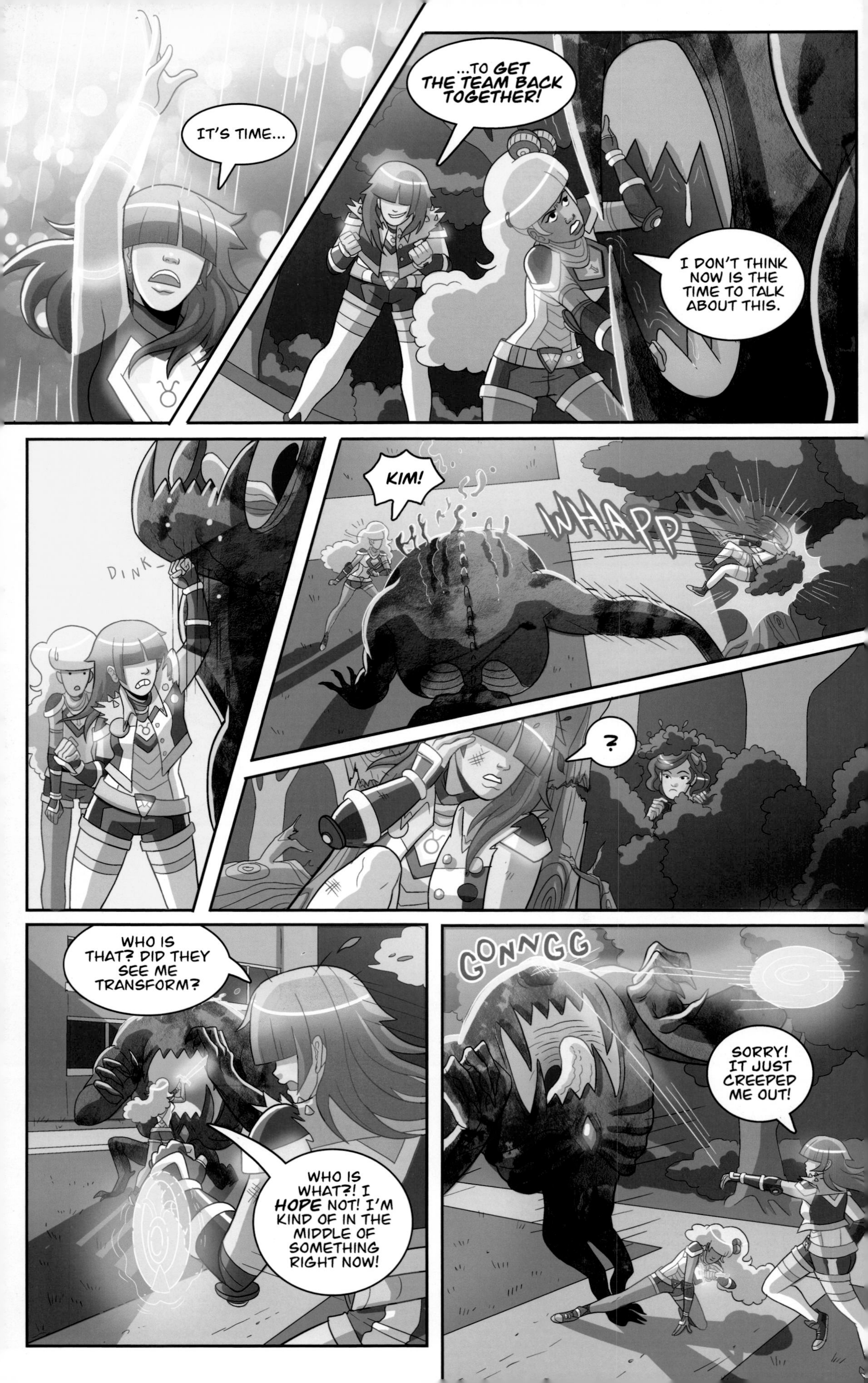
IT'S TIME...
...TO GET THE TEAM BACK TOGETHER!
I DON'T THINK NOW IS THE TIME TO TALK ABOUT THIS.
DINK
KIM!
WHAPP
?
WHO IS THAT? DID THEY SEE ME TRANSFORM?
WHO IS WHAT?! I HOPE NOT! I'M KIND OF IN THE MIDDLE OF SOMETHING RIGHT NOW!
GONNGG
SORRY! IT JUST CREEPED ME OUT!

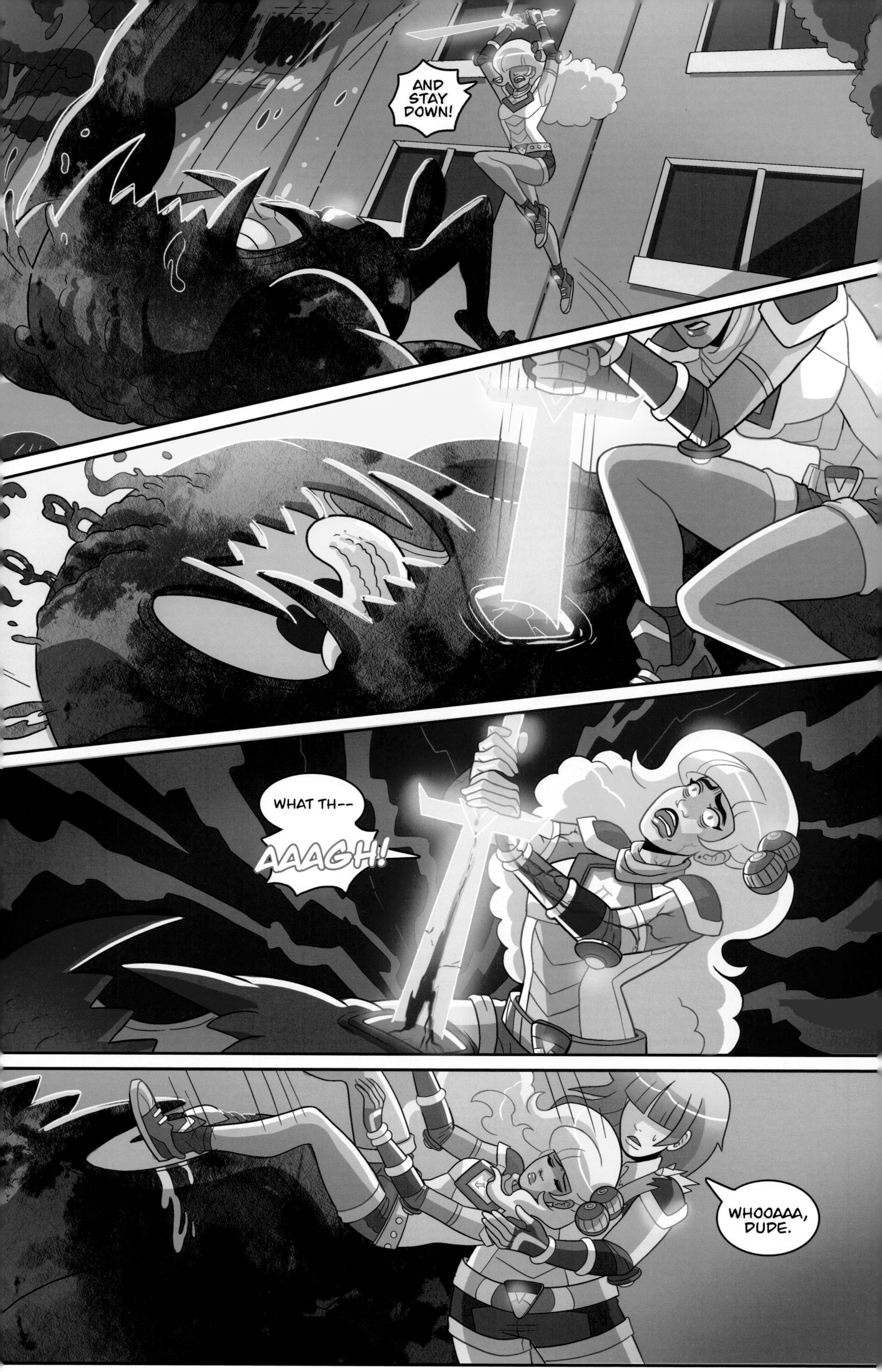
AND STAY DOWN!
WHAT TH--
AAAGH!
WHOOAAA, DUDE.

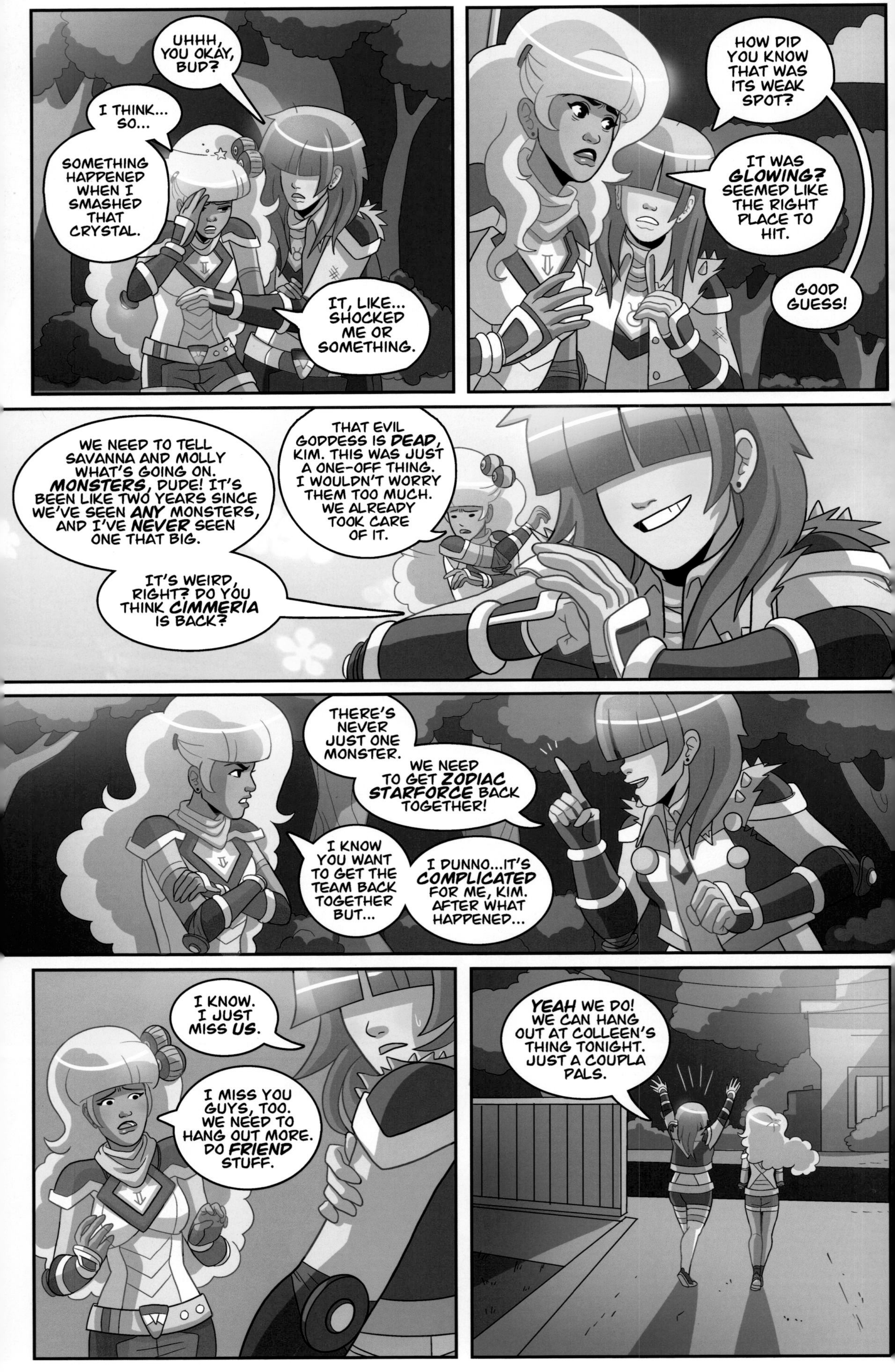
UHHH, YOU OKAY, BUD?
I THINK... SO...
SOMETHING HAPPENED WHEN I SMASHED THAT CRYSTAL.
IT, LIKE... SHOCKED ME OR SOMETHING.
HOW DID YOU KNOW THAT WAS ITS WEAK SPOT?
IT WAS GLOWING? SEEMED LIKE THE RIGHT PLACE TO HIT.
GOOD GUESS!
WE NEED TO TELL SAVANNA AND MOLLY WHAT'S GOING ON. MONSTERS, DUDE! IT'S BEEN LIKE TWO YEARS SINCE WE'VE SEEN ANY MONSTERS, AND I'VE NEVER SEEN ONE THAT BIG.
IT'S WEIRD, RIGHT? DO YOU THINK CIMMERIA IS BACK?
THAT EVIL GODDESS IS DEAD, KIM. THIS WAS JUST A ONE-OFF THING. I WOULDN'T WORRY THEM TOO MUCH. WE ALREADY TOOK CARE OF IT.
THERE'S NEVER JUST ONE MONSTER.
WE NEED TO GET ZODIAC STARFORCE BACK TOGETHER!
I KNOW YOU WANT TO GET THE TEAM BACK TOGETHER BUT...
I DUNNO...IT'S COMPLICATED FOR ME, KIM. AFTER WHAT HAPPENED...
I KNOW. I JUST MISS US.
I MISS YOU GUYS, TOO. WE NEED TO HANG OUT MORE. DO FRIEND STUFF.
YEAH WE DO! WE CAN HANG OUT AT COLLEEN'S THING TONIGHT. JUST A COUPLA PALS.

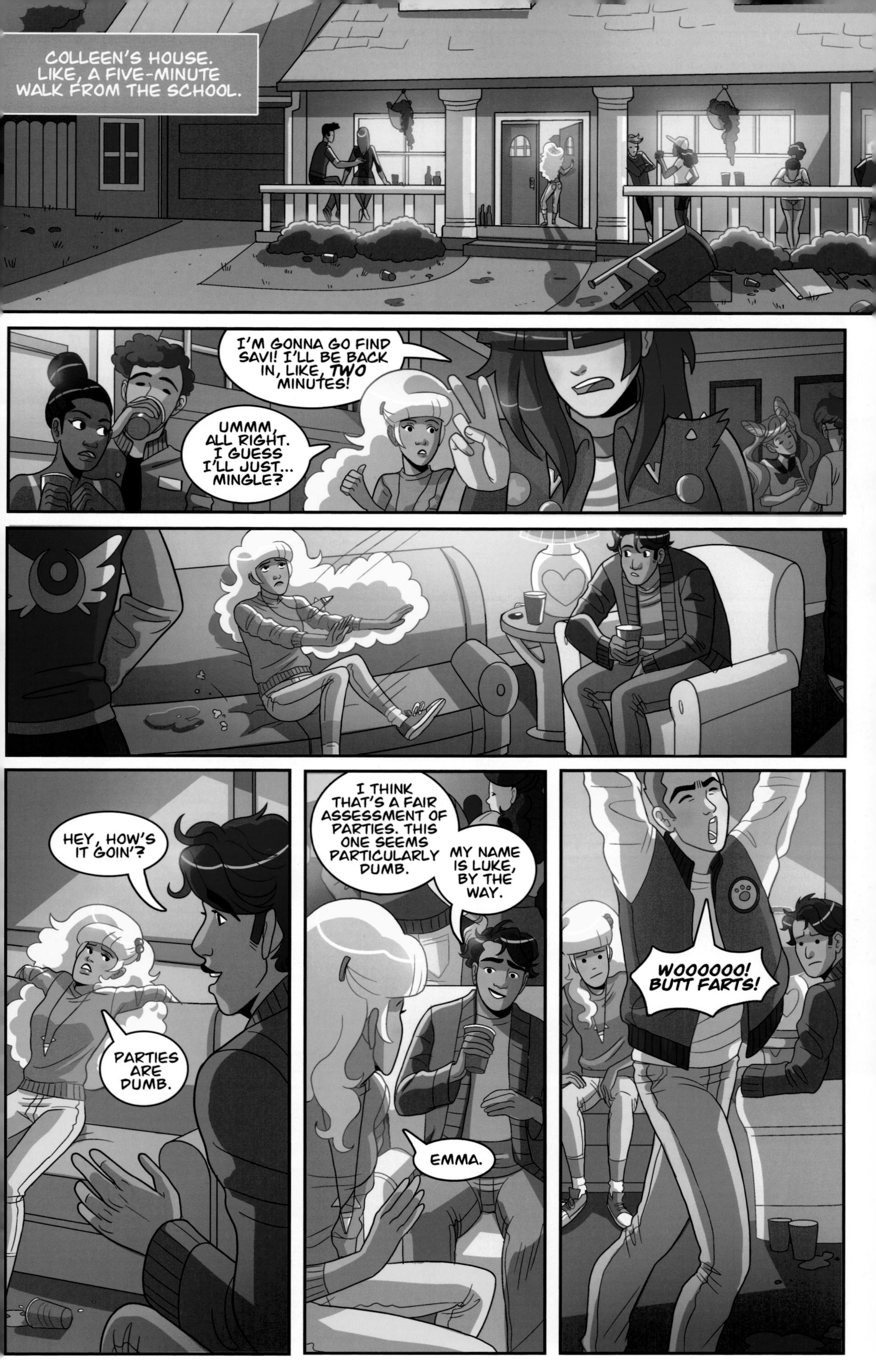

COLLEEN'S HOUSE. LIKE, A FIVE-MINUTE WALK FROM THE SCHOOL.
I'M GONNA GO FIND SAVI! I'LL BE BACK IN, LIKE, *TWO* MINUTES!
UMMM, ALL RIGHT. I GUESS I'LL JUST... MINGLE?
HEY, HOW'S IT GOIN'?
PARTIES ARE DUMB.
I THINK THAT'S A FAIR ASSESSMENT OF PARTIES. THIS ONE SEEMS PARTICULARLY DUMB.
MY NAME IS LUKE, BY THE WAY.
EMMA.
WOOOOOO! BUTT FARTS!

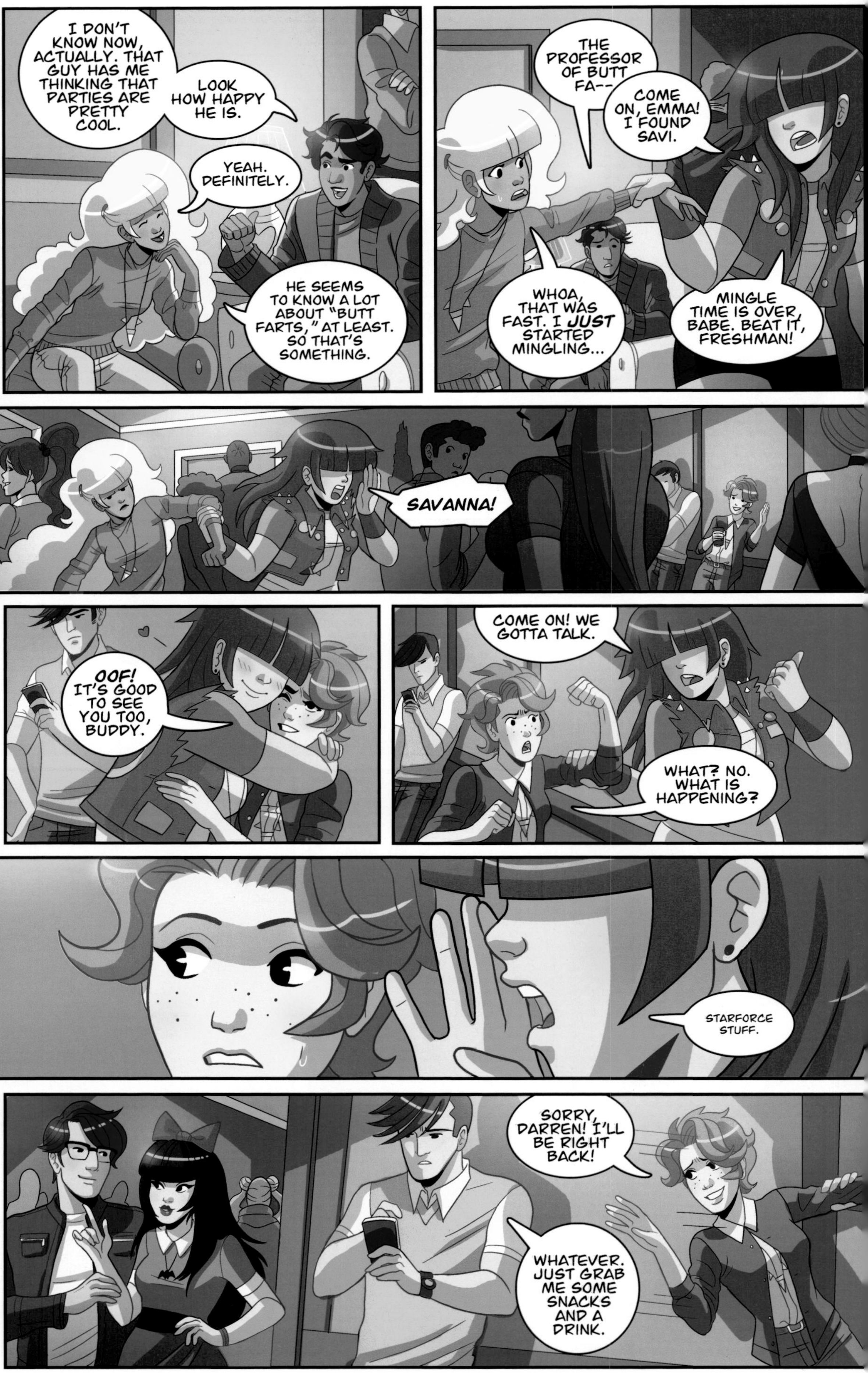
I DON'T KNOW NOW, ACTUALLY. THAT GUY HAS ME THINKING THAT PARTIES ARE PRETTY COOL.
LOOK HOW HAPPY HE IS.
YEAH. DEFINITELY.
HE SEEMS TO KNOW A LOT ABOUT "BUTT FARTS," AT LEAST. SO THAT'S SOMETHING.
THE PROFESSOR OF BUTT FA--
COME ON, EMMA! I FOUND SAVI.
WHOA, THAT WAS FAST. I JUST STARTED MINGLING...
MINGLE TIME IS OVER, BABE. BEAT IT, FRESHMAN!
SAVANNA!
OOF! IT'S GOOD TO SEE YOU TOO, BUDDY.
COME ON! WE GOTTA TALK.
WHAT? NO. WHAT IS HAPPENING?
STARFORCE STUFF.
SORRY, DARREN! I'LL BE RIGHT BACK!
WHATEVER. JUST GRAB ME SOME SNACKS AND A DRINK.

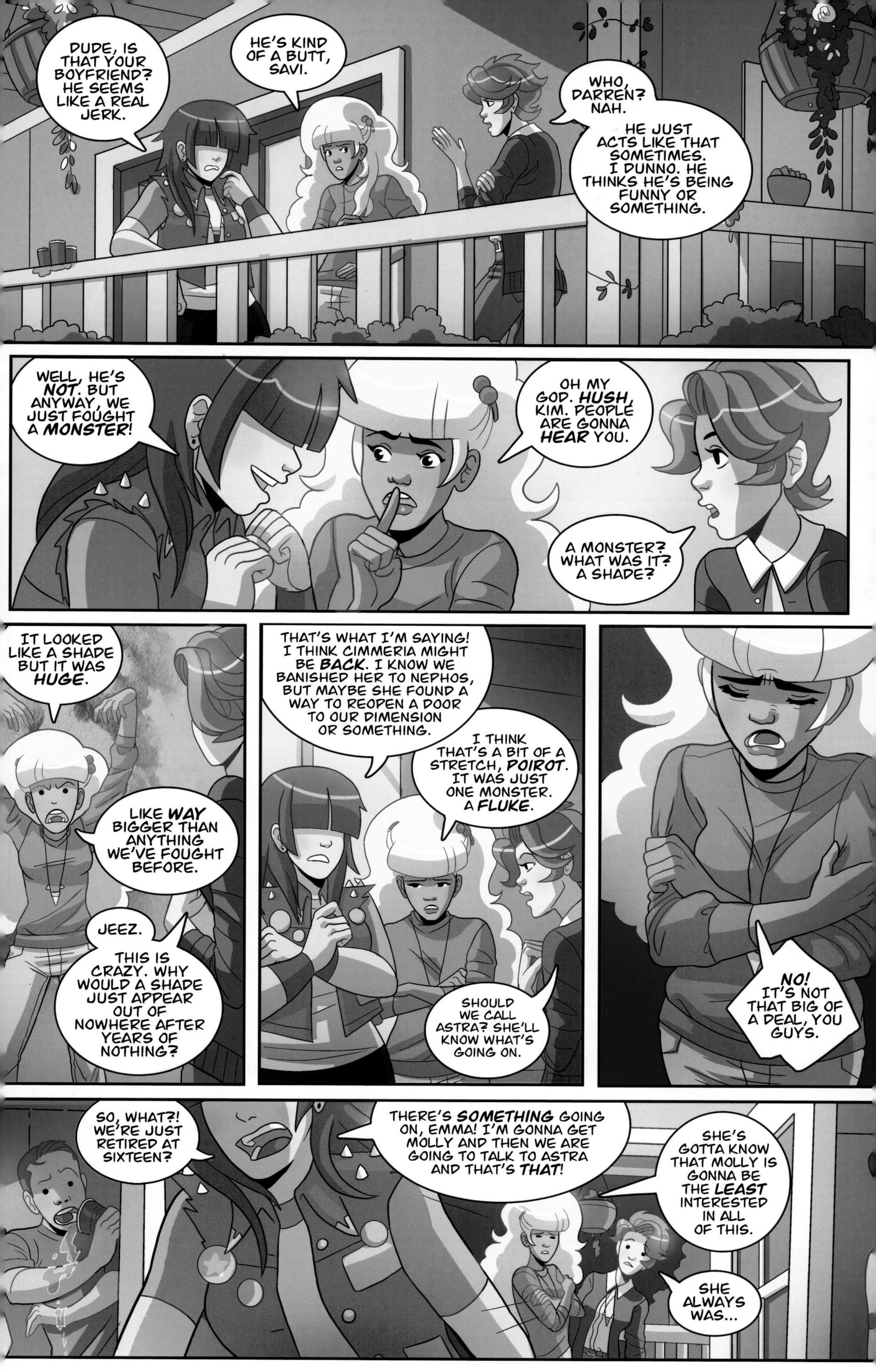
DUDE, IS THAT YOUR BOYFRIEND? HE SEEMS LIKE A REAL JERK.
HE'S KIND OF A BUTT, SAVI.
WHO, DARREN? NAH.
HE JUST ACTS LIKE THAT SOMETIMES. I DUNNO. HE THINKS HE'S BEING FUNNY OR SOMETHING.
WELL, HE'S NOT. BUT ANYWAY, WE JUST FOUGHT A MONSTER!
OH MY GOD. HUSH, KIM. PEOPLE ARE GONNA HEAR YOU.
A MONSTER? WHAT WAS IT? A SHADE?
IT LOOKED LIKE A SHADE BUT IT WAS HUGE.
LIKE WAY BIGGER THAN ANYTHING WE'VE FOUGHT BEFORE.
JEEZ.
THIS IS CRAZY. WHY WOULD A SHADE JUST APPEAR OUT OF NOWHERE AFTER YEARS OF NOTHING?
THAT'S WHAT I'M SAYING! I THINK CIMMERIA MIGHT BE BACK. I KNOW WE BANISHED HER TO NEPHOS, BUT MAYBE SHE FOUND A WAY TO REOPEN A DOOR TO OUR DIMENSION OR SOMETHING.
I THINK THAT'S A BIT OF A STRETCH, POIROT. IT WAS JUST ONE MONSTER. A FLUKE.
SHOULD WE CALL ASTRA? SHE'LL KNOW WHAT'S GOING ON.
NO! IT'S NOT THAT BIG OF A DEAL, YOU GUYS.
SO, WHAT?! WE'RE JUST RETIRED AT SIXTEEN?
THERE'S SOMETHING GOING ON, EMMA! I'M GONNA GET MOLLY AND THEN WE ARE GOING TO TALK TO ASTRA AND THAT'S THAT!
SHE'S GOTTA KNOW THAT MOLLY IS GONNA BE THE LEAST INTERESTED IN ALL OF THIS.
SHE ALWAYS WAS...

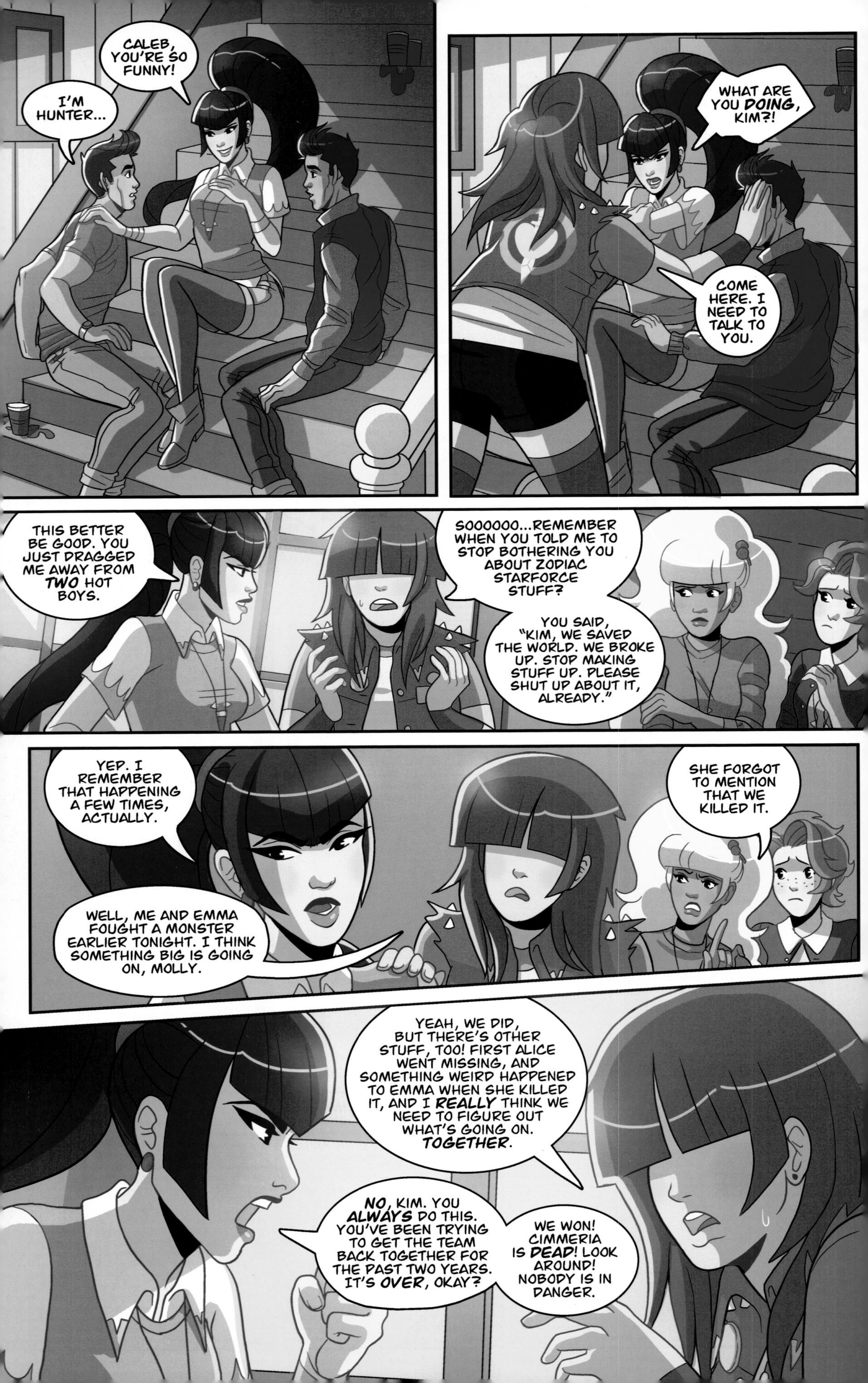
CALEB, YOU'RE SO FUNNY!
I'M HUNTER...
WHAT ARE YOU DOING, KIM?!
COME HERE. I NEED TO TALK TO YOU.
THIS BETTER BE GOOD. YOU JUST DRAGGED ME AWAY FROM TWO HOT BOYS.
SOOOOOO...REMEMBER WHEN YOU TOLD ME TO STOP BOTHERING YOU ABOUT ZODIAC STARFORCE STUFF?
YOU SAID, "KIM, WE SAVED THE WORLD. WE BROKE UP. STOP MAKING STUFF UP. PLEASE SHUT UP ABOUT IT, ALREADY."
YEP. I REMEMBER THAT HAPPENING A FEW TIMES, ACTUALLY.
WELL, ME AND EMMA FOUGHT A MONSTER EARLIER TONIGHT. I THINK SOMETHING BIG IS GOING ON, MOLLY.
SHE FORGOT TO MENTION THAT WE KILLED IT.
YEAH, WE DID, BUT THERE'S OTHER STUFF, TOO! FIRST ALICE WENT MISSING, AND SOMETHING WEIRD HAPPENED TO EMMA WHEN SHE KILLED IT, AND I REALLY THINK WE NEED TO FIGURE OUT WHAT'S GOING ON. TOGETHER.
NO, KIM. YOU ALWAYS DO THIS. YOU'VE BEEN TRYING TO GET THE TEAM BACK TOGETHER FOR THE PAST TWO YEARS. IT'S OVER, OKAY?
WE WON! CIMMERIA IS DEAD! LOOK AROUND! NOBODY IS IN DANGER.

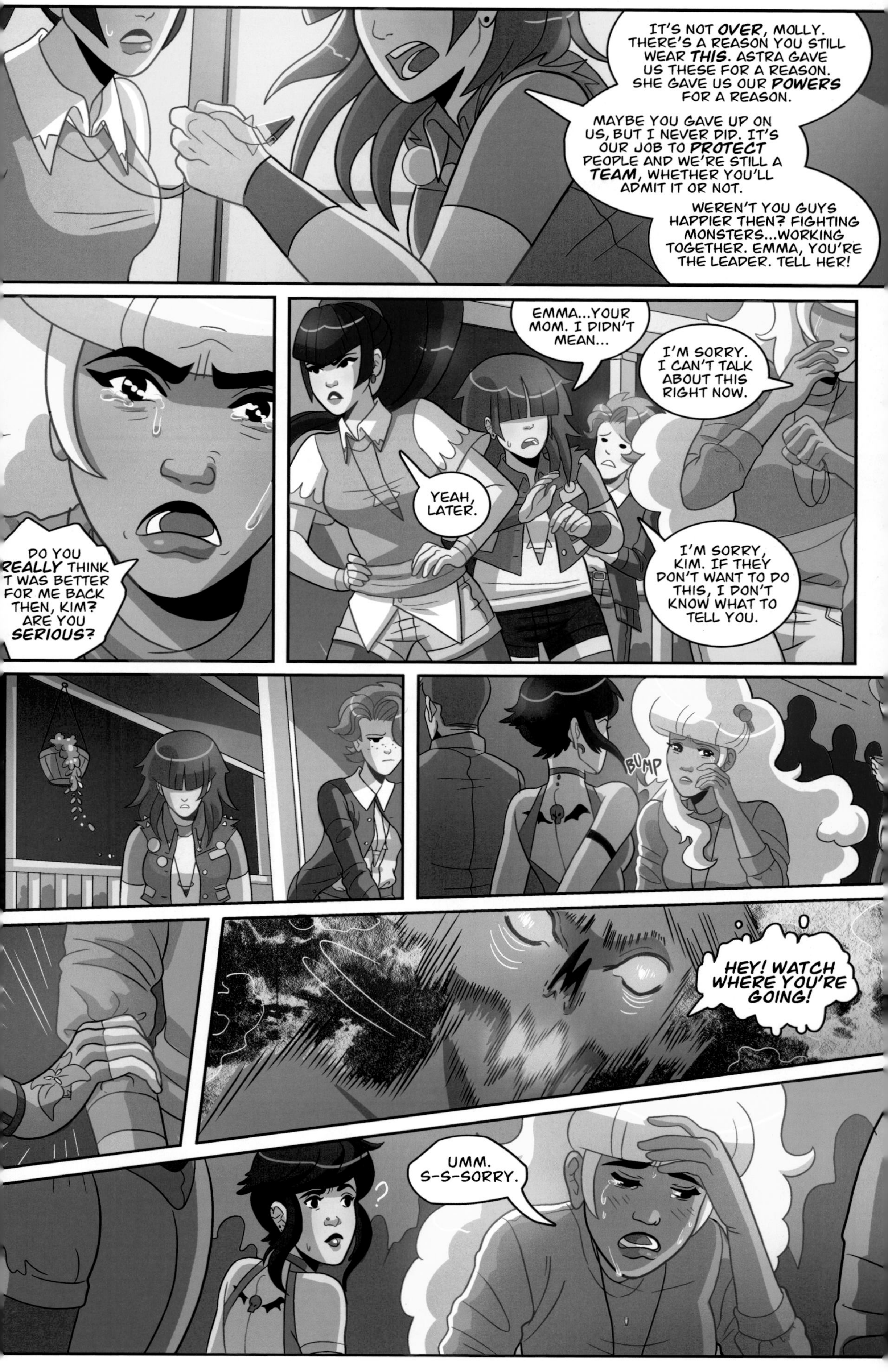
IT'S NOT OVER, MOLLY. THERE'S A REASON YOU STILL WEAR THIS. ASTRA GAVE US THESE FOR A REASON. SHE GAVE US OUR POWERS FOR A REASON.
MAYBE YOU GAVE UP ON US, BUT I NEVER DID. IT'S OUR JOB TO PROTECT PEOPLE AND WE'RE STILL A TEAM, WHETHER YOU'LL ADMIT IT OR NOT.
WEREN'T YOU GUYS HAPPIER THEN? FIGHTING MONSTERS...WORKING TOGETHER. EMMA, YOU'RE THE LEADER. TELL HER!
DO YOU REALLY THINK IT WAS BETTER FOR ME BACK THEN, KIM? ARE YOU SERIOUS?
EMMA...YOUR MOM. I DIDN'T MEAN...
I'M SORRY. I CAN'T TALK ABOUT THIS RIGHT NOW.
YEAH, LATER.
I'M SORRY, KIM. IF THEY DON'T WANT TO DO THIS, I DON'T KNOW WHAT TO TELL YOU.
BUMP
HEY! WATCH WHERE YOU'RE GOING!
UMM. S-S-SORRY.

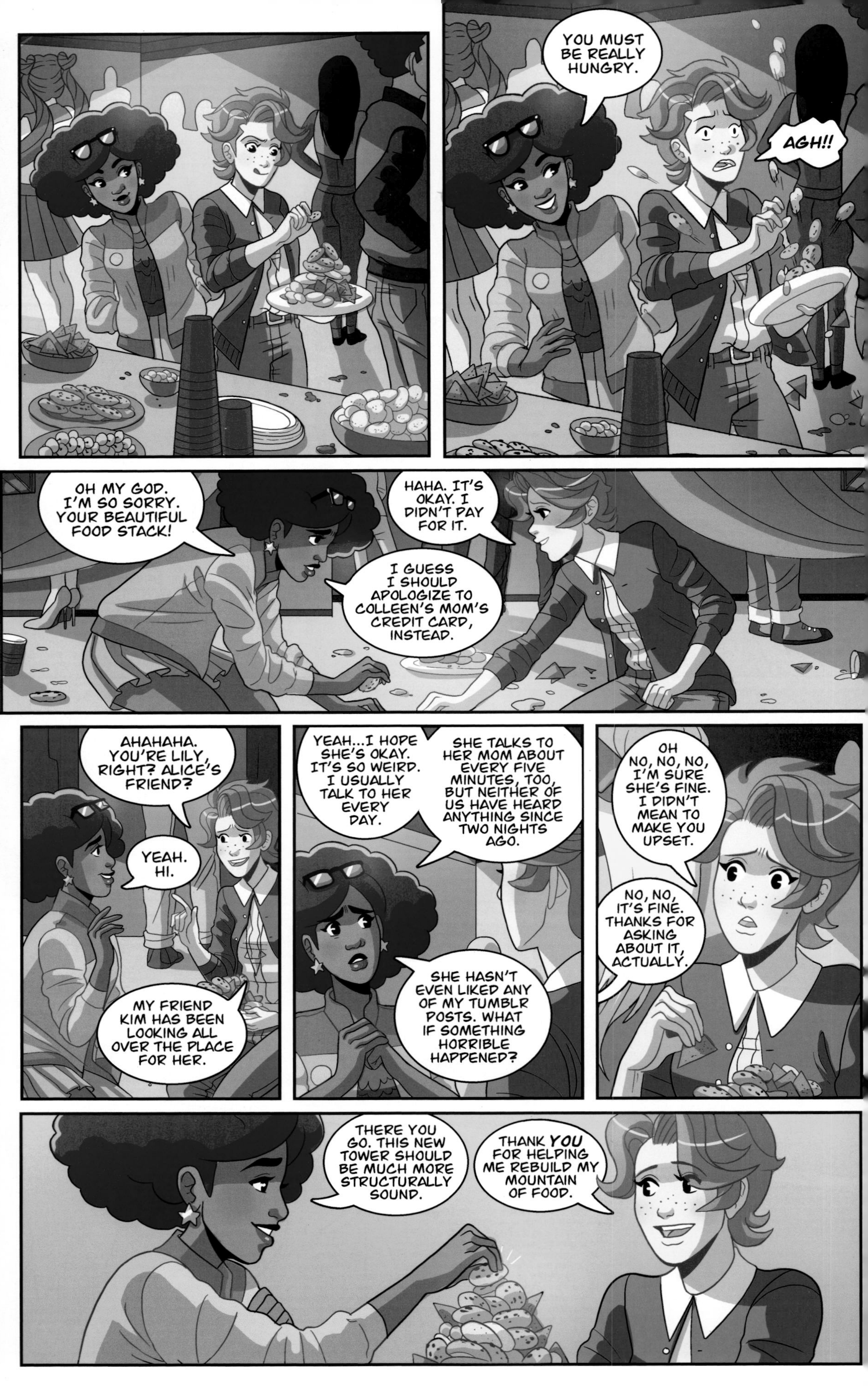
YOU MUST BE REALLY HUNGRY.
AGH!!
OH MY GOD. I'M SO SORRY. YOUR BEAUTIFUL FOOD STACK!
HAHA. IT'S OKAY. I DIDN'T PAY FOR IT.
I GUESS I SHOULD APOLOGIZE TO COLLEEN'S MOM'S CREDIT CARD, INSTEAD.
AHAHAHA. YOU'RE LILY, RIGHT? ALICE'S FRIEND?
YEAH. HI.
MY FRIEND KIM HAS BEEN LOOKING ALL OVER THE PLACE FOR HER.
YEAH...I HOPE SHE'S OKAY. IT'S SO WEIRD. I USUALLY TALK TO HER EVERY DAY.
SHE TALKS TO HER MOM ABOUT EVERY FIVE MINUTES, TOO, BUT NEITHER OF US HAVE HEARD ANYTHING SINCE TWO NIGHTS AGO.
SHE HASN'T EVEN LIKED ANY OF MY TUMBLR POSTS. WHAT IF SOMETHING HORRIBLE HAPPENED?
OH NO, NO, NO, I'M SURE SHE'S FINE. I DIDN'T MEAN TO MAKE YOU UPSET.
NO, NO, IT'S FINE. THANKS FOR ASKING ABOUT IT, ACTUALLY.
THERE YOU GO. THIS NEW TOWER SHOULD BE MUCH MORE STRUCTURALLY SOUND.
THANK *YOU* FOR HELPING ME REBUILD MY MOUNTAIN OF FOOD.

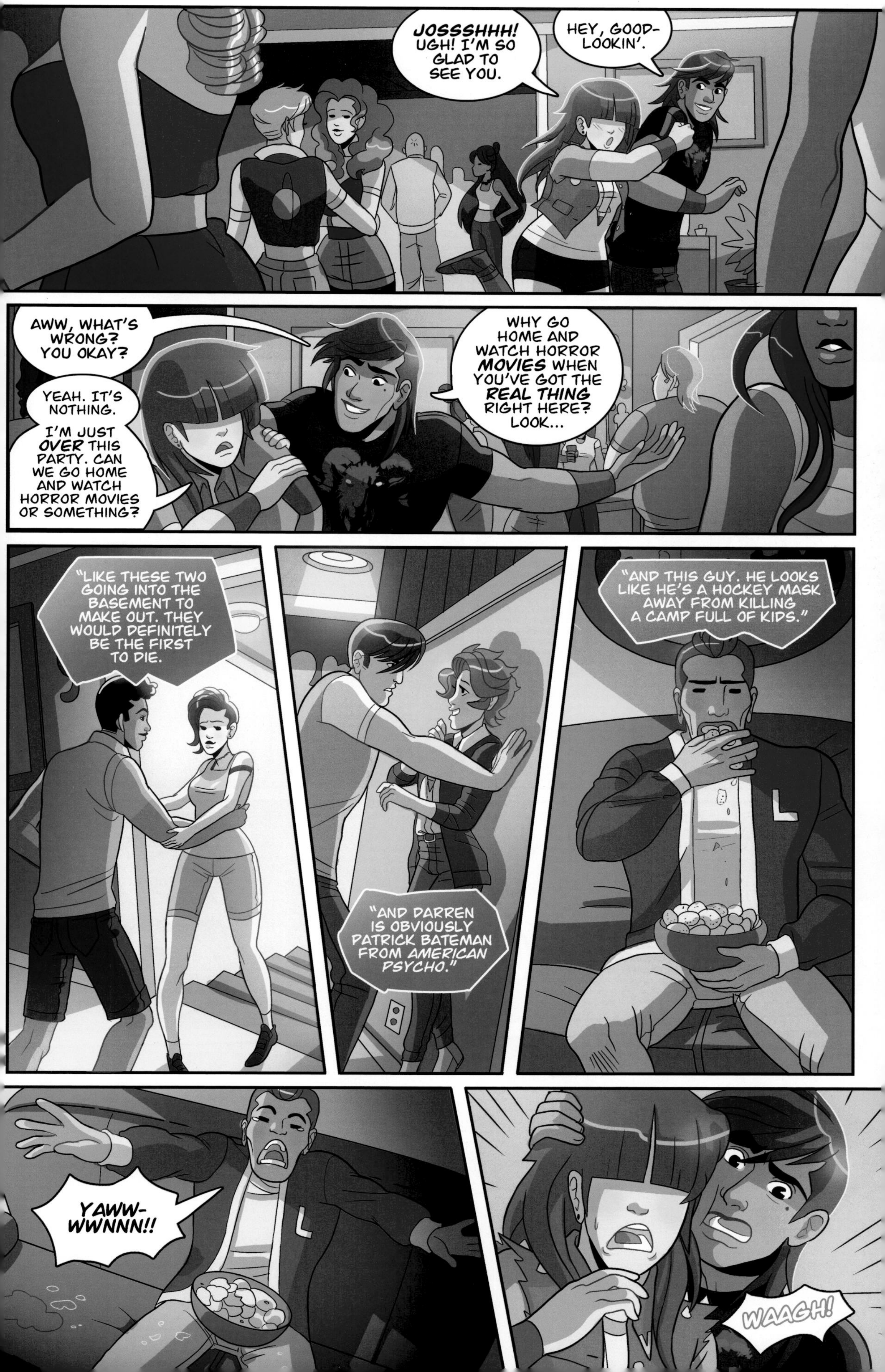
JOSSSHHH! UGH! I'M SO GLAD TO SEE YOU.
HEY, GOOD-LOOKIN'.
AWW, WHAT'S WRONG? YOU OKAY?
YEAH. IT'S NOTHING.
I'M JUST OVER THIS PARTY. CAN WE GO HOME AND WATCH HORROR MOVIES OR SOMETHING?
WHY GO HOME AND WATCH HORROR MOVIES WHEN YOU'VE GOT THE REAL THING RIGHT HERE? LOOK...
"LIKE THESE TWO GOING INTO THE BASEMENT TO MAKE OUT. THEY WOULD DEFINITELY BE THE FIRST TO DIE.
"AND DARREN IS OBVIOUSLY PATRICK BATEMAN FROM AMERICAN PSYCHO."
"AND THIS GUY. HE LOOKS LIKE HE'S A HOCKEY MASK AWAY FROM KILLING A CAMP FULL OF KIDS."
YAWW-WWNNN!!
WAAGH!

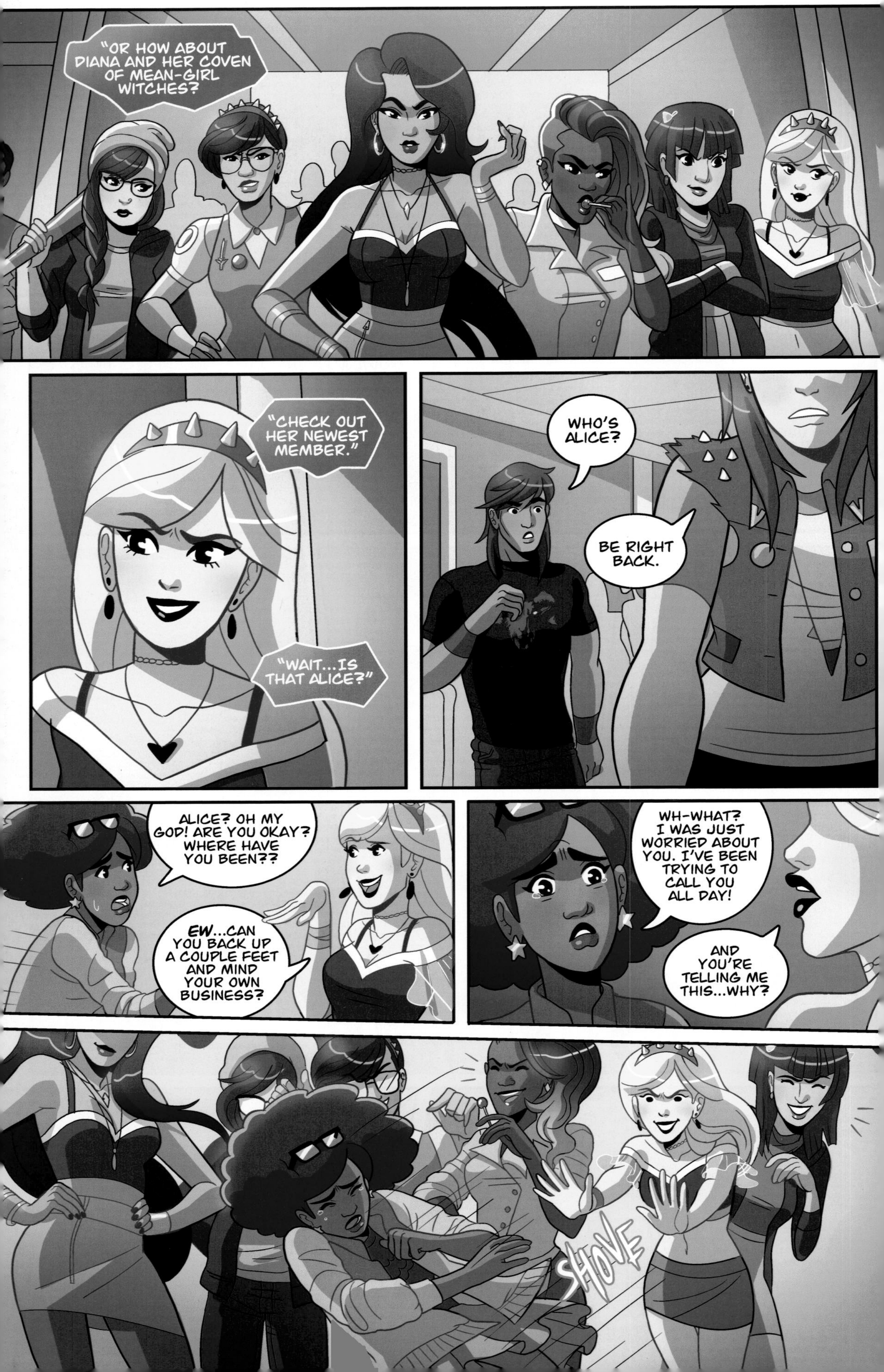
"OR HOW ABOUT DIANA AND HER COVEN OF MEAN-GIRL WITCHES?
"CHECK OUT HER NEWEST MEMBER."
"WAIT...IS THAT ALICE?"
WHO'S ALICE?
BE RIGHT BACK.
ALICE? OH MY GOD! ARE YOU OKAY? WHERE HAVE YOU BEEN??
EW...CAN YOU BACK UP A COUPLE FEET AND MIND YOUR OWN BUSINESS?
WH-WHAT? I WAS JUST WORRIED ABOUT YOU. I'VE BEEN TRYING TO CALL YOU ALL DAY!
AND YOU'RE TELLING ME THIS...WHY?
SHOVE

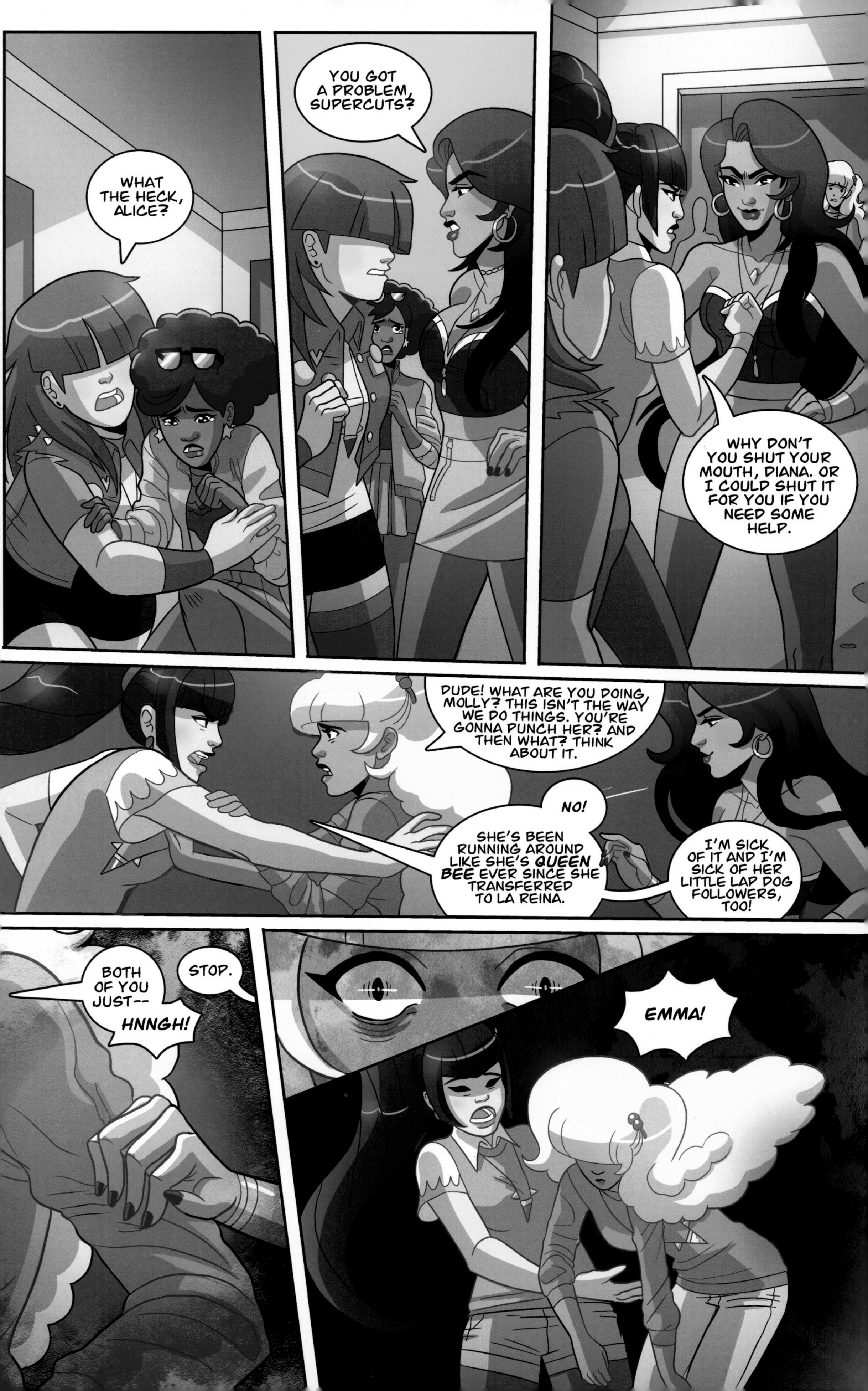
WHAT THE HECK, ALICE?
YOU GOT A PROBLEM, SUPERCUTS?
WHY DON'T YOU SHUT YOUR MOUTH, DIANA. OR I COULD SHUT IT FOR YOU IF YOU NEED SOME HELP.
DUDE! WHAT ARE YOU DOING, MOLLY? THIS ISN'T THE WAY WE DO THINGS. YOU'RE GONNA PUNCH HER? AND THEN WHAT? THINK ABOUT IT.
NO!
SHE'S BEEN RUNNING AROUND LIKE SHE'S QUEEN BEE EVER SINCE SHE TRANSFERRED TO LA REINA.
I'M SICK OF IT AND I'M SICK OF HER LITTLE LAP DOG FOLLOWERS, TOO!
BOTH OF YOU JUST-- HNNGH!
STOP.
EMMA!

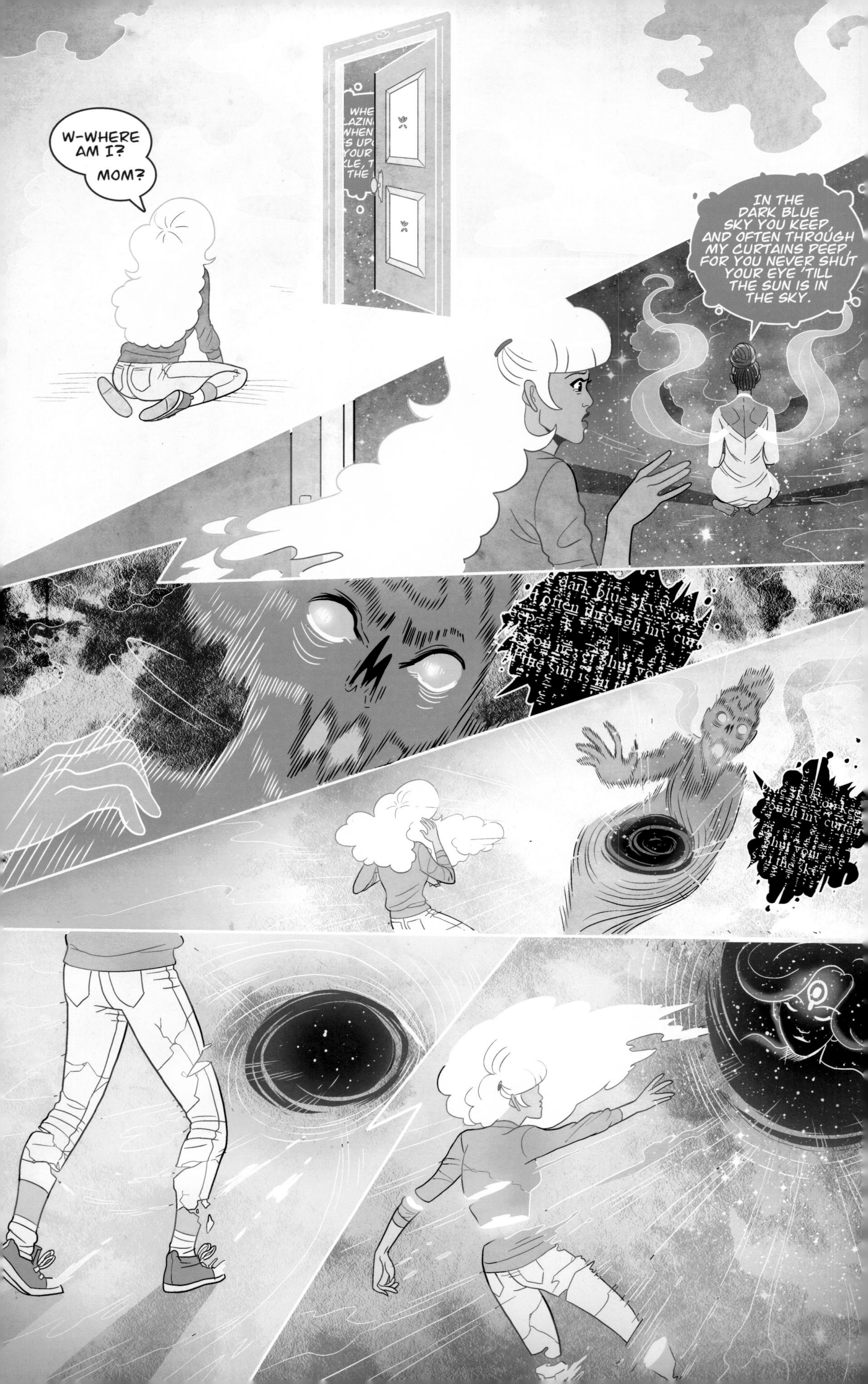
W-WHERE AM I?
MOM?
IN THE DARK BLUE SKY YOU KEEP, AND OFTEN THROUGH MY CURTAINS PEEP, FOR YOU NEVER SHUT YOUR EYE 'TILL THE SUN IS IN THE SKY.

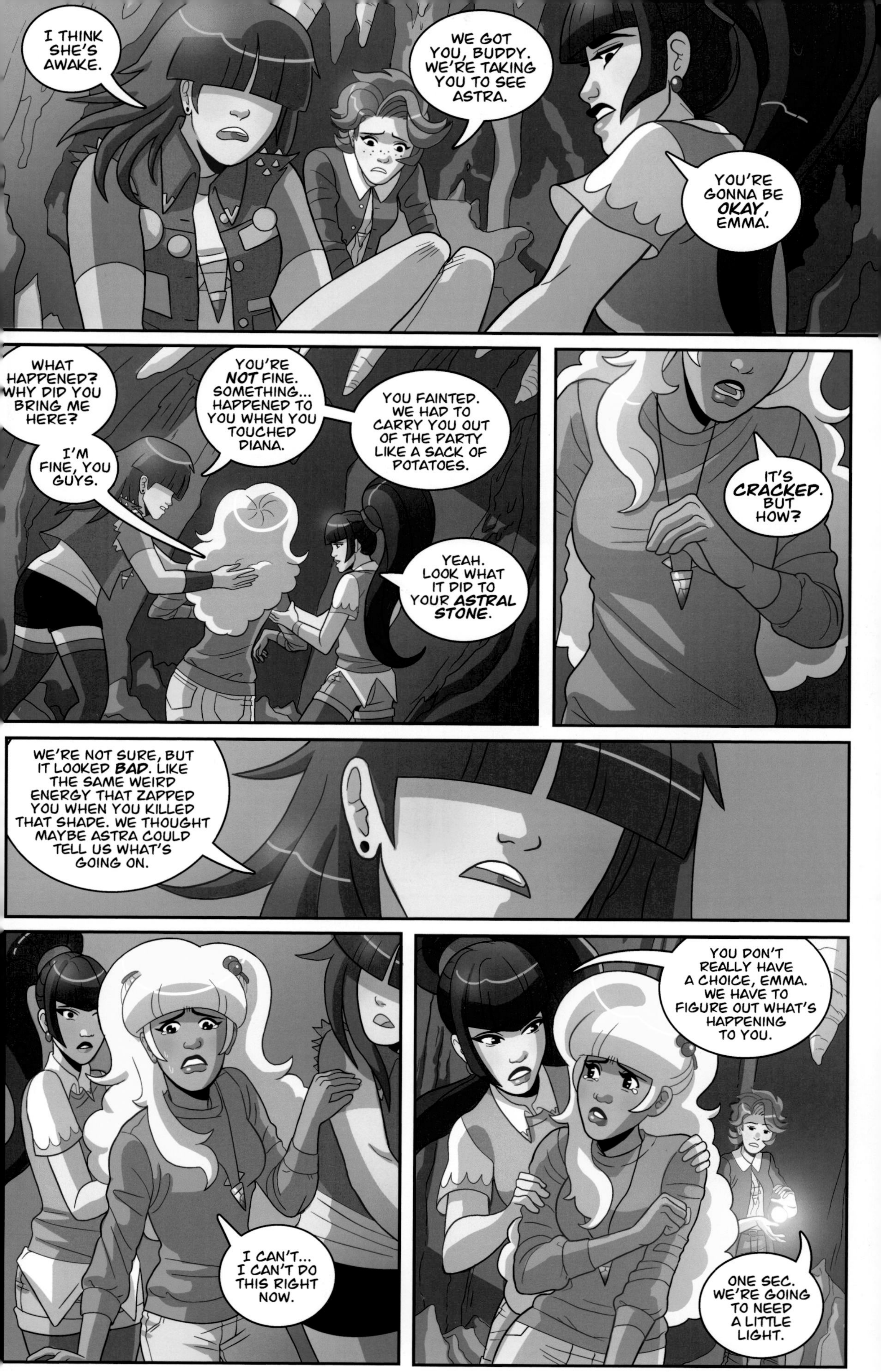
I THINK SHE'S AWAKE.
WE GOT YOU, BUDDY. WE'RE TAKING YOU TO SEE ASTRA.
YOU'RE GONNA BE OKAY, EMMA.
WHAT HAPPENED? WHY DID YOU BRING ME HERE?
I'M FINE, YOU GUYS.
YOU'RE NOT FINE. SOMETHING... HAPPENED TO YOU WHEN YOU TOUCHED DIANA.
YOU FAINTED. WE HAD TO CARRY YOU OUT OF THE PARTY LIKE A SACK OF POTATOES.
YEAH. LOOK WHAT IT DID TO YOUR ASTRAL STONE.
IT'S CRACKED. BUT HOW?
WE'RE NOT SURE, BUT IT LOOKED BAD. LIKE THE SAME WEIRD ENERGY THAT ZAPPED YOU WHEN YOU KILLED THAT SHADE. WE THOUGHT MAYBE ASTRA COULD TELL US WHAT'S GOING ON.
I CAN'T... I CAN'T DO THIS RIGHT NOW.
YOU DON'T REALLY HAVE A CHOICE, EMMA. WE HAVE TO FIGURE OUT WHAT'S HAPPENING TO YOU.
ONE SEC. WE'RE GOING TO NEED A LITTLE LIGHT.

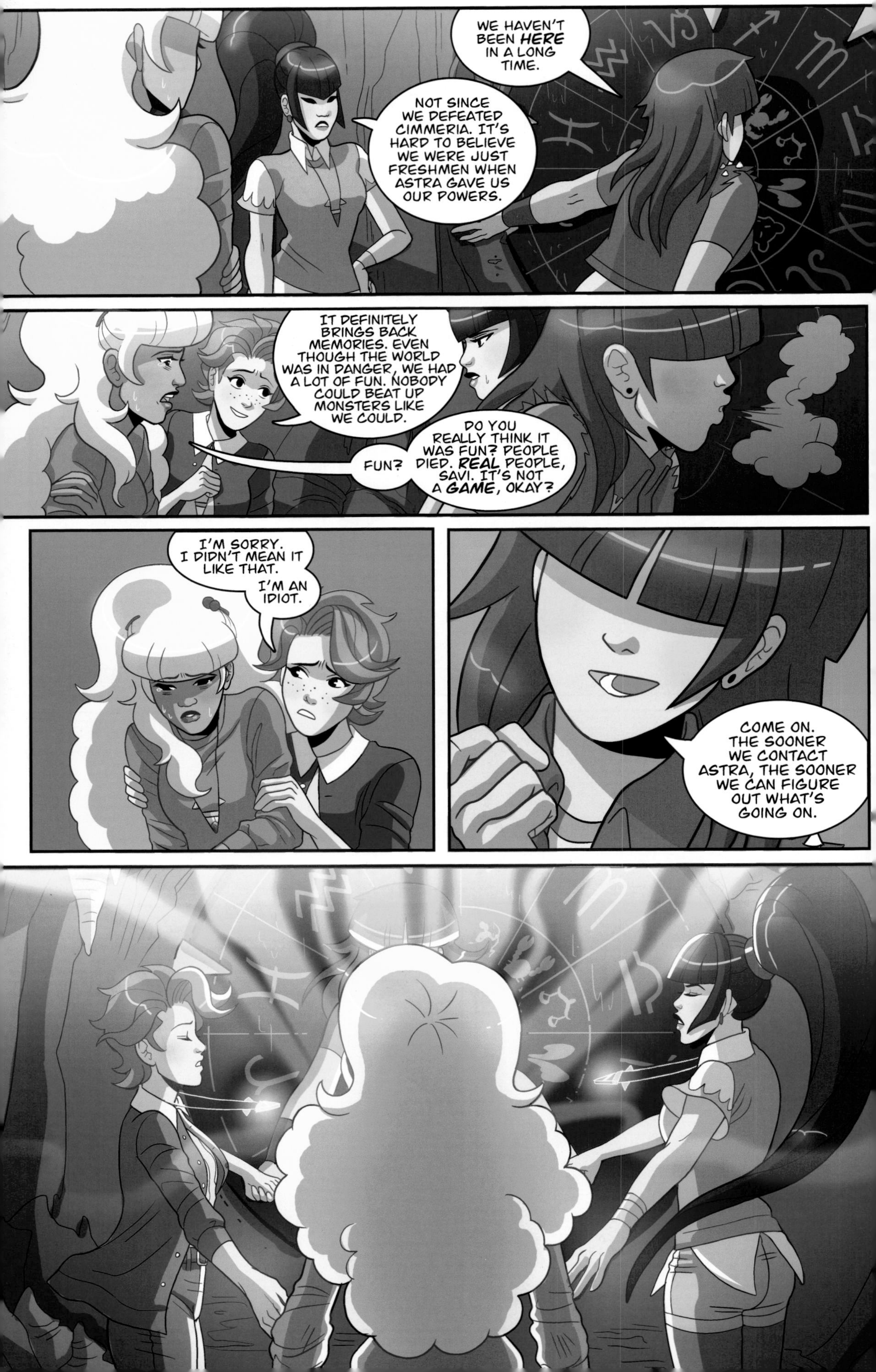
WE HAVEN'T BEEN HERE IN A LONG TIME.
NOT SINCE WE DEFEATED CIMMERIA. IT'S HARD TO BELIEVE WE WERE JUST FRESHMEN WHEN ASTRA GAVE US OUR POWERS.
IT DEFINITELY BRINGS BACK MEMORIES. EVEN THOUGH THE WORLD WAS IN DANGER, WE HAD A LOT OF FUN. NOBODY COULD BEAT UP MONSTERS LIKE WE COULD.
FUN?
DO YOU REALLY THINK IT WAS FUN? PEOPLE DIED. REAL PEOPLE, SAVI. IT'S NOT A GAME, OKAY?
I'M SORRY. I DIDN'T MEAN IT LIKE THAT.
I'M AN IDIOT.
COME ON. THE SOONER WE CONTACT ASTRA, THE SOONER WE CAN FIGURE OUT WHAT'S GOING ON.

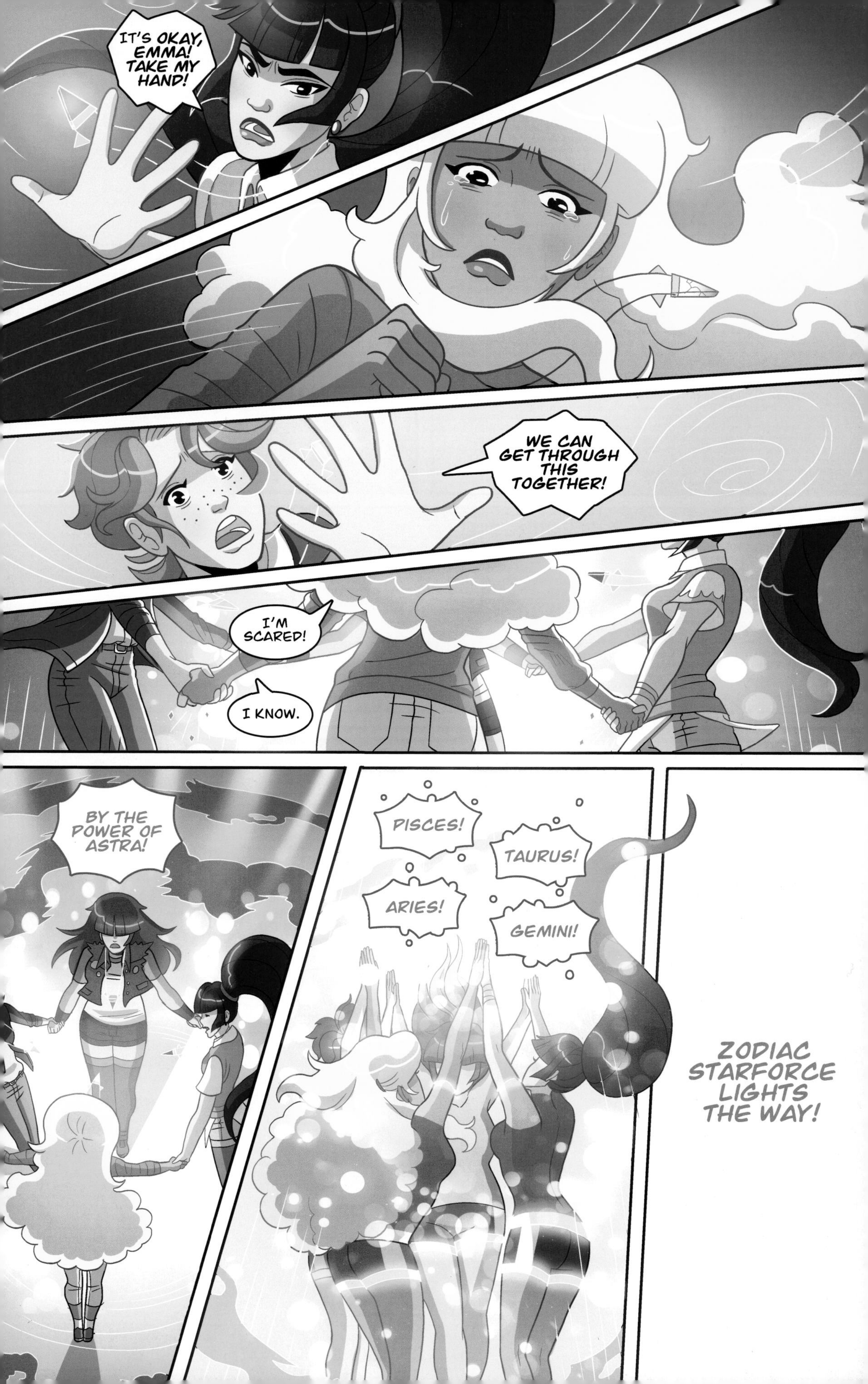
IT'S OKAY, EMMA! TAKE MY HAND!
WE CAN GET THROUGH THIS TOGETHER!
I'M SCARED!
I KNOW.
BY THE POWER OF ASTRA!
PISCES!
TAURUS!
ARIES!
GEMINI!
ZODIAC STARFORCE LIGHTS THE WAY!

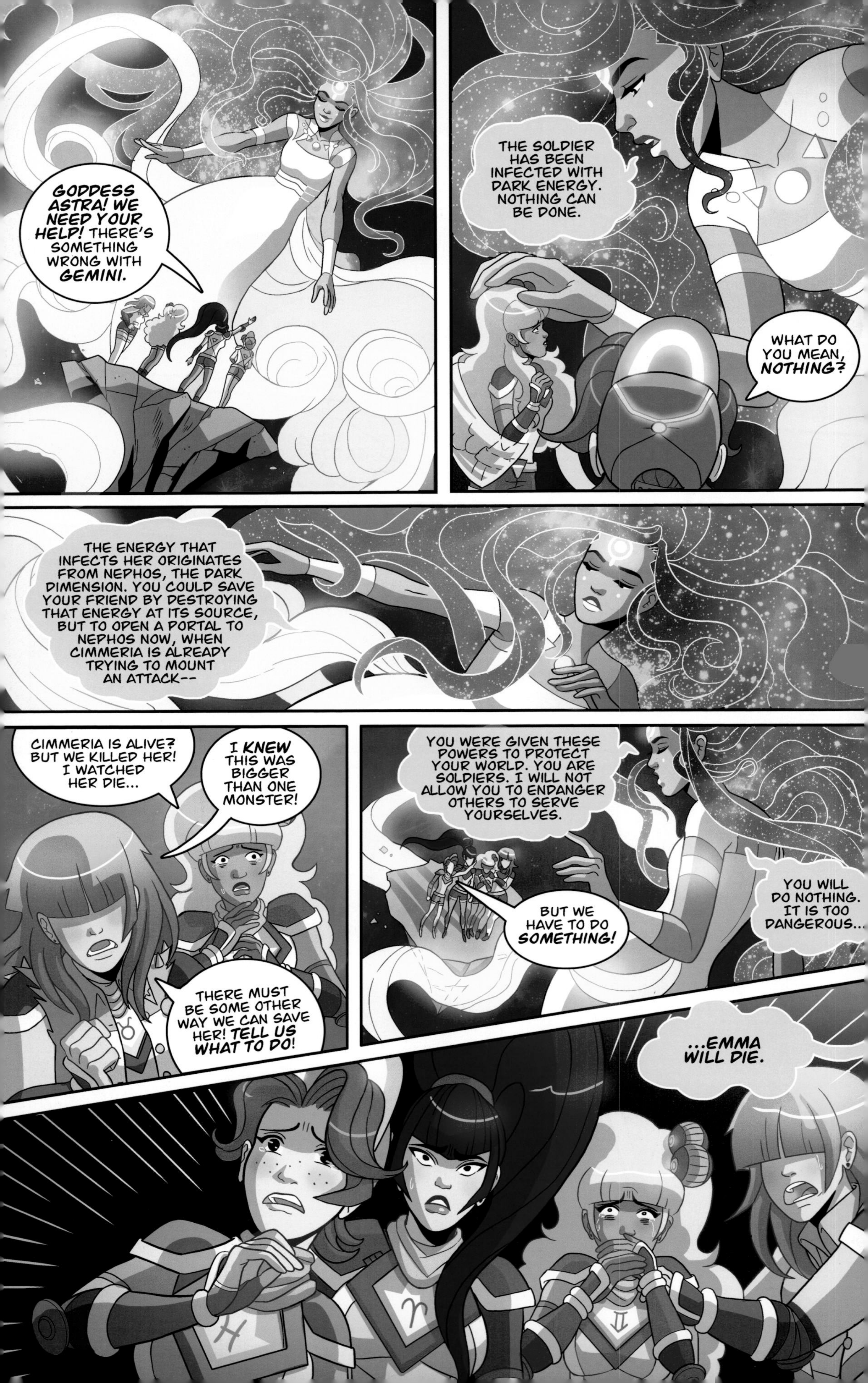
GODDESS ASTRA! WE NEED YOUR HELP! THERE'S SOMETHING WRONG WITH GEMINI.
THE SOLDIER HAS BEEN INFECTED WITH DARK ENERGY. NOTHING CAN BE DONE.
WHAT DO YOU MEAN, NOTHING?
THE ENERGY THAT INFECTS HER ORIGINATES FROM NEPHOS, THE DARK DIMENSION. YOU COULD SAVE YOUR FRIEND BY DESTROYING THAT ENERGY AT ITS SOURCE, BUT TO OPEN A PORTAL TO NEPHOS NOW, WHEN CIMMERIA IS ALREADY TRYING TO MOUNT AN ATTACK--
CIMMERIA IS ALIVE? BUT WE KILLED HER! I WATCHED HER DIE...
I KNEW THIS WAS BIGGER THAN ONE MONSTER!
THERE MUST BE SOME OTHER WAY WE CAN SAVE HER! TELL US WHAT TO DO!
YOU WERE GIVEN THESE POWERS TO PROTECT YOUR WORLD. YOU ARE SOLDIERS. I WILL NOT ALLOW YOU TO ENDANGER OTHERS TO SERVE YOURSELVES.
BUT WE HAVE TO DO SOMETHING!
YOU WILL DO NOTHING. IT IS TOO DANGEROUS...
...EMMA WILL DIE.

CHAPTER TWO

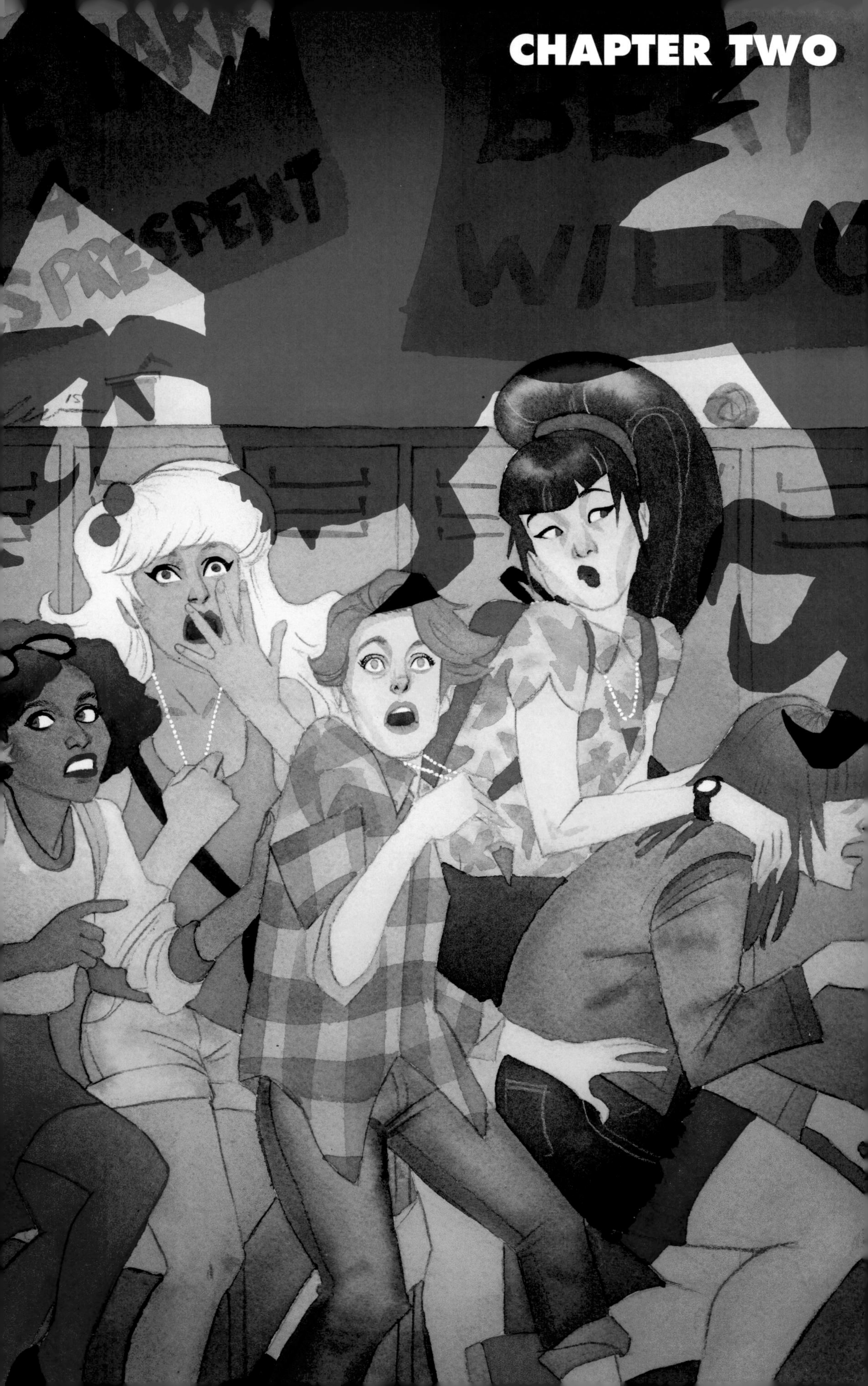

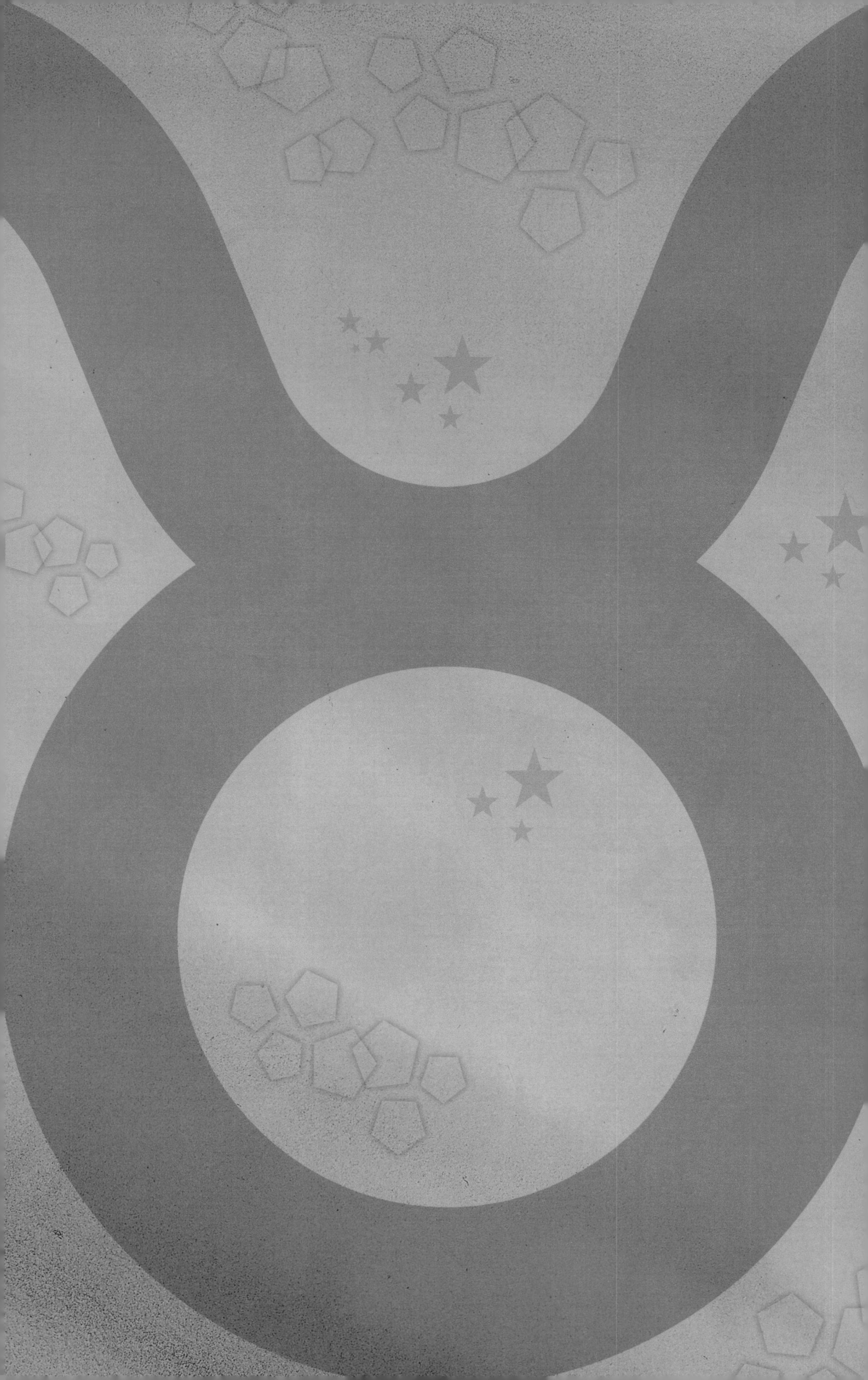

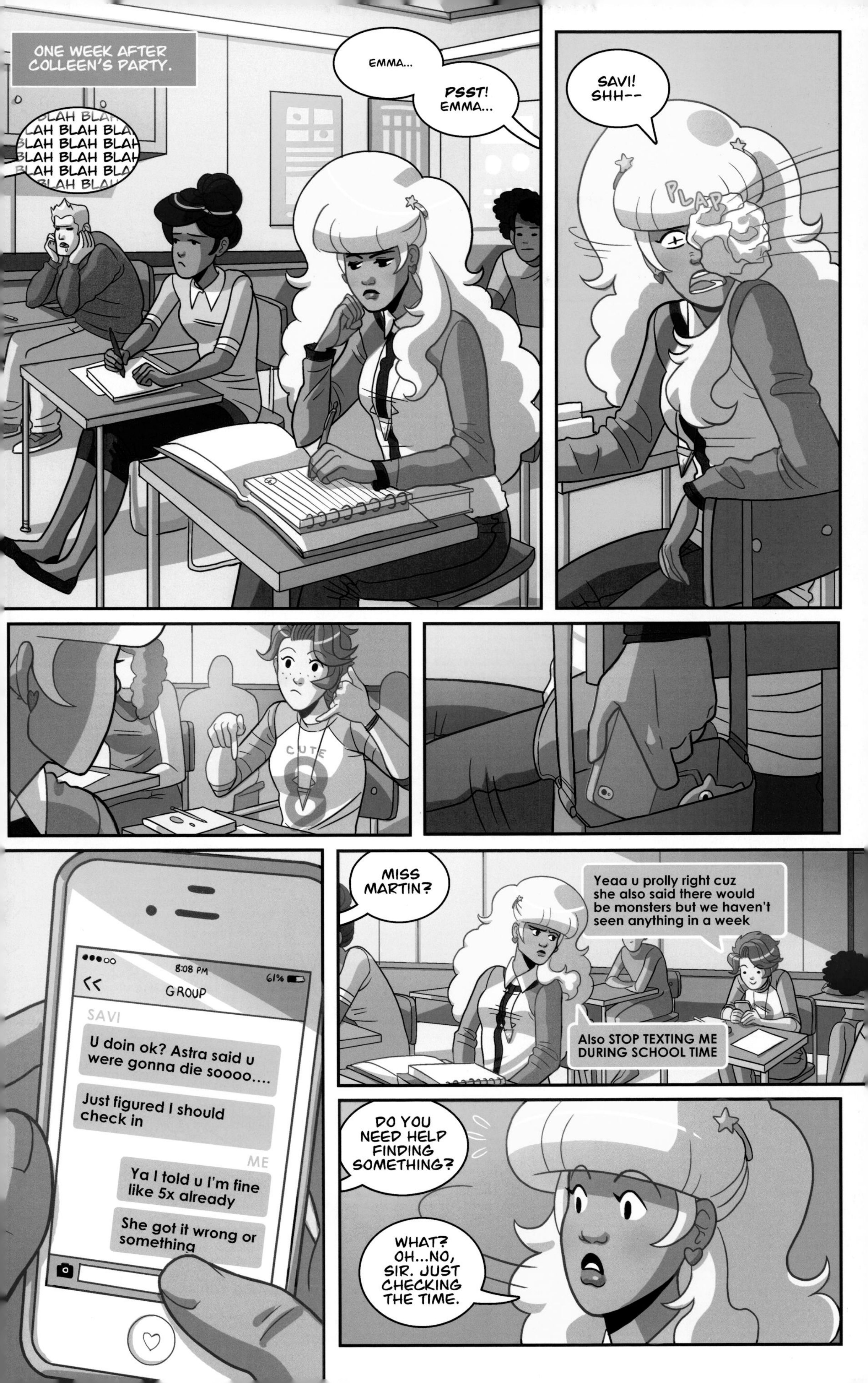
ONE WEEK AFTER COLLEEN'S PARTY.
BLAH BLAH BLAH BLAH BLAH BLAH BLAH BLAH BLAH BLAH BLAH BLAH BLAH BLAH
EMMA...
PSST! EMMA...
SAVI! SHH--
PLAP
MISS MARTIN?
Yeaa u prolly right cuz she also said there would be monsters but we haven't seen anything in a week
Also STOP TEXTING ME DURING SCHOOL TIME
8:08 PM
61%
GROUP
SAVI
U doin ok? Astra said u were gonna die soooo....
Just figured I should check in
ME
Ya I told u I'm fine like 5x already
She got it wrong or something
DO YOU NEED HELP FINDING SOMETHING?
WHAT? OH...NO, SIR. JUST CHECKING THE TIME.

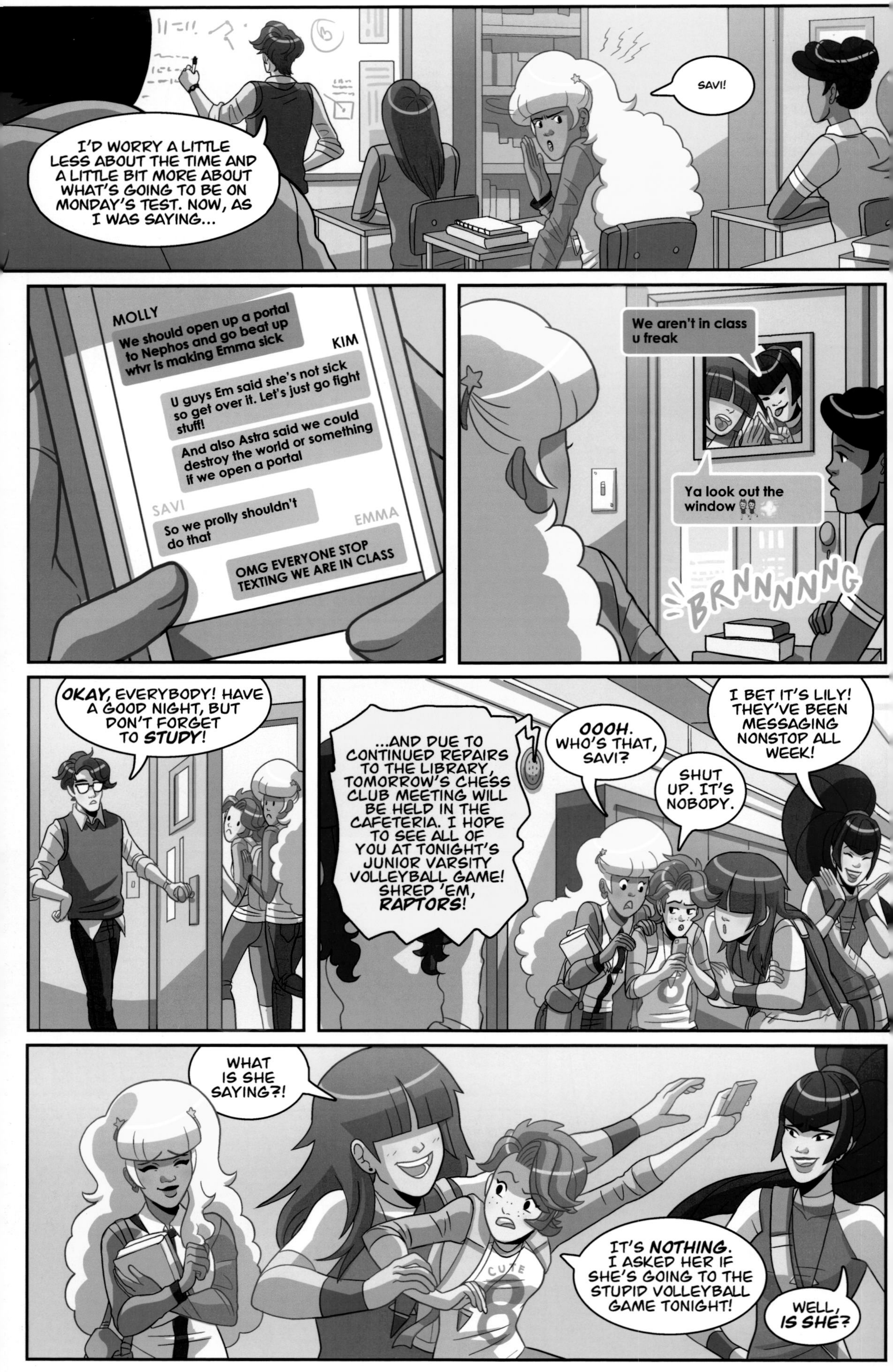

I'D WORRY A LITTLE LESS ABOUT THE TIME AND A LITTLE BIT MORE ABOUT WHAT'S GOING TO BE ON MONDAY'S TEST. NOW, AS I WAS SAYING...
SAVI!
MOLLY
We should open up a portal to Nephos and go beat up wtvr is making Emma sick
KIM
U guys Em said she's not sick so get over it. Let's just go fight stuff!
And also Astra said we could destroy the world or something if we open a portal
SAVI
So we prolly shouldn't do that
EMMA
OMG EVERYONE STOP TEXTING WE ARE IN CLASS
We aren't in class u freak
Ya look out the window
BRNNNNNG
OKAY, EVERYBODY! HAVE A GOOD NIGHT, BUT DON'T FORGET TO STUDY!
...AND DUE TO CONTINUED REPAIRS TO THE LIBRARY, TOMORROW'S CHESS CLUB MEETING WILL BE HELD IN THE CAFETERIA. I HOPE TO SEE ALL OF YOU AT TONIGHT'S JUNIOR VARSITY VOLLEYBALL GAME! SHRED 'EM, RAPTORS!
OOOH. WHO'S THAT, SAVI?
I BET IT'S LILY! THEY'VE BEEN MESSAGING NONSTOP ALL WEEK!
SHUT UP. IT'S NOBODY.
WHAT IS SHE SAYING?!
CUTE
IT'S NOTHING. I ASKED HER IF SHE'S GOING TO THE STUPID VOLLEYBALL GAME TONIGHT!
WELL, IS SHE?

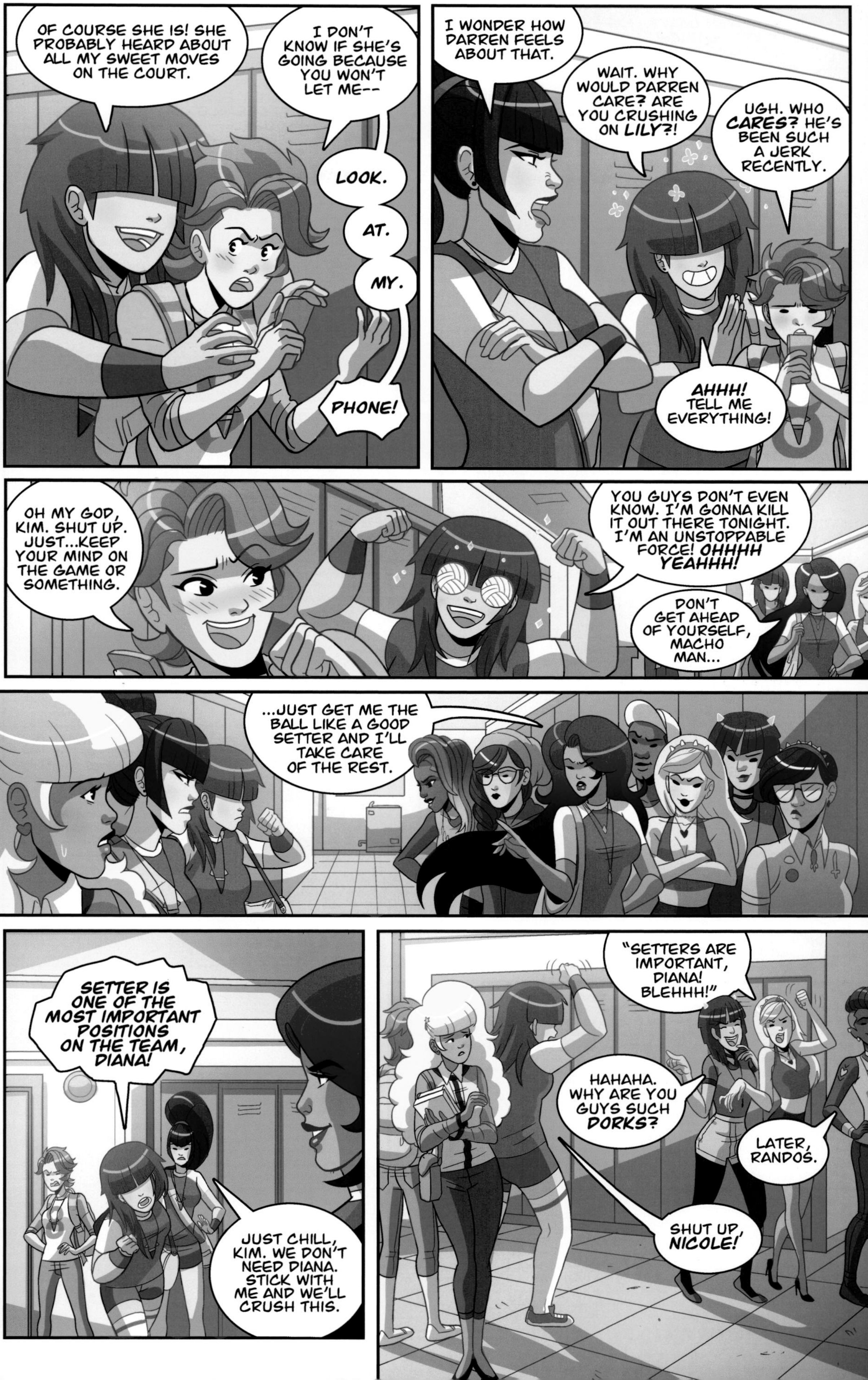
OF COURSE SHE IS! SHE PROBABLY HEARD ABOUT ALL MY SWEET MOVES ON THE COURT.
I DON'T KNOW IF SHE'S GOING BECAUSE YOU WON'T LET ME--
LOOK.
AT.
MY.
PHONE!
I WONDER HOW DARREN FEELS ABOUT THAT.
WAIT. WHY WOULD DARREN CARE? ARE YOU CRUSHING ON LILY?!
UGH. WHO CARES? HE'S BEEN SUCH A JERK RECENTLY.
AHHH! TELL ME EVERYTHING!
OH MY GOD, KIM. SHUT UP. JUST...KEEP YOUR MIND ON THE GAME OR SOMETHING.
YOU GUYS DON'T EVEN KNOW. I'M GONNA KILL IT OUT THERE TONIGHT. I'M AN UNSTOPPABLE FORCE! OHHHH YEAHHH!
DON'T GET AHEAD OF YOURSELF, MACHO MAN...
...JUST GET ME THE BALL LIKE A GOOD SETTER AND I'LL TAKE CARE OF THE REST.
SETTER IS ONE OF THE MOST IMPORTANT POSITIONS ON THE TEAM, DIANA!
JUST CHILL, KIM. WE DON'T NEED DIANA. STICK WITH ME AND WE'LL CRUSH THIS.
"SETTERS ARE IMPORTANT, DIANA! BLEHHH!"
HAHAHA. WHY ARE YOU GUYS SUCH DORKS?
LATER, RANDOS.
SHUT UP, NICOLE!

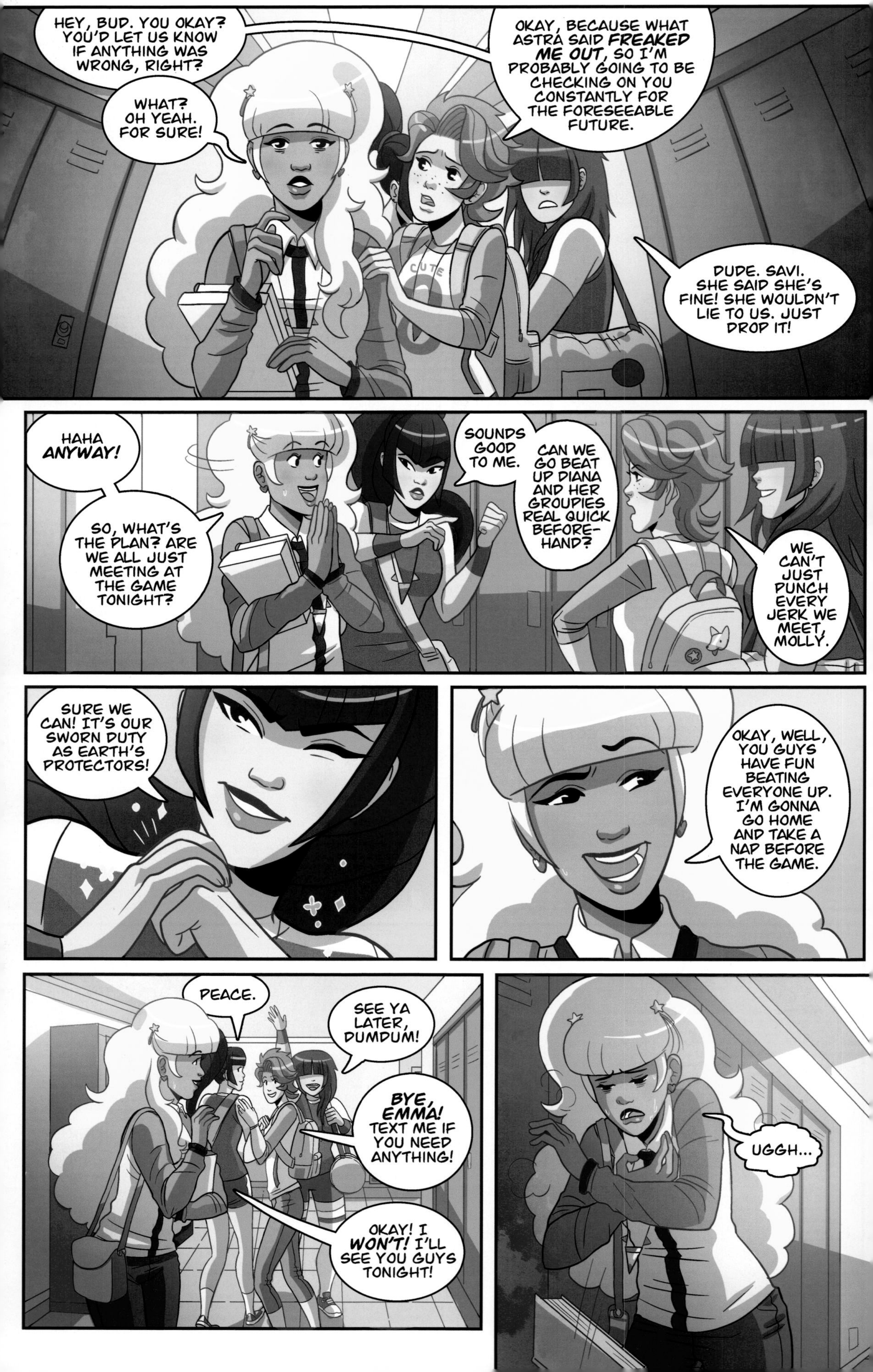
HEY, BUD. YOU OKAY? YOU'D LET US KNOW IF ANYTHING WAS WRONG, RIGHT?
OKAY, BECAUSE WHAT ASTRA SAID FREAKED ME OUT, SO I'M PROBABLY GOING TO BE CHECKING ON YOU CONSTANTLY FOR THE FORESEEABLE FUTURE.
WHAT? OH YEAH. FOR SURE!
DUDE. SAVI. SHE SAID SHE'S FINE! SHE WOULDN'T LIE TO US. JUST DROP IT!
HAHA ANYWAY!
SO, WHAT'S THE PLAN? ARE WE ALL JUST MEETING AT THE GAME TONIGHT?
SOUNDS GOOD TO ME.
CAN WE GO BEAT UP DIANA AND HER GROUPIES REAL QUICK BEFORE-HAND?
WE CAN'T JUST PUNCH EVERY JERK WE MEET, MOLLY.
SURE WE CAN! IT'S OUR SWORN DUTY AS EARTH'S PROTECTORS!
OKAY, WELL, YOU GUYS HAVE FUN BEATING EVERYONE UP. I'M GONNA GO HOME AND TAKE A NAP BEFORE THE GAME.
PEACE.
SEE YA LATER, DUMDUM!
BYE, EMMA! TEXT ME IF YOU NEED ANYTHING!
OKAY! I WON'T! I'LL SEE YOU GUYS TONIGHT!
UGGH...

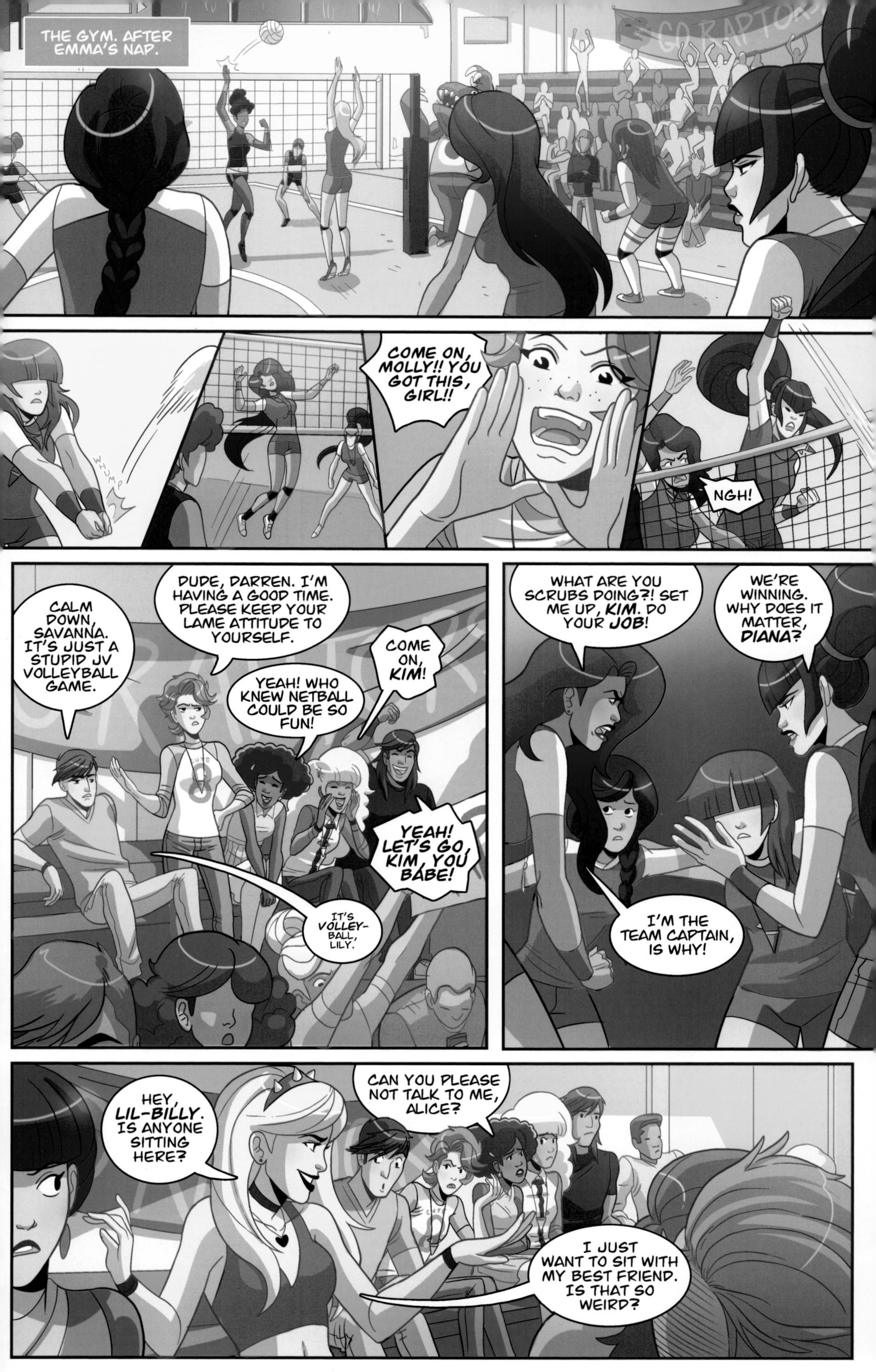
THE GYM. AFTER EMMA'S NAP.
GO RAPTORS
WHUMP
COME ON, MOLLY!! YOU GOT THIS, GIRL!!
NGH!
CALM DOWN, SAVANNA. IT'S JUST A STUPID JV VOLLEYBALL GAME.
DUDE, DARREN. I'M HAVING A GOOD TIME. PLEASE KEEP YOUR LAME ATTITUDE TO YOURSELF.
YEAH! WHO KNEW NETBALL COULD BE SO FUN!
COME ON, KIM!
YEAH! LET'S GO, KIM, YOU BABE!
IT'S VOLLEY-BALL, LILY.
WHAT ARE YOU SCRUBS DOING?! SET ME UP, KIM. DO YOUR JOB!
WE'RE WINNING. WHY DOES IT MATTER, DIANA?
I'M THE TEAM CAPTAIN, IS WHY!
HEY, LIL-BILLY. IS ANYONE SITTING HERE?
CAN YOU PLEASE NOT TALK TO ME, ALICE?
I JUST WANT TO SIT WITH MY BEST FRIEND. IS THAT SO WEIRD?

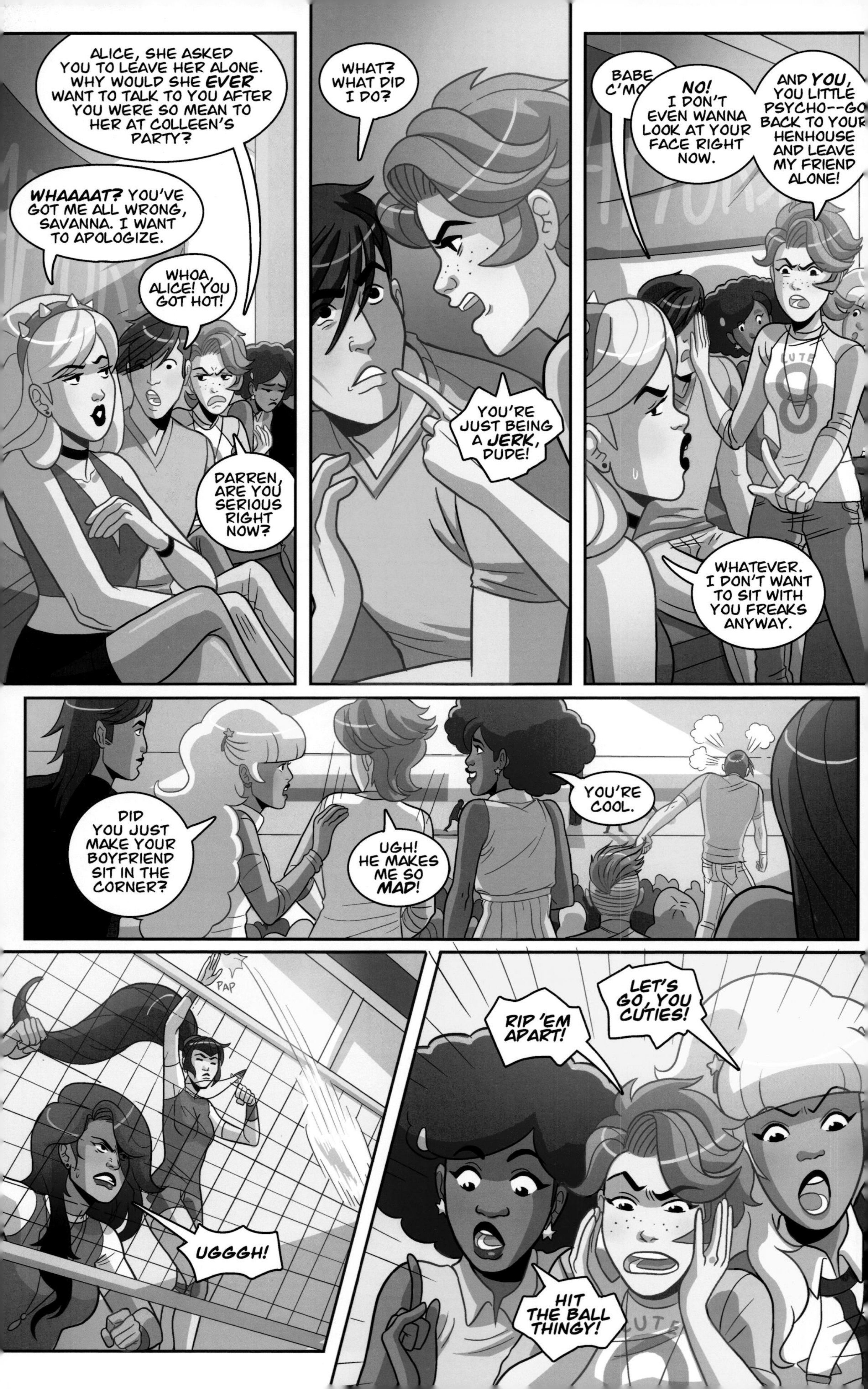

ALICE, SHE ASKED YOU TO LEAVE HER ALONE. WHY WOULD SHE EVER WANT TO TALK TO YOU AFTER YOU WERE SO MEAN TO HER AT COLLEEN'S PARTY?
WHAAAAT? YOU'VE GOT ME ALL WRONG, SAVANNA. I WANT TO APOLOGIZE.
WHOA, ALICE! YOU GOT HOT!
DARREN, ARE YOU SERIOUS RIGHT NOW?
WHAT? WHAT DID I DO?
YOU'RE JUST BEING A JERK, DUDE!
BABE, C'MO
NO! I DON'T EVEN WANNA LOOK AT YOUR FACE RIGHT NOW.
AND YOU, YOU LITTLE PSYCHO--GO BACK TO YOUR HENHOUSE AND LEAVE MY FRIEND ALONE!
WHATEVER. I DON'T WANT TO SIT WITH YOU FREAKS ANYWAY.
DID YOU JUST MAKE YOUR BOYFRIEND SIT IN THE CORNER?
UGH! HE MAKES ME SO MAD!
YOU'RE COOL.
PAP
UGGGH!
RIP 'EM APART!
LET'S GO, YOU CUTIES!
HIT THE BALL THINGY!

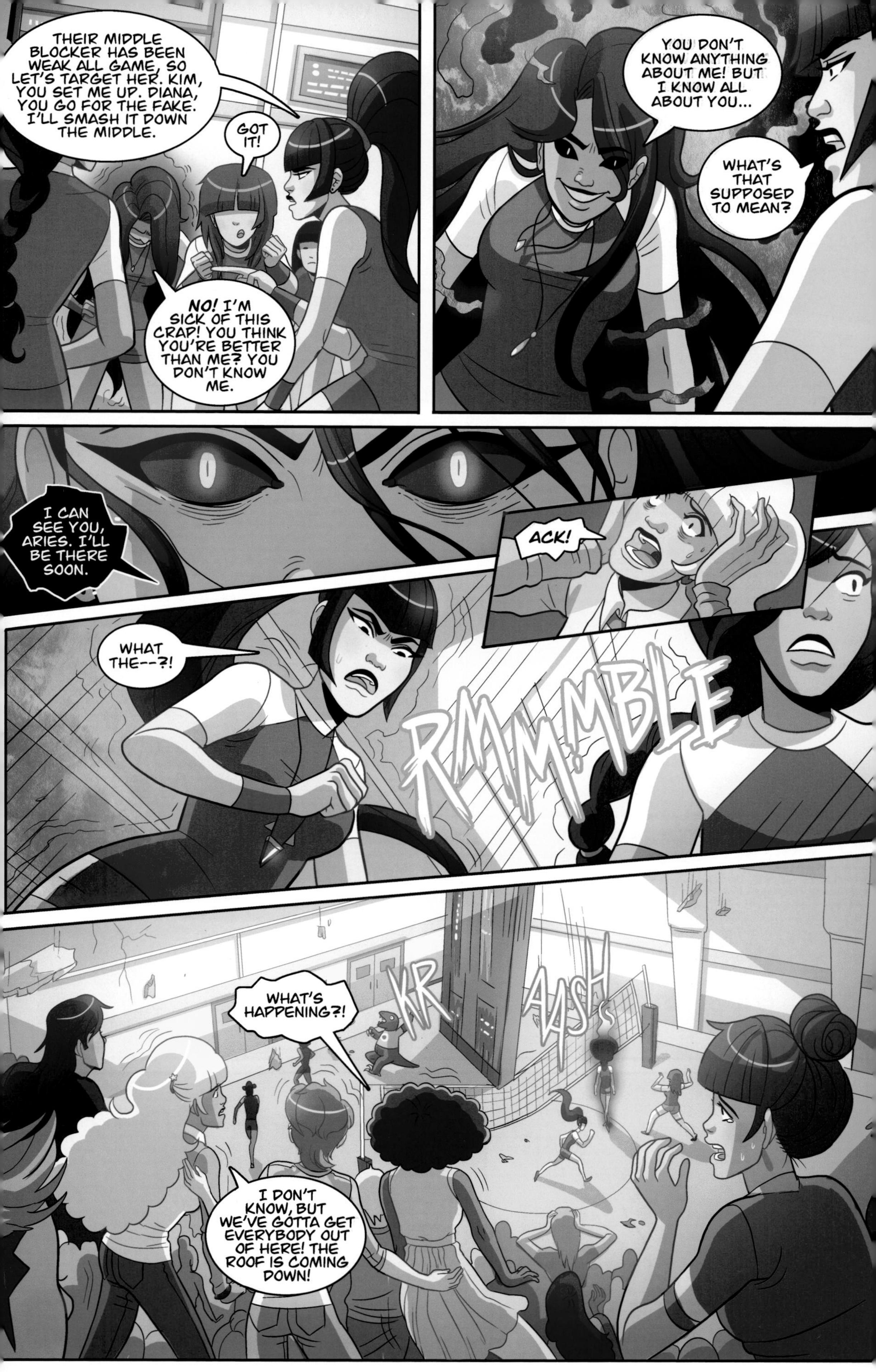
THEIR MIDDLE BLOCKER HAS BEEN WEAK ALL GAME, SO LET'S TARGET HER. KIM, YOU SET ME UP. DIANA, YOU GO FOR THE FAKE. I'LL SMASH IT DOWN THE MIDDLE.
GOT IT!
NO! I'M SICK OF THIS CRAP! YOU THINK YOU'RE BETTER THAN ME? YOU DON'T KNOW ME.
YOU DON'T KNOW ANYTHING ABOUT ME! BUT I KNOW ALL ABOUT YOU...
WHAT'S THAT SUPPOSED TO MEAN?
I CAN SEE YOU, ARIES. I'LL BE THERE SOON.
ACK!
WHAT THE--?!
RMMMBLE
KR
AASH
WHAT'S HAPPENING?!
I DON'T KNOW, BUT WE'VE GOTTA GET EVERYBODY OUT OF HERE! THE ROOF IS COMING DOWN!

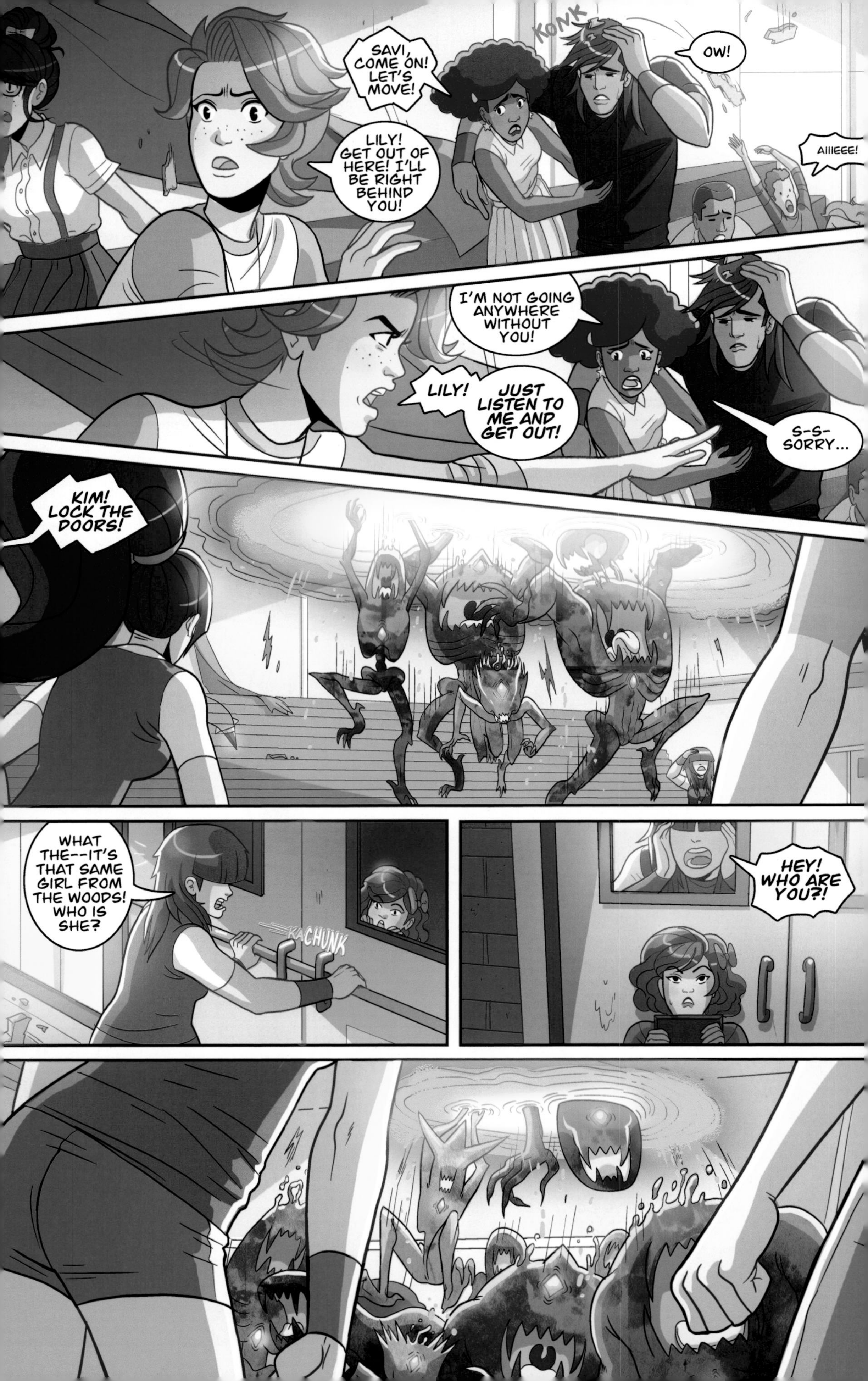
SAVI, COME ON! LET'S MOVE!
KONK
OW!
LILY! GET OUT OF HERE! I'LL BE RIGHT BEHIND YOU!
AIIIEEE!
I'M NOT GOING ANYWHERE WITHOUT YOU!
LILY!
JUST LISTEN TO ME AND GET OUT!
S-S-SORRY...
KIM! LOCK THE DOORS!
WHAT THE--IT'S THAT SAME GIRL FROM THE WOODS! WHO IS SHE?
KACHUNK
HEY! WHO ARE YOU?!

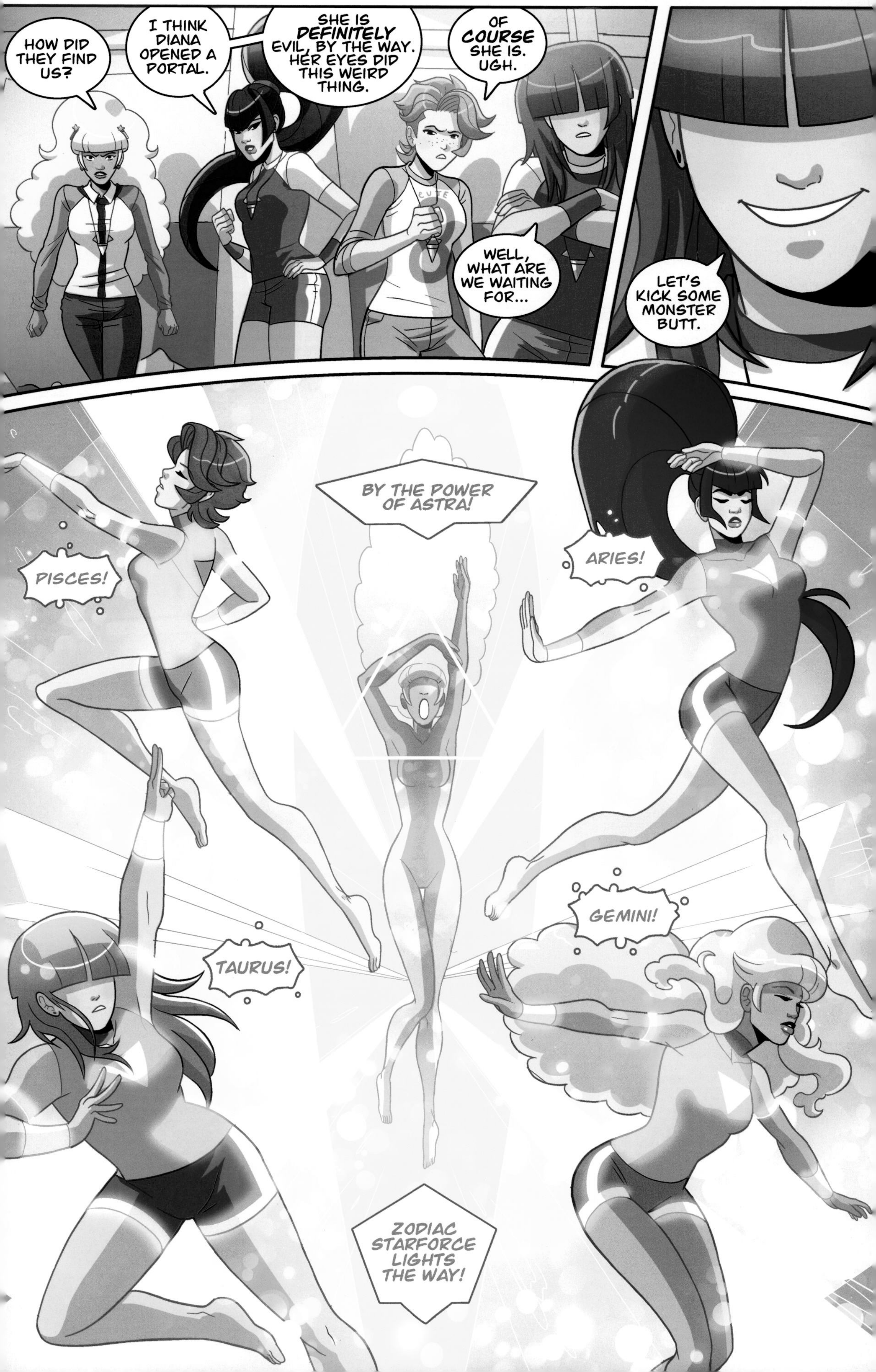
HOW DID THEY FIND US?
I THINK DIANA OPENED A PORTAL.
SHE IS **DEFINITELY** EVIL, BY THE WAY. HER EYES DID THIS WEIRD THING.
OF **COURSE** SHE IS. UGH.
WELL, WHAT ARE WE WAITING FOR...
LET'S KICK SOME MONSTER BUTT.
BY THE POWER OF ASTRA!
PISCES!
ARIES!
TAURUS!
GEMINI!
ZODIAC STARFORCE LIGHTS THE WAY!

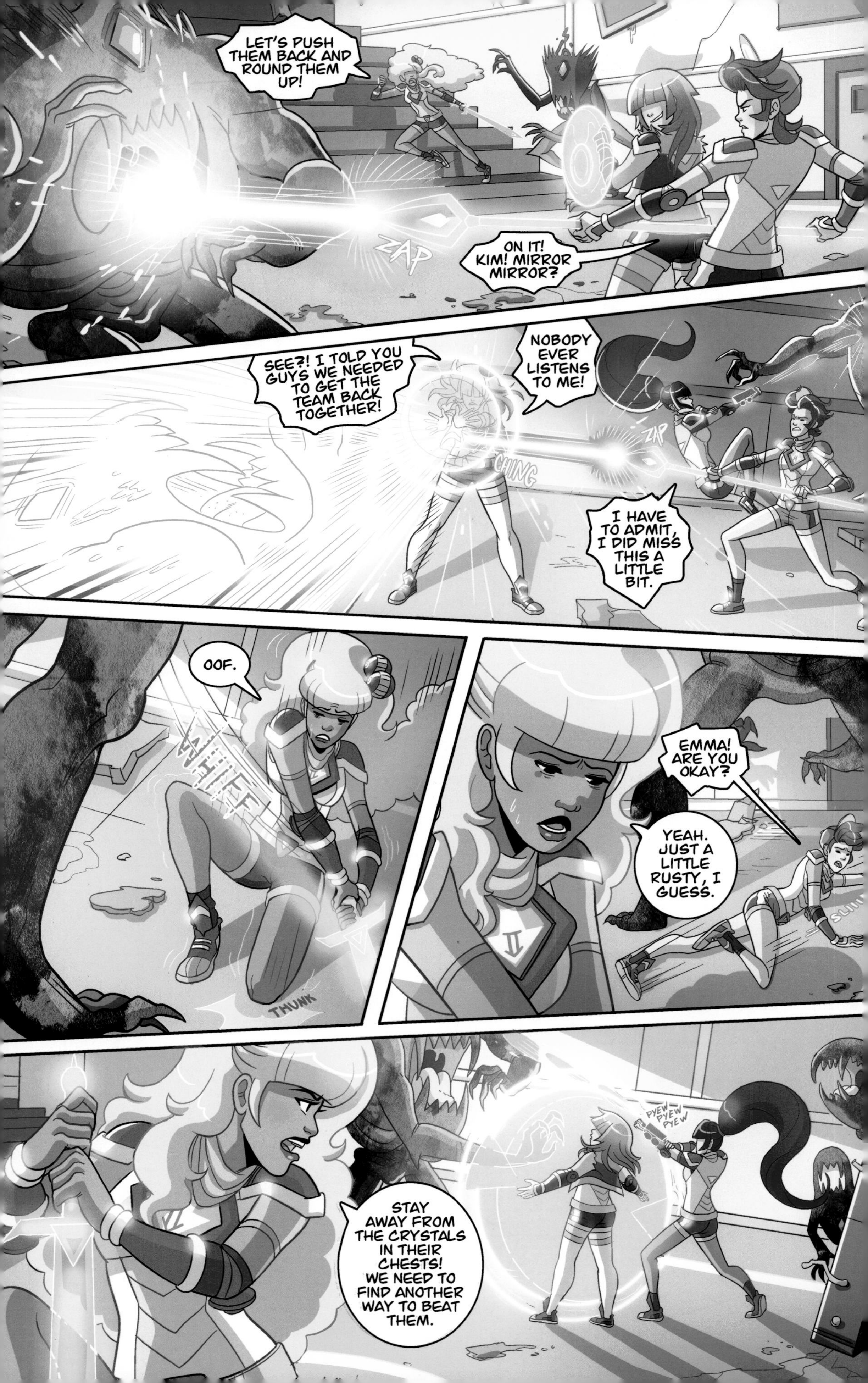
LET'S PUSH THEM BACK AND ROUND THEM UP!
ZAP
ON IT! KIM! MIRROR MIRROR?
SEE?! I TOLD YOU GUYS WE NEEDED TO GET THE TEAM BACK TOGETHER!
NOBODY EVER LISTENS TO ME!
ZAP
CHING
I HAVE TO ADMIT, I DID MISS THIS A LITTLE BIT.
OOF.
WHIFF
THUNK
EMMA! ARE YOU OKAY?
YEAH. JUST A LITTLE RUSTY, I GUESS.
PYEW PYEW PYEW
STAY AWAY FROM THE CRYSTALS IN THEIR CHESTS! WE NEED TO FIND ANOTHER WAY TO BEAT THEM.

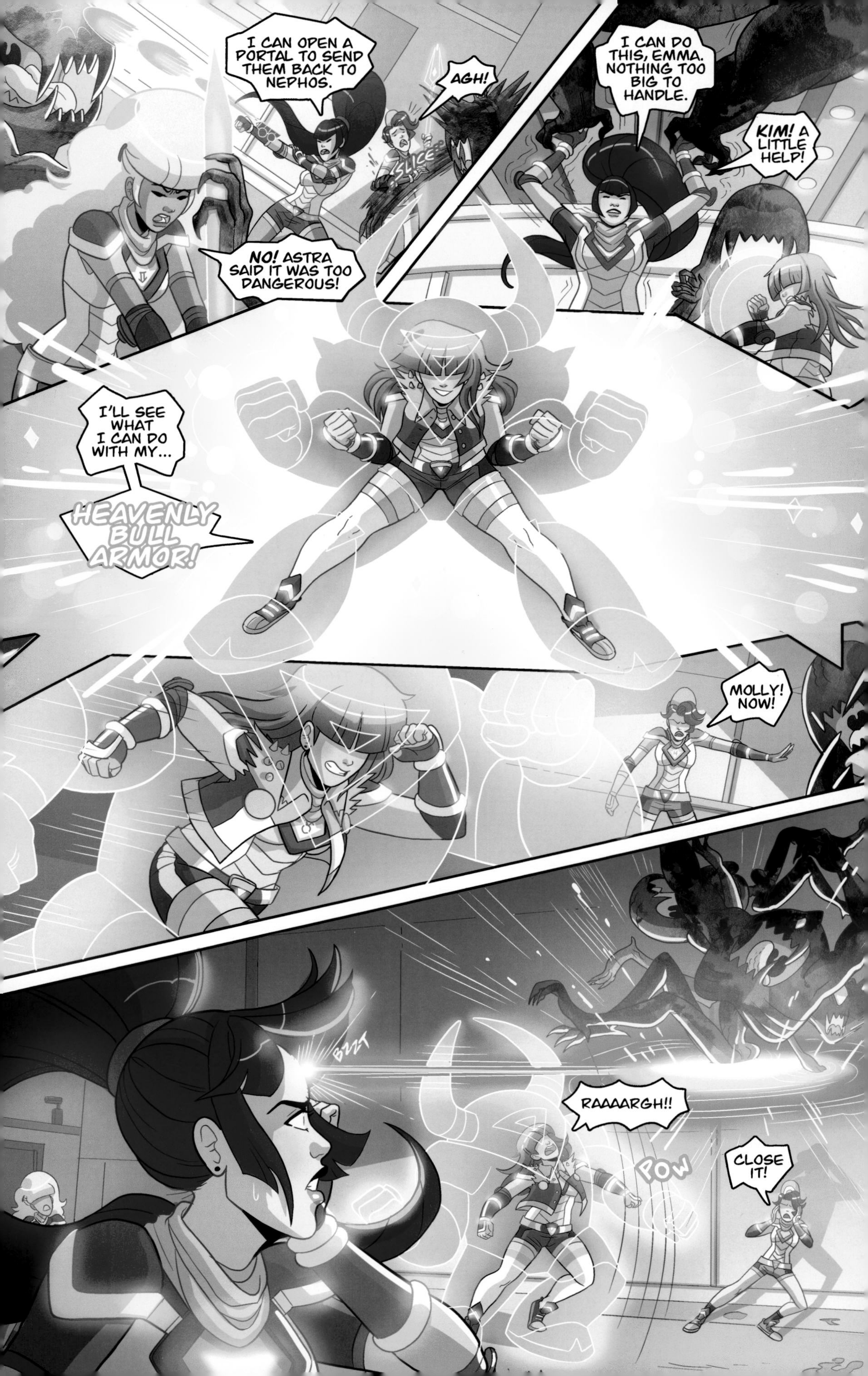
I CAN OPEN A PORTAL TO SEND THEM BACK TO NEPHOS.
AGH!
SLICE
NO! ASTRA SAID IT WAS TOO DANGEROUS!
I CAN DO THIS, EMMA. NOTHING TOO BIG TO HANDLE.
KIM! A LITTLE HELP!
I'LL SEE WHAT I CAN DO WITH MY...
HEAVENLY BULL ARMOR!
MOLLY! NOW!
BZZT
RAAAARGH!!
POW
CLOSE IT!

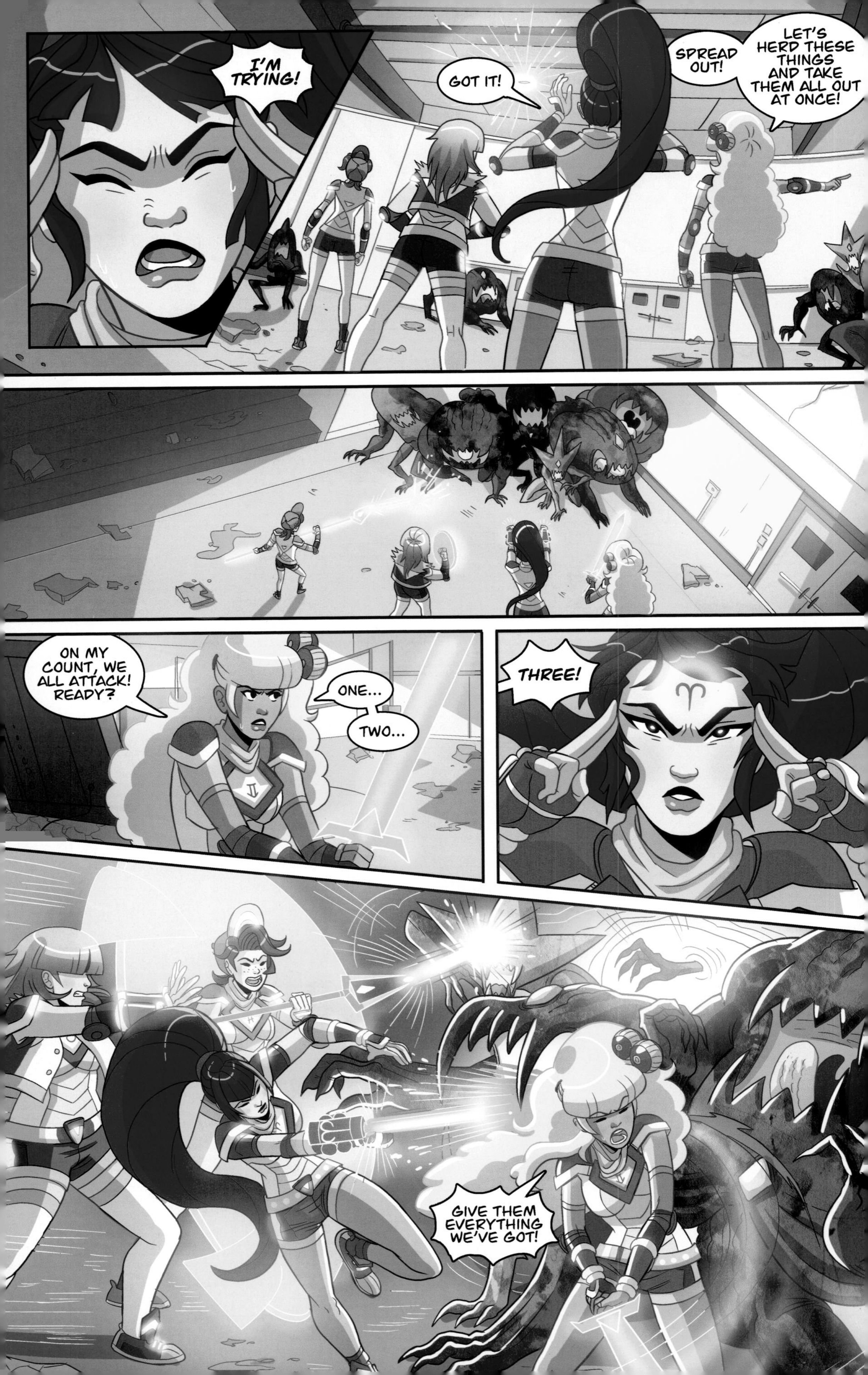
I'M TRYING!
GOT IT!
SPREAD OUT!
LET'S HERD THESE THINGS AND TAKE THEM ALL OUT AT ONCE!
ON MY COUNT, WE ALL ATTACK! READY?
ONE...
TWO...
THREE!
GIVE THEM EVERYTHING WE'VE GOT!

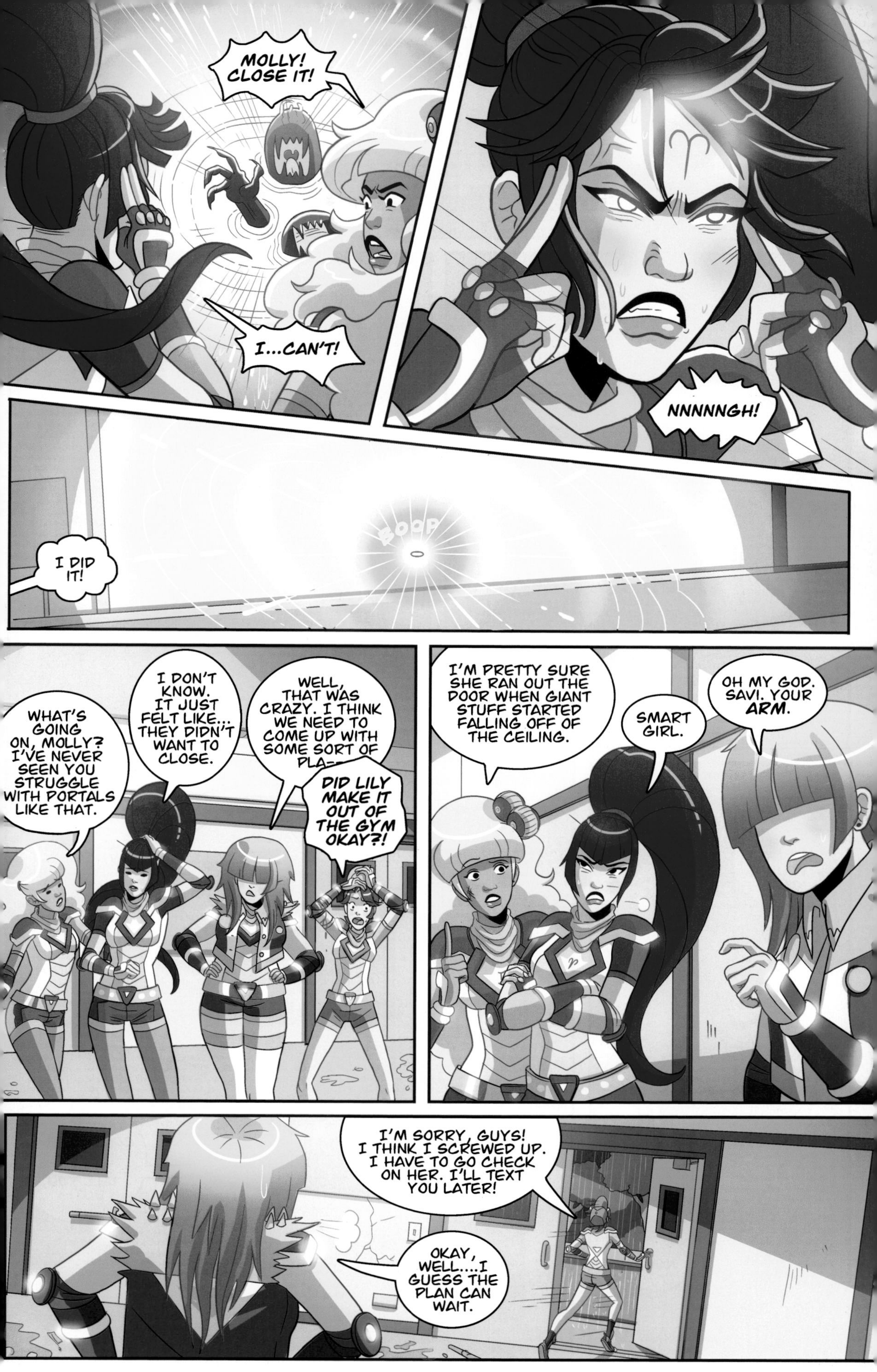
MOLLY! CLOSE IT!
I...CAN'T!
NNNNNGH!
BOOP
I DID IT!
WHAT'S GOING ON, MOLLY? I'VE NEVER SEEN YOU STRUGGLE WITH PORTALS LIKE THAT.
I DON'T KNOW. IT JUST FELT LIKE... THEY DIDN'T WANT TO CLOSE.
WELL, THAT WAS CRAZY. I THINK WE NEED TO COME UP WITH SOME SORT OF PLA--
DID LILY MAKE IT OUT OF THE GYM OKAY?!
I'M PRETTY SURE SHE RAN OUT THE DOOR WHEN GIANT STUFF STARTED FALLING OFF OF THE CEILING.
SMART GIRL.
OH MY GOD. SAVI. YOUR ARM.
I'M SORRY, GUYS! I THINK I SCREWED UP. I HAVE TO GO CHECK ON HER. I'LL TEXT YOU LATER!
OKAY, WELL....I GUESS THE PLAN CAN WAIT.

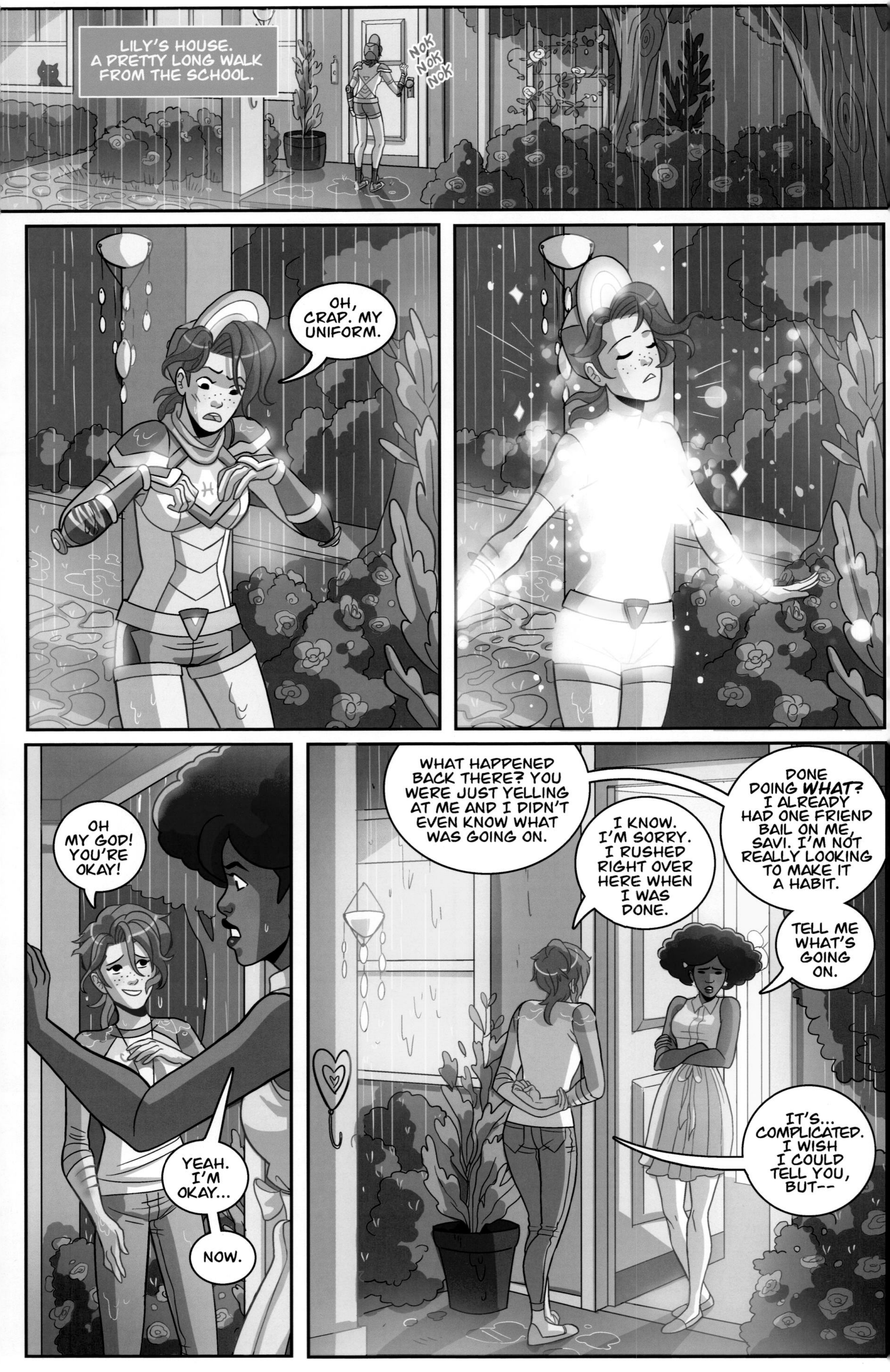

LILY'S HOUSE. A PRETTY LONG WALK FROM THE SCHOOL.
NOK NOK NOK
OH, CRAP. MY UNIFORM.
OH MY GOD! YOU'RE OKAY!
YEAH. I'M OKAY...
NOW.
WHAT HAPPENED BACK THERE? YOU WERE JUST YELLING AT ME AND I DIDN'T EVEN KNOW WHAT WAS GOING ON.
I KNOW. I'M SORRY. I RUSHED RIGHT OVER HERE WHEN I WAS DONE.
DONE DOING *WHAT*? I ALREADY HAD ONE FRIEND BAIL ON ME, SAVI. I'M NOT REALLY LOOKING TO MAKE IT A HABIT.
TELL ME WHAT'S GOING ON.
IT'S... COMPLICATED. I WISH I COULD TELL YOU, BUT--

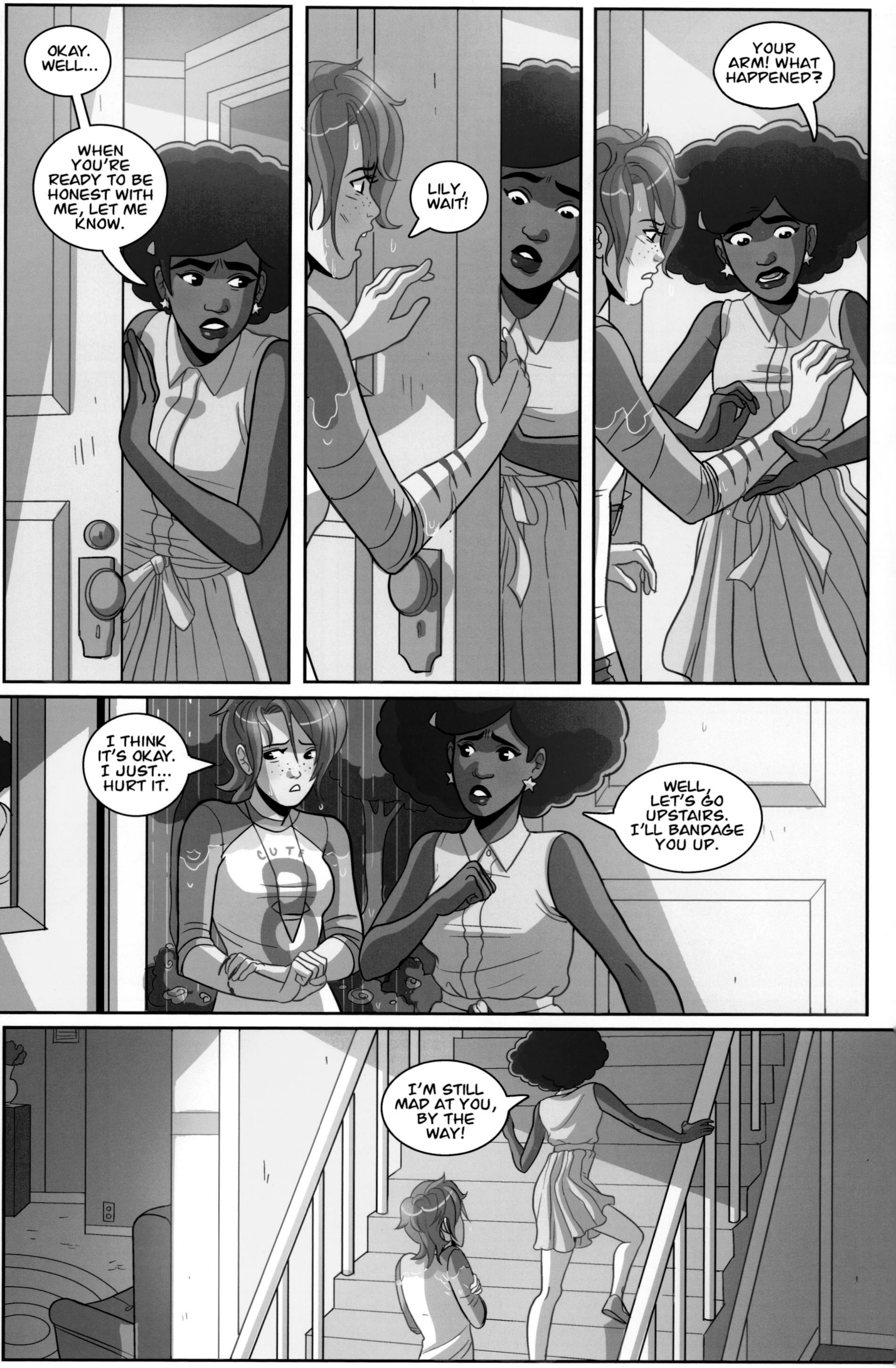
OKAY. WELL...
WHEN YOU'RE READY TO BE HONEST WITH ME, LET ME KNOW.
LILY, WAIT!
YOUR ARM! WHAT HAPPENED?
I THINK IT'S OKAY. I JUST... HURT IT.
WELL, LET'S GO UPSTAIRS. I'LL BANDAGE YOU UP.
I'M STILL MAD AT YOU, BY THE WAY!

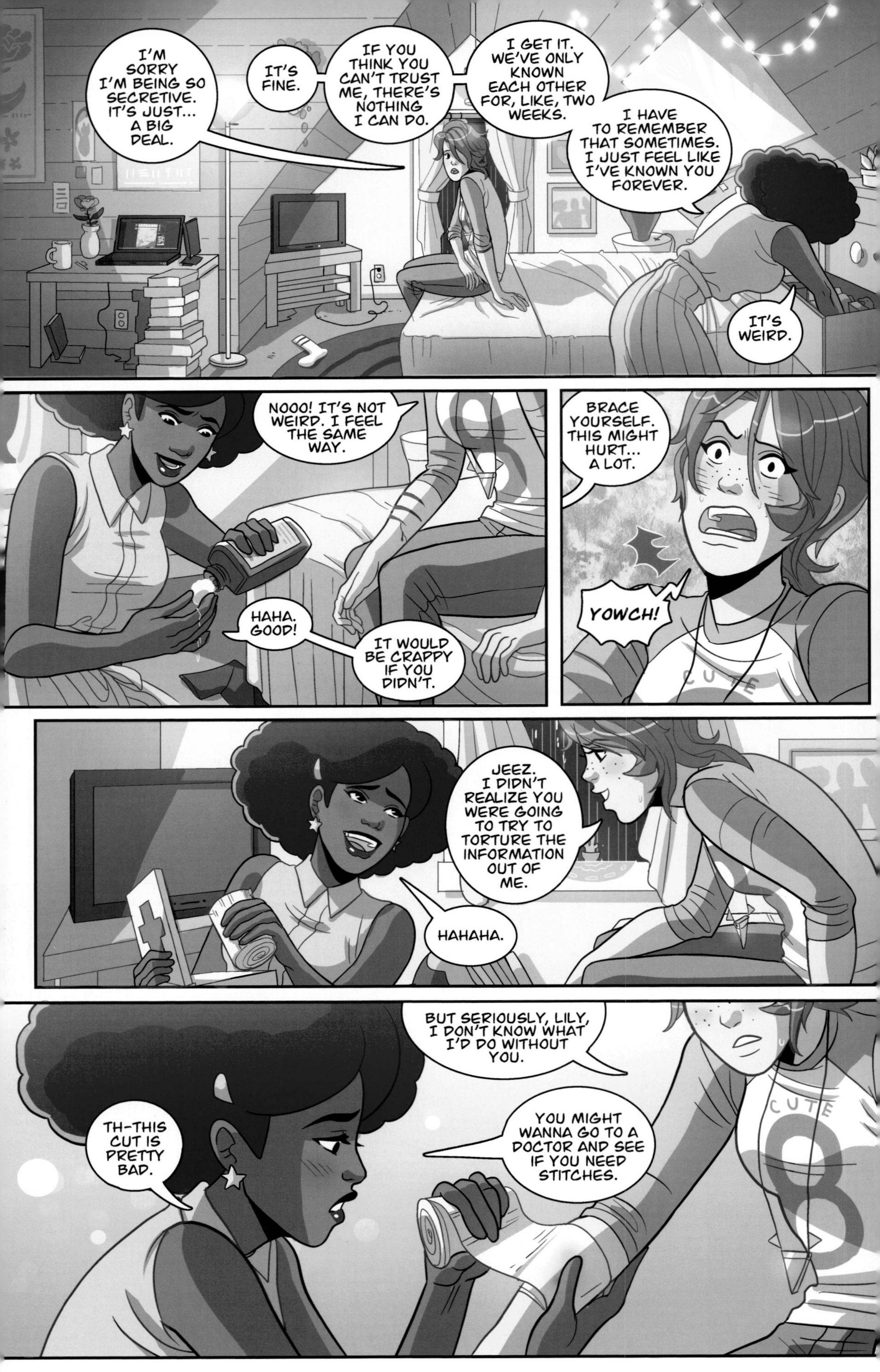
I'M SORRY I'M BEING SO SECRETIVE. IT'S JUST... A BIG DEAL.
IT'S FINE.
IF YOU THINK YOU CAN'T TRUST ME, THERE'S NOTHING I CAN DO.
I GET IT. WE'VE ONLY KNOWN EACH OTHER FOR, LIKE, TWO WEEKS.
I HAVE TO REMEMBER THAT SOMETIMES. I JUST FEEL LIKE I'VE KNOWN YOU FOREVER.
IT'S WEIRD.
NOOO! IT'S NOT WEIRD. I FEEL THE SAME WAY.
HAHA. GOOD!
IT WOULD BE CRAPPY IF YOU DIDN'T.
BRACE YOURSELF. THIS MIGHT HURT... A LOT.
YOWCH!
CUTE
JEEZ. I DIDN'T REALIZE YOU WERE GOING TO TRY TO TORTURE THE INFORMATION OUT OF ME.
HAHAHA.
BUT SERIOUSLY, LILY, I DON'T KNOW WHAT I'D DO WITHOUT YOU.
TH-THIS CUT IS PRETTY BAD.
YOU MIGHT WANNA GO TO A DOCTOR AND SEE IF YOU NEED STITCHES.
CUTE

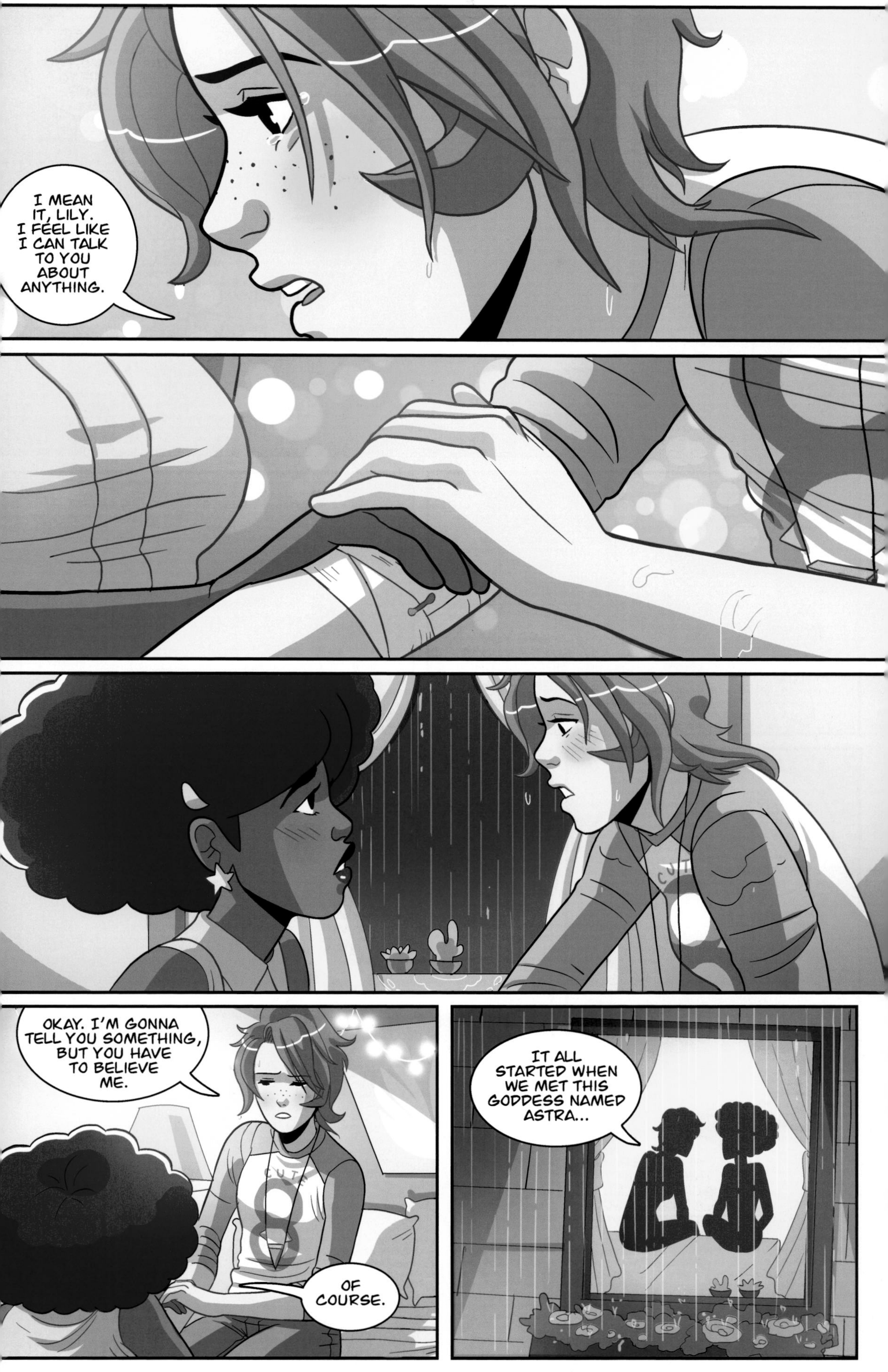
I MEAN IT, LILY. I FEEL LIKE I CAN TALK TO YOU ABOUT ANYTHING.
OKAY. I'M GONNA TELL YOU SOMETHING, BUT YOU HAVE TO BELIEVE ME.
OF COURSE.
IT ALL STARTED WHEN WE MET THIS GODDESS NAMED ASTRA...

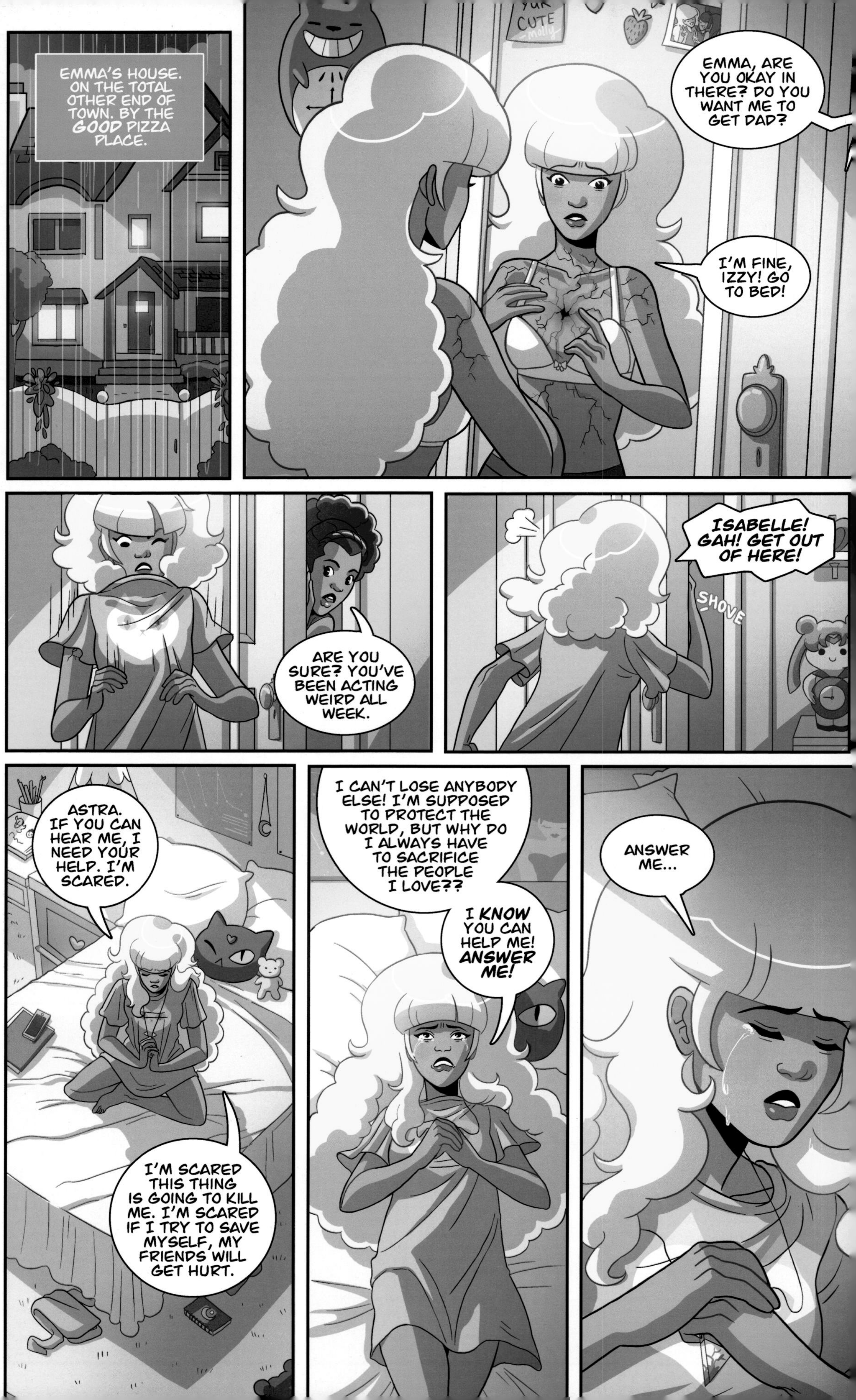
EMMA'S HOUSE. ON THE TOTAL OTHER END OF TOWN. BY THE GOOD PIZZA PLACE.
UR CUTE -molly
EMMA, ARE YOU OKAY IN THERE? DO YOU WANT ME TO GET DAD?
I'M FINE, IZZY! GO TO BED!
ARE YOU SURE? YOU'VE BEEN ACTING WEIRD ALL WEEK.
ISABELLE! GAH! GET OUT OF HERE!
SHOVE
ASTRA. IF YOU CAN HEAR ME, I NEED YOUR HELP. I'M SCARED.
I'M SCARED THIS THING IS GOING TO KILL ME. I'M SCARED IF I TRY TO SAVE MYSELF, MY FRIENDS WILL GET HURT.
I CAN'T LOSE ANYBODY ELSE! I'M SUPPOSED TO PROTECT THE WORLD, BUT WHY DO I ALWAYS HAVE TO SACRIFICE THE PEOPLE I LOVE??
I KNOW YOU CAN HELP ME! ANSWER ME!
ANSWER ME...

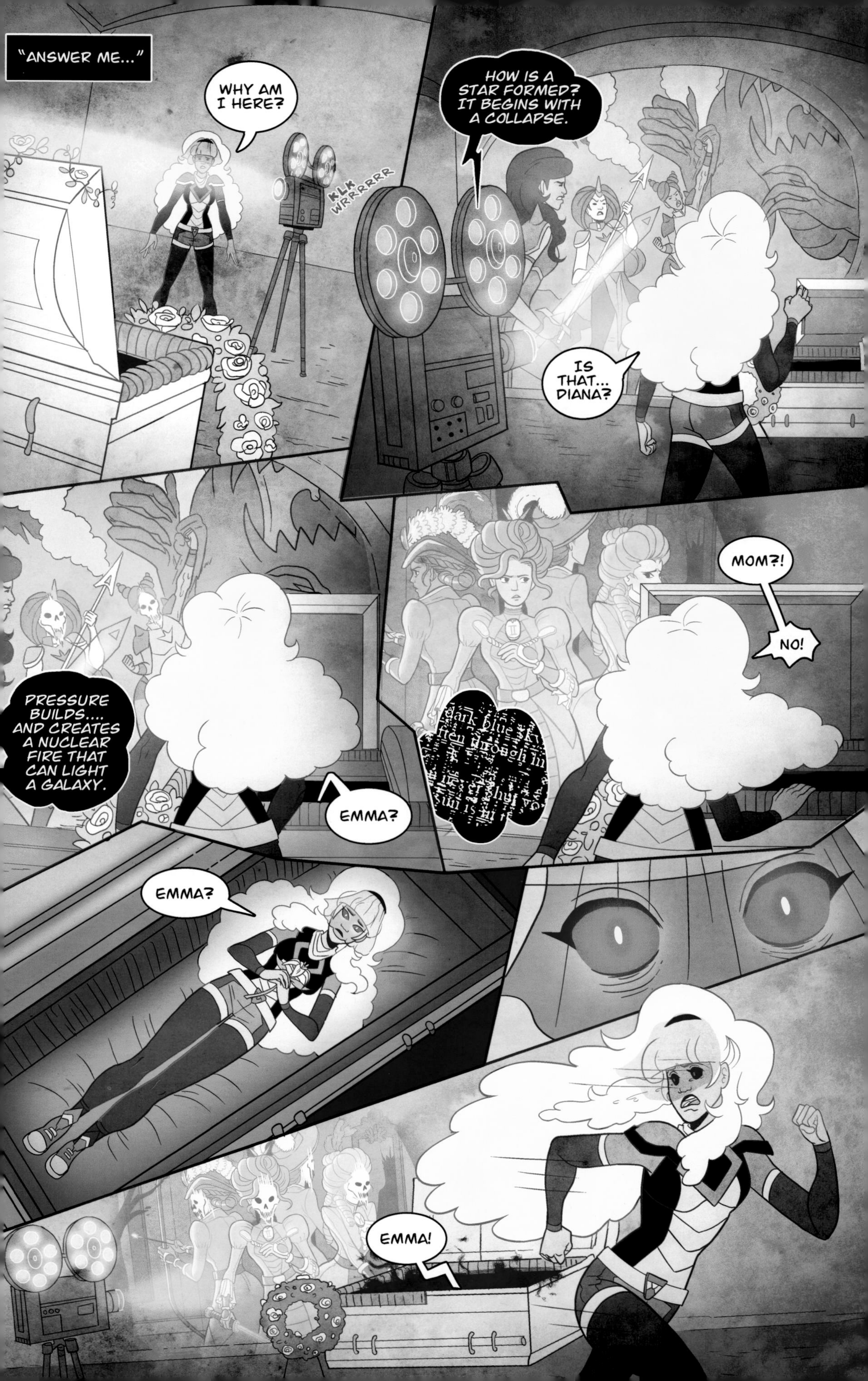
"ANSWER ME..."
WHY AM I HERE?
KLK WRRRRRR
HOW IS A STAR FORMED? IT BEGINS WITH A COLLAPSE.
IS THAT... DIANA?
PRESSURE BUILDS.... AND CREATES A NUCLEAR FIRE THAT CAN LIGHT A GALAXY.
EMMA?
MOM?!
NO!
EMMA?
EMMA!

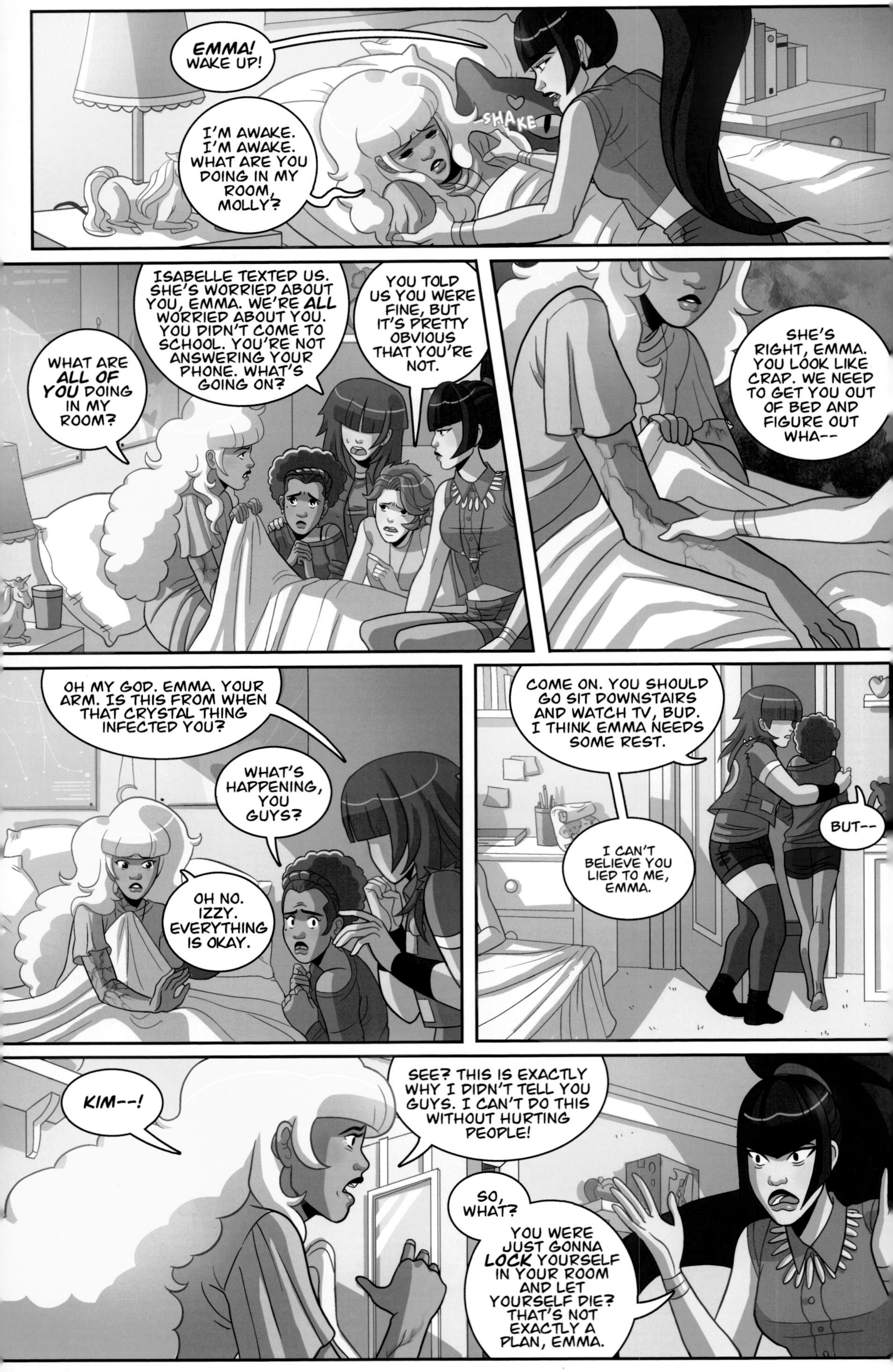
EMMA! WAKE UP!
SHAKE
I'M AWAKE. I'M AWAKE. WHAT ARE YOU DOING IN MY ROOM, MOLLY?
WHAT ARE ALL OF YOU DOING IN MY ROOM?
ISABELLE TEXTED US. SHE'S WORRIED ABOUT YOU, EMMA. WE'RE ALL WORRIED ABOUT YOU. YOU DIDN'T COME TO SCHOOL. YOU'RE NOT ANSWERING YOUR PHONE. WHAT'S GOING ON?
YOU TOLD US YOU WERE FINE, BUT IT'S PRETTY OBVIOUS THAT YOU'RE NOT.
SHE'S RIGHT, EMMA. YOU LOOK LIKE CRAP. WE NEED TO GET YOU OUT OF BED AND FIGURE OUT WHA--
OH MY GOD. EMMA. YOUR ARM. IS THIS FROM WHEN THAT CRYSTAL THING INFECTED YOU?
WHAT'S HAPPENING, YOU GUYS?
OH NO. IZZY. EVERYTHING IS OKAY.
COME ON. YOU SHOULD GO SIT DOWNSTAIRS AND WATCH TV, BUD. I THINK EMMA NEEDS SOME REST.
BUT--
I CAN'T BELIEVE YOU LIED TO ME, EMMA.
KIM--!
SEE? THIS IS EXACTLY WHY I DIDN'T TELL YOU GUYS. I CAN'T DO THIS WITHOUT HURTING PEOPLE!
SO, WHAT?
YOU WERE JUST GONNA LOCK YOURSELF IN YOUR ROOM AND LET YOURSELF DIE? THAT'S NOT EXACTLY A PLAN, EMMA.

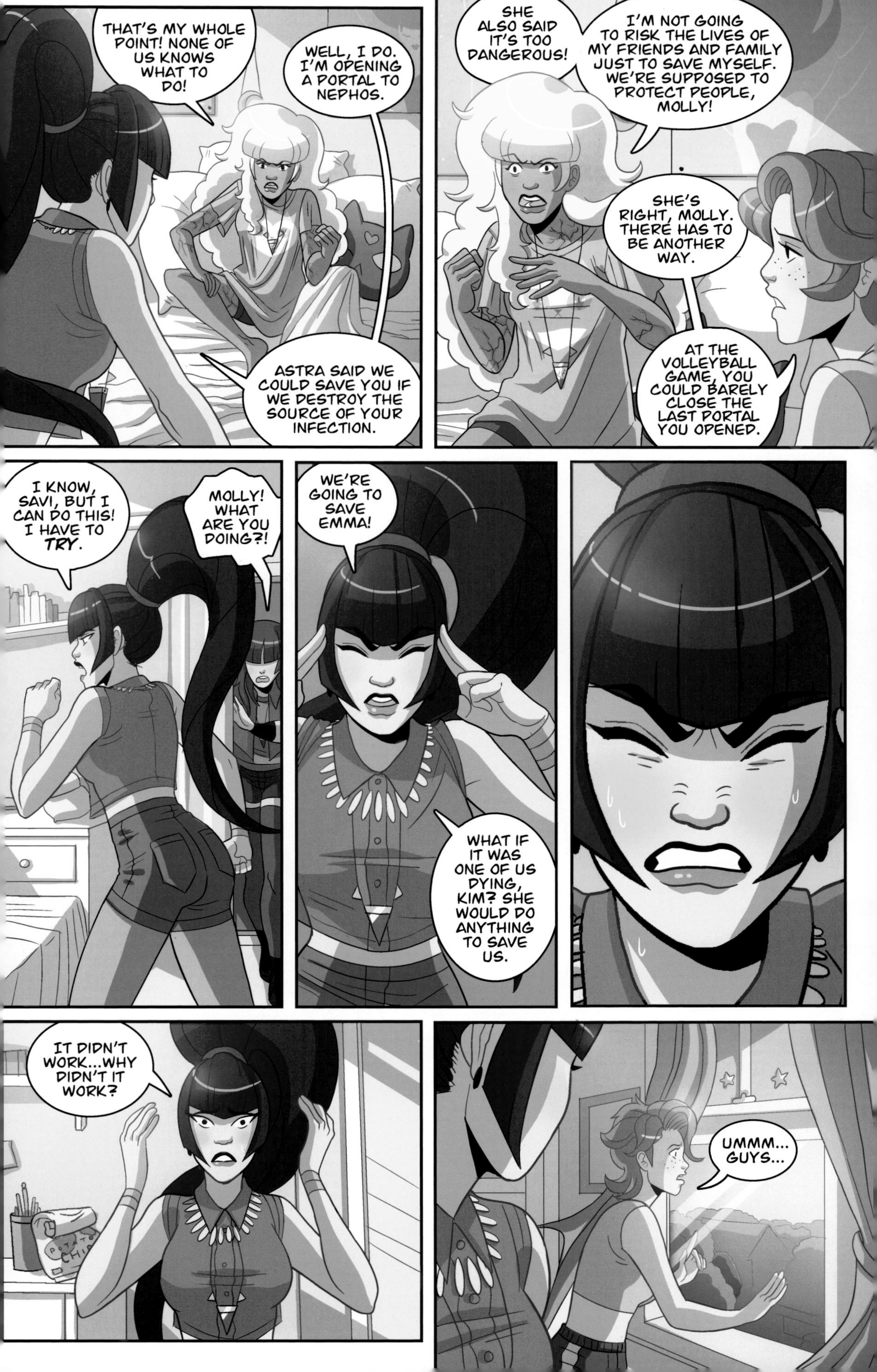
THAT'S MY WHOLE POINT! NONE OF US KNOWS WHAT TO DO!
WELL, I DO. I'M OPENING A PORTAL TO NEPHOS.
ASTRA SAID WE COULD SAVE YOU IF WE DESTROY THE SOURCE OF YOUR INFECTION.
SHE ALSO SAID IT'S TOO DANGEROUS!
I'M NOT GOING TO RISK THE LIVES OF MY FRIENDS AND FAMILY JUST TO SAVE MYSELF. WE'RE SUPPOSED TO PROTECT PEOPLE, MOLLY!
SHE'S RIGHT, MOLLY. THERE HAS TO BE ANOTHER WAY.
AT THE VOLLEYBALL GAME, YOU COULD BARELY CLOSE THE LAST PORTAL YOU OPENED.
I KNOW, SAVI, BUT I CAN DO THIS! I HAVE TO *TRY*.
MOLLY! WHAT ARE YOU DOING?!
WE'RE GOING TO SAVE EMMA!
WHAT IF IT WAS ONE OF US DYING, KIM? SHE WOULD DO ANYTHING TO SAVE US.
IT DIDN'T WORK...WHY DIDN'T IT WORK?
UMMM... GUYS...

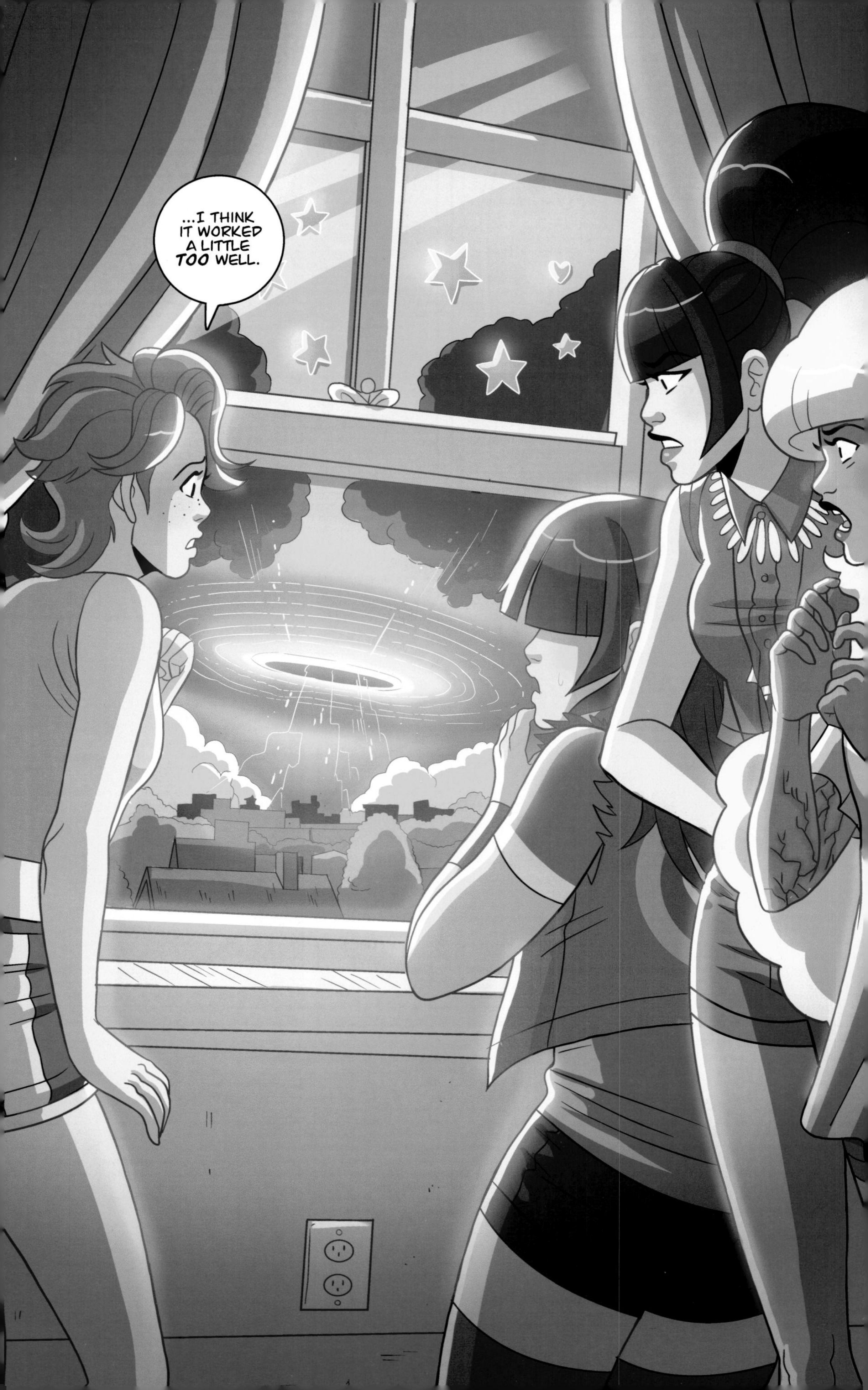
...I THINK IT WORKED A LITTLE *TOO* WELL.

CHAPTER THREE

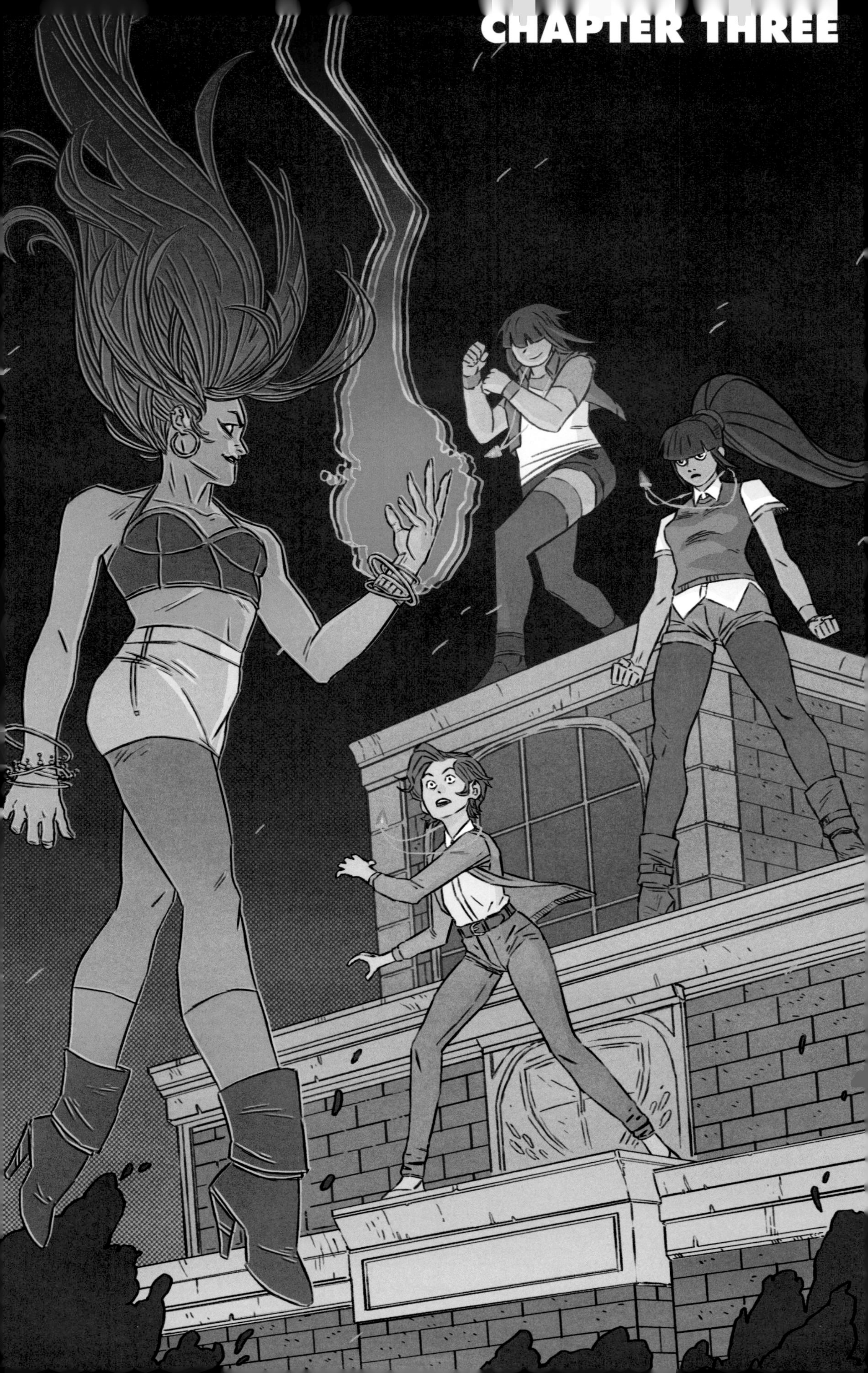

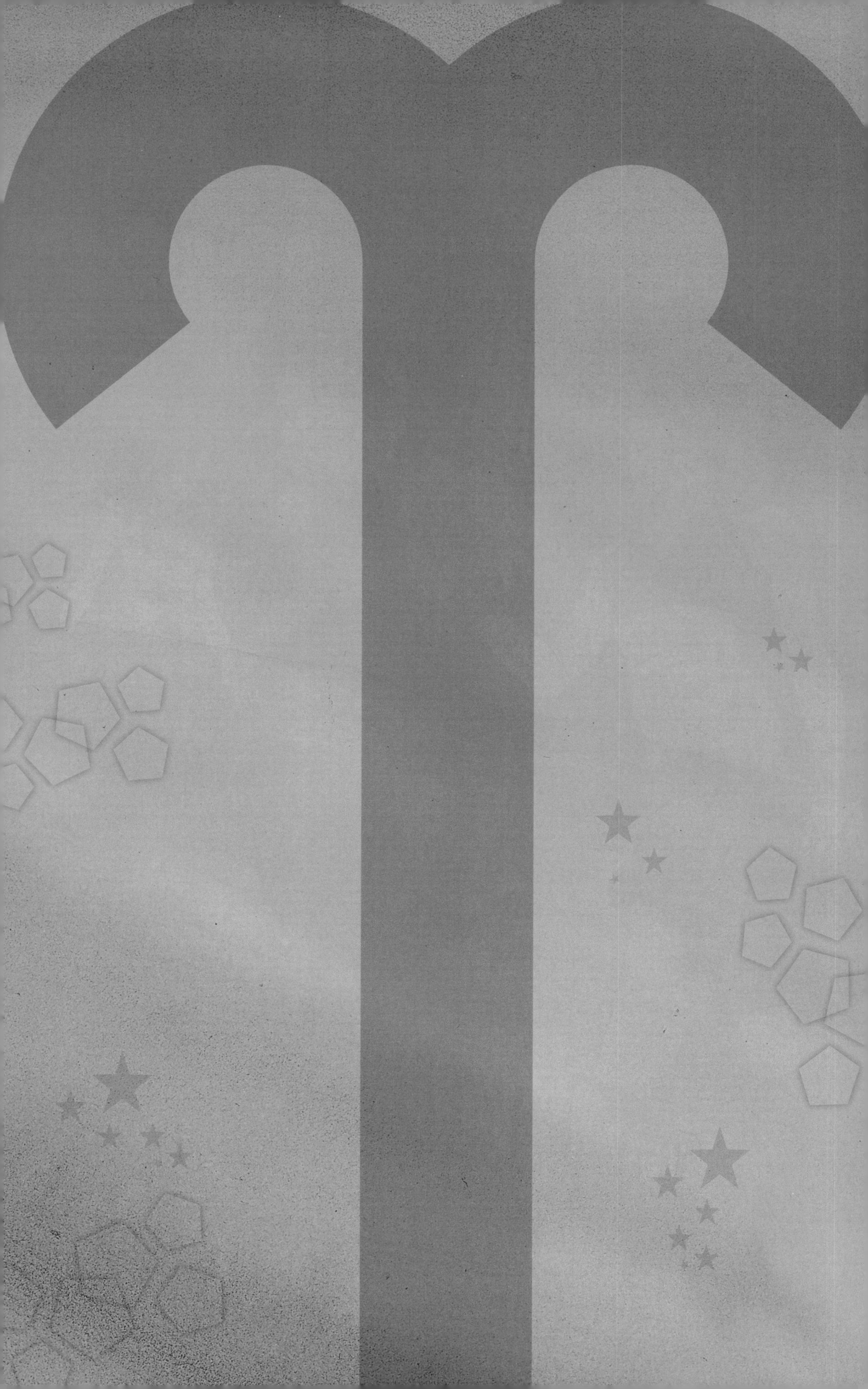

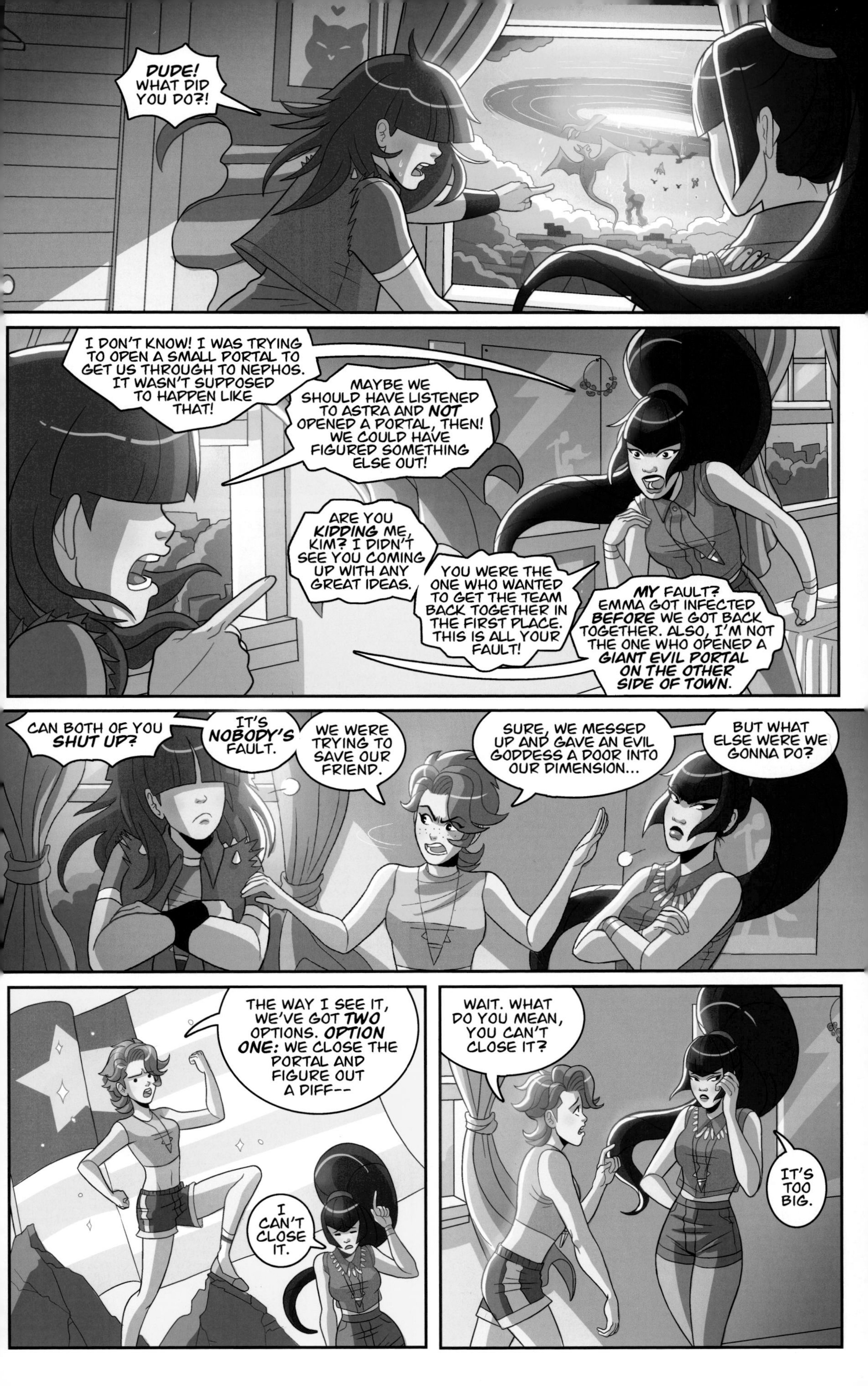
DUDE! WHAT DID YOU DO?!
I DON'T KNOW! I WAS TRYING TO OPEN A SMALL PORTAL TO GET US THROUGH TO NEPHOS. IT WASN'T SUPPOSED TO HAPPEN LIKE THAT!
MAYBE WE SHOULD HAVE LISTENED TO ASTRA AND NOT OPENED A PORTAL, THEN! WE COULD HAVE FIGURED SOMETHING ELSE OUT!
ARE YOU KIDDING ME, KIM? I DIDN'T SEE YOU COMING UP WITH ANY GREAT IDEAS.
YOU WERE THE ONE WHO WANTED TO GET THE TEAM BACK TOGETHER IN THE FIRST PLACE. THIS IS ALL YOUR FAULT!
MY FAULT? EMMA GOT INFECTED BEFORE WE GOT BACK TOGETHER. ALSO, I'M NOT THE ONE WHO OPENED A GIANT EVIL PORTAL ON THE OTHER SIDE OF TOWN.
CAN BOTH OF YOU SHUT UP?
IT'S NOBODY'S FAULT.
WE WERE TRYING TO SAVE OUR FRIEND.
SURE, WE MESSED UP AND GAVE AN EVIL GODDESS A DOOR INTO OUR DIMENSION...
BUT WHAT ELSE WERE WE GONNA DO?
THE WAY I SEE IT, WE'VE GOT TWO OPTIONS. OPTION ONE: WE CLOSE THE PORTAL AND FIGURE OUT A DIFF--
I CAN'T CLOSE IT.
WAIT. WHAT DO YOU MEAN, YOU CAN'T CLOSE IT?
IT'S TOO BIG.

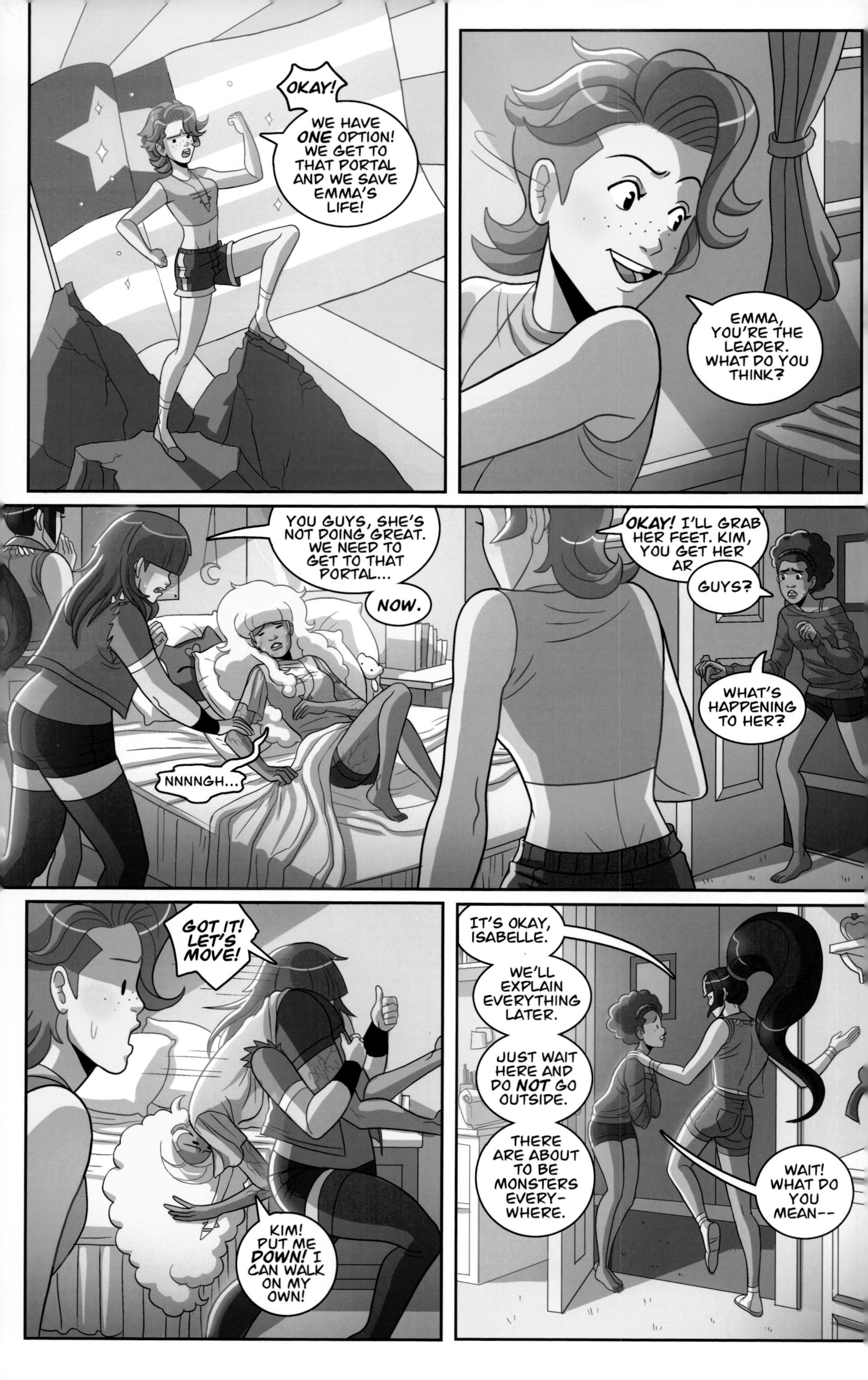
OKAY!
WE HAVE ONE OPTION! WE GET TO THAT PORTAL AND WE SAVE EMMA'S LIFE!
EMMA, YOU'RE THE LEADER. WHAT DO YOU THINK?
YOU GUYS, SHE'S NOT DOING GREAT. WE NEED TO GET TO THAT PORTAL...
NOW.
NNNNGH...
OKAY! I'LL GRAB HER FEET. KIM, YOU GET HER AR
GUYS?
WHAT'S HAPPENING TO HER?
GOT IT! LET'S MOVE!
KIM! PUT ME DOWN! I CAN WALK ON MY OWN!
IT'S OKAY, ISABELLE.
WE'LL EXPLAIN EVERYTHING LATER.
JUST WAIT HERE AND DO NOT GO OUTSIDE.
THERE ARE ABOUT TO BE MONSTERS EVERY-WHERE.
WAIT! WHAT DO YOU MEAN--

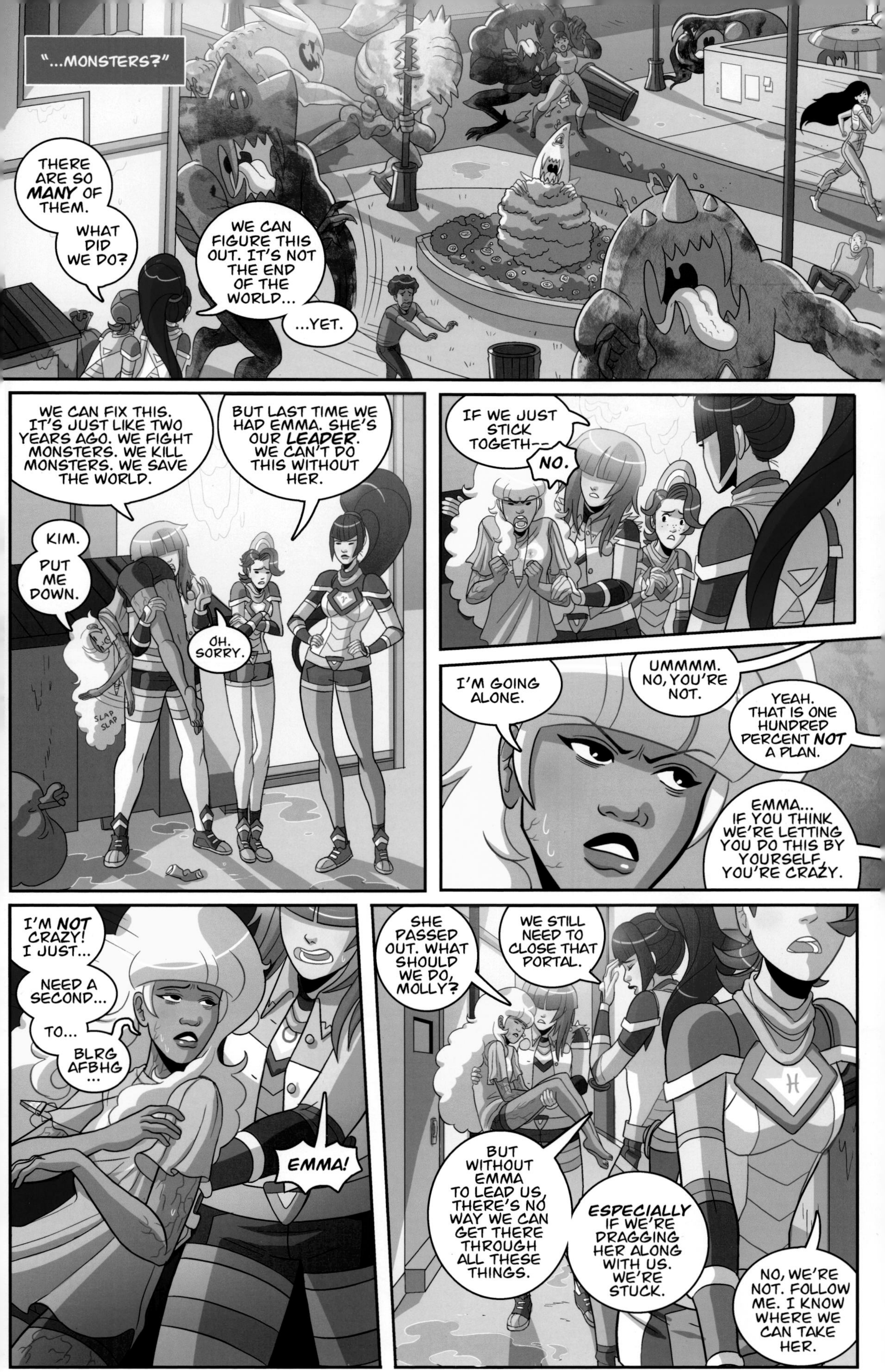
"...MONSTERS?"
THERE ARE SO MANY OF THEM.
WHAT DID WE DO?
WE CAN FIGURE THIS OUT. IT'S NOT THE END OF THE WORLD...
...YET.
WE CAN FIX THIS. IT'S JUST LIKE TWO YEARS AGO. WE FIGHT MONSTERS. WE KILL MONSTERS. WE SAVE THE WORLD.
BUT LAST TIME WE HAD EMMA. SHE'S OUR LEADER. WE CAN'T DO THIS WITHOUT HER.
KIM.
PUT ME DOWN.
SLAP SLAP
OH. SORRY.
IF WE JUST STICK TOGETH--
NO.
I'M GOING ALONE.
UMMMM. NO, YOU'RE NOT.
YEAH. THAT IS ONE HUNDRED PERCENT NOT A PLAN.
EMMA... IF YOU THINK WE'RE LETTING YOU DO THIS BY YOURSELF, YOU'RE CRAZY.
I'M NOT CRAZY! I JUST...
NEED A SECOND...
TO...
BLRG AFBHG ...
EMMA!
SHE PASSED OUT. WHAT SHOULD WE DO, MOLLY?
WE STILL NEED TO CLOSE THAT PORTAL.
BUT WITHOUT EMMA TO LEAD US, THERE'S NO WAY WE CAN GET THERE THROUGH ALL THESE THINGS.
ESPECIALLY IF WE'RE DRAGGING HER ALONG WITH US. WE'RE STUCK.
NO, WE'RE NOT. FOLLOW ME. I KNOW WHERE WE CAN TAKE HER.

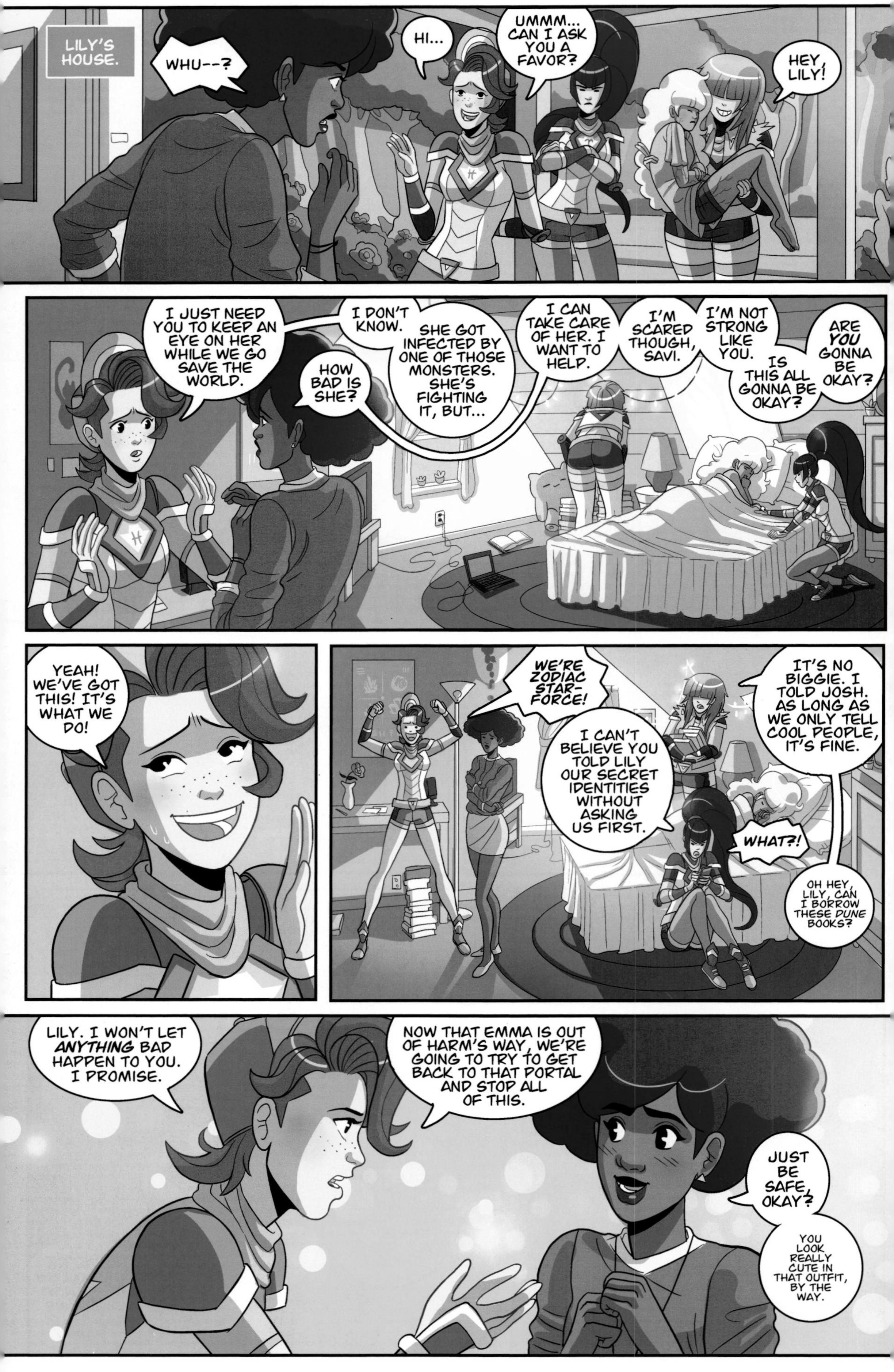
LILY'S HOUSE.
WHU--?
HI...
UMMM... CAN I ASK YOU A FAVOR?
HEY, LILY!
I JUST NEED YOU TO KEEP AN EYE ON HER WHILE WE GO SAVE THE WORLD.
HOW BAD IS SHE?
I DON'T KNOW.
SHE GOT INFECTED BY ONE OF THOSE MONSTERS. SHE'S FIGHTING IT, BUT...
I CAN TAKE CARE OF HER. I WANT TO HELP.
I'M SCARED THOUGH, SAVI.
I'M NOT STRONG LIKE YOU.
IS THIS ALL GONNA BE OKAY?
ARE *YOU* GONNA BE OKAY?
YEAH! WE'VE GOT THIS! IT'S WHAT WE DO!
WE'RE ZODIAC STARFORCE!
I CAN'T BELIEVE YOU TOLD LILY OUR SECRET IDENTITIES WITHOUT ASKING US FIRST.
IT'S NO BIGGIE. I TOLD JOSH. AS LONG AS WE ONLY TELL COOL PEOPLE, IT'S FINE.
WHAT?!
OH HEY, LILY, CAN I BORROW THESE *DUNE* BOOKS?
LILY. I WON'T LET ***ANYTHING*** BAD HAPPEN TO YOU. I PROMISE.
NOW THAT EMMA IS OUT OF HARM'S WAY, WE'RE GOING TO TRY TO GET BACK TO THAT PORTAL AND STOP ALL OF THIS.
JUST BE SAFE, OKAY?
YOU LOOK REALLY CUTE IN THAT OUTFIT, BY THE WAY.

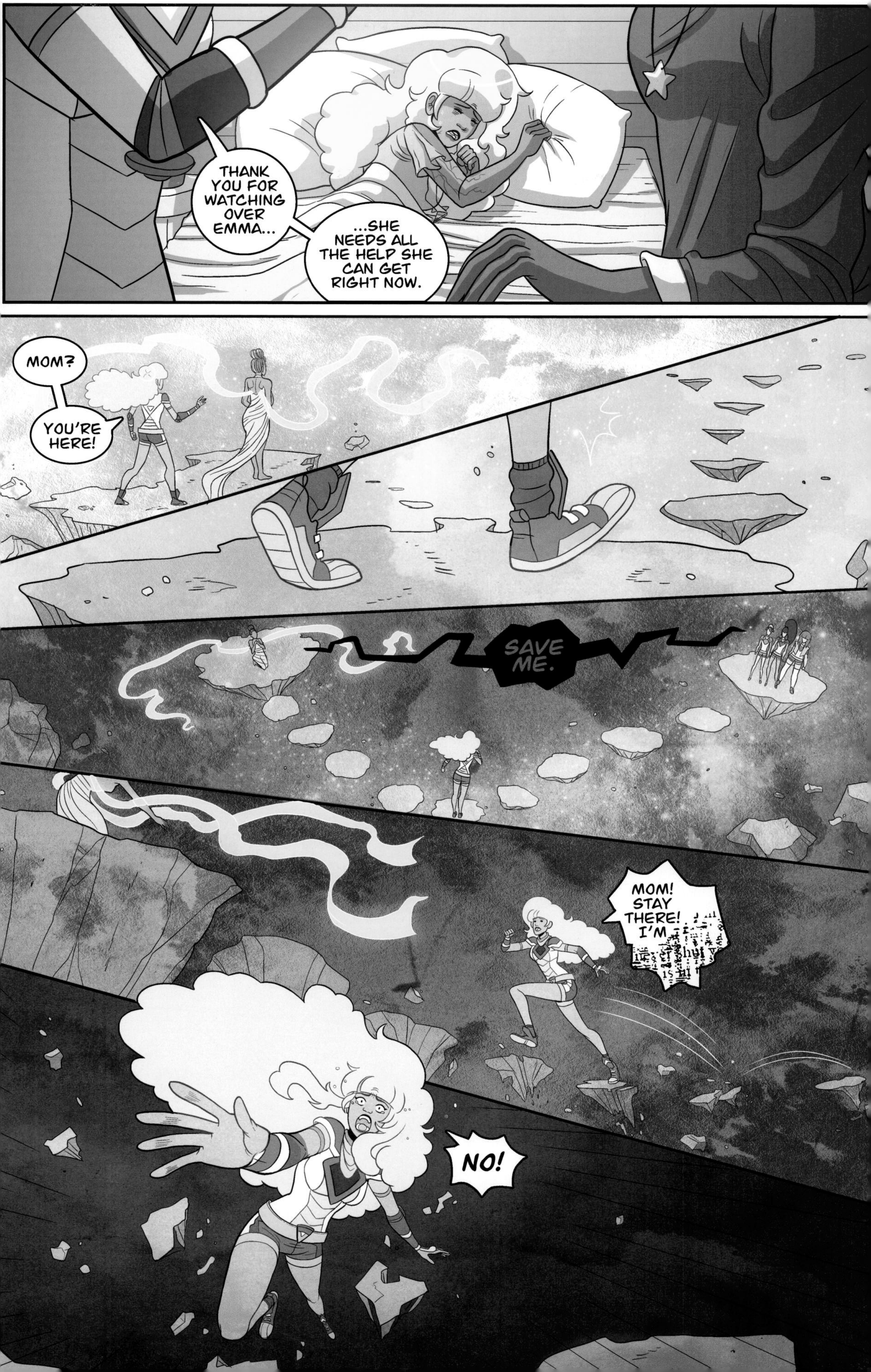
THANK YOU FOR WATCHING OVER EMMA...
...SHE NEEDS ALL THE HELP SHE CAN GET RIGHT NOW.
MOM?
YOU'RE HERE!
SAVE ME.
MOM! STAY THERE! I'M
NO!

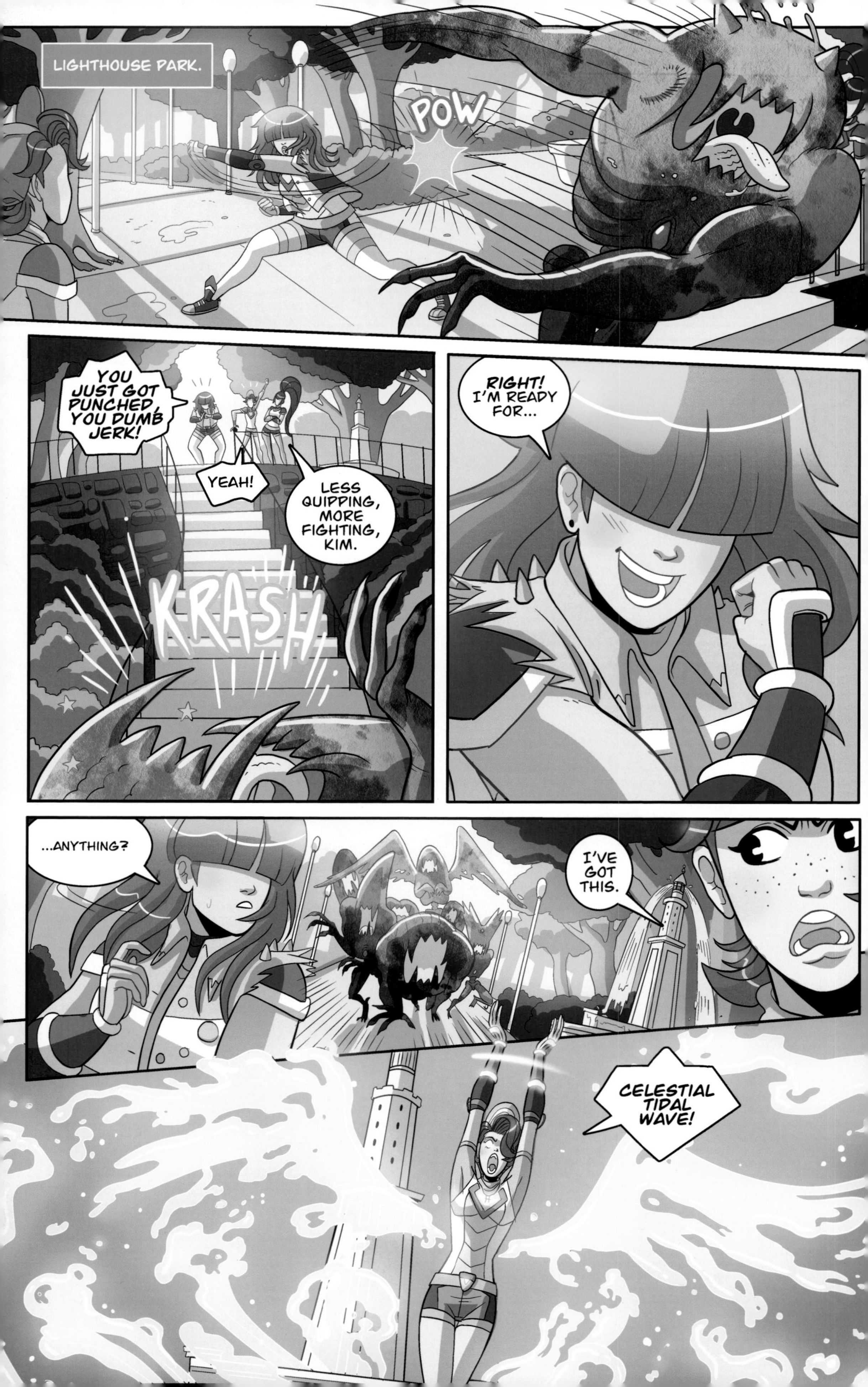
LIGHTHOUSE PARK.
POW
YOU JUST GOT PUNCHED, YOU DUMB JERK!
YEAH!
LESS QUIPPING, MORE FIGHTING, KIM.
KRASH
RIGHT! I'M READY FOR...
...ANYTHING?
I'VE GOT THIS.
CELESTIAL TIDAL WAVE!

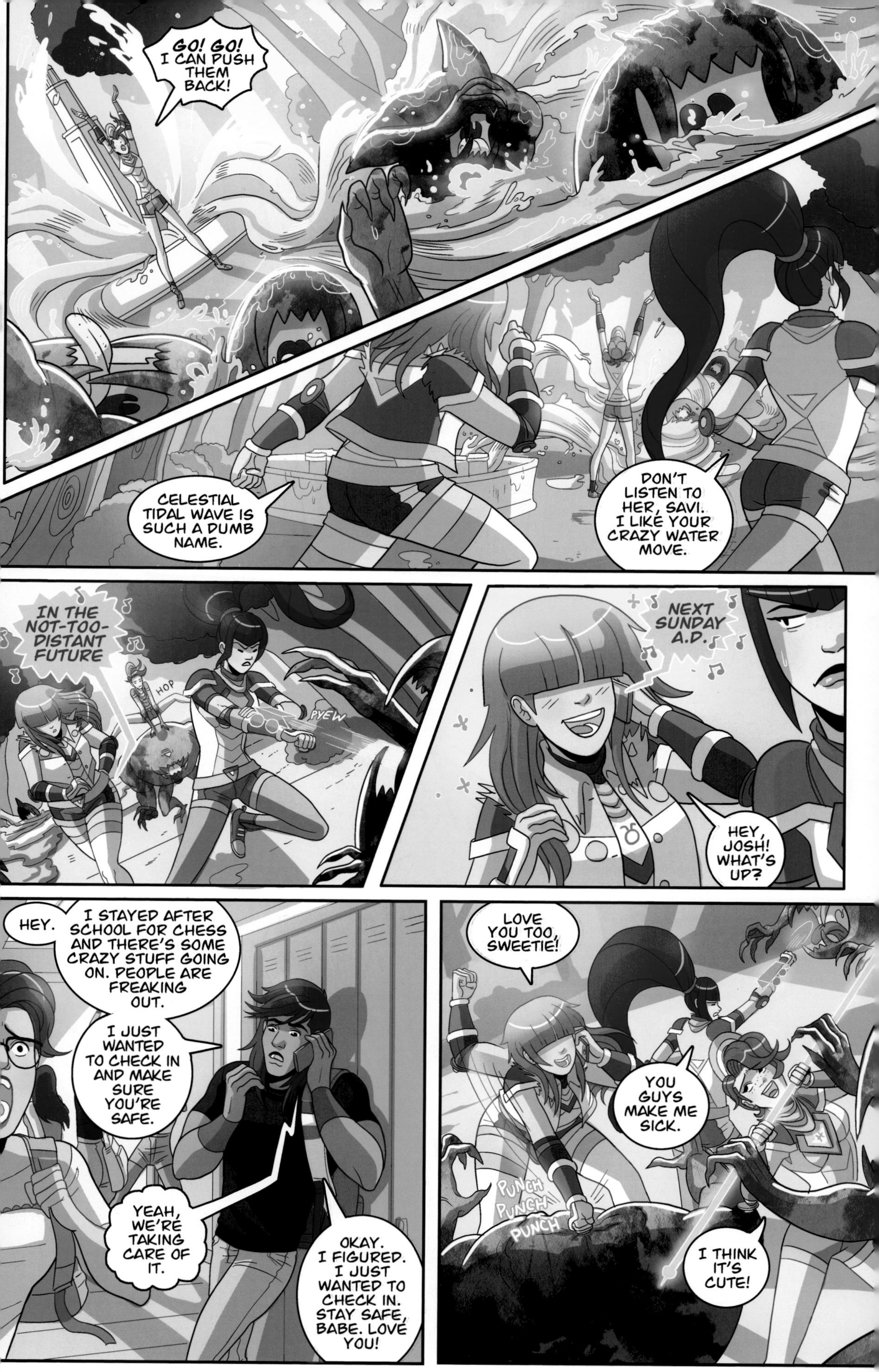
GO! GO! I CAN PUSH THEM BACK!
CELESTIAL TIDAL WAVE IS SUCH A DUMB NAME.
DON'T LISTEN TO HER, SAVI. I LIKE YOUR CRAZY WATER MOVE.
IN THE NOT-TOO-DISTANT FUTURE
HOP
PYEW
NEXT SUNDAY A.D.
HEY, JOSH! WHAT'S UP?
HEY.
I STAYED AFTER SCHOOL FOR CHESS AND THERE'S SOME CRAZY STUFF GOING ON. PEOPLE ARE FREAKING OUT.
I JUST WANTED TO CHECK IN AND MAKE SURE YOU'RE SAFE.
YEAH, WE'RE TAKING CARE OF IT.
OKAY. I FIGURED. I JUST WANTED TO CHECK IN. STAY SAFE, BABE. LOVE YOU!
LOVE YOU TOO, SWEETIE!
YOU GUYS MAKE ME SICK.
PUNCH PUNCH PUNCH
I THINK IT'S CUTE!

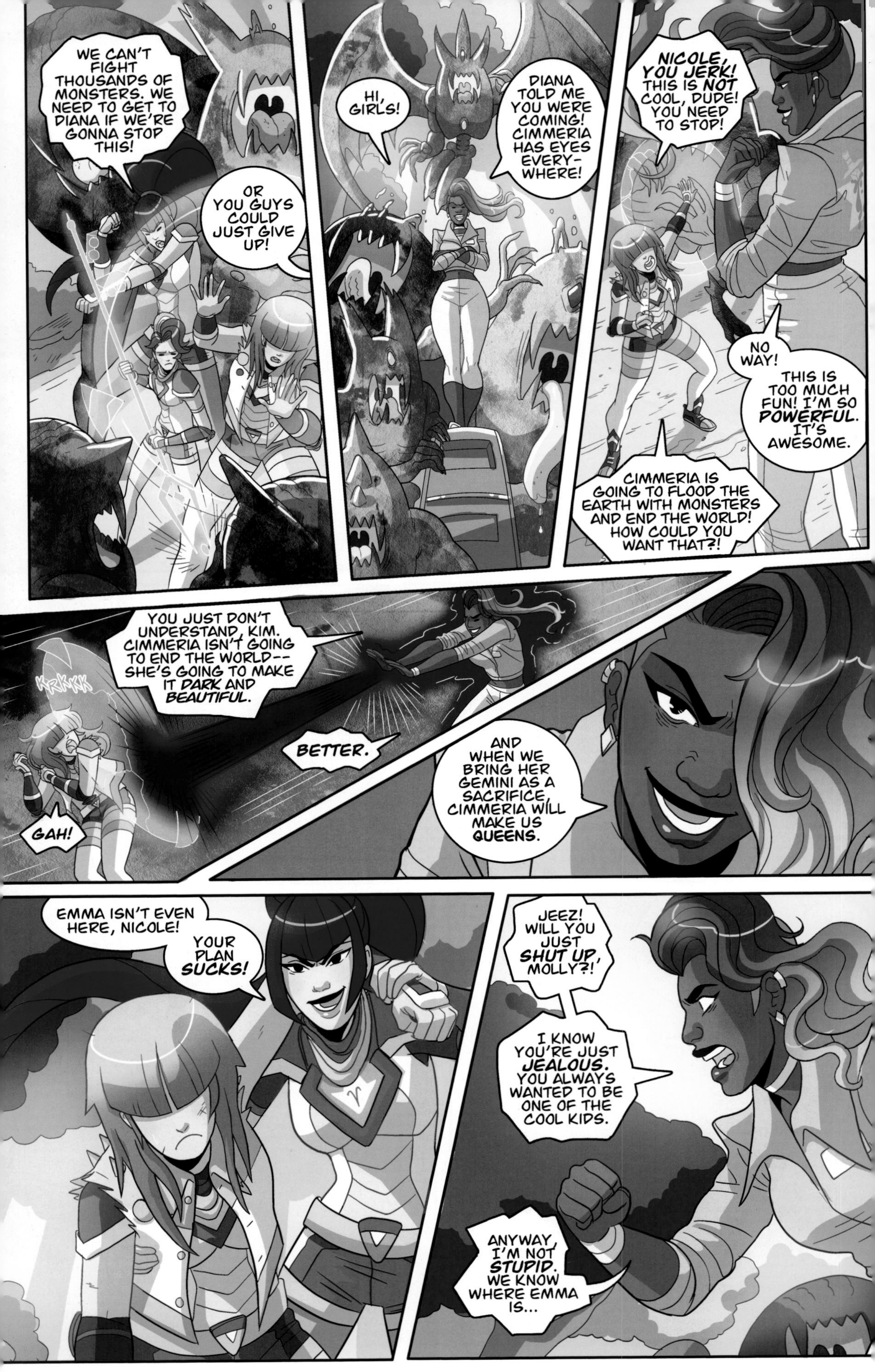

WE CAN'T FIGHT THOUSANDS OF MONSTERS. WE NEED TO GET TO DIANA IF WE'RE GONNA STOP THIS!
OR YOU GUYS COULD JUST GIVE UP!
HI, GIRLS!
DIANA TOLD ME YOU WERE COMING! CIMMERIA HAS EYES EVERY-WHERE!
NICOLE, YOU JERK! THIS IS NOT COOL, DUDE! YOU NEED TO STOP!
NO WAY!
THIS IS TOO MUCH FUN! I'M SO POWERFUL. IT'S AWESOME.
CIMMERIA IS GOING TO FLOOD THE EARTH WITH MONSTERS AND END THE WORLD! HOW COULD YOU WANT THAT?!
YOU JUST DON'T UNDERSTAND, KIM. CIMMERIA ISN'T GOING TO END THE WORLD-- SHE'S GOING TO MAKE IT DARK AND BEAUTIFUL.
KRAKKK
BETTER.
GAH!
AND WHEN WE BRING HER GEMINI AS A SACRIFICE, CIMMERIA WILL MAKE US QUEENS.
EMMA ISN'T EVEN HERE, NICOLE!
YOUR PLAN SUCKS!
JEEZ! WILL YOU JUST SHUT UP, MOLLY?!
I KNOW YOU'RE JUST JEALOUS. YOU ALWAYS WANTED TO BE ONE OF THE COOL KIDS.
ANYWAY, I'M NOT STUPID. WE KNOW WHERE EMMA IS...

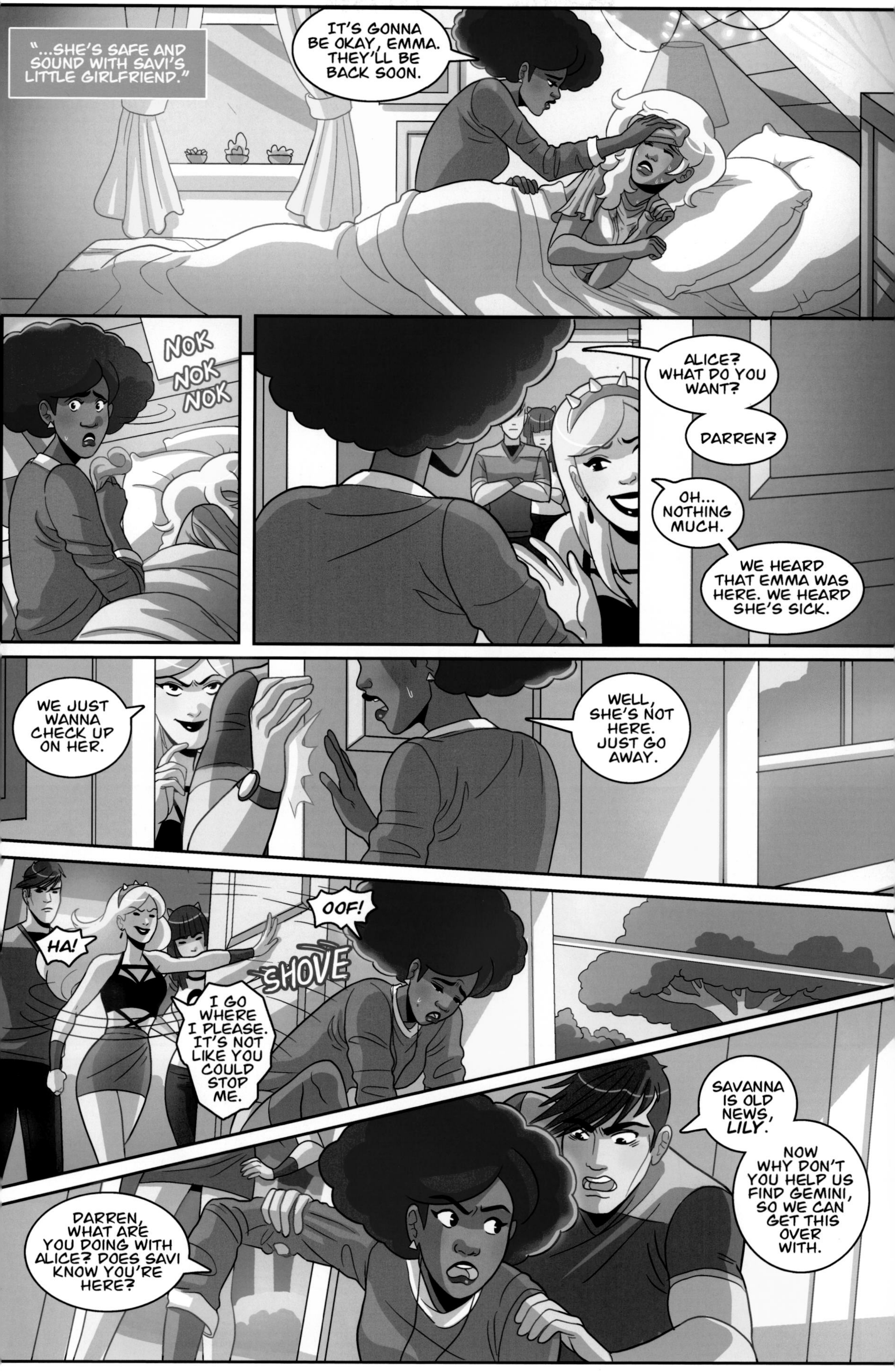
"...SHE'S SAFE AND SOUND WITH SAVI'S LITTLE GIRLFRIEND."
IT'S GONNA BE OKAY, EMMA. THEY'LL BE BACK SOON.
NOK NOK NOK
ALICE? WHAT DO YOU WANT?
DARREN?
OH... NOTHING MUCH.
WE HEARD THAT EMMA WAS HERE. WE HEARD SHE'S SICK.
WE JUST WANNA CHECK UP ON HER.
WELL, SHE'S NOT HERE. JUST GO AWAY.
OOF!
HA!
SHOVE
I GO WHERE I PLEASE. IT'S NOT LIKE YOU COULD STOP ME.
SAVANNA IS OLD NEWS, LILY.
NOW WHY DON'T YOU HELP US FIND GEMINI, SO WE CAN GET THIS OVER WITH.
DARREN, WHAT ARE YOU DOING WITH ALICE? DOES SAVI KNOW YOU'RE HERE?

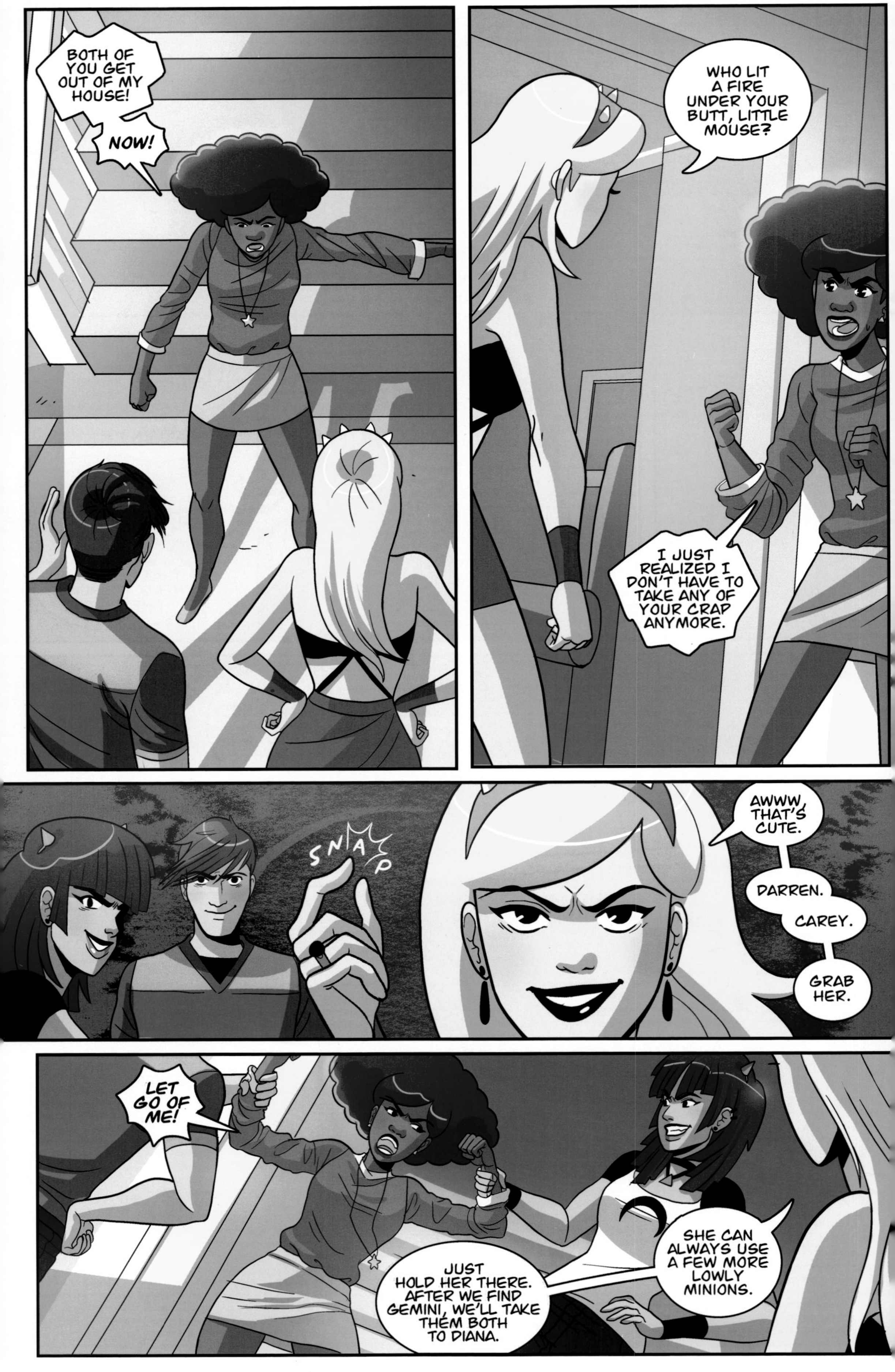
BOTH OF YOU GET OUT OF MY HOUSE!
NOW!
WHO LIT A FIRE UNDER YOUR BUTT, LITTLE MOUSE?
I JUST REALIZED I DON'T HAVE TO TAKE ANY OF YOUR CRAP ANYMORE.
SNAP
AWWW, THAT'S CUTE.
DARREN.
CAREY.
GRAB HER.
LET GO OF ME!
JUST HOLD HER THERE. AFTER WE FIND GEMINI, WE'LL TAKE THEM BOTH TO DIANA.
SHE CAN ALWAYS USE A FEW MORE LOWLY MINIONS.

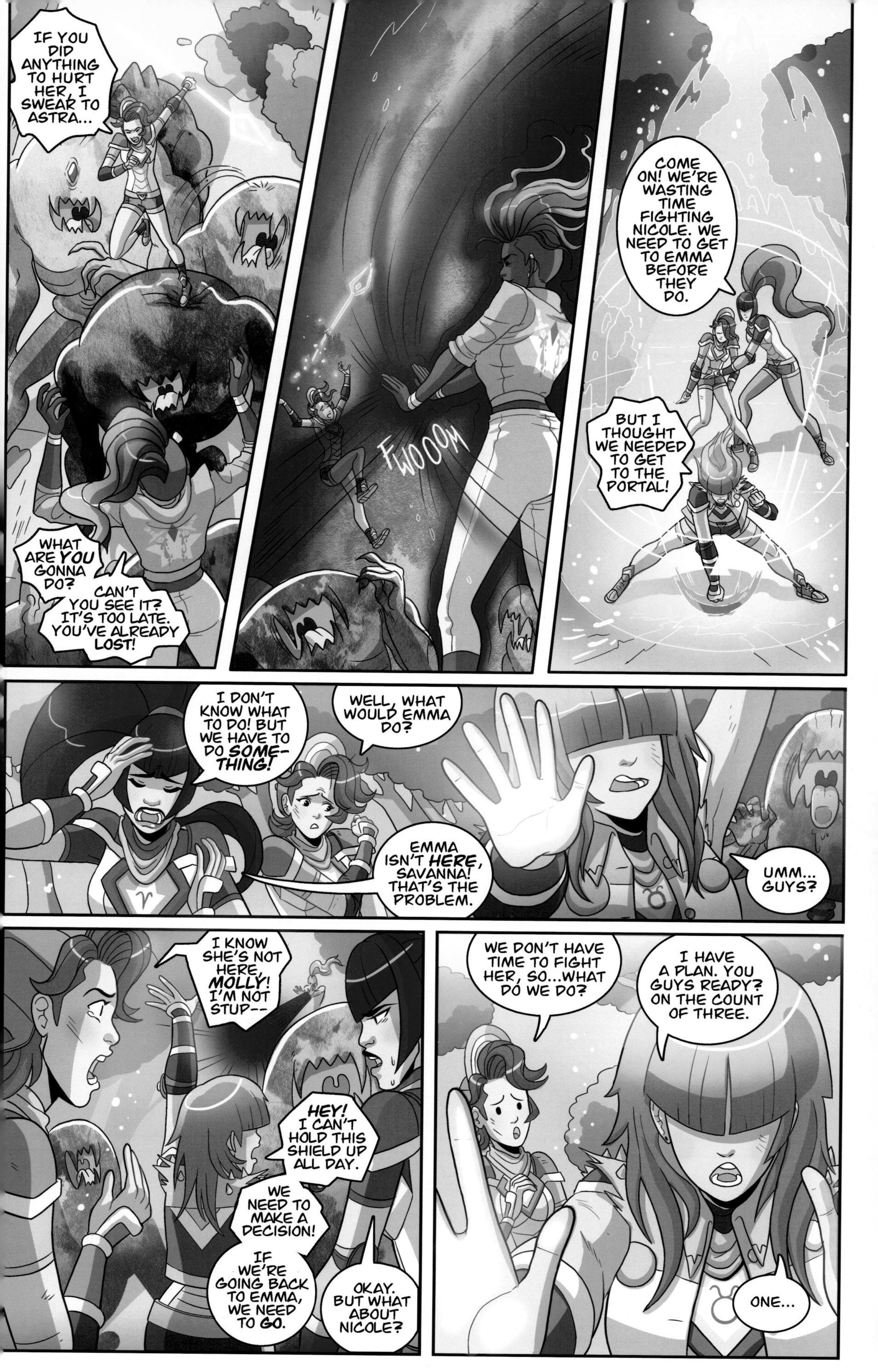

IF YOU DID ANYTHING TO HURT HER, I SWEAR TO ASTRA...
WHAT ARE YOU GONNA DO?
CAN'T YOU SEE IT? IT'S TOO LATE. YOU'VE ALREADY LOST!
FWOOOM
COME ON! WE'RE WASTING TIME FIGHTING NICOLE. WE NEED TO GET TO EMMA BEFORE THEY DO.
BUT I THOUGHT WE NEEDED TO GET TO THE PORTAL!
I DON'T KNOW WHAT TO DO! BUT WE HAVE TO DO SOMETHING!
WELL, WHAT WOULD EMMA DO?
EMMA ISN'T HERE, SAVANNA! THAT'S THE PROBLEM.
UMM... GUYS?
I KNOW SHE'S NOT HERE, MOLLY! I'M NOT STUP--
HEY! I CAN'T HOLD THIS SHIELD UP ALL DAY.
WE NEED TO MAKE A DECISION!
IF WE'RE GOING BACK TO EMMA, WE NEED TO GO.
OKAY. BUT WHAT ABOUT NICOLE?
WE DON'T HAVE TIME TO FIGHT HER, SO...WHAT DO WE DO?
I HAVE A PLAN. YOU GUYS READY? ON THE COUNT OF THREE.
ONE...

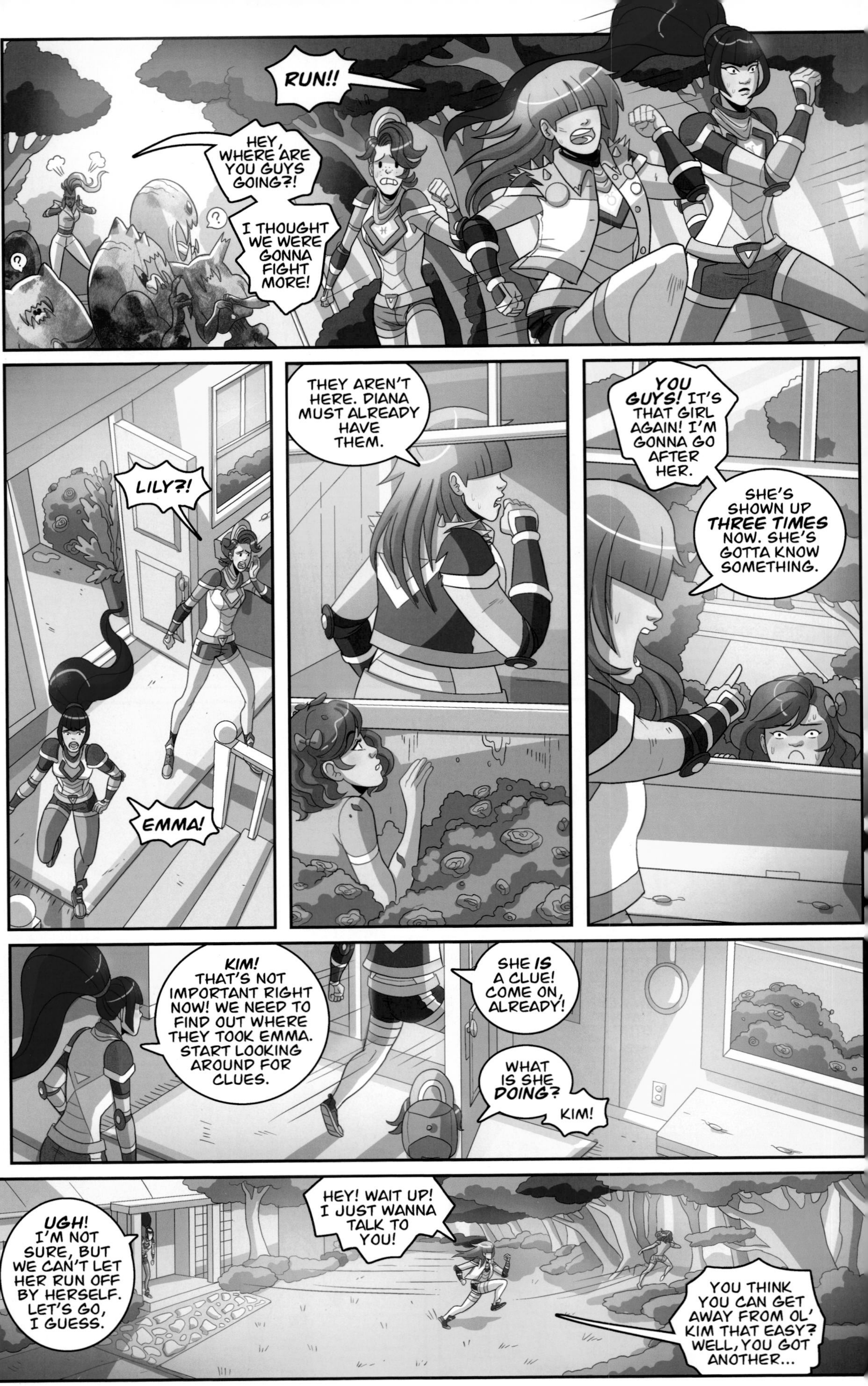
RUN!!
HEY, WHERE ARE YOU GUYS GOING?!
I THOUGHT WE WERE GONNA FIGHT MORE!
LILY?!
EMMA!
THEY AREN'T HERE. DIANA MUST ALREADY HAVE THEM.
YOU GUYS! IT'S THAT GIRL AGAIN! I'M GONNA GO AFTER HER.
SHE'S SHOWN UP THREE TIMES NOW. SHE'S GOTTA KNOW SOMETHING.
KIM! THAT'S NOT IMPORTANT RIGHT NOW! WE NEED TO FIND OUT WHERE THEY TOOK EMMA. START LOOKING AROUND FOR CLUES.
SHE IS A CLUE! COME ON, ALREADY!
WHAT IS SHE DOING?
KIM!
UGH! I'M NOT SURE, BUT WE CAN'T LET HER RUN OFF BY HERSELF. LET'S GO, I GUESS.
HEY! WAIT UP! I JUST WANNA TALK TO YOU!
YOU THINK YOU CAN GET AWAY FROM OL' KIM THAT EASY? WELL, YOU GOT ANOTHER...

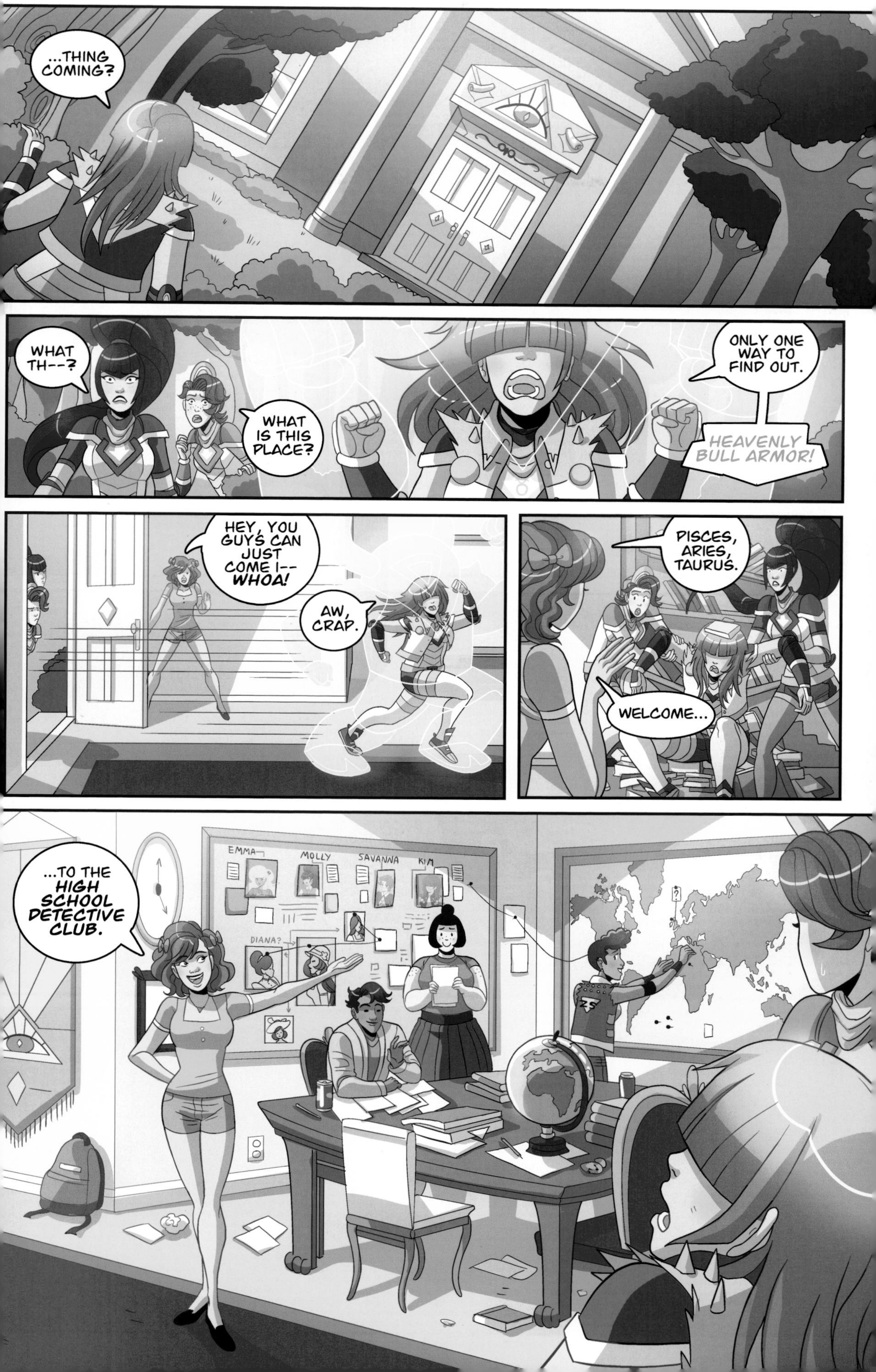
...THING COMING?
WHAT TH--?
WHAT IS THIS PLACE?
ONLY ONE WAY TO FIND OUT.
HEAVENLY BULL ARMOR!
HEY, YOU GUY'S CAN JUST COME I-- WHOA!
AW, CRAP.
PISCES, ARIES, TAURUS.
WELCOME...
...TO THE HIGH SCHOOL DETECTIVE CLUB.
EMMA
MOLLY
SAVANNA
KIM
DIANA?

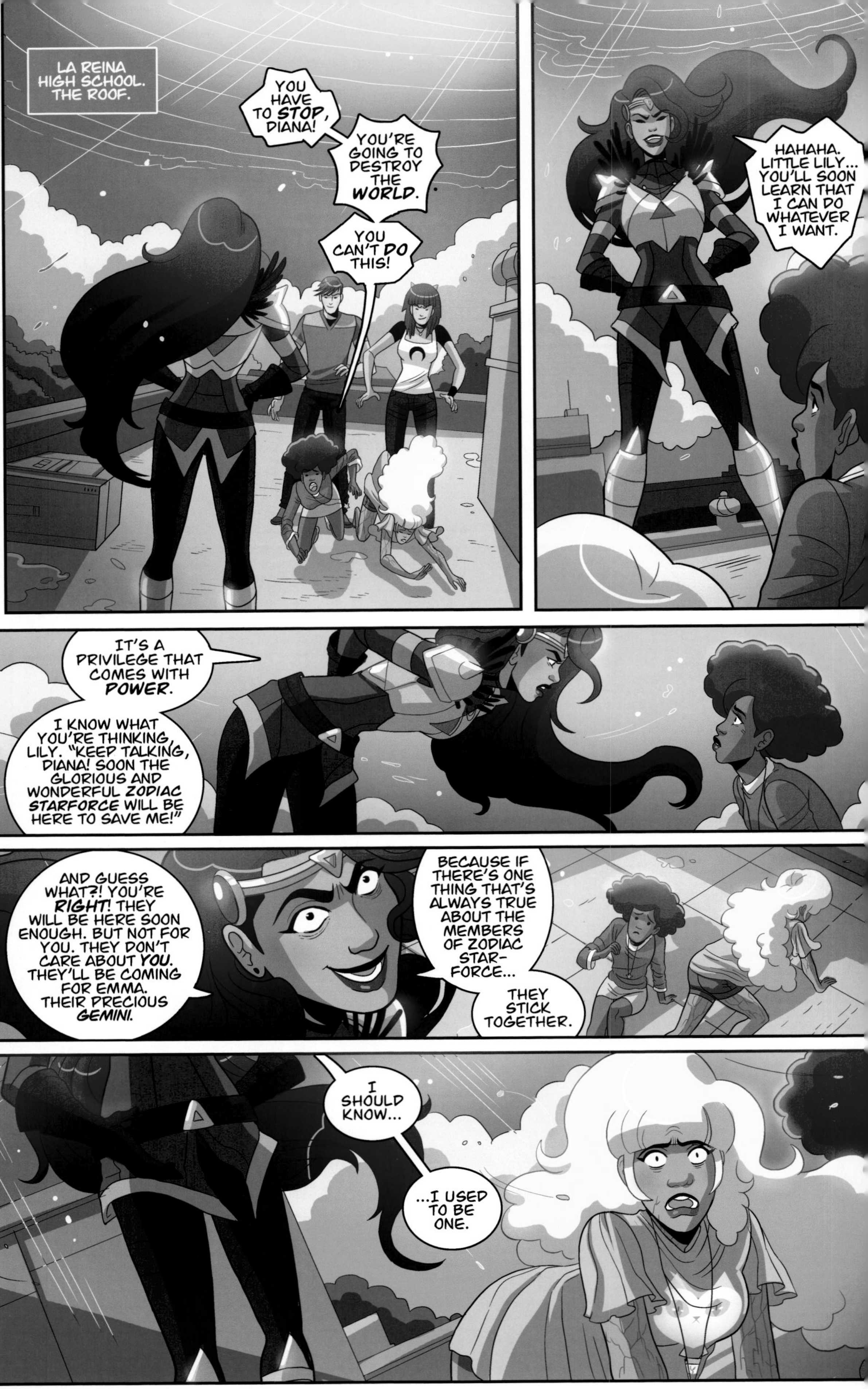
LA REINA HIGH SCHOOL. THE ROOF.
YOU HAVE TO STOP, DIANA!
YOU'RE GOING TO DESTROY THE WORLD.
YOU CAN'T DO THIS!
HAHAHA. LITTLE LILY... YOU'LL SOON LEARN THAT I CAN DO WHATEVER I WANT.
IT'S A PRIVILEGE THAT COMES WITH POWER.
I KNOW WHAT YOU'RE THINKING, LILY. "KEEP TALKING, DIANA! SOON THE GLORIOUS AND WONDERFUL ZODIAC STARFORCE WILL BE HERE TO SAVE ME!"
AND GUESS WHAT?! YOU'RE RIGHT! THEY WILL BE HERE SOON ENOUGH. BUT NOT FOR YOU. THEY DON'T CARE ABOUT YOU. THEY'LL BE COMING FOR EMMA. THEIR PRECIOUS GEMINI.
BECAUSE IF THERE'S ONE THING THAT'S ALWAYS TRUE ABOUT THE MEMBERS OF ZODIAC STAR-FORCE...
THEY STICK TOGETHER.
I SHOULD KNOW...
...I USED TO BE ONE.

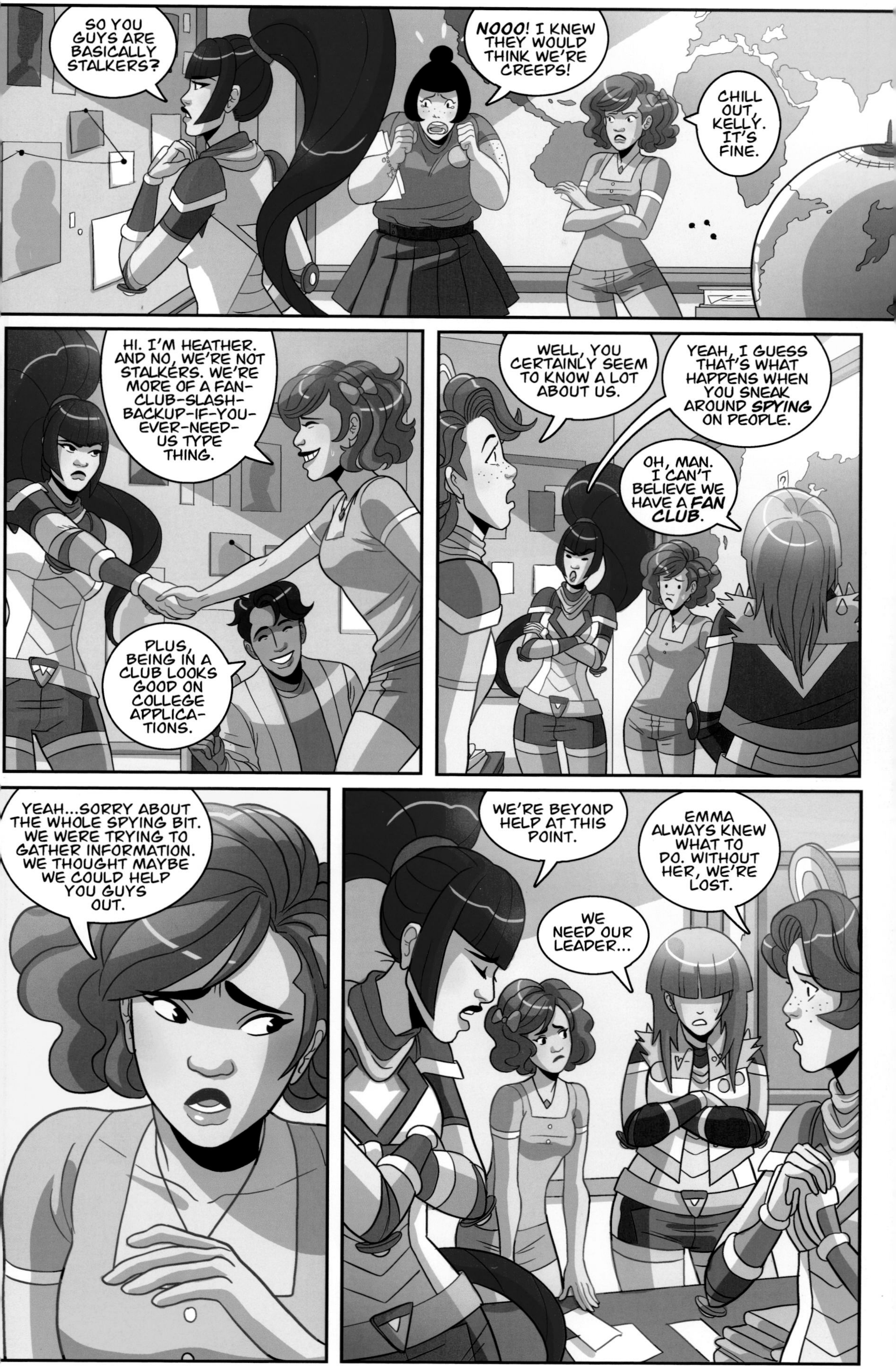
SO YOU GUYS ARE BASICALLY STALKERS?
NOOO! I KNEW THEY WOULD THINK WE'RE CREEPS!
CHILL OUT, KELLY. IT'S FINE.
HI. I'M HEATHER. AND NO, WE'RE NOT STALKERS. WE'RE MORE OF A FAN-CLUB-SLASH-BACKUP-IF-YOU-EVER-NEED-US TYPE THING.
PLUS, BEING IN A CLUB LOOKS GOOD ON COLLEGE APPLICATIONS.
WELL, YOU CERTAINLY SEEM TO KNOW A LOT ABOUT US.
YEAH, I GUESS THAT'S WHAT HAPPENS WHEN YOU SNEAK AROUND SPYING ON PEOPLE.
OH, MAN. I CAN'T BELIEVE WE HAVE A FAN CLUB.
YEAH...SORRY ABOUT THE WHOLE SPYING BIT. WE WERE TRYING TO GATHER INFORMATION. WE THOUGHT MAYBE WE COULD HELP YOU GUYS OUT.
WE'RE BEYOND HELP AT THIS POINT.
EMMA ALWAYS KNEW WHAT TO DO. WITHOUT HER, WE'RE LOST.
WE NEED OUR LEADER...

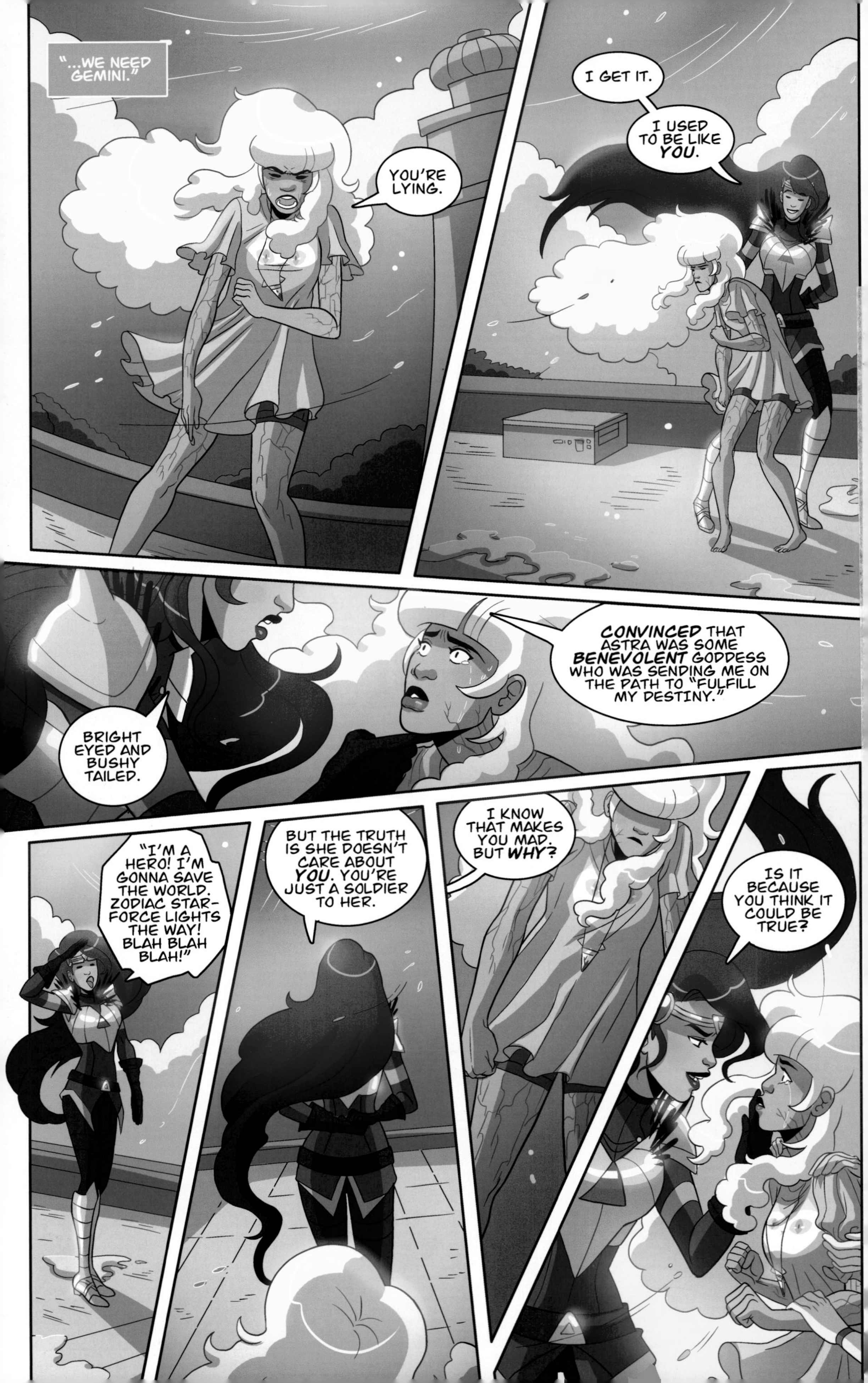
"...WE NEED GEMINI."
YOU'RE LYING.
I GET IT.
I USED TO BE LIKE YOU.
BRIGHT EYED AND BUSHY TAILED.
CONVINCED THAT ASTRA WAS SOME BENEVOLENT GODDESS WHO WAS SENDING ME ON THE PATH TO "FULFILL MY DESTINY."
"I'M A HERO! I'M GONNA SAVE THE WORLD. ZODIAC STAR-FORCE LIGHTS THE WAY! BLAH BLAH BLAH!"
BUT THE TRUTH IS SHE DOESN'T CARE ABOUT YOU. YOU'RE JUST A SOLDIER TO HER.
I KNOW THAT MAKES YOU MAD. BUT WHY?
IS IT BECAUSE YOU THINK IT COULD BE TRUE?

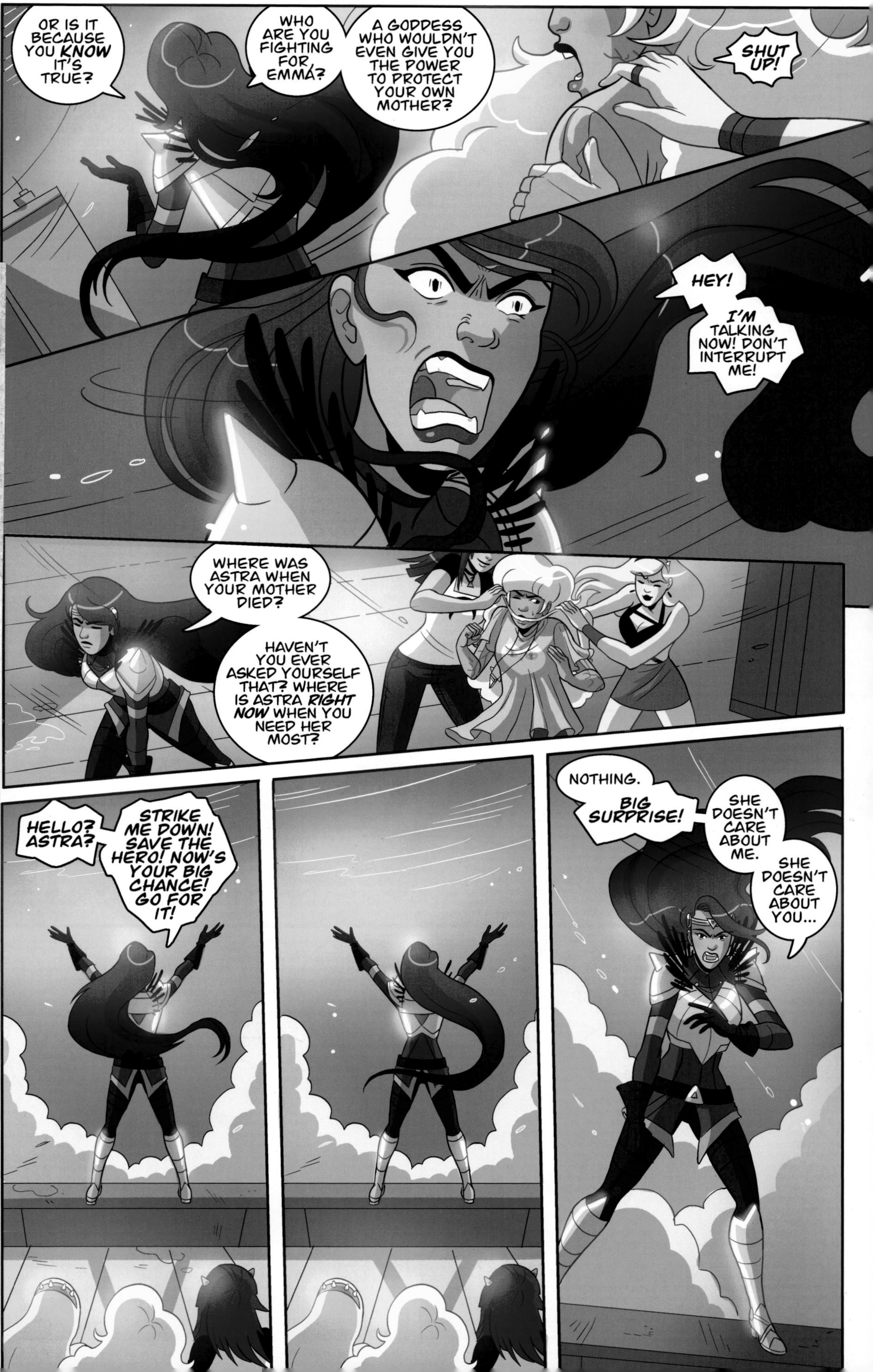

OR IS IT BECAUSE YOU **KNOW** IT'S TRUE?
WHO ARE YOU FIGHTING FOR, EMMA?
A GODDESS WHO WOULDN'T EVEN GIVE YOU THE POWER TO PROTECT YOUR OWN MOTHER?
SHUT UP!
HEY!
I'M TALKING NOW! DON'T INTERRUPT ME!
WHERE WAS ASTRA WHEN YOUR MOTHER DIED?
HAVEN'T YOU EVER ASKED YOURSELF THAT? WHERE IS ASTRA *RIGHT NOW* WHEN YOU NEED HER MOST?
HELLO? ASTRA?
STRIKE ME DOWN! SAVE THE HERO! NOW'S YOUR BIG CHANCE! GO FOR IT!
NOTHING.
BIG SURPRISE!
SHE DOESN'T CARE ABOUT ME.
SHE DOESN'T CARE ABOUT YOU...

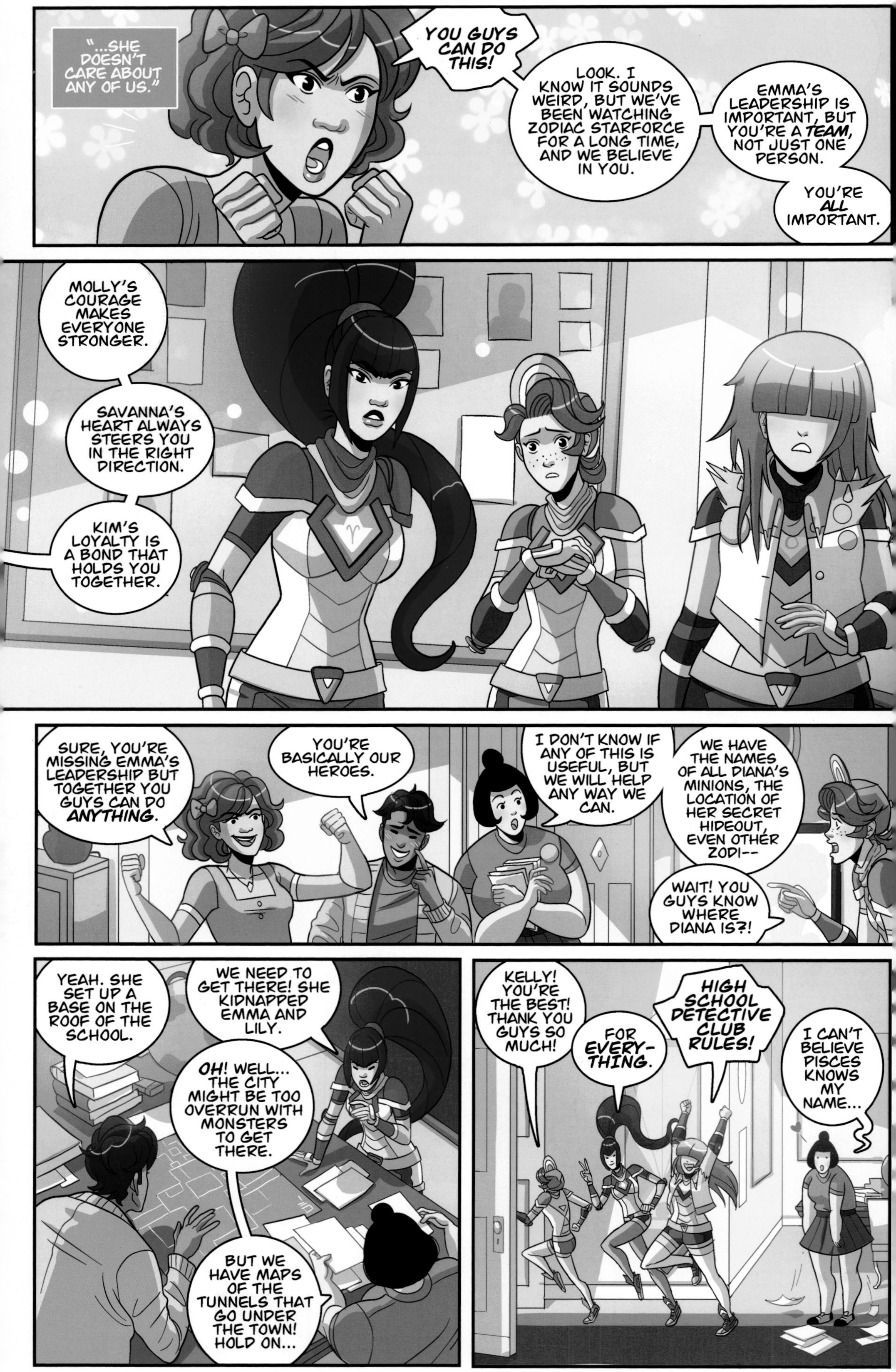
"...SHE DOESN'T CARE ABOUT ANY OF US."
YOU GUYS CAN DO THIS!
LOOK. I KNOW IT SOUNDS WEIRD, BUT WE'VE BEEN WATCHING ZODIAC STARFORCE FOR A LONG TIME, AND WE BELIEVE IN YOU.
EMMA'S LEADERSHIP IS IMPORTANT, BUT YOU'RE A *TEAM,* NOT JUST ONE PERSON.
YOU'RE *ALL* IMPORTANT.
MOLLY'S COURAGE MAKES EVERYONE STRONGER.
SAVANNA'S HEART ALWAYS STEERS YOU IN THE RIGHT DIRECTION.
KIM'S LOYALTY IS A BOND THAT HOLDS YOU TOGETHER.
SURE, YOU'RE MISSING EMMA'S LEADERSHIP BUT TOGETHER YOU GUYS CAN DO **ANYTHING**.
YOU'RE BASICALLY OUR HEROES.
I DON'T KNOW IF ANY OF THIS IS USEFUL, BUT WE WILL HELP ANY WAY WE CAN.
WE HAVE THE NAMES OF ALL DIANA'S MINIONS, THE LOCATION OF HER SECRET HIDEOUT, EVEN OTHER ZODI--
WAIT! YOU GUYS KNOW WHERE DIANA IS?!
YEAH. SHE SET UP A BASE ON THE ROOF OF THE SCHOOL.
WE NEED TO GET THERE! SHE KIDNAPPED EMMA AND LILY.
OH! WELL... THE CITY MIGHT BE TOO OVERRUN WITH MONSTERS TO GET THERE.
BUT WE HAVE MAPS OF THE TUNNELS THAT GO UNDER THE TOWN! HOLD ON...
KELLY! YOU'RE THE BEST! THANK YOU GUYS SO MUCH!
FOR **EVERY-THING**.
HIGH SCHOOL DETECTIVE CLUB RULES!
I CAN'T BELIEVE PISCES KNOWS MY NAME...

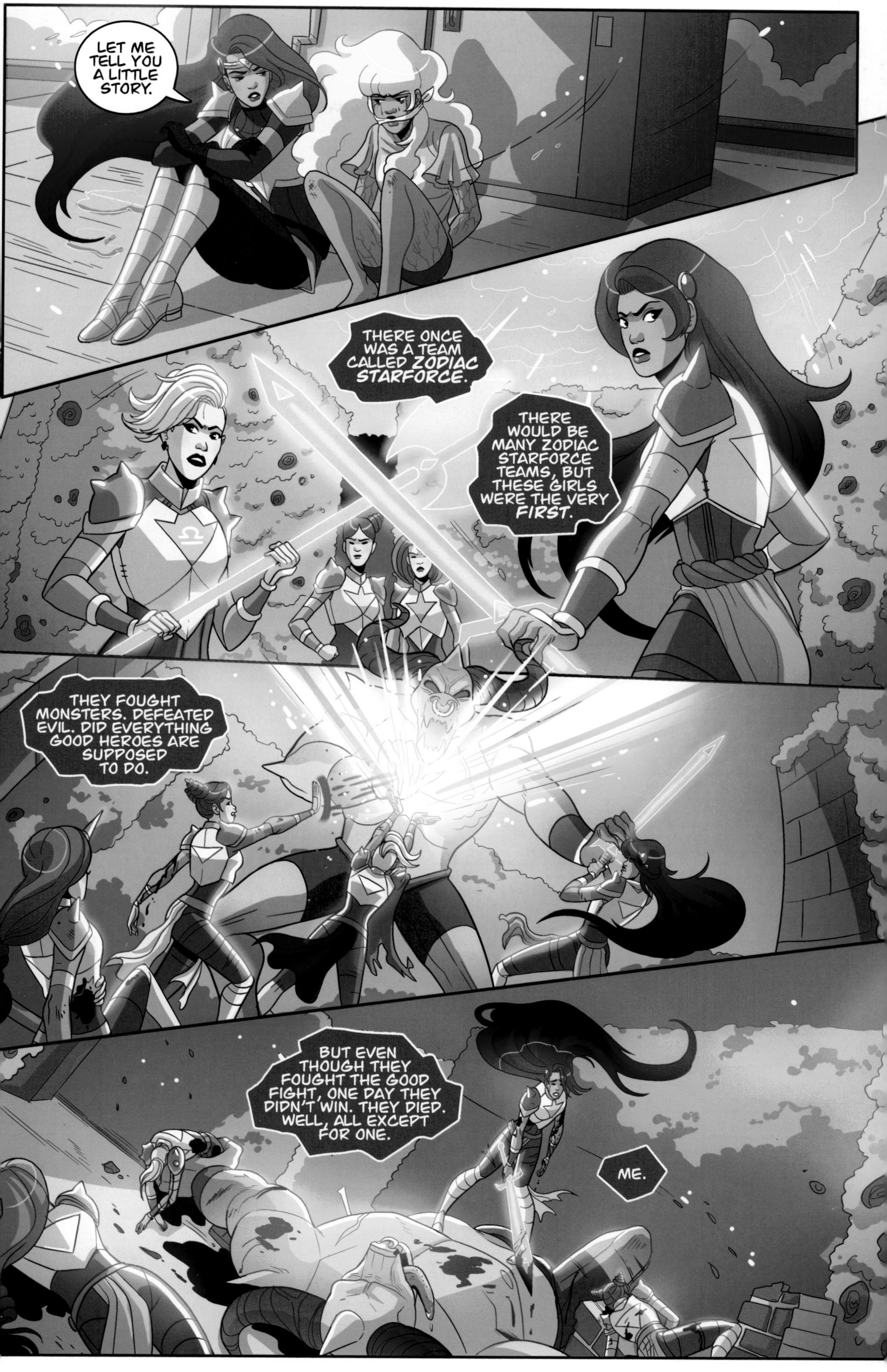
LET ME TELL YOU A LITTLE STORY.
THERE ONCE WAS A TEAM CALLED ZODIAC STARFORCE.
THERE WOULD BE MANY ZODIAC STARFORCE TEAMS, BUT THESE GIRLS WERE THE VERY FIRST.
THEY FOUGHT MONSTERS. DEFEATED EVIL. DID EVERYTHING GOOD HEROES ARE SUPPOSED TO DO.
BUT EVEN THOUGH THEY FOUGHT THE GOOD FIGHT, ONE DAY THEY DIDN'T WIN. THEY DIED. WELL, ALL EXCEPT FOR ONE.
ME.

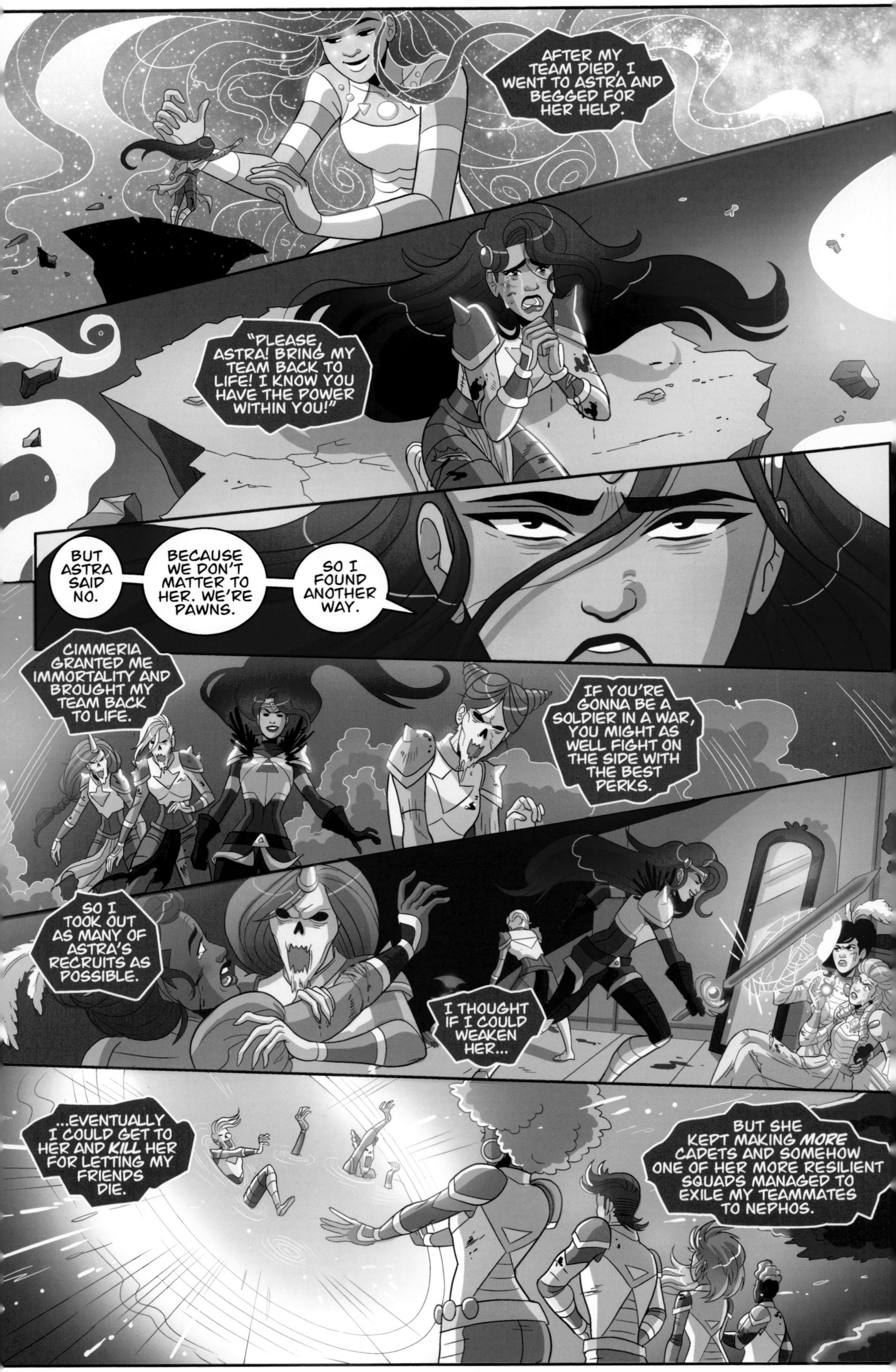
AFTER MY TEAM DIED, I WENT TO ASTRA AND BEGGED FOR HER HELP.
"PLEASE, ASTRA! BRING MY TEAM BACK TO LIFE! I KNOW YOU HAVE THE POWER WITHIN YOU!"
BUT ASTRA SAID NO.
BECAUSE WE DON'T MATTER TO HER. WE'RE PAWNS.
SO I FOUND ANOTHER WAY.
CIMMERIA GRANTED ME IMMORTALITY AND BROUGHT MY TEAM BACK TO LIFE.
IF YOU'RE GONNA BE A SOLDIER IN A WAR, YOU MIGHT AS WELL FIGHT ON THE SIDE WITH THE BEST PERKS.
SO I TOOK OUT AS MANY OF ASTRA'S RECRUITS AS POSSIBLE.
I THOUGHT IF I COULD WEAKEN HER...
...EVENTUALLY I COULD GET TO HER AND KILL HER FOR LETTING MY FRIENDS DIE.
BUT SHE KEPT MAKING MORE CADETS AND SOMEHOW ONE OF HER MORE RESILIENT SQUADS MANAGED TO EXILE MY TEAMMATES TO NEPHOS.

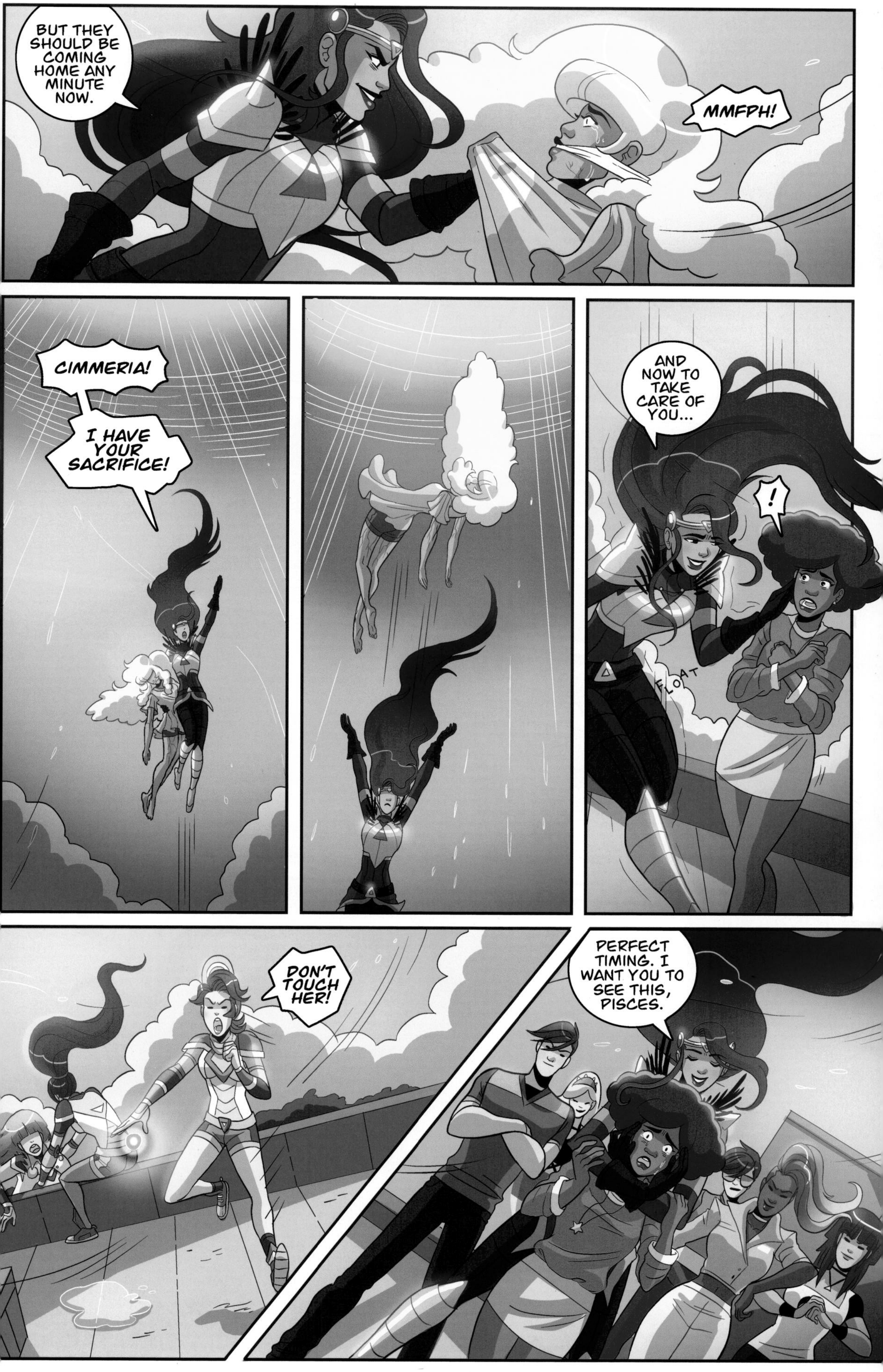
BUT THEY SHOULD BE COMING HOME ANY MINUTE NOW.
MMFPH!
CIMMERIA!
I HAVE YOUR SACRIFICE!
AND NOW TO TAKE CARE OF YOU...
!
FLOAT
DON'T TOUCH HER!
PERFECT TIMING. I WANT YOU TO SEE THIS, PISCES.

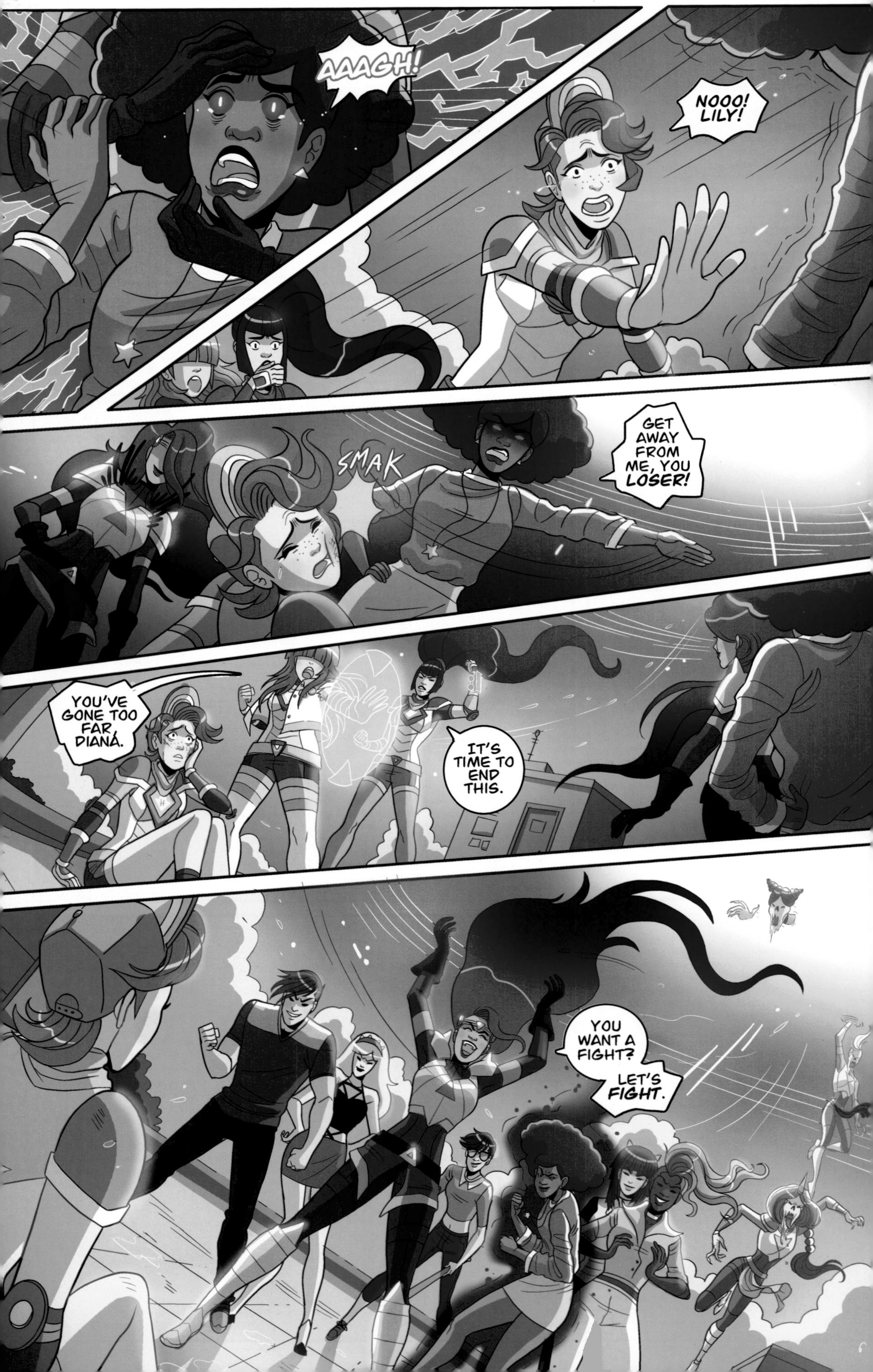
AAAGH!
NOOO! LILY!
SMAK
GET AWAY FROM ME, YOU **LOSER!**
YOU'VE GONE TOO FAR, DIANA.
IT'S TIME TO END THIS.
YOU WANT A FIGHT?
LET'S **FIGHT.**

CHAPTER FOUR

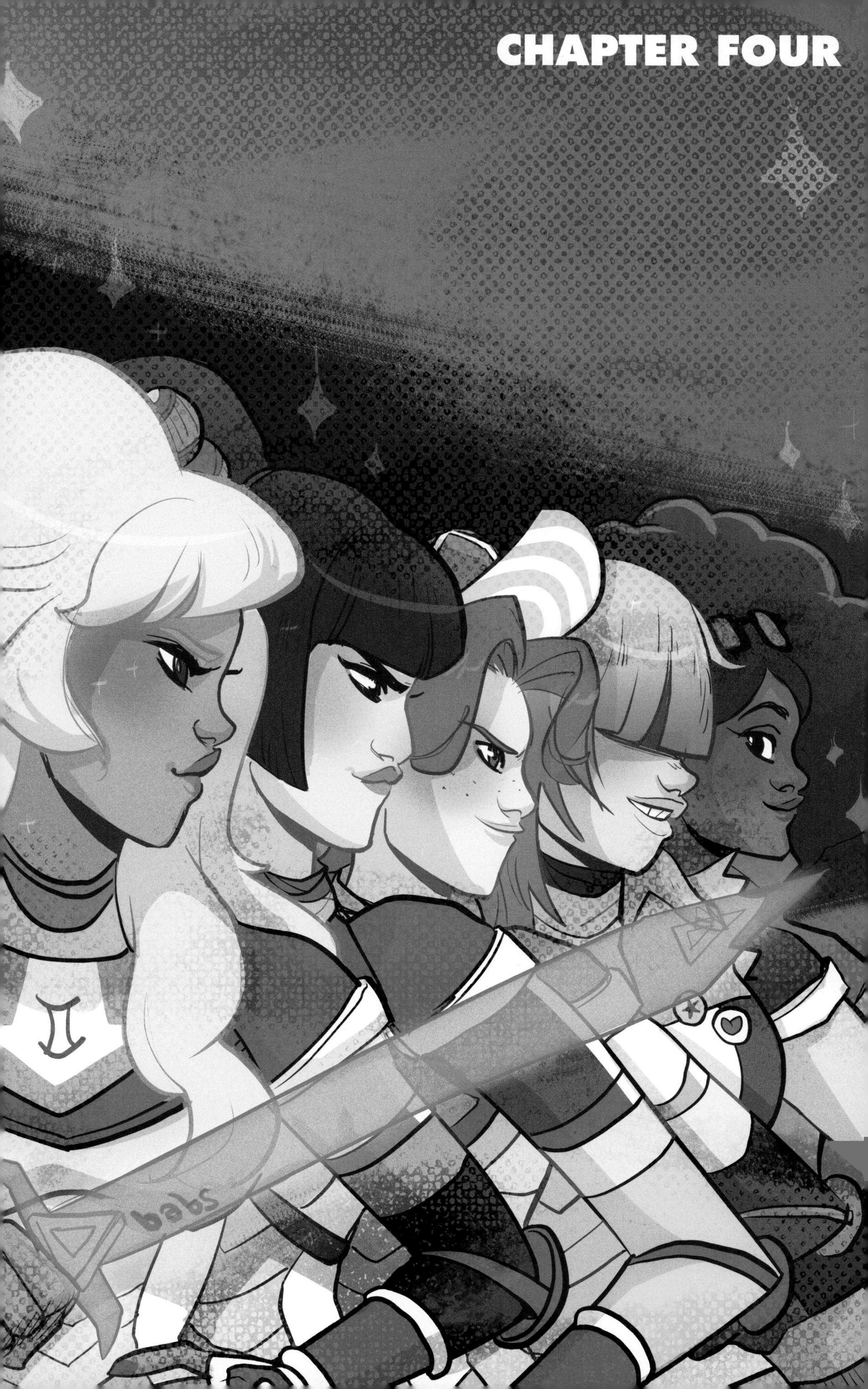

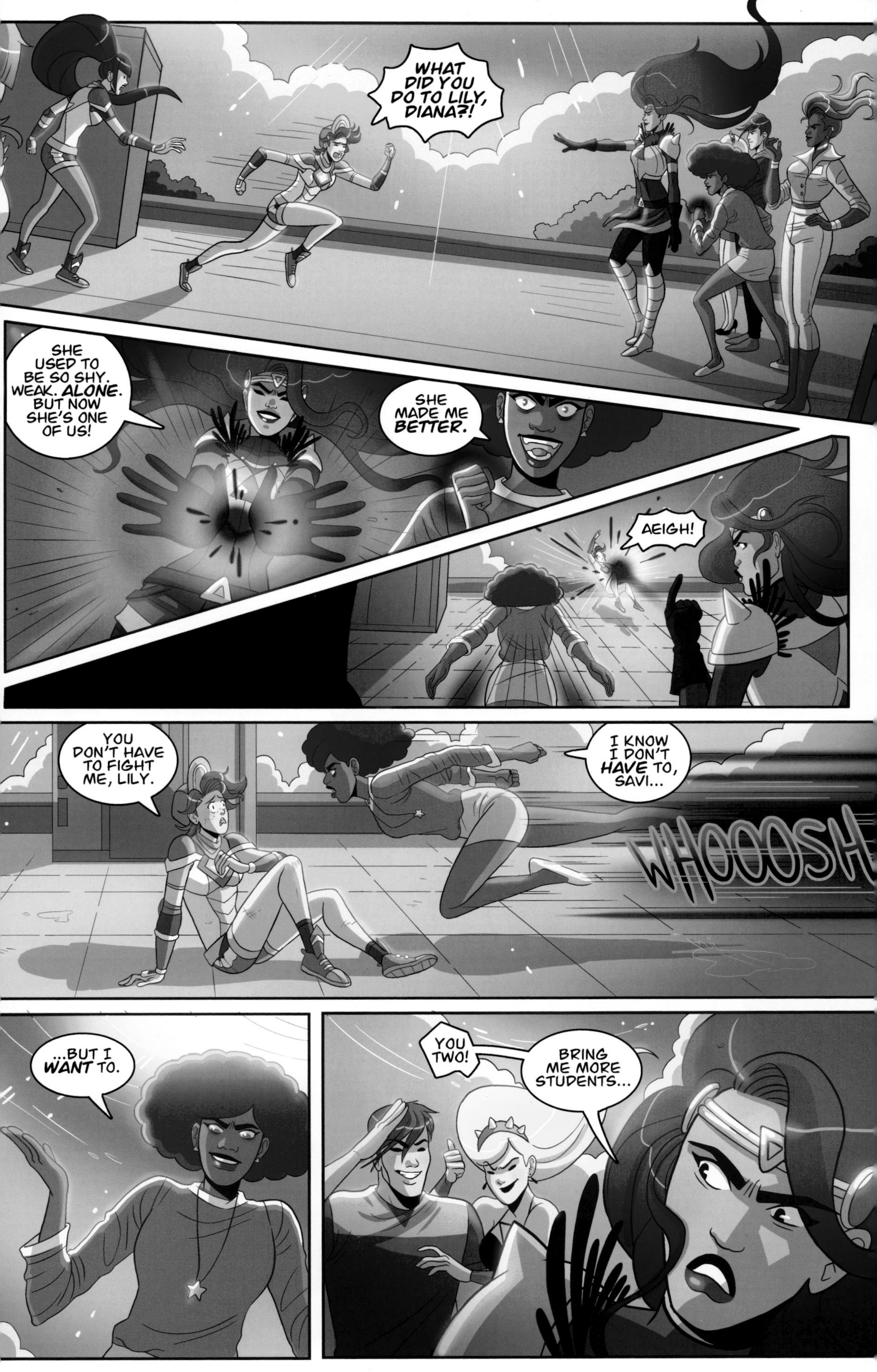
WHAT DID YOU DO TO LILY, DIANA?!
SHE USED TO BE SO SHY. WEAK. ALONE. BUT NOW SHE'S ONE OF US!
SHE MADE ME BETTER.
AEIGH!
YOU DON'T HAVE TO FIGHT ME, LILY.
I KNOW I DON'T HAVE TO, SAVI...
WHOOOSH
...BUT I WANT TO.
YOU TWO!
BRING ME MORE STUDENTS...

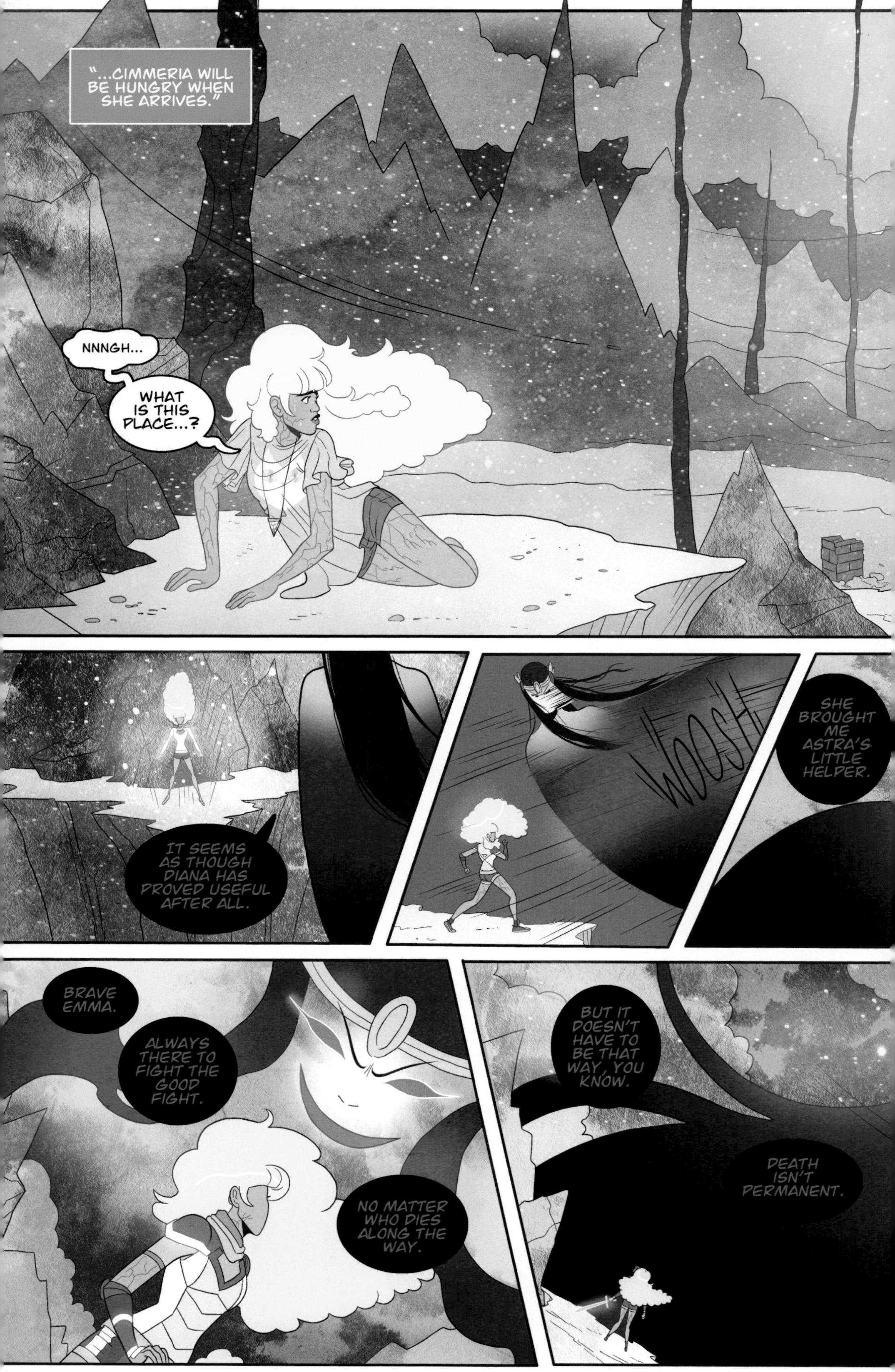
"...CIMMERIA WILL BE HUNGRY WHEN SHE ARRIVES."
NNNGH...
WHAT IS THIS PLACE...?
IT SEEMS AS THOUGH DIANA HAS PROVED USEFUL AFTER ALL.
WOOSH
SHE BROUGHT ME ASTRA'S LITTLE HELPER.
BRAVE EMMA.
ALWAYS THERE TO FIGHT THE GOOD FIGHT.
NO MATTER WHO DIES ALONG THE WAY.
BUT IT DOESN'T HAVE TO BE THAT WAY, YOU KNOW.
DEATH ISN'T PERMANENT.

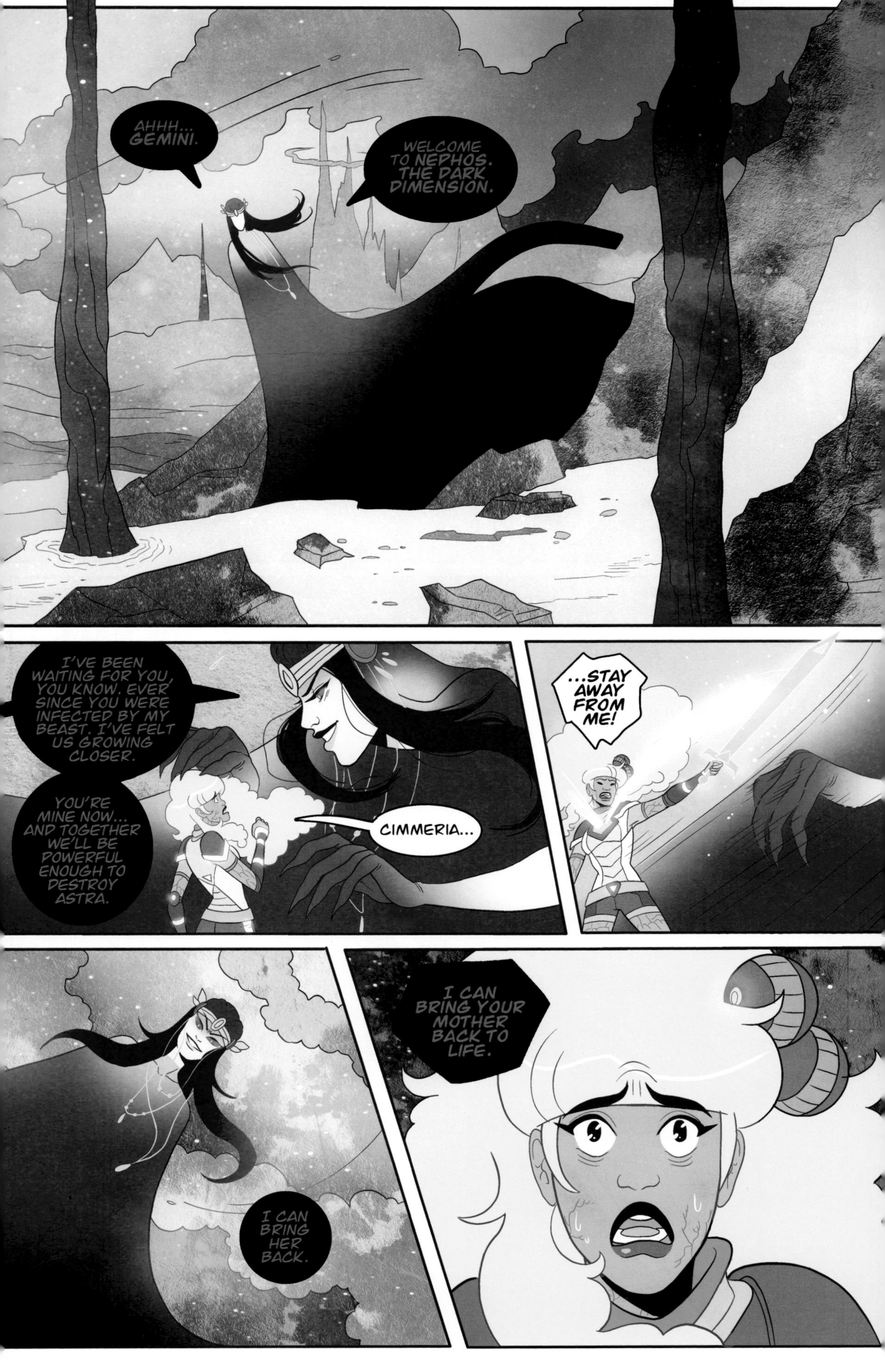
AHHH... GEMINI.
WELCOME TO NEPHOS. THE DARK DIMENSION.
I'VE BEEN WAITING FOR YOU, YOU KNOW. EVER SINCE YOU WERE INFECTED BY MY BEAST. I'VE FELT US GROWING CLOSER.
YOU'RE MINE NOW... AND TOGETHER WE'LL BE POWERFUL ENOUGH TO DESTROY ASTRA.
CIMMERIA...
...STAY AWAY FROM ME!
I CAN BRING HER BACK.
I CAN BRING YOUR MOTHER BACK TO LIFE.

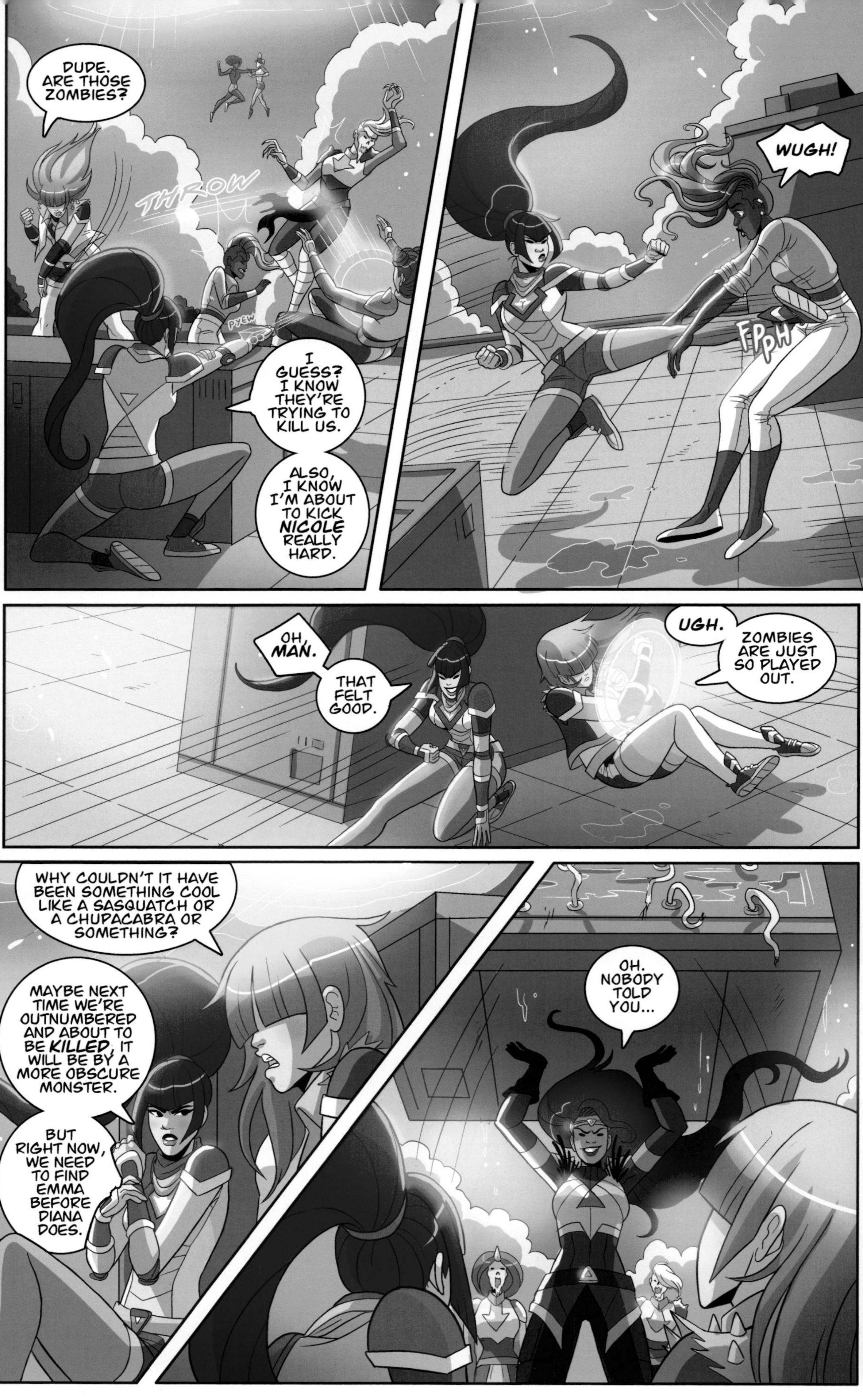
DUDE. ARE THOSE ZOMBIES?
THROW
PYEW
I GUESS? I KNOW THEY'RE TRYING TO KILL US.
ALSO, I KNOW I'M ABOUT TO KICK NICOLE REALLY HARD.
WUGH!
FPPH
OH MAN.
THAT FELT GOOD.
UGH.
ZOMBIES ARE JUST SO PLAYED OUT.
WHY COULDN'T IT HAVE BEEN SOMETHING COOL LIKE A SASQUATCH OR A CHUPACABRA OR SOMETHING?
MAYBE NEXT TIME WE'RE OUTNUMBERED AND ABOUT TO BE KILLED, IT WILL BE BY A MORE OBSCURE MONSTER.
BUT RIGHT NOW, WE NEED TO FIND EMMA BEFORE DIANA DOES.
OH. NOBODY TOLD YOU...

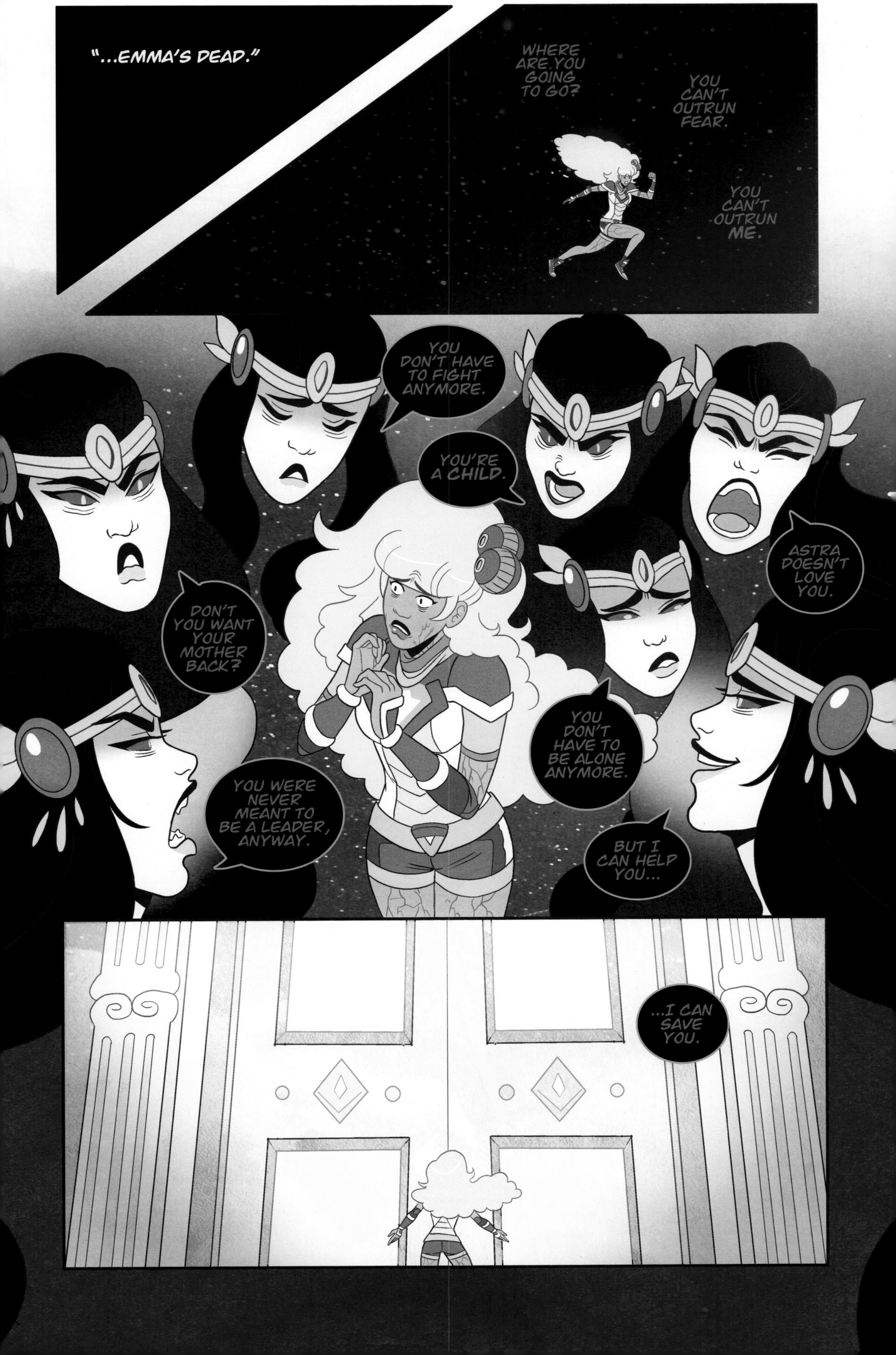
"...EMMA'S DEAD."
WHERE ARE YOU GOING TO GO?
YOU CAN'T OUTRUN FEAR.
YOU CAN'T OUTRUN ME.
YOU DON'T HAVE TO FIGHT ANYMORE.
YOU'RE A CHILD.
ASTRA DOESN'T LOVE YOU.
DON'T YOU WANT YOUR MOTHER BACK?
YOU WERE NEVER MEANT TO BE A LEADER, ANYWAY.
YOU DON'T HAVE TO BE ALONE ANYMORE.
BUT I CAN HELP YOU...
...I CAN SAVE YOU.

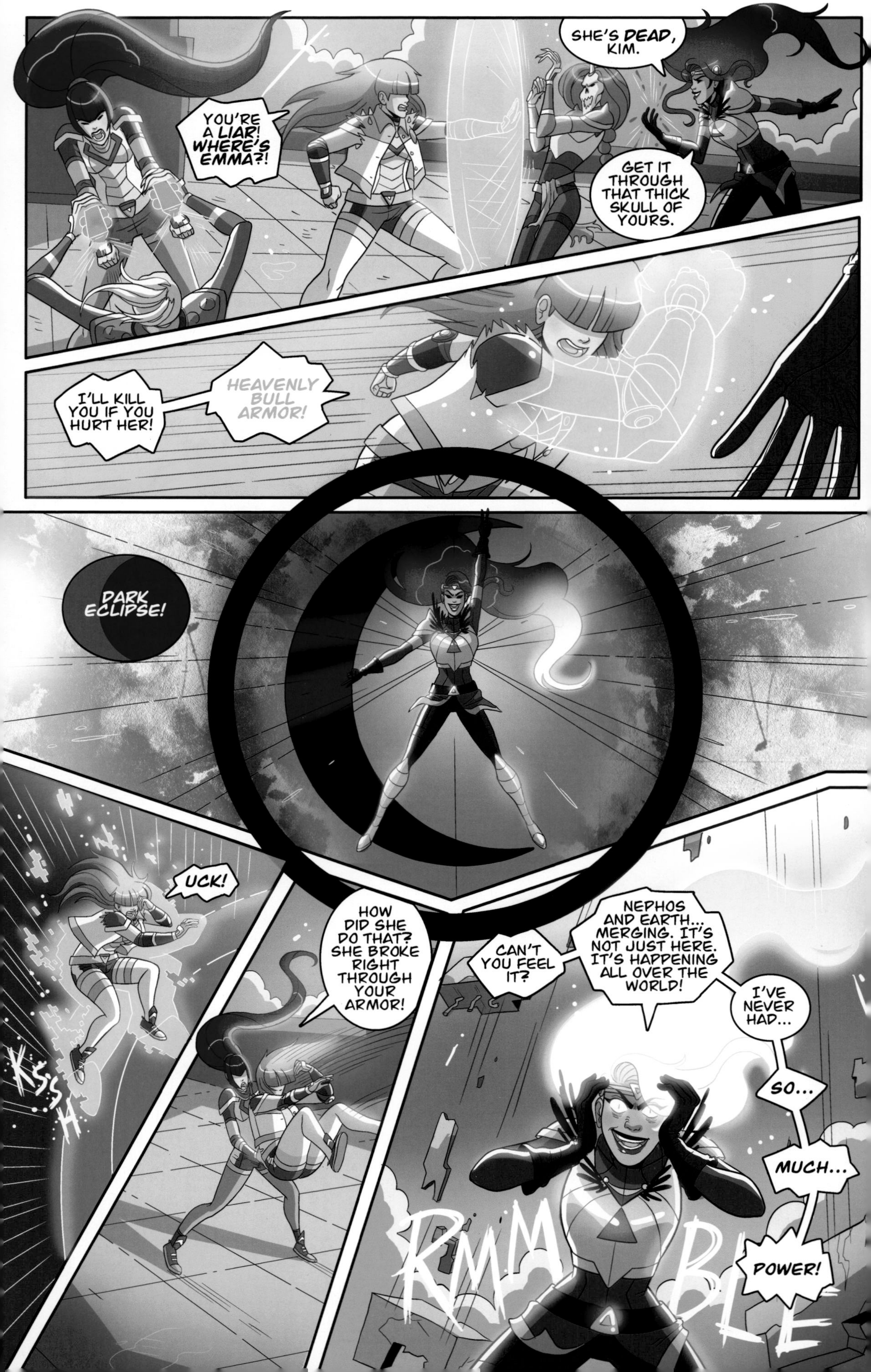
YOU'RE A LIAR! WHERE'S EMMA?!
SHE'S DEAD, KIM.
GET IT THROUGH THAT THICK SKULL OF YOURS.
I'LL KILL YOU IF YOU HURT HER!
HEAVENLY BULL ARMOR!
DARK ECLIPSE!
UCK!
KSSH
HOW DID SHE DO THAT? SHE BROKE RIGHT THROUGH YOUR ARMOR!
CAN'T YOU FEEL IT?
NEPHOS AND EARTH... MERGING. IT'S NOT JUST HERE. IT'S HAPPENING ALL OVER THE WORLD!
I'VE NEVER HAD...
SO...
MUCH...
POWER!
RMMBLE

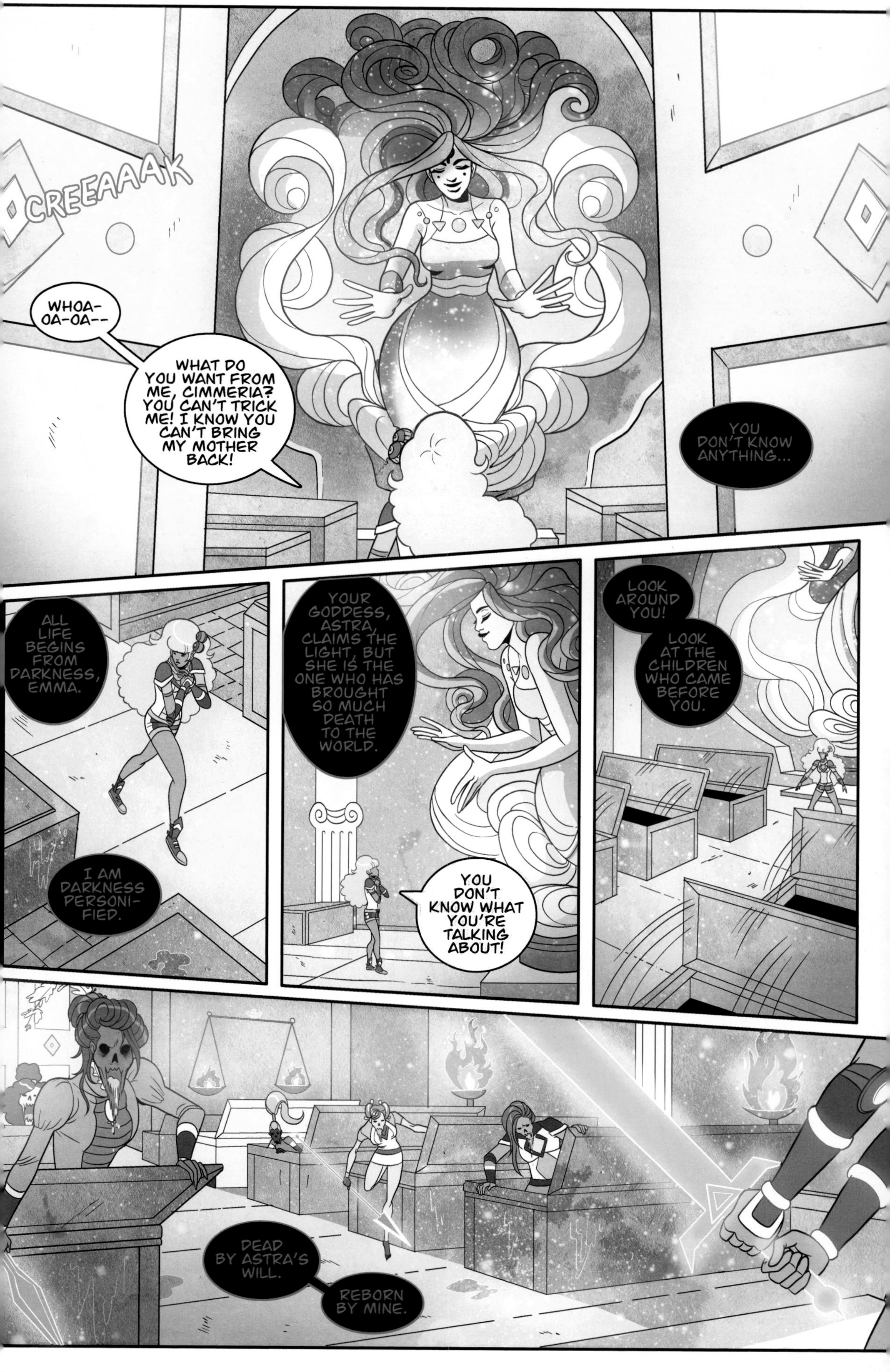
CREEAAAK
WHOA-OA-OA--
WHAT DO YOU WANT FROM ME, CIMMERIA? YOU CAN'T TRICK ME! I KNOW YOU CAN'T BRING MY MOTHER BACK!
YOU DON'T KNOW ANYTHING...
ALL LIFE BEGINS FROM DARKNESS, EMMA.
I AM DARKNESS PERSONIFIED.
YOUR GODDESS, ASTRA, CLAIMS THE LIGHT, BUT SHE IS THE ONE WHO HAS BROUGHT SO MUCH DEATH TO THE WORLD.
YOU DON'T KNOW WHAT YOU'RE TALKING ABOUT!
LOOK AROUND YOU!
LOOK AT THE CHILDREN WHO CAME BEFORE YOU.
DEAD BY ASTRA'S WILL.
REBORN BY MINE.

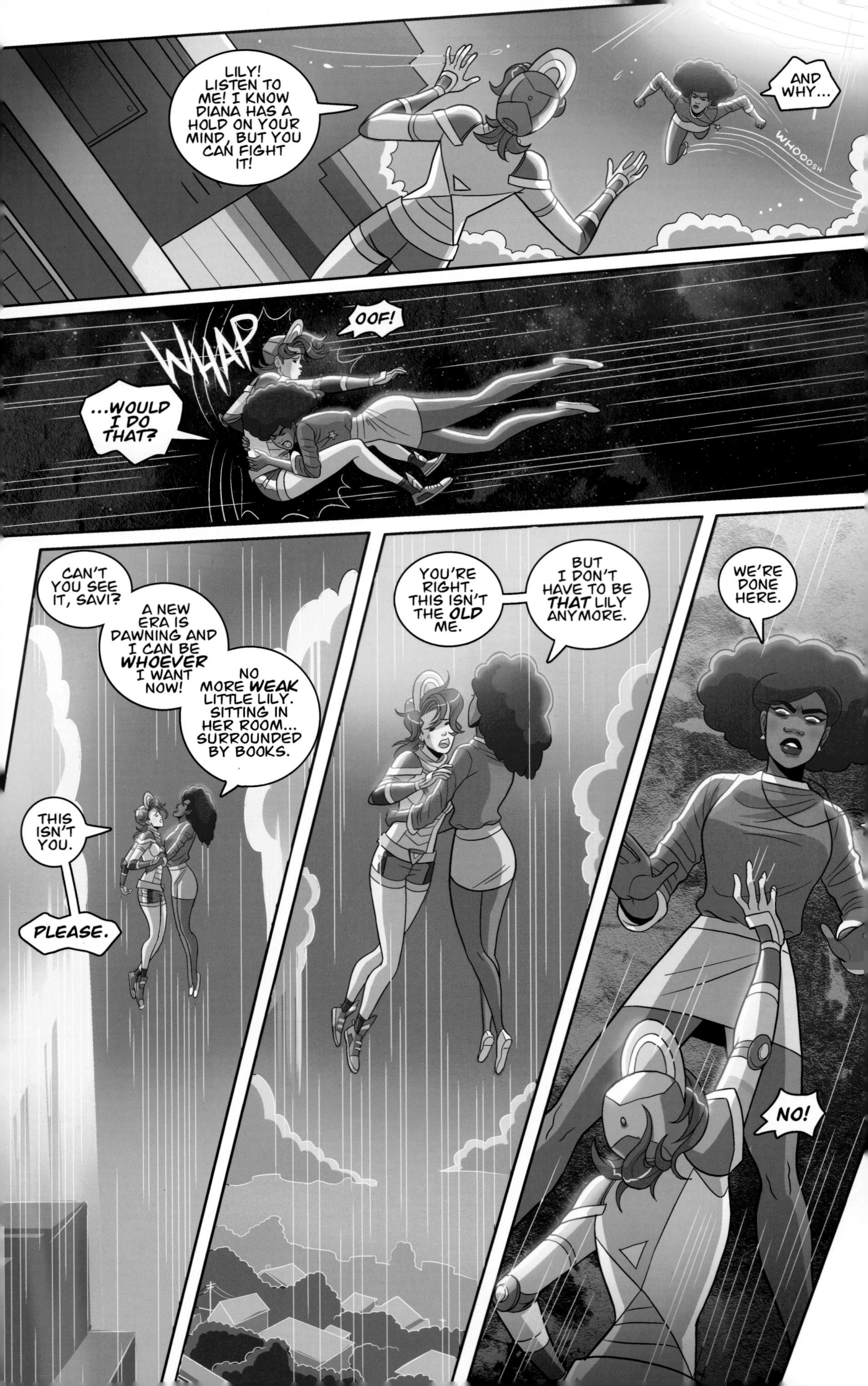
LILY! LISTEN TO ME! I KNOW DIANA HAS A HOLD ON YOUR MIND, BUT YOU CAN FIGHT IT!
AND WHY...
WHOOOSH
WHAP
OOF!
...WOULD I DO THAT?
CAN'T YOU SEE IT, SAVI?
A NEW ERA IS DAWNING AND I CAN BE WHOEVER I WANT NOW!
NO MORE WEAK LITTLE LILY. SITTING IN HER ROOM... SURROUNDED BY BOOKS.
THIS ISN'T YOU.
PLEASE.
YOU'RE RIGHT. THIS ISN'T THE OLD ME.
BUT I DON'T HAVE TO BE THAT LILY ANYMORE.
WE'RE DONE HERE.
NO!

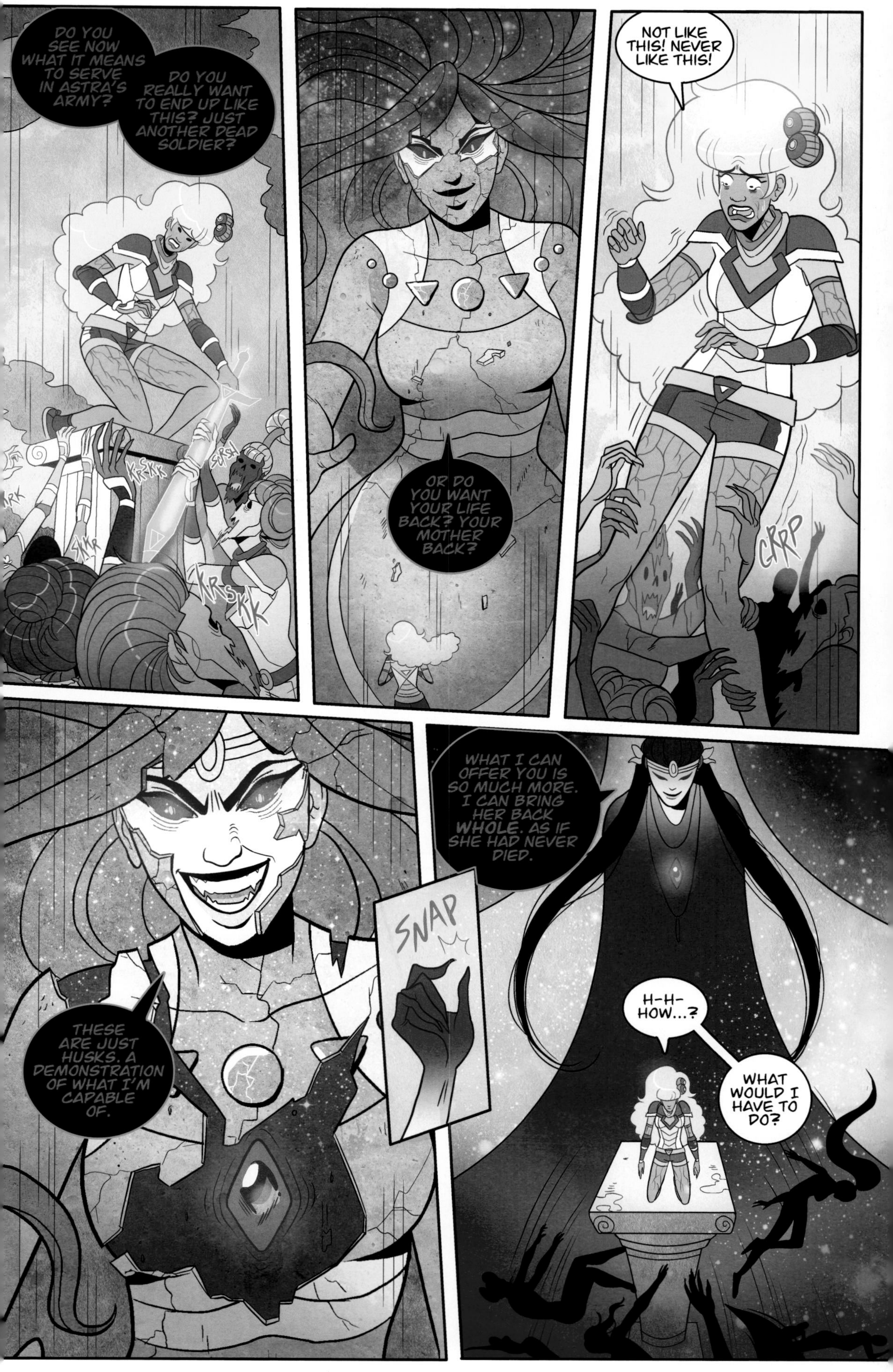
DO YOU SEE NOW WHAT IT MEANS TO SERVE IN ASTRA'S ARMY?
DO YOU REALLY WANT TO END UP LIKE THIS? JUST ANOTHER DEAD SOLDIER?
KRSKK
SURSH
SKKR
KRSKK
OR DO YOU WANT YOUR LIFE BACK? YOUR MOTHER BACK?
NOT LIKE THIS! NEVER LIKE THIS!
CRRP
THESE ARE JUST HUSKS. A DEMONSTRATION OF WHAT I'M CAPABLE OF.
SNAP
WHAT I CAN OFFER YOU IS SO MUCH MORE. I CAN BRING HER BACK WHOLE. AS IF SHE HAD NEVER DIED.
H-H-HOW...?
WHAT WOULD I HAVE TO DO?

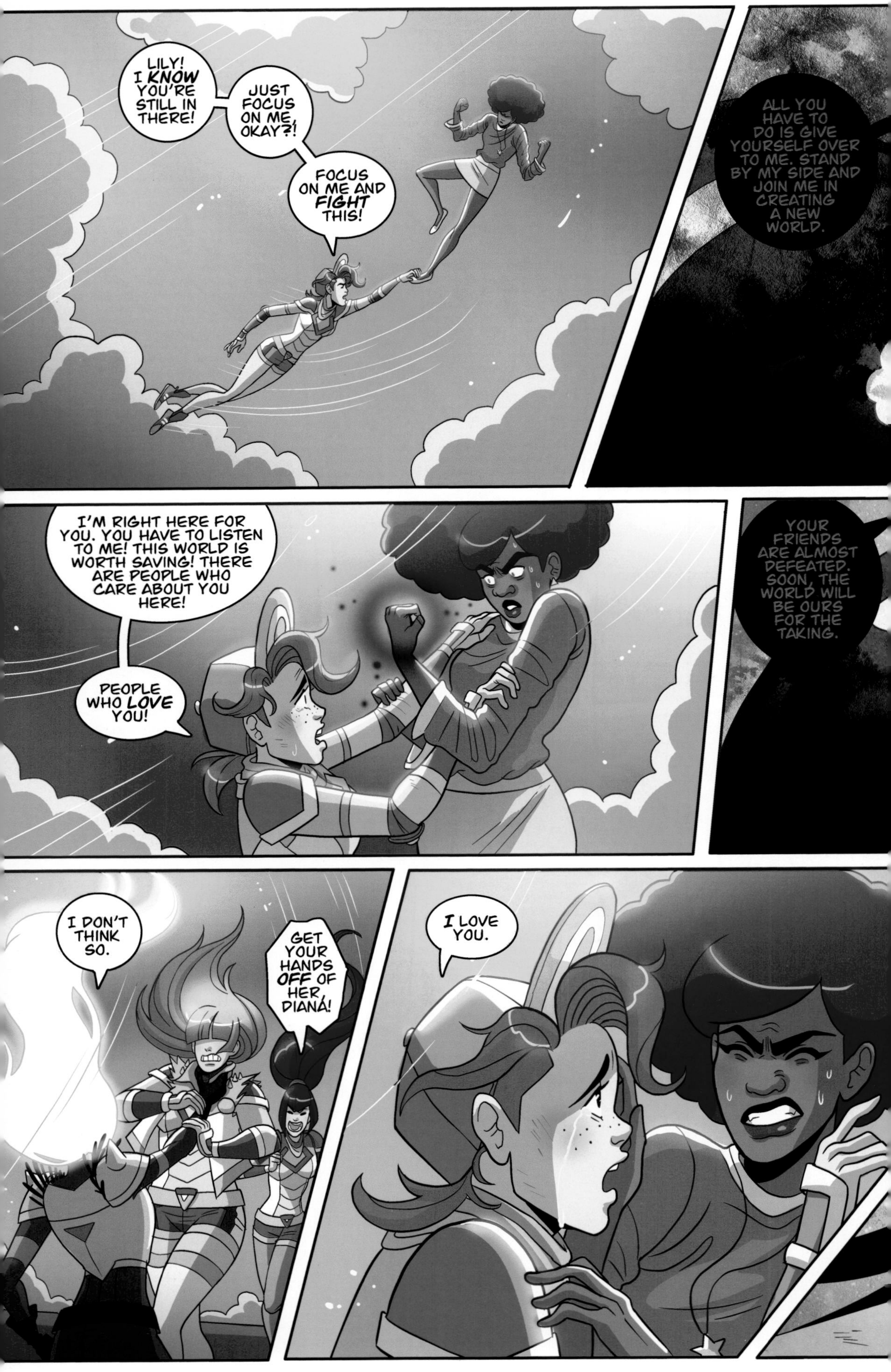
LILY! I KNOW YOU'RE STILL IN THERE!
JUST FOCUS ON ME, OKAY?!
FOCUS ON ME AND FIGHT THIS!
ALL YOU HAVE TO DO IS GIVE YOURSELF OVER TO ME. STAND BY MY SIDE AND JOIN ME IN CREATING A NEW WORLD.
I'M RIGHT HERE FOR YOU. YOU HAVE TO LISTEN TO ME! THIS WORLD IS WORTH SAVING! THERE ARE PEOPLE WHO CARE ABOUT YOU HERE!
PEOPLE WHO LOVE YOU!
YOUR FRIENDS ARE ALMOST DEFEATED. SOON, THE WORLD WILL BE OURS FOR THE TAKING.
I DON'T THINK SO.
GET YOUR HANDS OFF OF HER, DIANA!
I LOVE YOU.

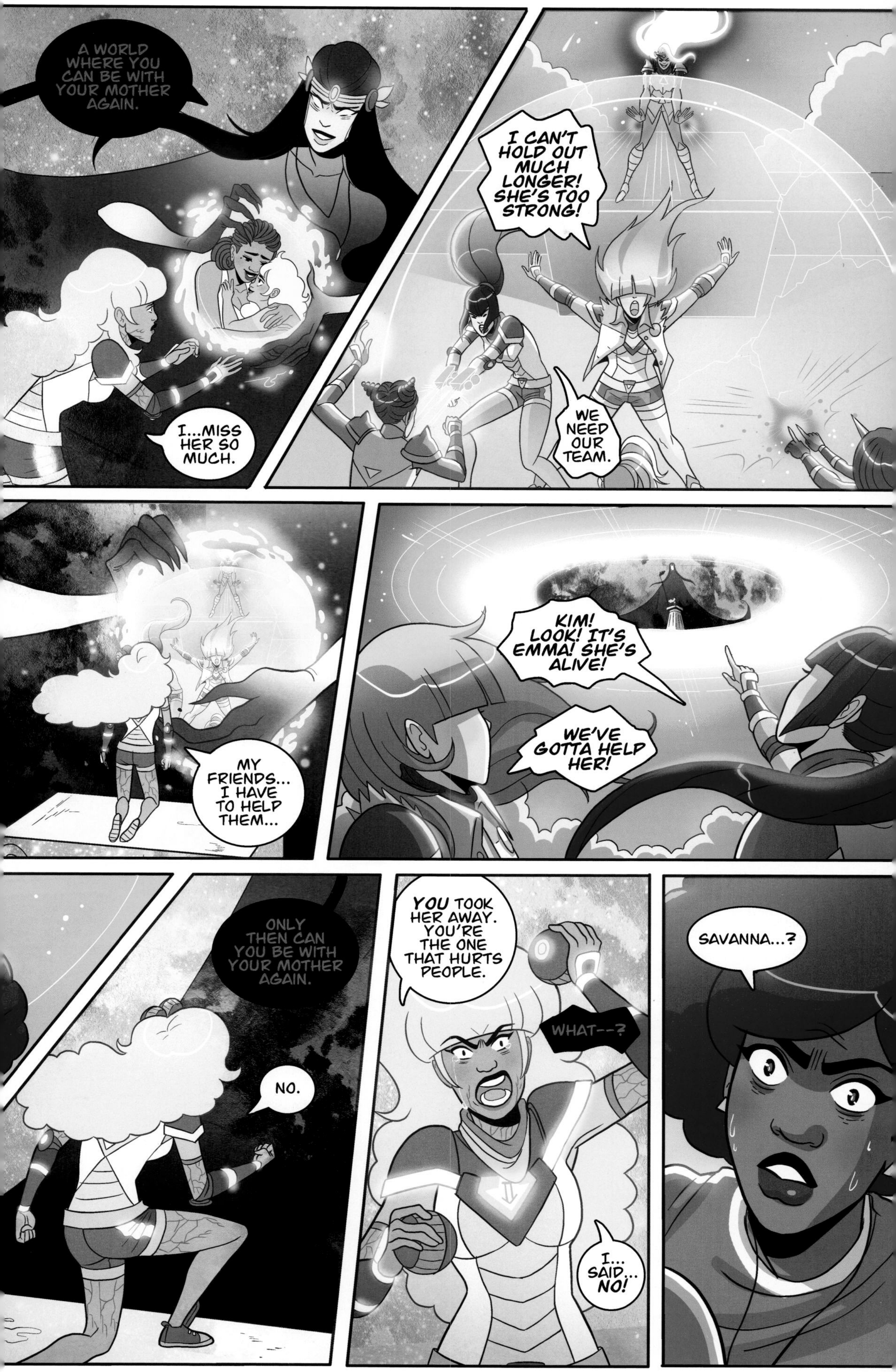
A WORLD WHERE YOU CAN BE WITH YOUR MOTHER AGAIN.
I...MISS HER SO MUCH.
I CAN'T HOLD OUT MUCH LONGER! SHE'S TOO STRONG!
WE NEED OUR TEAM.
MY FRIENDS... I HAVE TO HELP THEM...
KIM! LOOK! IT'S EMMA! SHE'S ALIVE!
WE'VE GOTTA HELP HER!
ONLY THEN CAN YOU BE WITH YOUR MOTHER AGAIN.
NO.
YOU TOOK HER AWAY. YOU'RE THE ONE THAT HURTS PEOPLE.
WHAT--?
I... SAID... NO!
SAVANNA...?

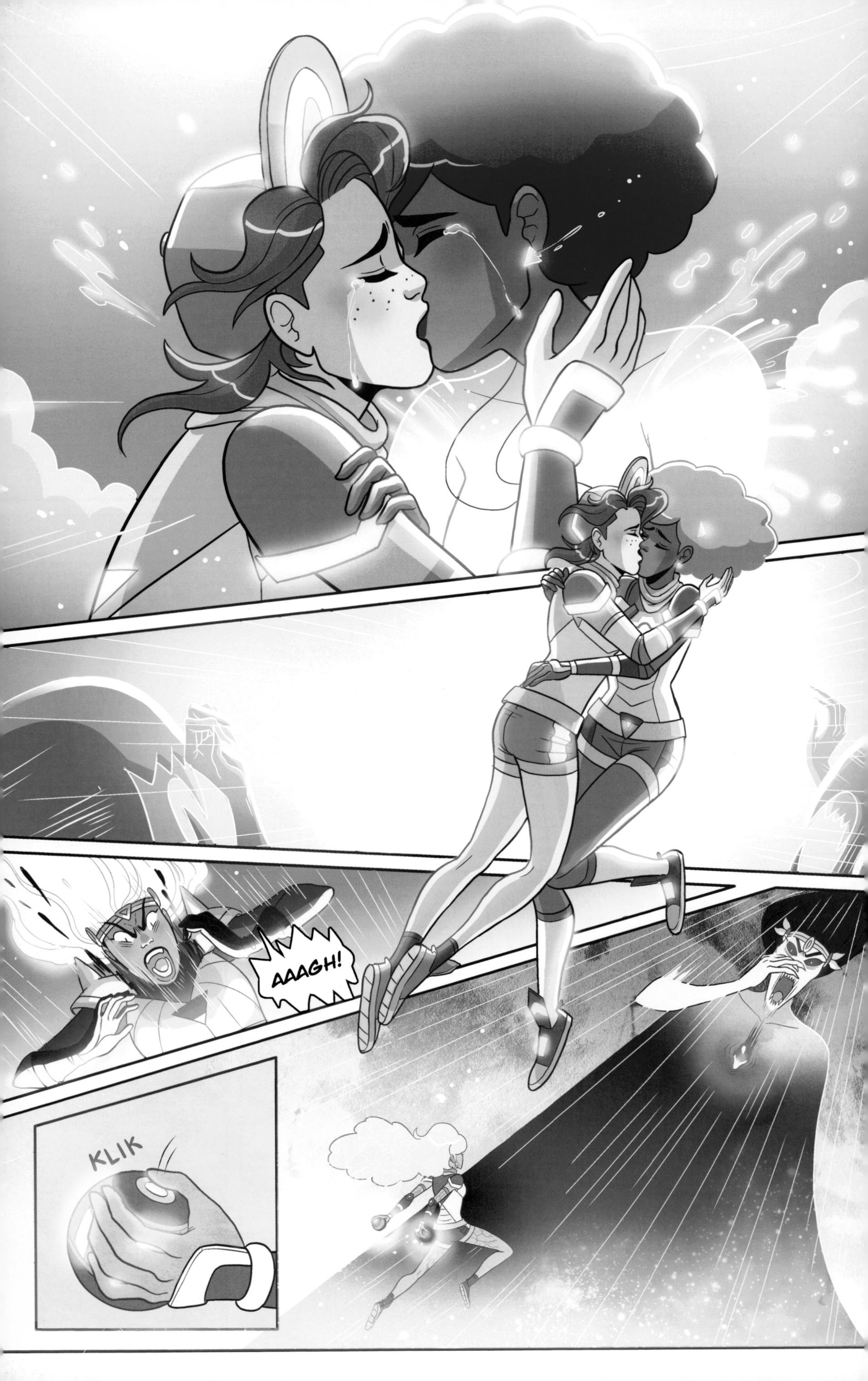
AAAGH!
KLIK

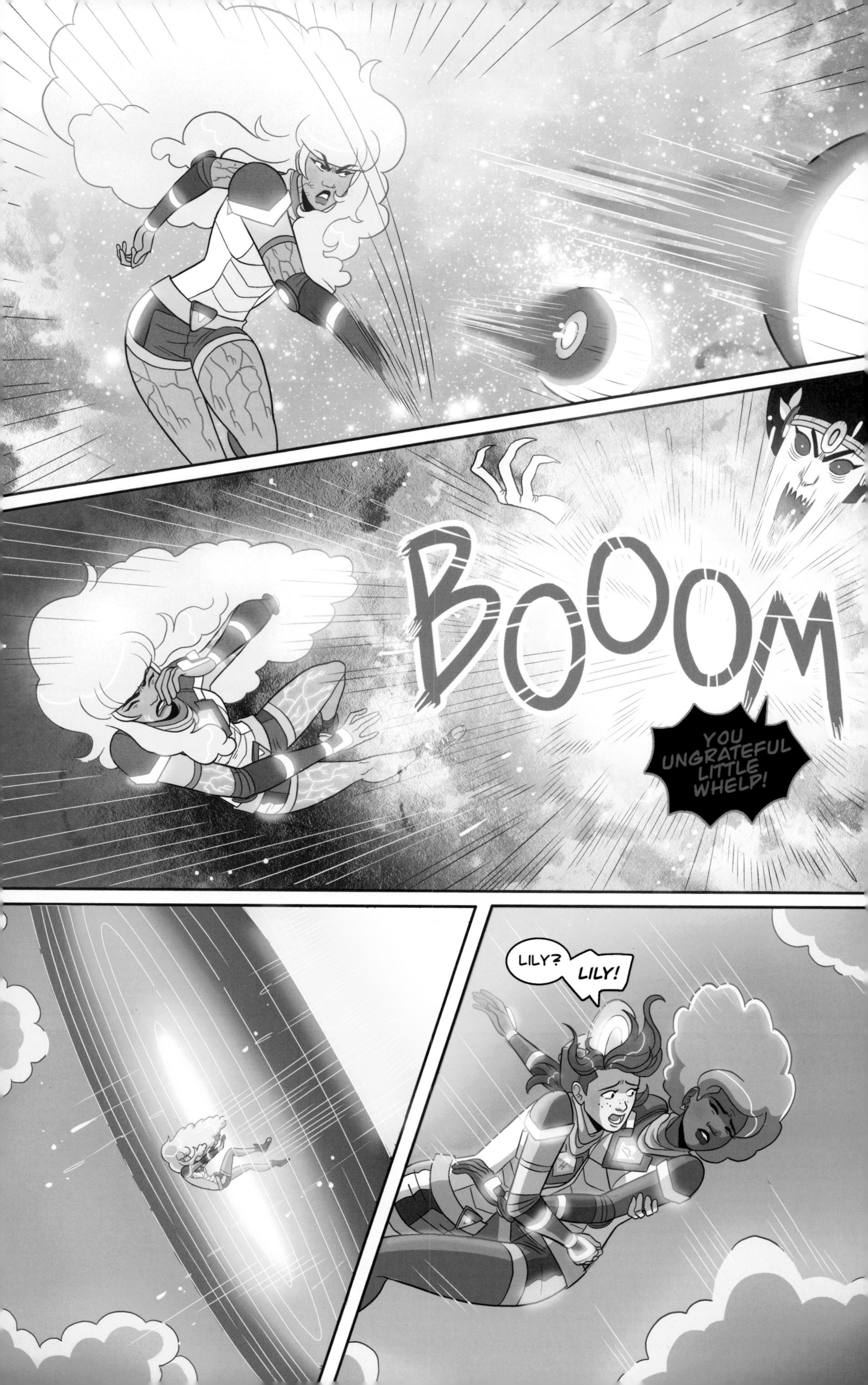
BOOOM
YOU UNGRATEFUL LITTLE WHELP!
LILY?
LILY!

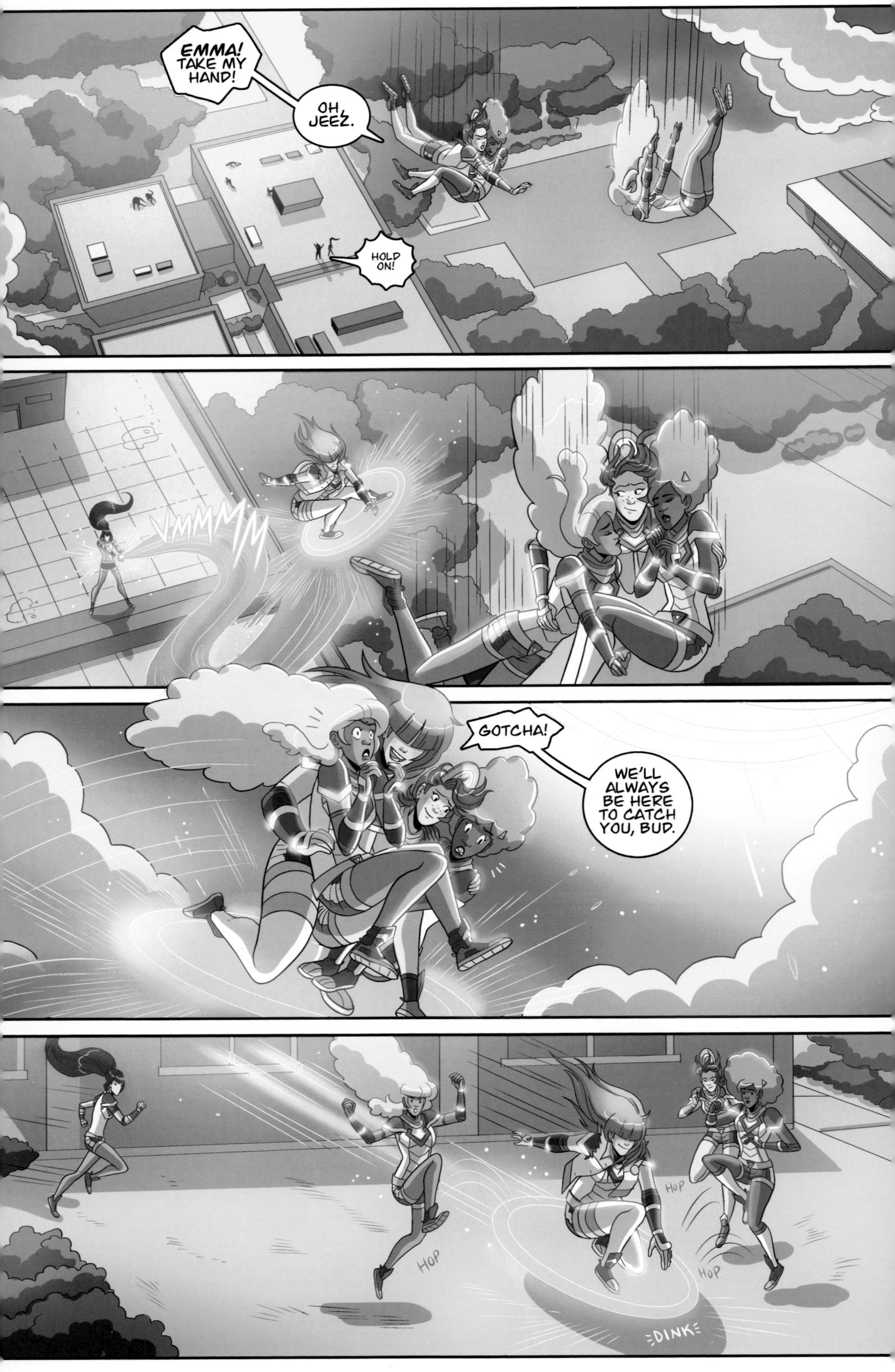
EMMA! TAKE MY HAND!
OH, JEEZ.
HOLD ON!
VMMMM
GOTCHA!
WE'LL ALWAYS BE HERE TO CATCH YOU, BUD.
HOP
HOP
HOP
DINK

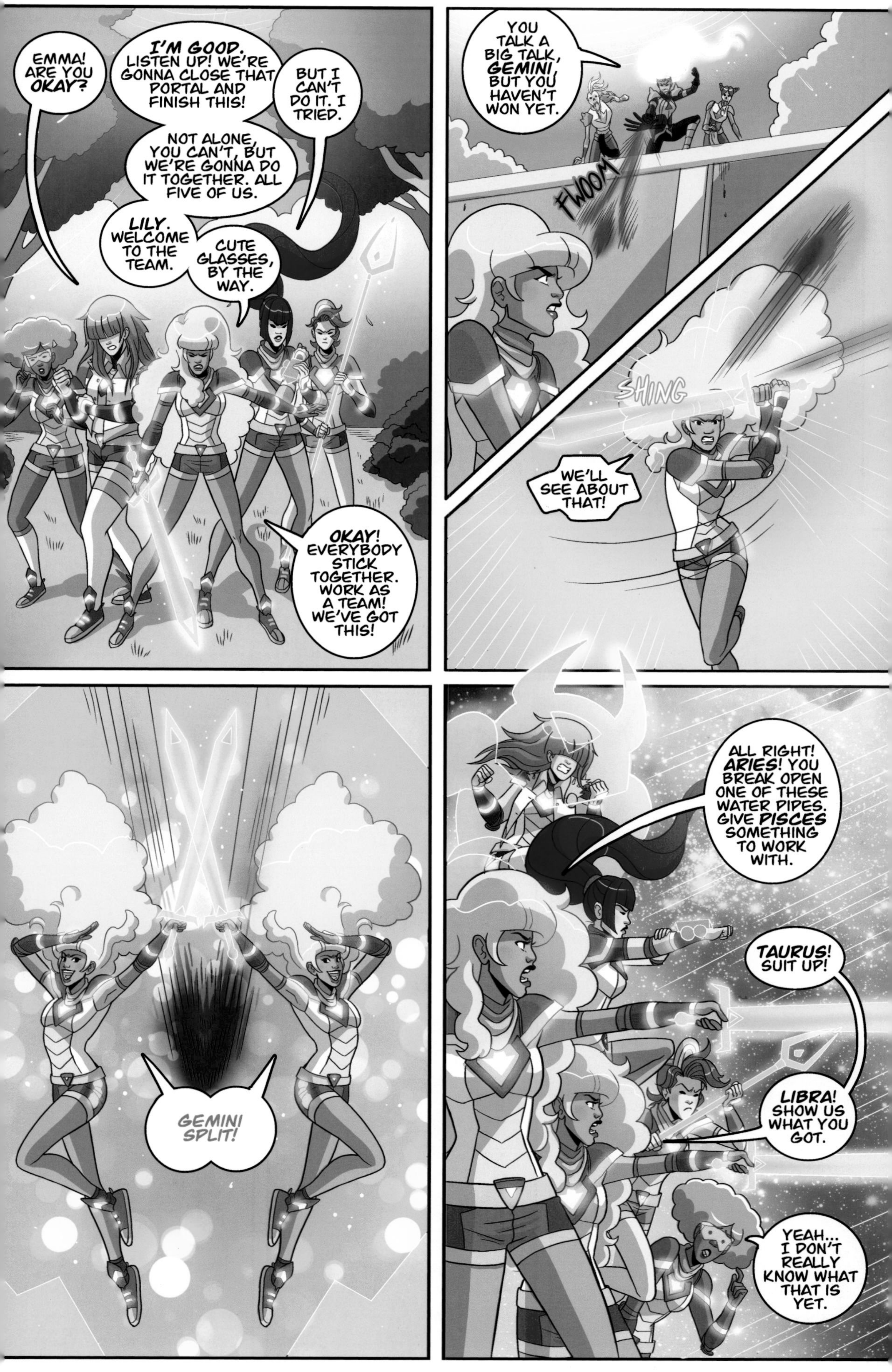
EMMA! ARE YOU OKAY?
I'M GOOD. LISTEN UP! WE'RE GONNA CLOSE THAT PORTAL AND FINISH THIS!
BUT I CAN'T DO IT. I TRIED.
NOT ALONE, YOU CAN'T, BUT WE'RE GONNA DO IT TOGETHER. ALL FIVE OF US.
LILY. WELCOME TO THE TEAM.
CUTE GLASSES, BY THE WAY.
OKAY! EVERYBODY STICK TOGETHER. WORK AS A TEAM! WE'VE GOT THIS!
YOU TALK A BIG TALK, GEMINI, BUT YOU HAVEN'T WON YET.
FWOOM
SHING
WE'LL SEE ABOUT THAT!
GEMINI SPLIT!
ALL RIGHT! ARIES! YOU BREAK OPEN ONE OF THESE WATER PIPES. GIVE PISCES SOMETHING TO WORK WITH.
TAURUS! SUIT UP!
LIBRA! SHOW US WHAT YOU GOT.
YEAH... I DON'T REALLY KNOW WHAT THAT IS YET.

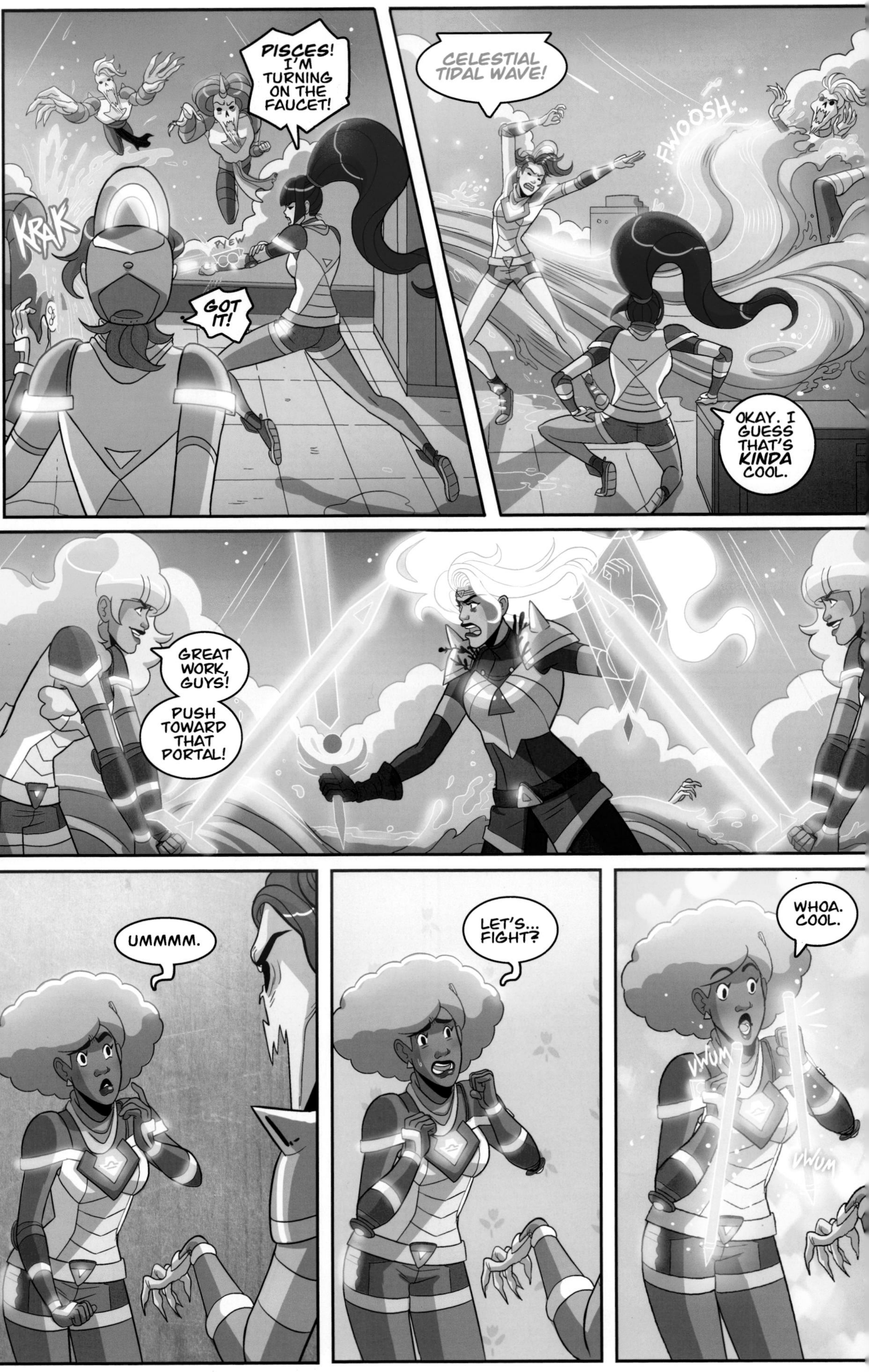
PISCES! I'M TURNING ON THE FAUCET!
KRAK
PYEW
GOT IT!
CELESTIAL TIDAL WAVE!
FWOOSH
OKAY. I GUESS THAT'S KINDA COOL.
GREAT WORK, GUYS!
PUSH TOWARD THAT PORTAL!
UMMMM.
LET'S... FIGHT?
WHOA. COOL.
VWUM
VWUM

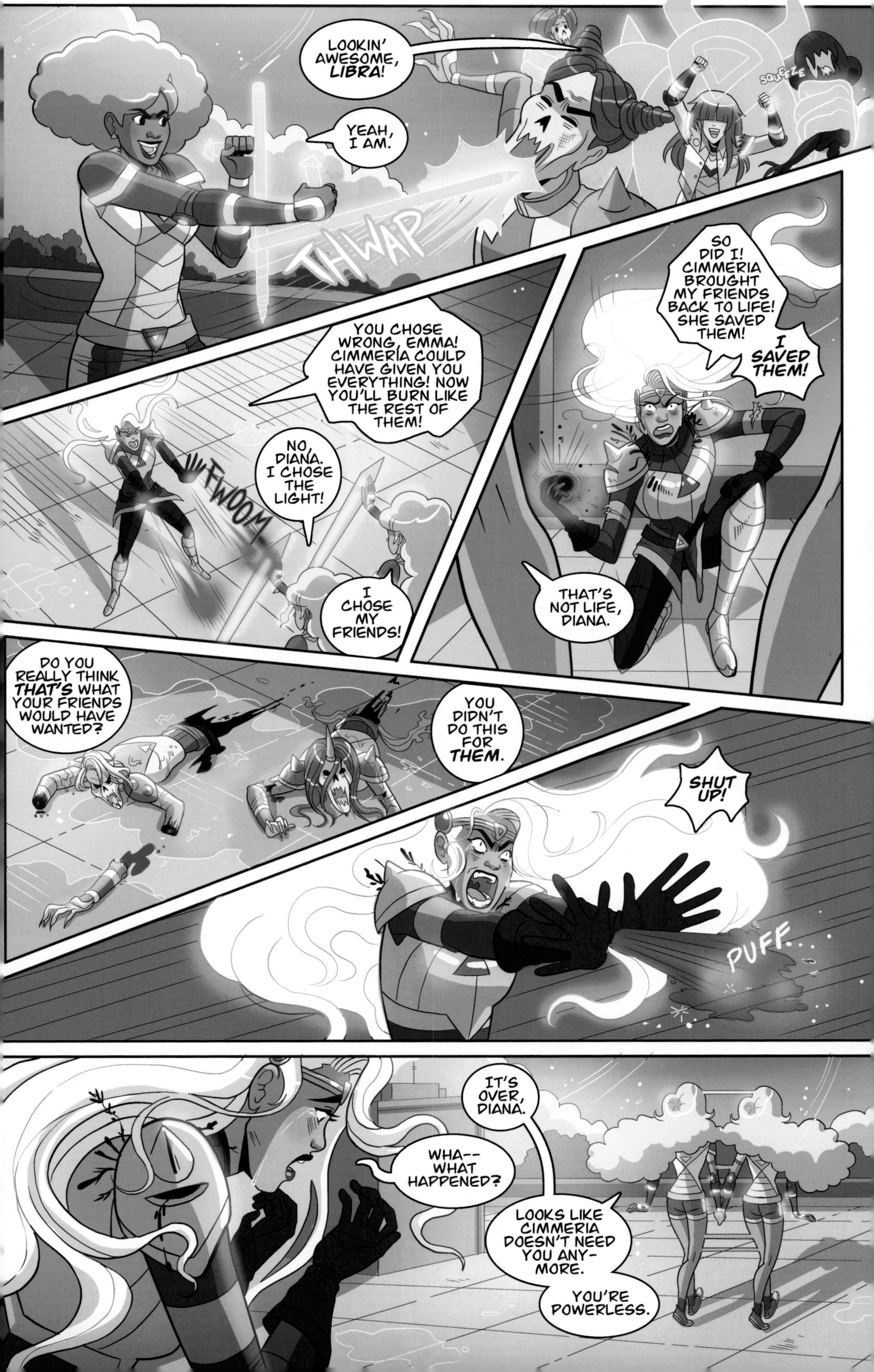
LOOKIN' AWESOME, LIBRA!
YEAH, I AM.
SQUEEZE
THWAP
YOU CHOSE WRONG, EMMA! CIMMERIA COULD HAVE GIVEN YOU EVERYTHING! NOW YOU'LL BURN LIKE THE REST OF THEM!
FWOOM
NO, DIANA. I CHOSE THE LIGHT!
I CHOSE MY FRIENDS!
SO DID I! CIMMERIA BROUGHT MY FRIENDS BACK TO LIFE! SHE SAVED THEM!
I SAVED THEM!
THAT'S NOT LIFE, DIANA.
DO YOU REALLY THINK THAT'S WHAT YOUR FRIENDS WOULD HAVE WANTED?
YOU DIDN'T DO THIS FOR THEM.
SHUT UP!
PUFF
IT'S OVER, DIANA.
WHA-- WHAT HAPPENED?
LOOKS LIKE CIMMERIA DOESN'T NEED YOU ANY-MORE.
YOU'RE POWERLESS.

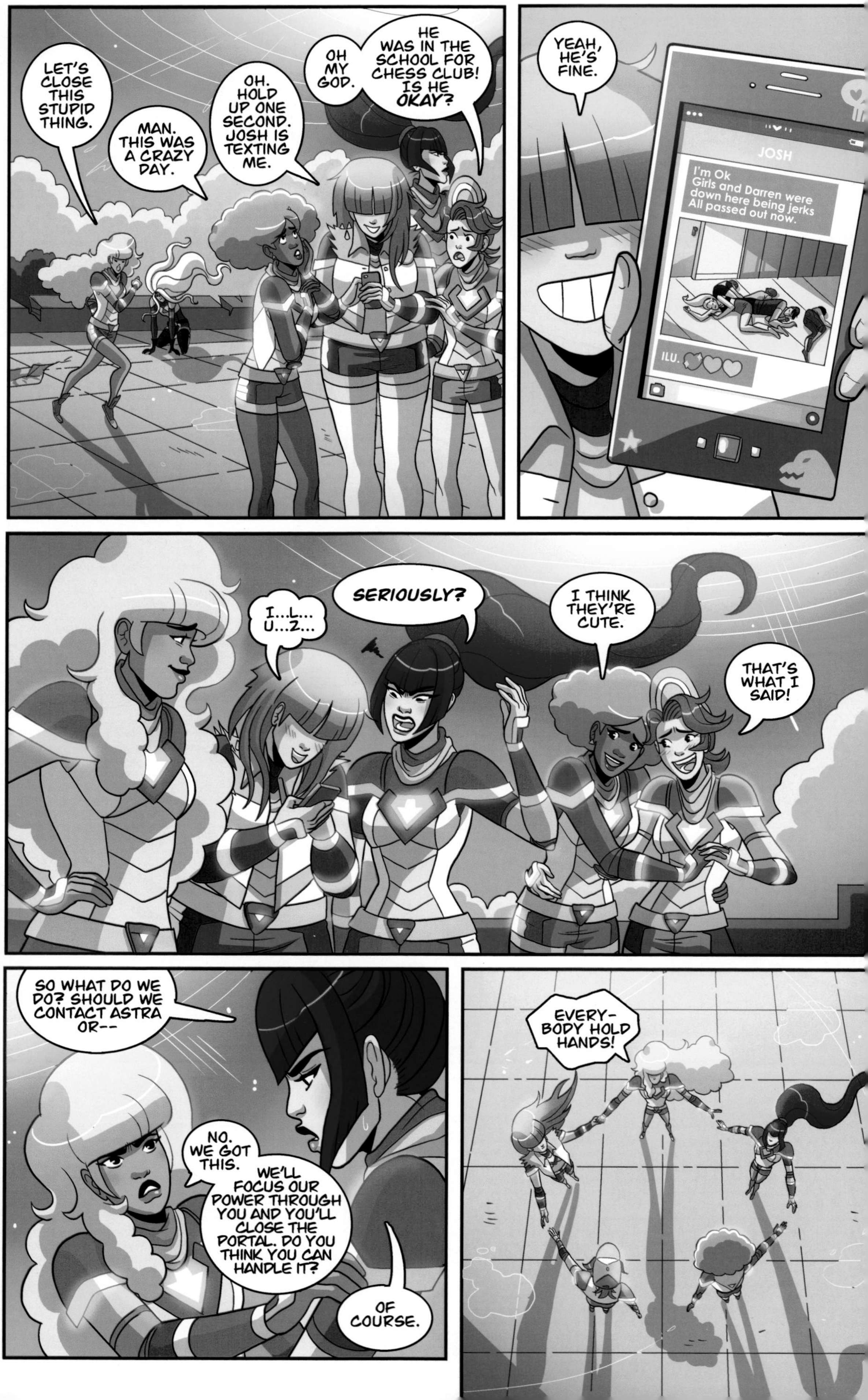
LET'S CLOSE THIS STUPID THING.
MAN. THIS WAS A CRAZY DAY.
OH. HOLD UP ONE SECOND. JOSH IS TEXTING ME.
OH MY GOD.
HE WAS IN THE SCHOOL FOR CHESS CLUB! IS HE OKAY?
YEAH, HE'S FINE.
JOSH
I'm Ok
Girls and Darren were down here being jerks
All passed out now.
ILU.
I...L... U...Z...
SERIOUSLY?
I THINK THEY'RE CUTE.
THAT'S WHAT I SAID!
SO WHAT DO WE DO? SHOULD WE CONTACT ASTRA OR--
NO. WE GOT THIS.
WE'LL FOCUS OUR POWER THROUGH YOU AND YOU'LL CLOSE THE PORTAL. DO YOU THINK YOU CAN HANDLE IT?
OF COURSE.
EVERY-BODY HOLD HANDS!

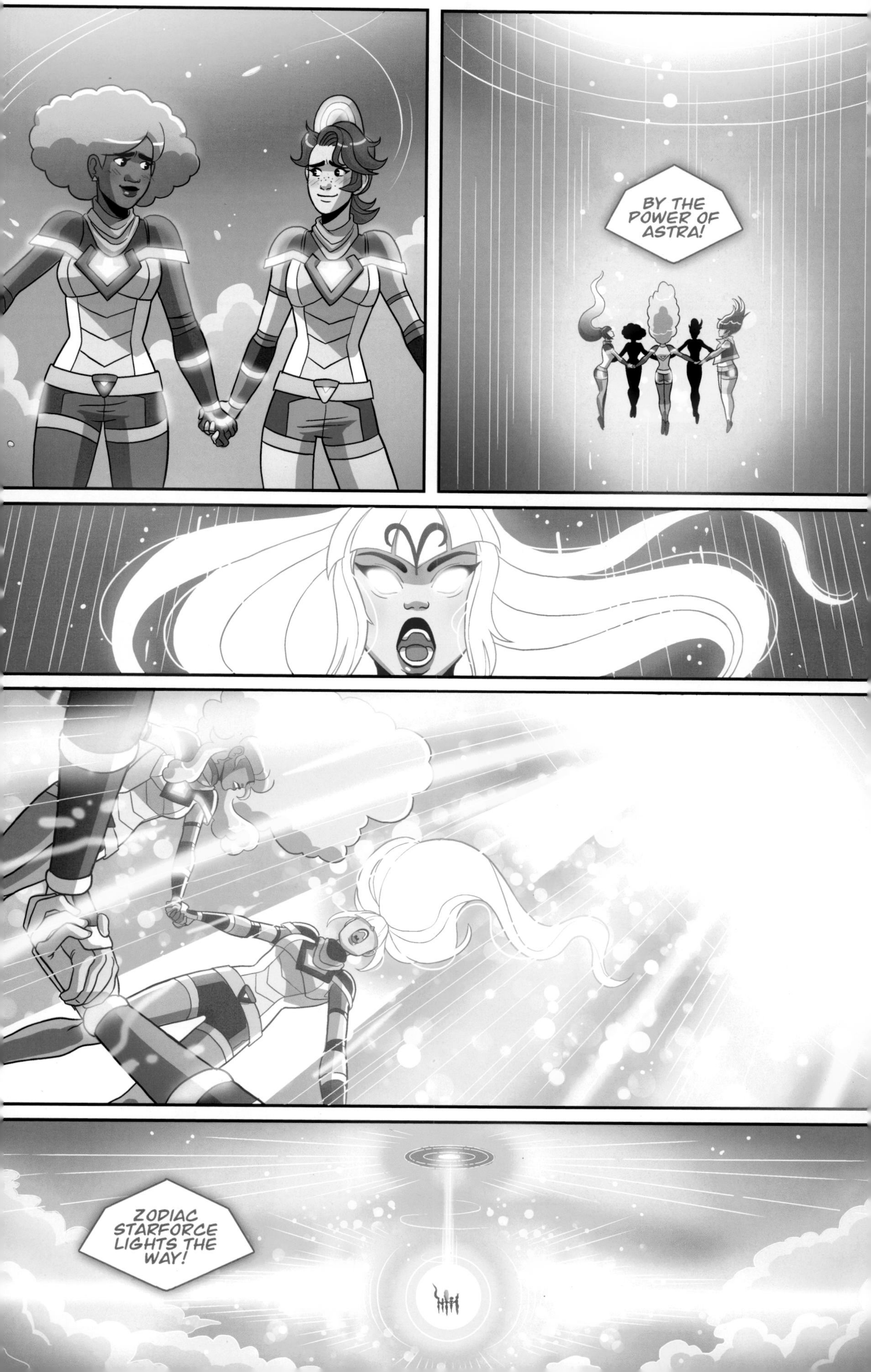
BY THE POWER OF ASTRA!
ZODIAC STARFORCE LIGHTS THE WAY!

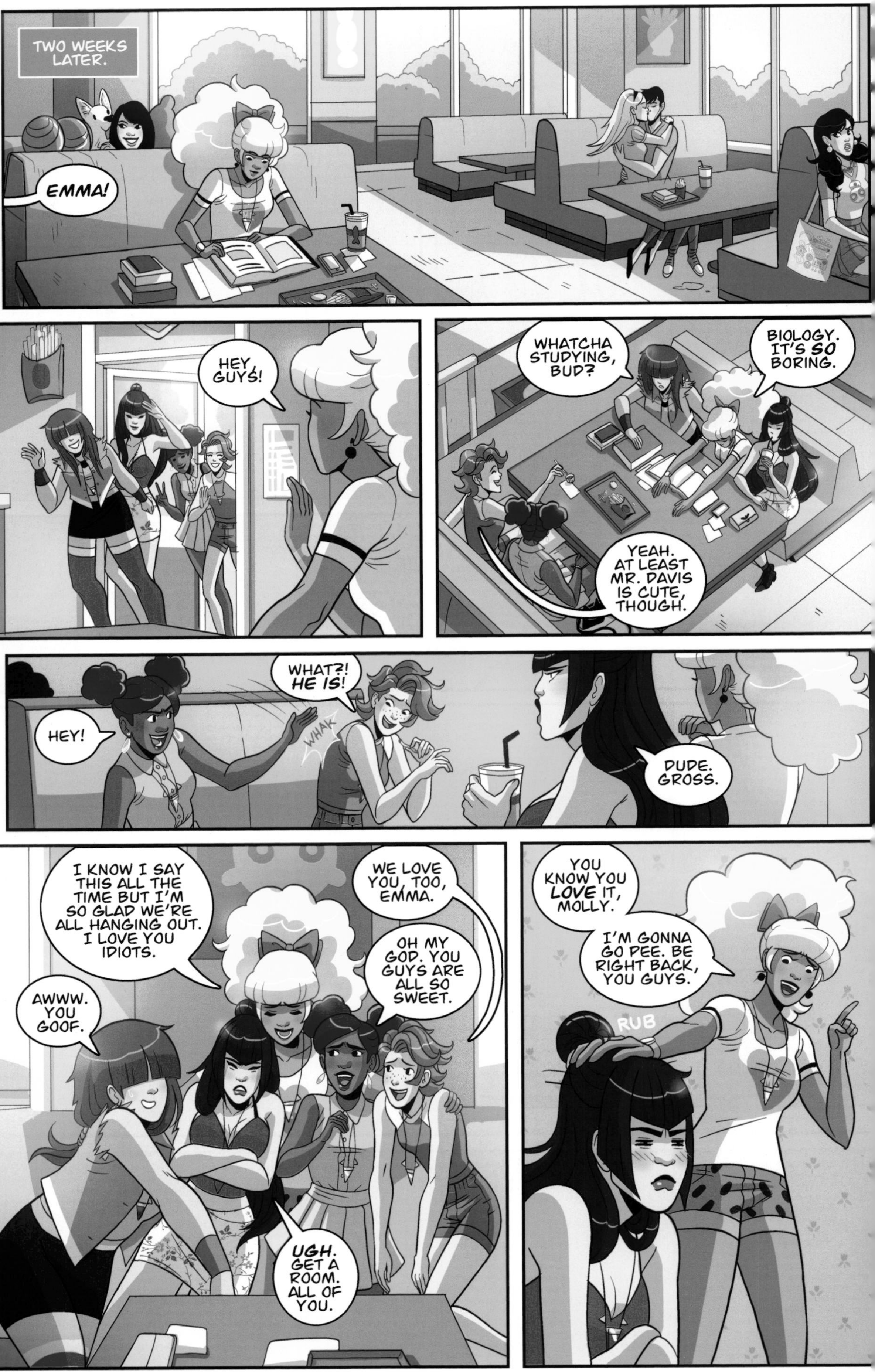
TWO WEEKS LATER.
EMMA!
HEY, GUYS!
WHATCHA STUDYING, BUD?
BIOLOGY. IT'S SO BORING.
YEAH. AT LEAST MR. DAVIS IS CUTE, THOUGH.
HEY!
WHAT?! HE IS!
WHAK
DUDE. GROSS.
I KNOW I SAY THIS ALL THE TIME BUT I'M SO GLAD WE'RE ALL HANGING OUT. I LOVE YOU IDIOTS.
WE LOVE YOU, TOO, EMMA.
AWWW. YOU GOOF.
OH MY GOD. YOU GUYS ARE ALL SO SWEET.
UGH. GET A ROOM. ALL OF YOU.
YOU KNOW YOU LOVE IT, MOLLY.
I'M GONNA GO PEE. BE RIGHT BACK, YOU GUYS.
RUB

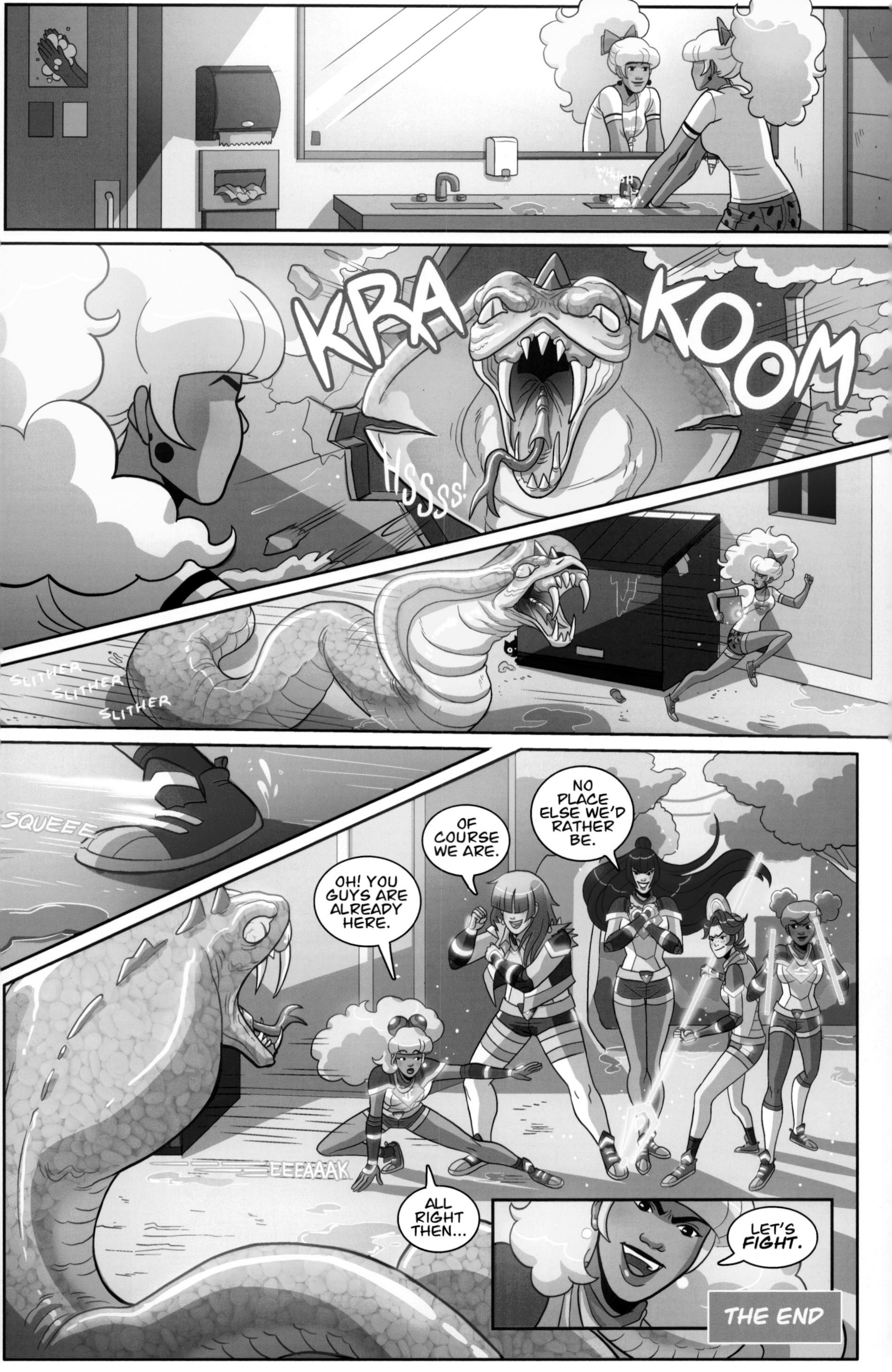

WHISH
KRA KOOM
HSSSS!
SLITHER SLITHER SLITHER
SQUEEEE
OH! YOU GUYS ARE ALREADY HERE.
OF COURSE WE ARE.
NO PLACE ELSE WE'D RATHER BE.
EEEAAAK
ALL RIGHT THEN...
LET'S FIGHT.
THE END

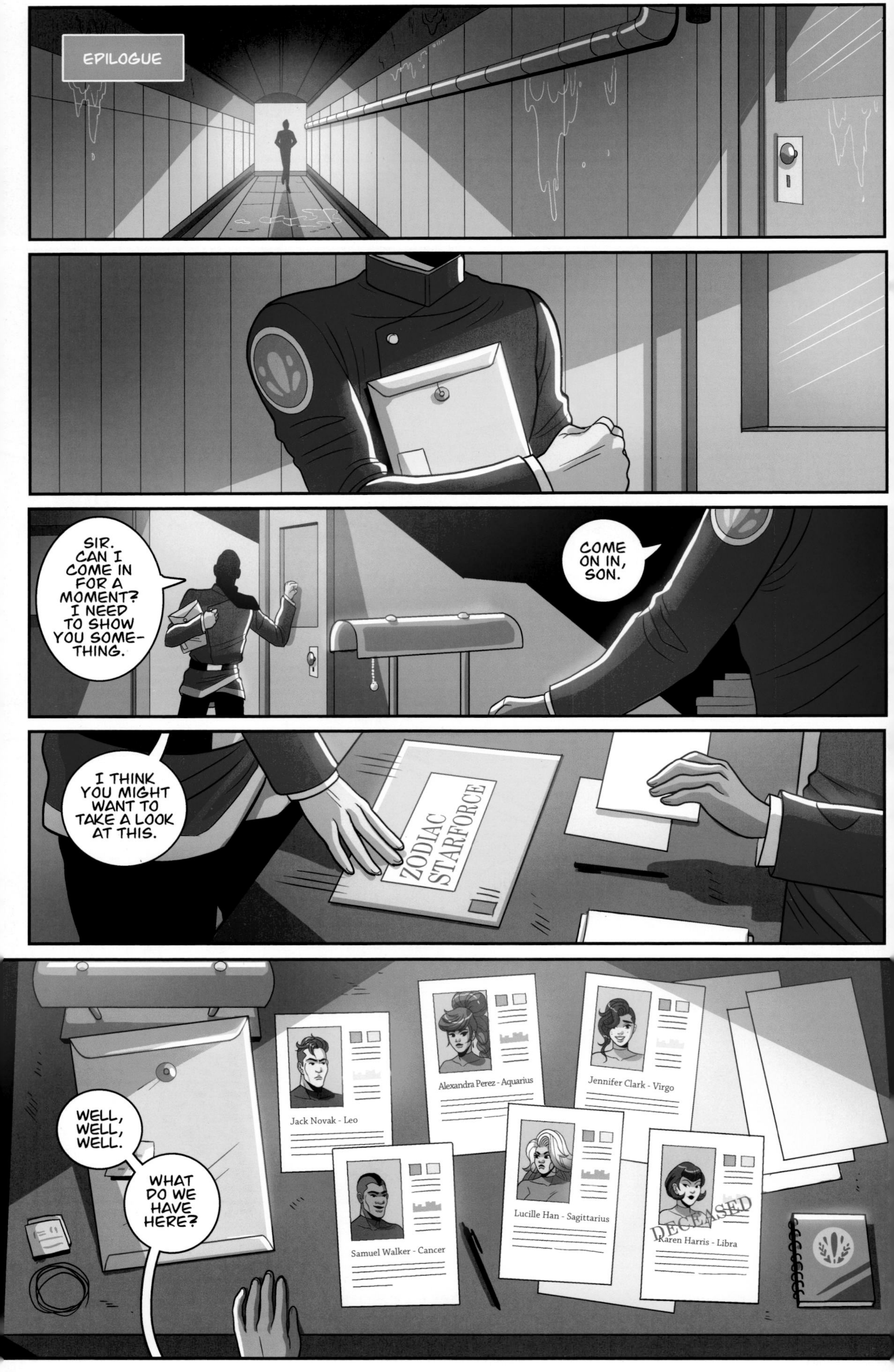
EPILOGUE
SIR. CAN I COME IN FOR A MOMENT? I NEED TO SHOW YOU SOME-THING.
COME ON IN, SON.
I THINK YOU MIGHT WANT TO TAKE A LOOK AT THIS.
ZODIAC STARFORCE
WELL, WELL, WELL.
WHAT DO WE HAVE HERE?
Jack Novak - Leo
Alexandra Perez - Aquarius
Jennifer Clark - Virgo
Samuel Walker - Cancer
Lucille Han - Sagittarius
DECEASED
Karen Harris - Libra

SKETCHBOOK

NOTES BY KEVIN AND PAULINA

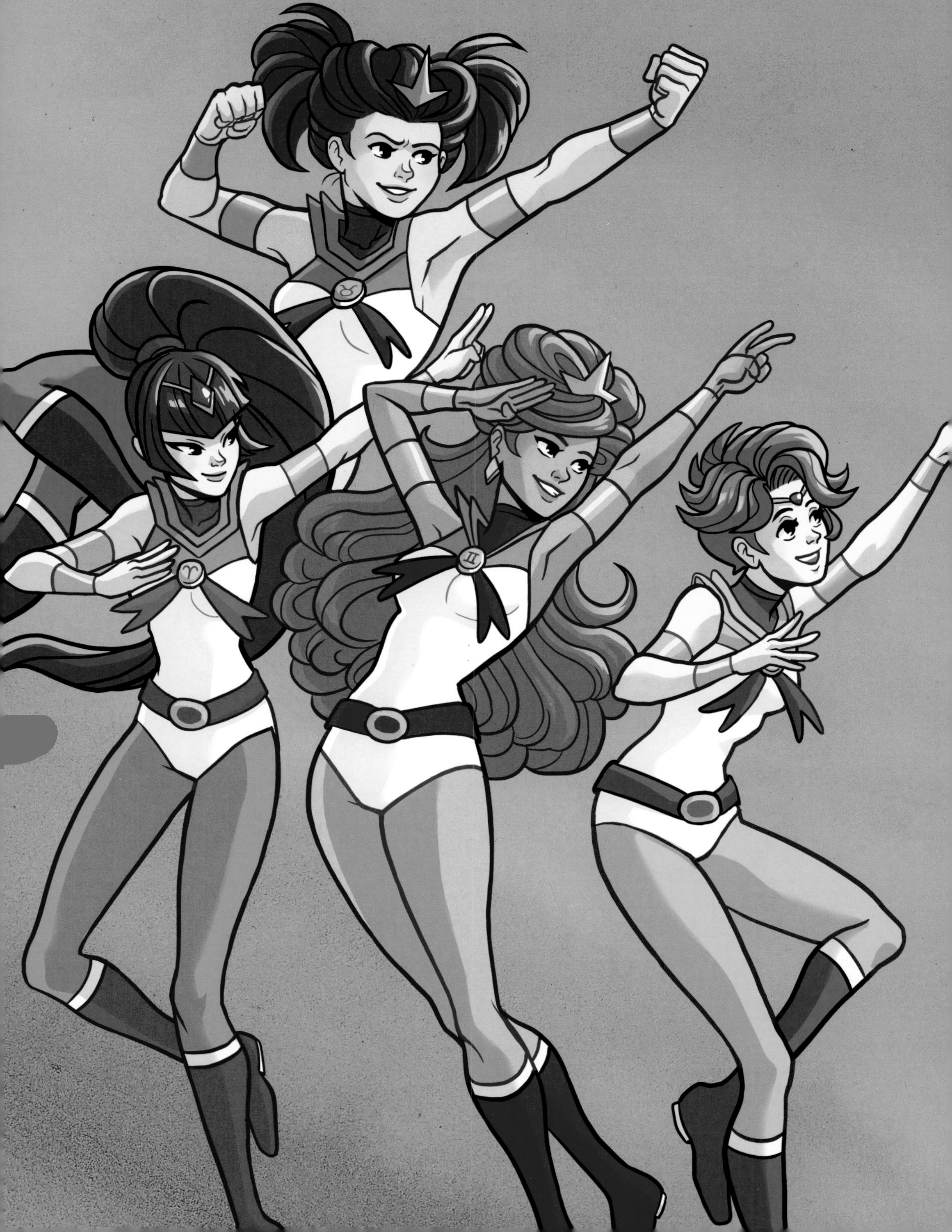

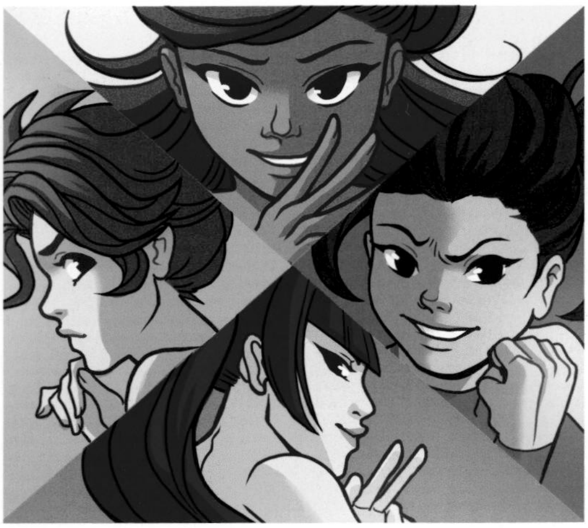

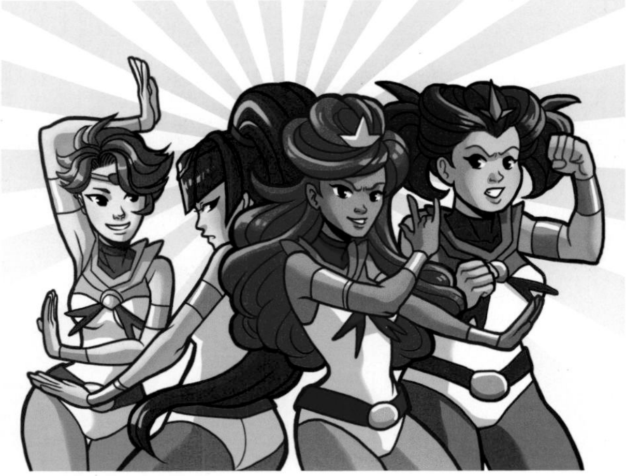

THE BIG PLANET AD

KEVIN: *Zodiac Starforce* has changed a lot since its original incarnation (an ad for Washington, DC, comic book store Big Planet Comics). Back then the girls were a crime-fighting rock band.

PAULINA: We like to call this our "Jem meets Scooby-Doo" phase.

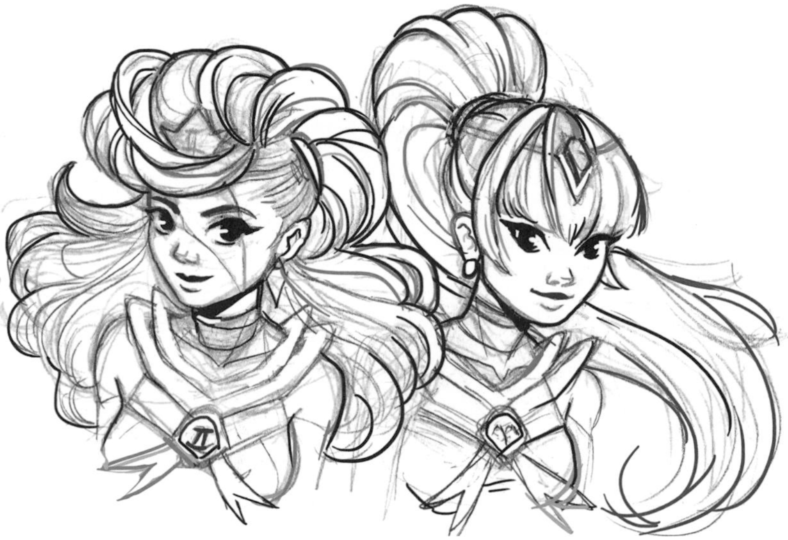

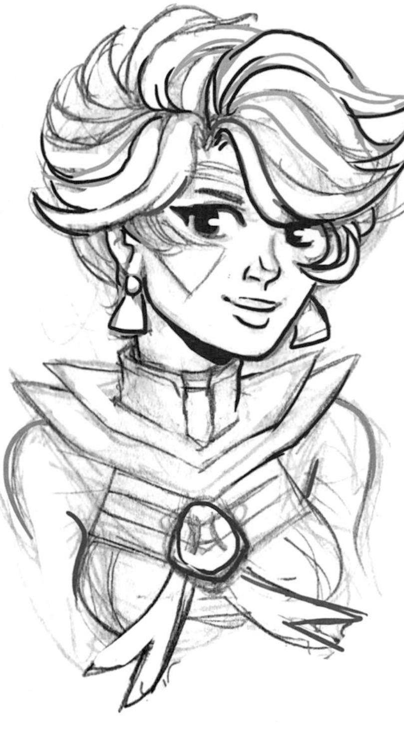

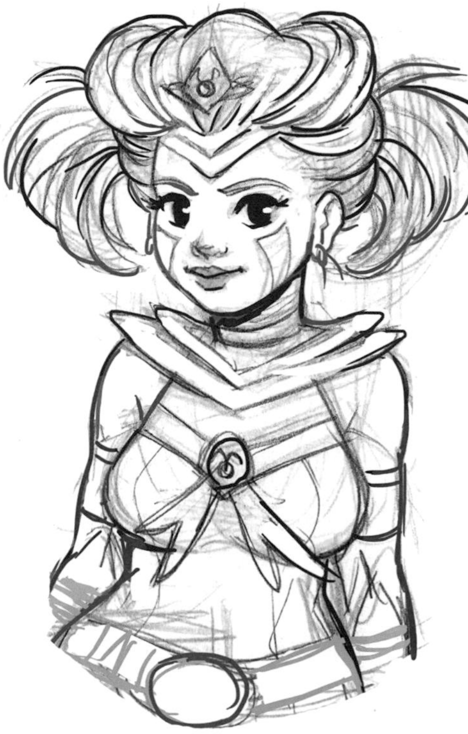

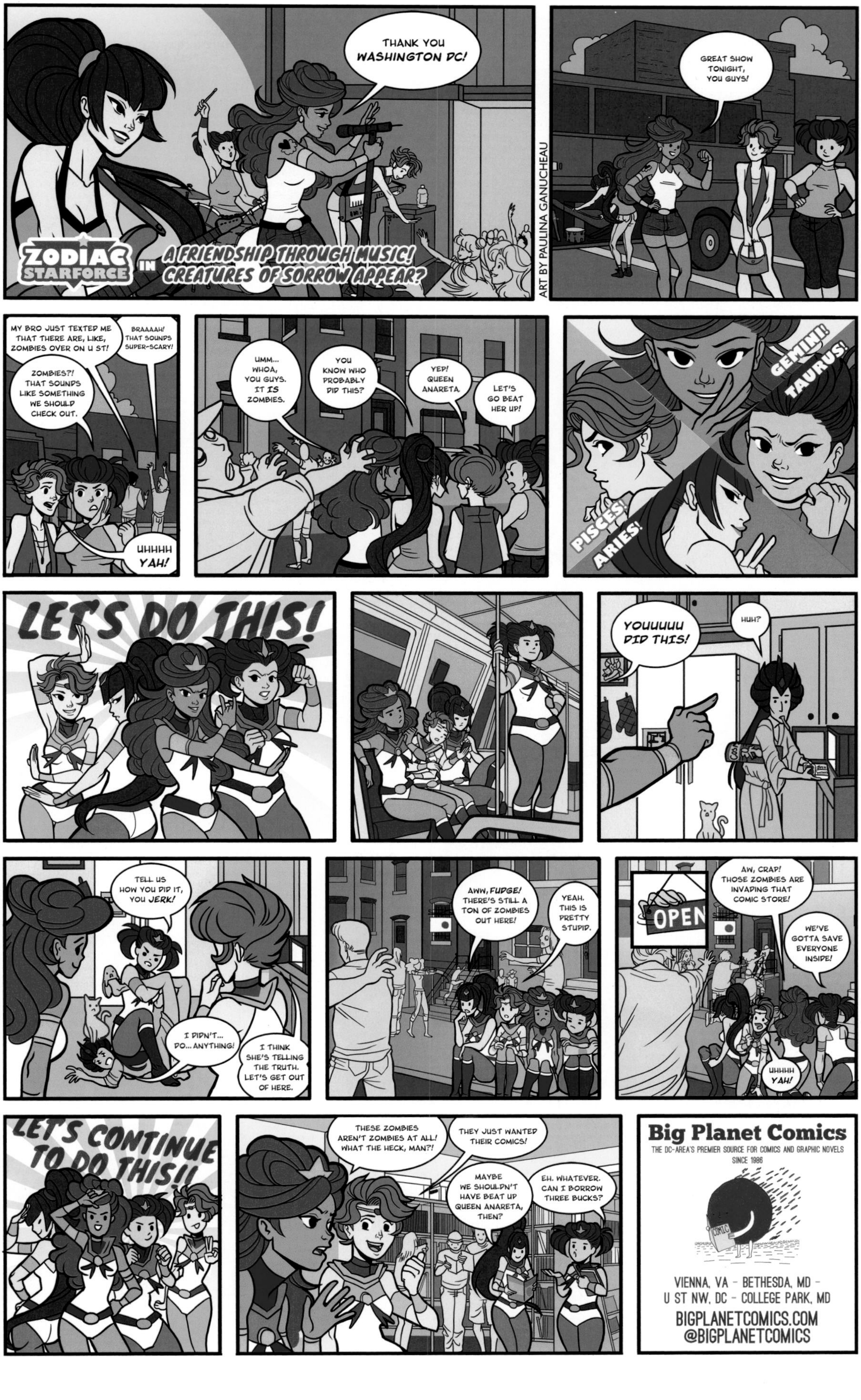
THANK YOU WASHINGTON DC!
ZODIAC STARFORCE IN A FRIENDSHIP THROUGH MUSIC! CREATURES OF SORROW APPEAR?
ART BY PAULINA GANUCHEAU
GREAT SHOW TONIGHT, YOU GUYS!
MY BRO JUST TEXTED ME THAT THERE ARE, LIKE, ZOMBIES OVER ON U ST!
BRAAAAH! THAT SOUNDS SUPER-SCARY!
ZOMBIES?! THAT SOUNDS LIKE SOMETHING WE SHOULD CHECK OUT.
UHHHH YAH!
UMM... WHOA, YOU GUYS. IT IS ZOMBIES.
YOU KNOW WHO PROBABLY DID THIS?
YEP! QUEEN ANARETA.
LET'S GO BEAT HER UP!
GEMINI!
TAURUS!
PISCES!
ARIES!
LET'S DO THIS!
YOUUUUU DID THIS!
HUH?
TELL US HOW YOU DID IT, YOU JERK!
I DIDN'T... DO... ANYTHING!
I THINK SHE'S TELLING THE TRUTH. LET'S GET OUT OF HERE.
AWW, FUDGE! THERE'S STILL A TON OF ZOMBIES OUT HERE!
YEAH. THIS IS PRETTY STUPID.
OPEN
AW, CRAP! THOSE ZOMBIES ARE INVADING THAT COMIC STORE!
WE'VE GOTTA SAVE EVERYONE INSIDE!
UHHHH YAH!
LET'S CONTINUE TO DO THIS!!
THESE ZOMBIES AREN'T ZOMBIES AT ALL! WHAT THE HECK, MAN?!
THEY JUST WANTED THEIR COMICS!
MAYBE WE SHOULDN'T HAVE BEAT UP QUEEN ANARETA, THEN?
EH. WHATEVER. CAN I BORROW THREE BUCKS?
Big Planet Comics
THE DC-AREA'S PREMIER SOURCE FOR COMICS AND GRAPHIC NOVELS
SINCE 1986
COMICS
VIENNA, VA - BETHESDA, MD -
U ST NW, DC - COLLEGE PARK, MD
BIGPLANETCOMICS.COM
@BIGPLANETCOMICS

THE WEB COMIC

K: Even though we only did five pages, the web comic was a ton of fun. It was all about how the girls got their powers, a much different story from what we told in the Dark Horse series.

P: It's interesting looking at these thumbnails for pages that never were!

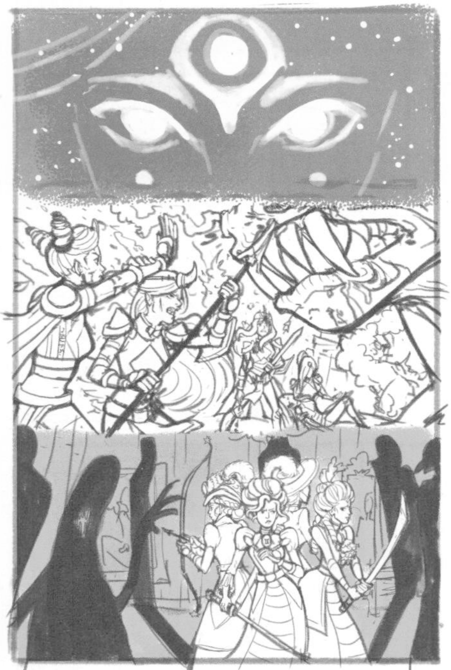

P6

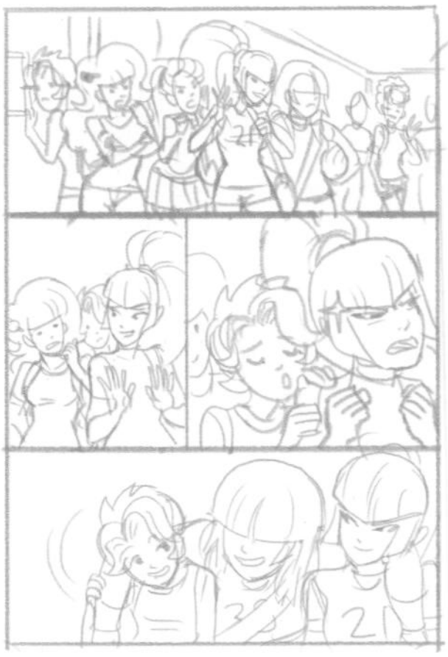

P7

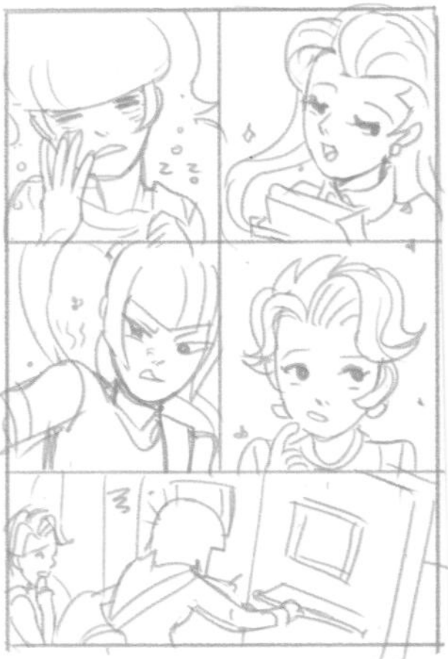

P8-9

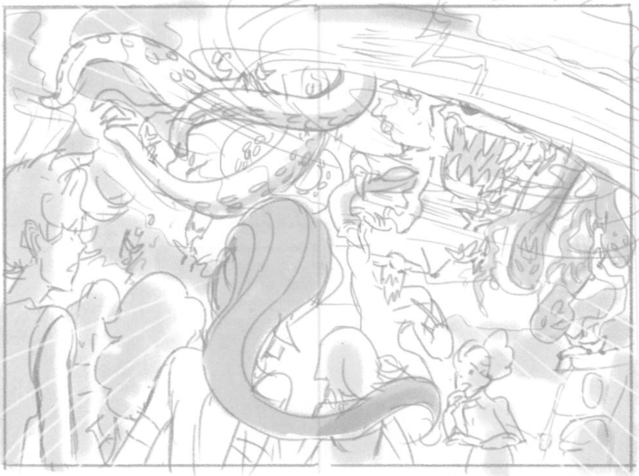

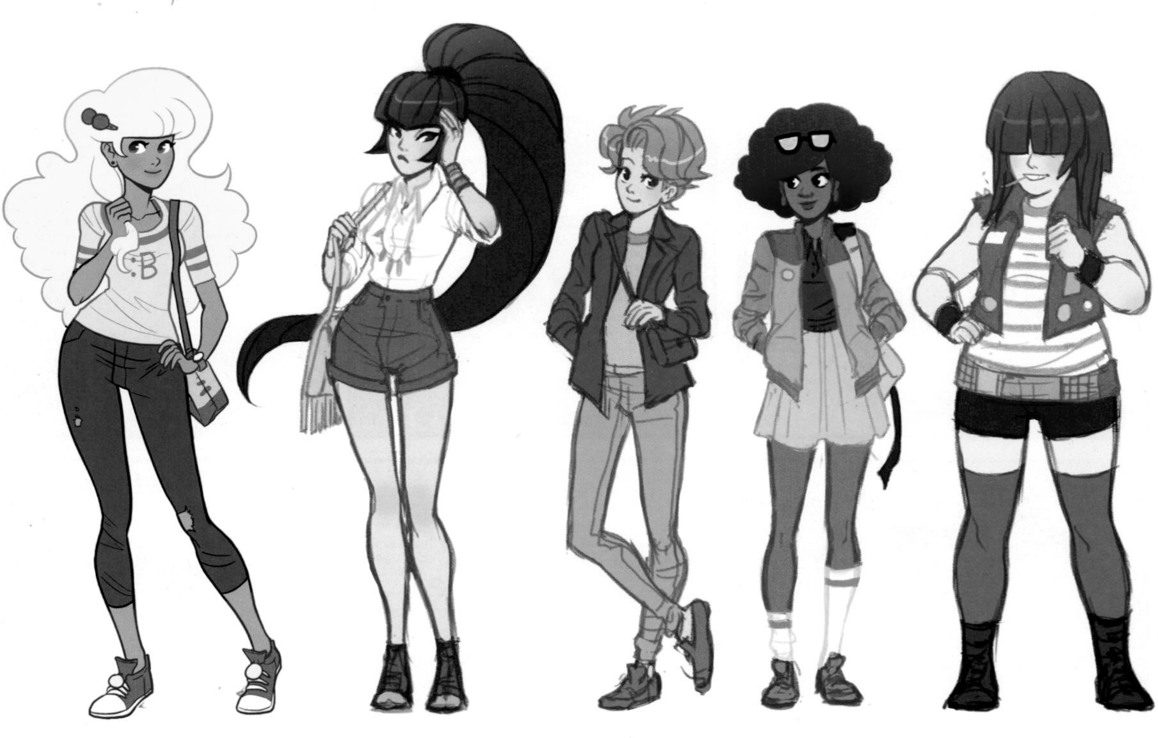

FINAL WEB COMIC DESIGNS

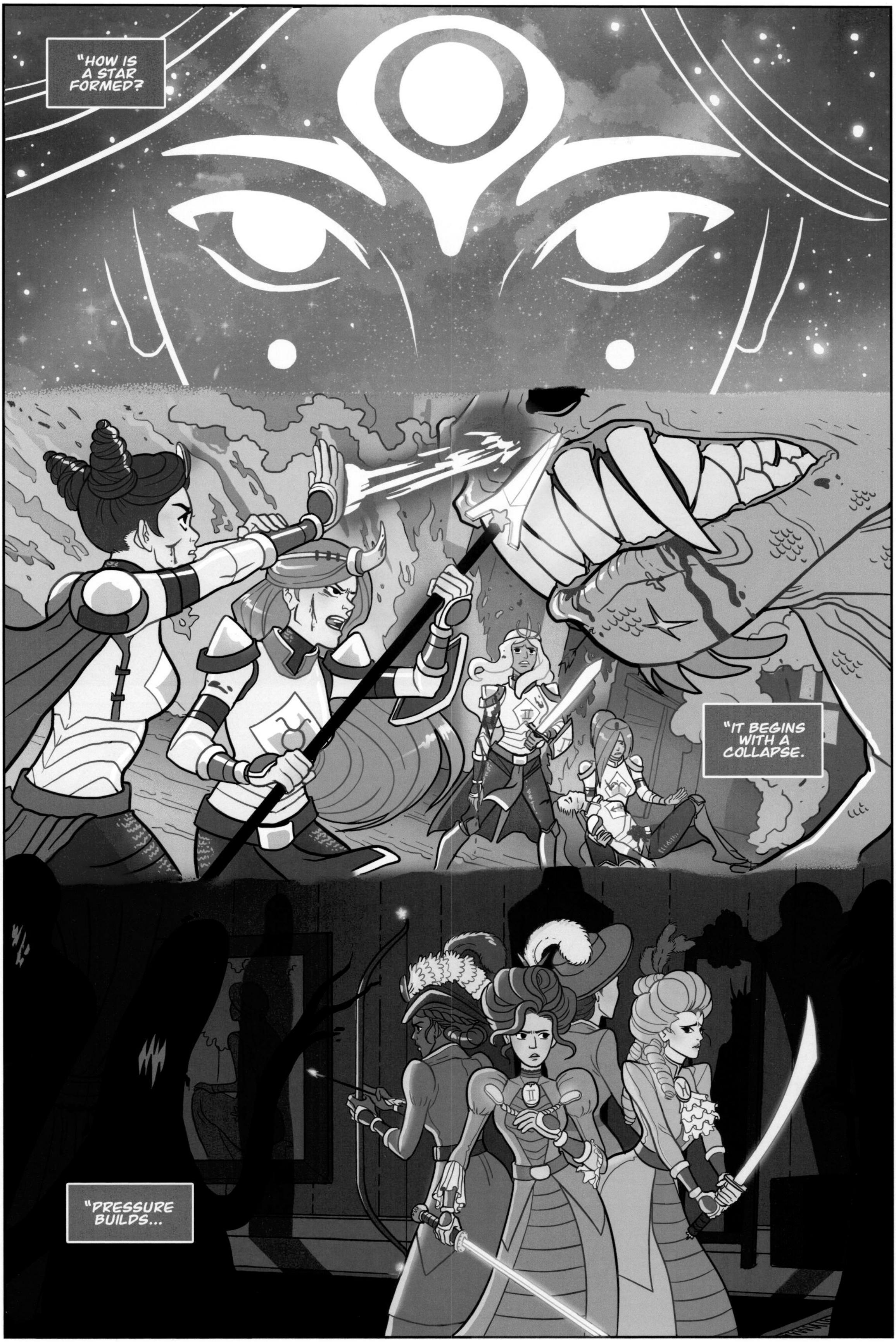
"HOW IS A STAR FORMED?
"IT BEGINS WITH A COLLAPSE.
"PRESSURE BUILDS...

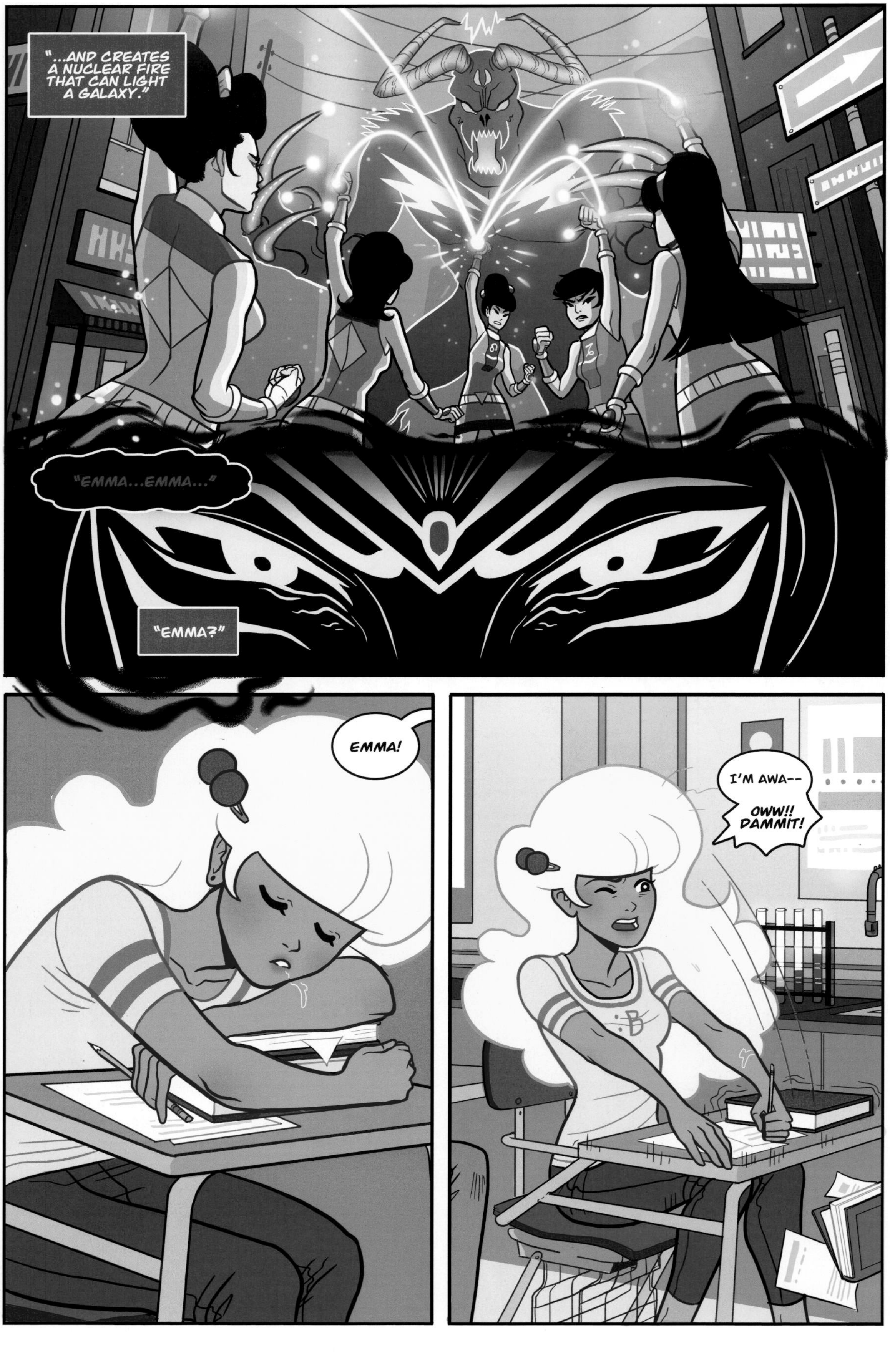
"...AND CREATES A NUCLEAR FIRE THAT CAN LIGHT A GALAXY."
"EMMA...EMMA..."
"EMMA?"
EMMA!
I'M AWA--
OWW!! DAMMIT!

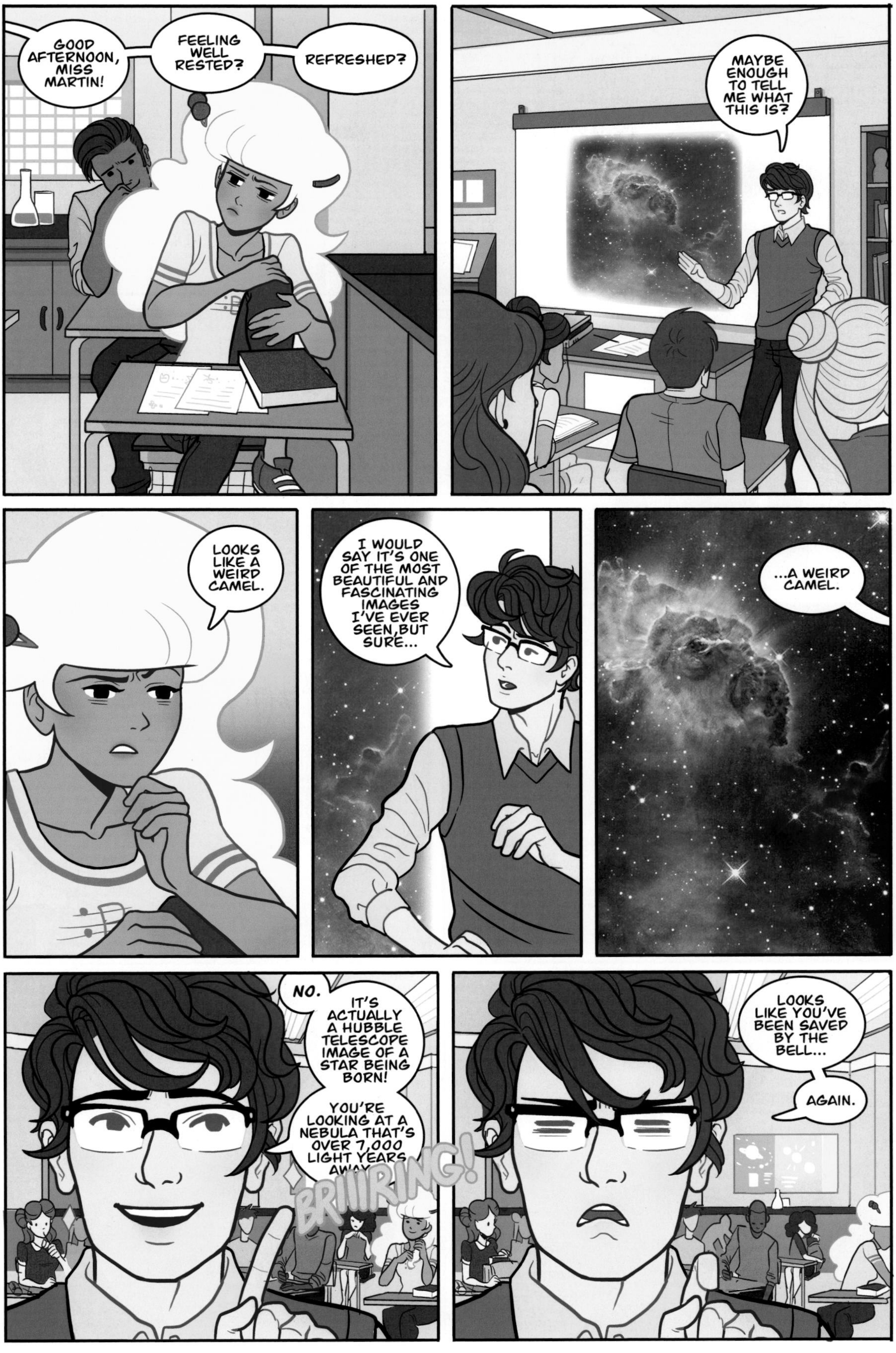
GOOD AFTERNOON, MISS MARTIN!
FEELING WELL RESTED?
REFRESHED?
MAYBE ENOUGH TO TELL ME WHAT THIS IS?
LOOKS LIKE A WEIRD CAMEL.
I WOULD SAY IT'S ONE OF THE MOST BEAUTIFUL AND FASCINATING IMAGES I'VE EVER SEEN,BUT SURE...
...A WEIRD CAMEL.
NO.
IT'S ACTUALLY A HUBBLE TELESCOPE IMAGE OF A STAR BEING BORN!
YOU'RE LOOKING AT A NEBULA THAT'S OVER 7,000 LIGHT YEARS AWAY
BRIIIRING!
LOOKS LIKE YOU'VE BEEN SAVED BY THE BELL...
AGAIN.

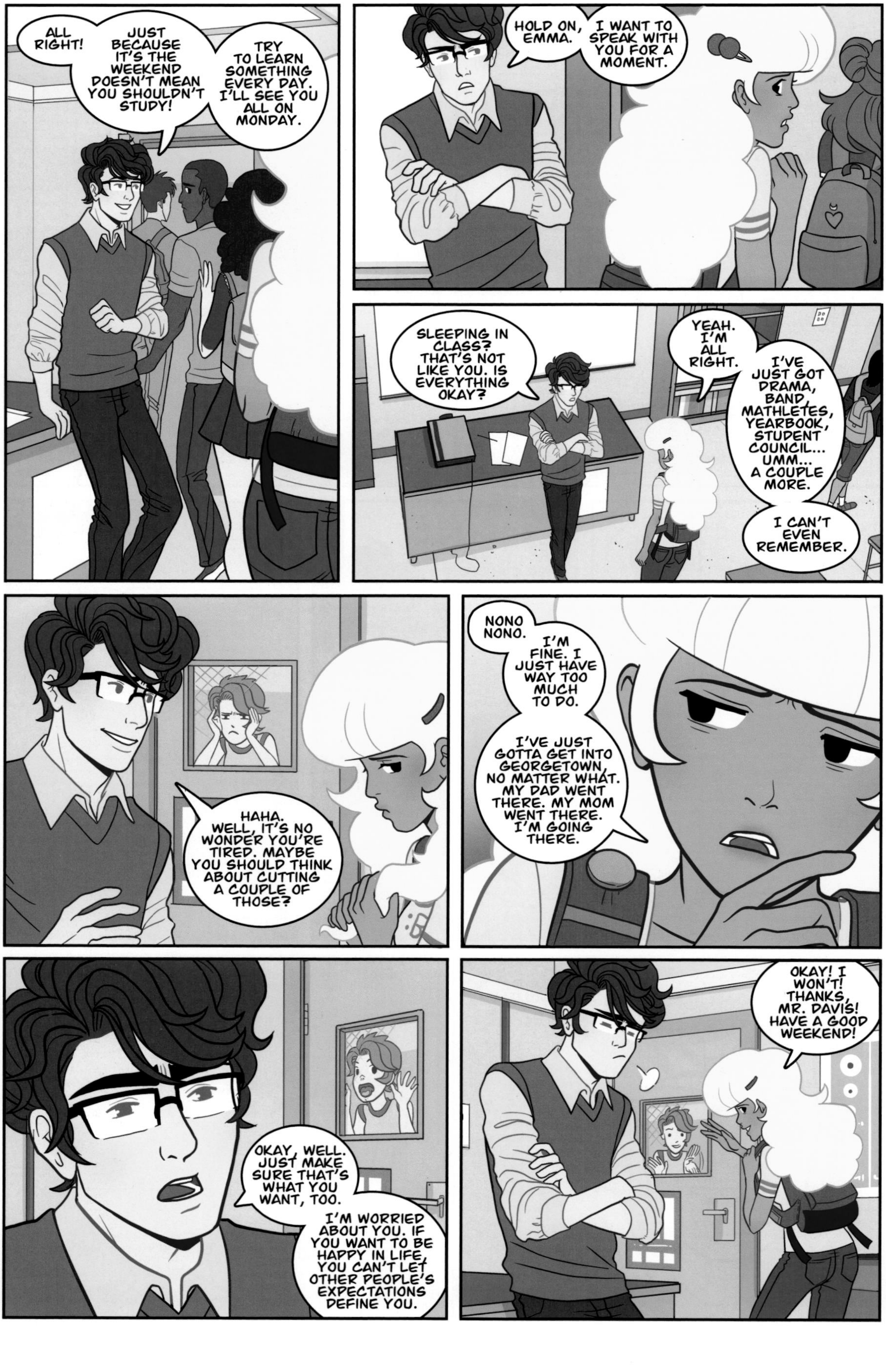
ALL RIGHT!
JUST BECAUSE IT'S THE WEEKEND DOESN'T MEAN YOU SHOULDN'T STUDY!
TRY TO LEARN SOMETHING EVERY DAY. I'LL SEE YOU ALL ON MONDAY.
HOLD ON, EMMA.
I WANT TO SPEAK WITH YOU FOR A MOMENT.
SLEEPING IN CLASS? THAT'S NOT LIKE YOU. IS EVERYTHING OKAY?
YEAH. I'M ALL RIGHT.
I'VE JUST GOT DRAMA, BAND, MATHLETES, YEARBOOK, STUDENT COUNCIL... UMM... A COUPLE MORE.
I CAN'T EVEN REMEMBER.
HAHA. WELL, IT'S NO WONDER YOU'RE TIRED. MAYBE YOU SHOULD THINK ABOUT CUTTING A COUPLE OF THOSE?
NONO NONO.
I'M FINE. I JUST HAVE WAY TOO MUCH TO DO.
I'VE JUST GOTTA GET INTO GEORGETOWN, NO MATTER WHAT. MY DAD WENT THERE. MY MOM WENT THERE. I'M GOING THERE.
OKAY, WELL. JUST MAKE SURE THAT'S WHAT YOU WANT, TOO.
I'M WORRIED ABOUT YOU. IF YOU WANT TO BE HAPPY IN LIFE, YOU CAN'T LET OTHER PEOPLE'S EXPECTATIONS DEFINE YOU.
OKAY! I WON'T! THANKS, MR. DAVIS! HAVE A GOOD WEEKEND!

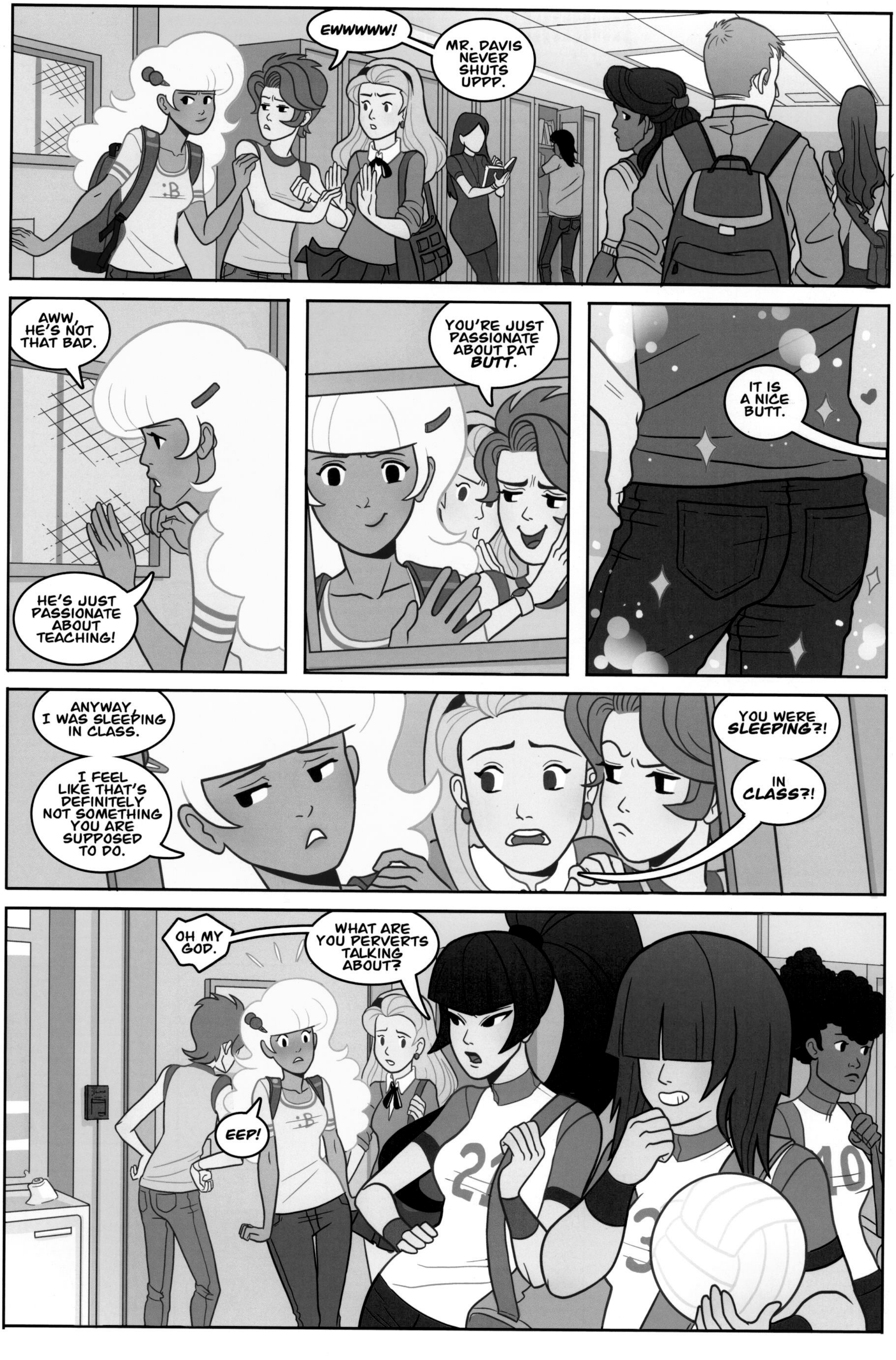
EWWWWW!
MR. DAVIS NEVER SHUTS UPPP.
AWW, HE'S NOT THAT BAD.
HE'S JUST PASSIONATE ABOUT TEACHING!
YOU'RE JUST PASSIONATE ABOUT DAT BUTT.
IT IS A NICE BUTT.
ANYWAY, I WAS SLEEPING IN CLASS.
I FEEL LIKE THAT'S DEFINITELY NOT SOMETHING YOU ARE SUPPOSED TO DO.
YOU WERE SLEEPING?!
IN CLASS?!
OH MY GOD.
WHAT ARE YOU PERVERTS TALKING ABOUT?
EEP!

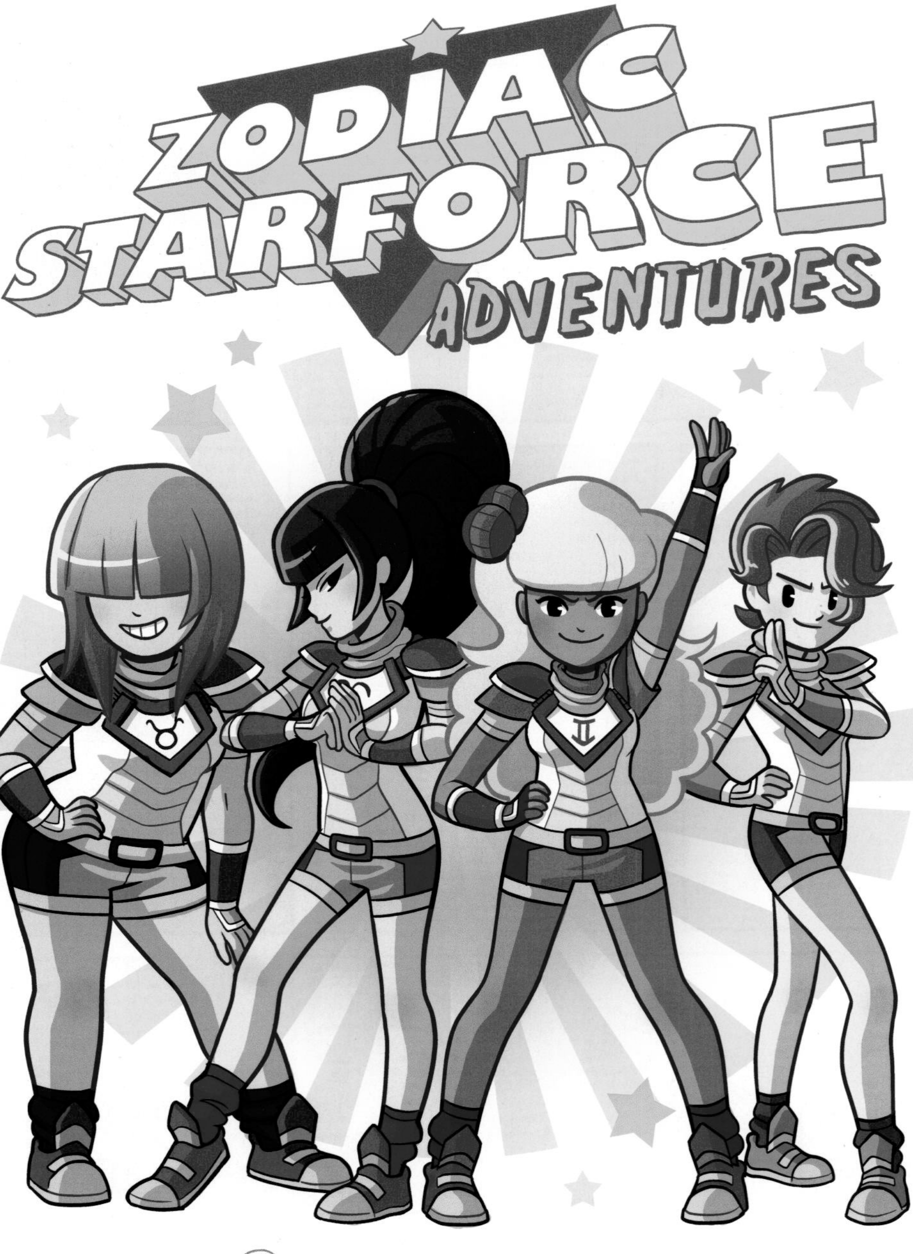
ZODIAC STARFORCE
ADVENTURES

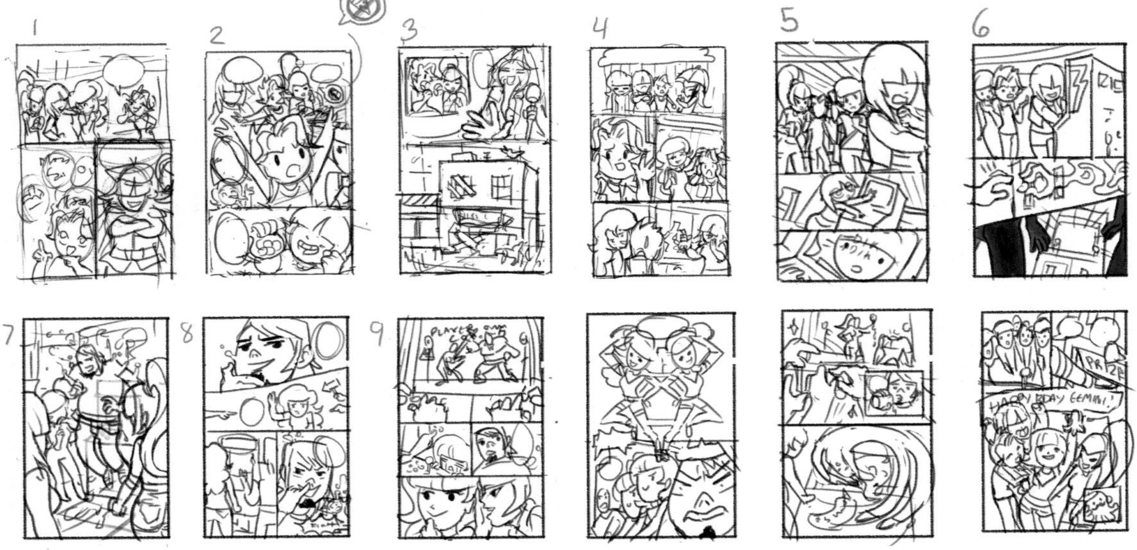

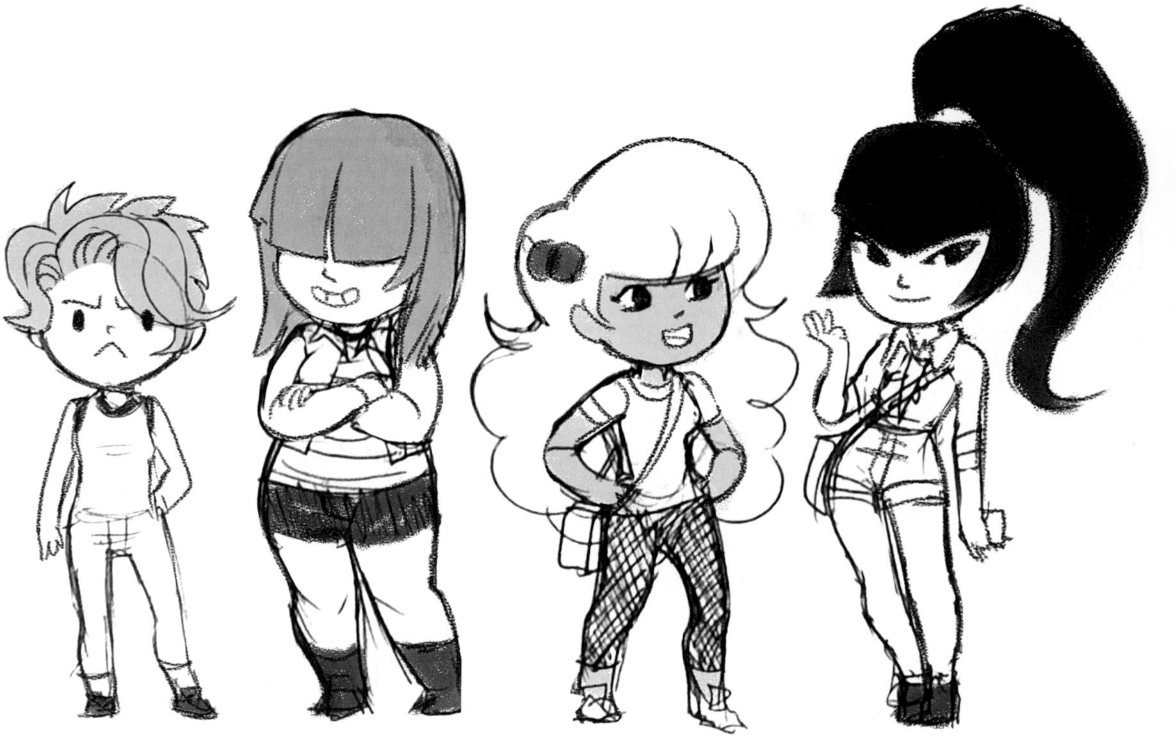

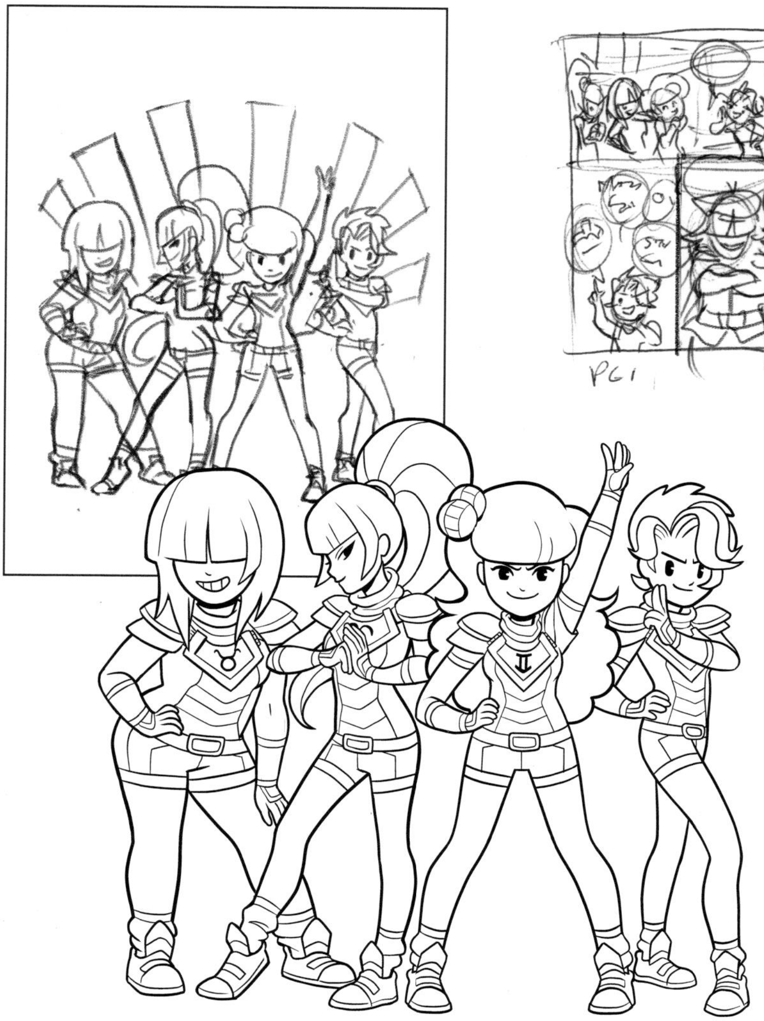

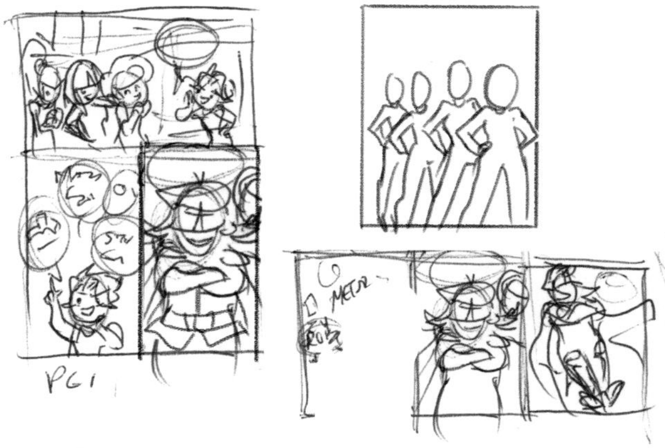

THE MINICOMIC

K: *Zodiac Starforce Adventures* was our first printed comic! We put it together in just a few weeks for the Small Press Expo. It's probably the most *Sailor Moon*-y thing we've done (haunted arcade machine!), but it turned out super cute and even had a shiny silver cover! (Special thanks to Paulina's sister, Savanna, for adding all the *shoujo* screen tones!)

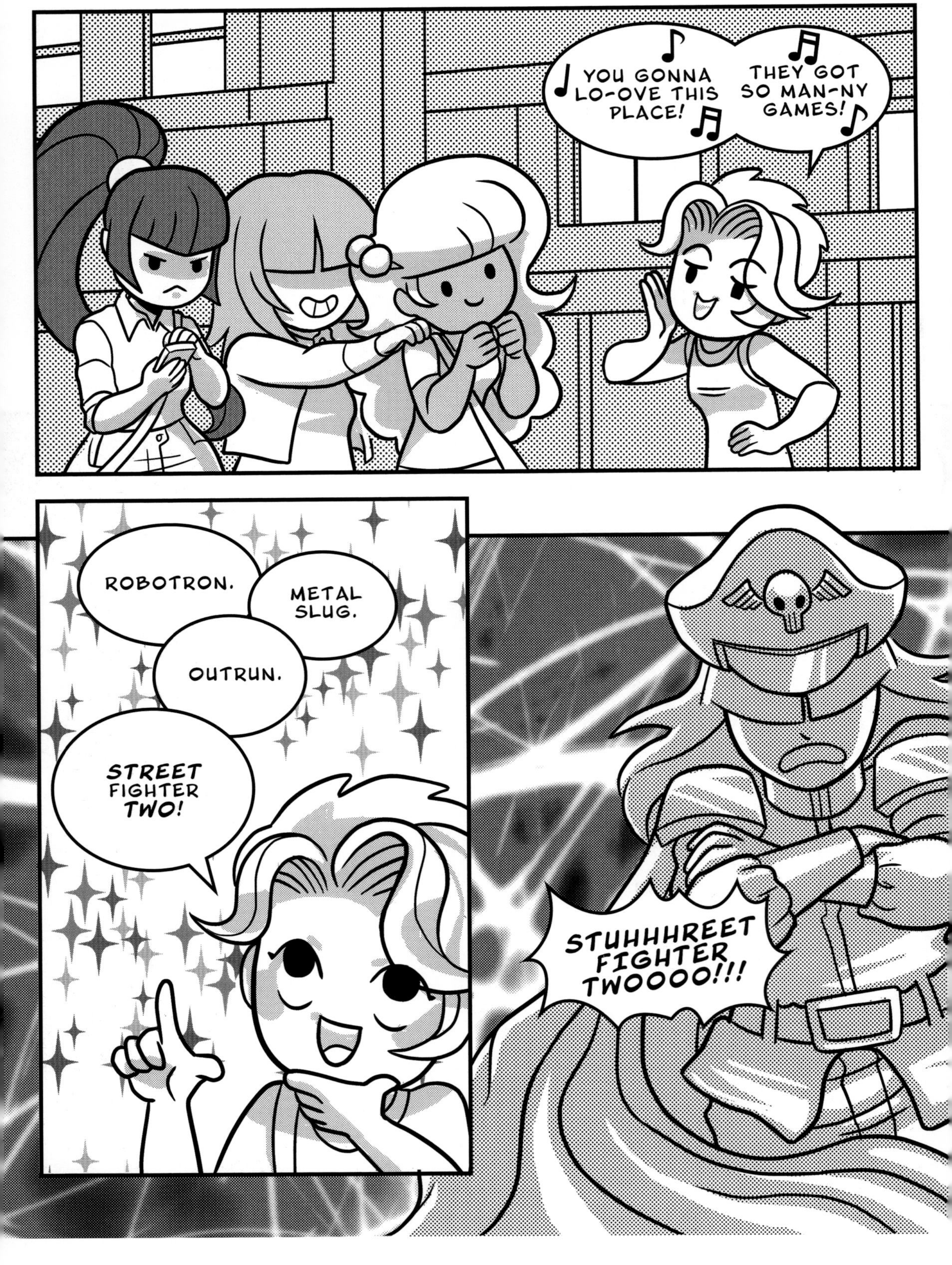
YOU GONNA LO-OVE THIS PLACE!
THEY GOT SO MAN-NY GAMES!
ROBOTRON.
METAL SLUG.
OUTRUN.
STREET FIGHTER TWO!
STUHHHREET FIGHTER TWOOOO!!!

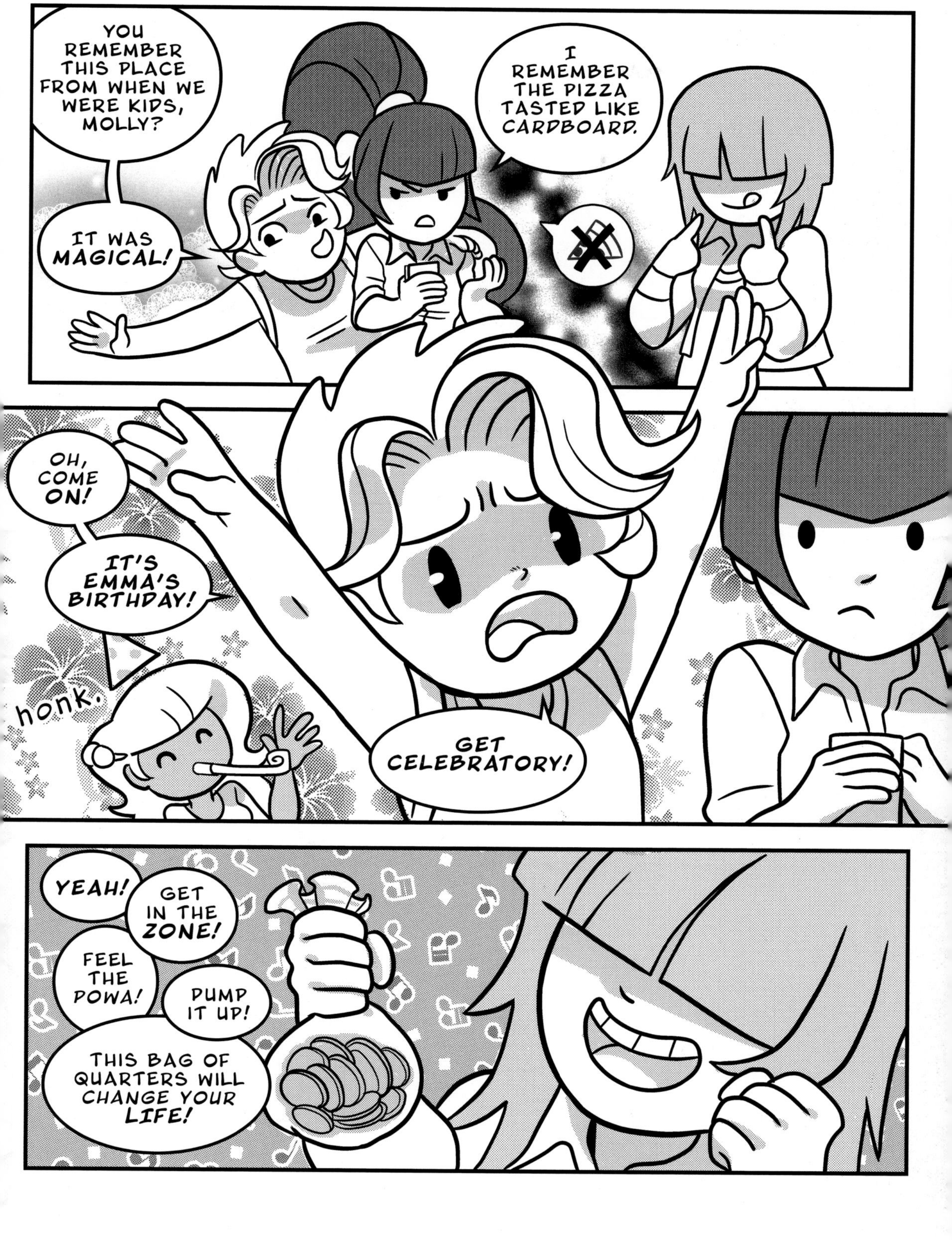
YOU REMEMBER THIS PLACE FROM WHEN WE WERE KIDS, MOLLY?
IT WAS MAGICAL!
I REMEMBER THE PIZZA TASTED LIKE CARDBOARD.
OH, COME ON!
IT'S EMMA'S BIRTHDAY!
honk.
GET CELEBRATORY!
YEAH!
GET IN THE ZONE!
FEEL THE POWA!
PUMP IT UP!
THIS BAG OF QUARTERS WILL CHANGE YOUR LIFE!

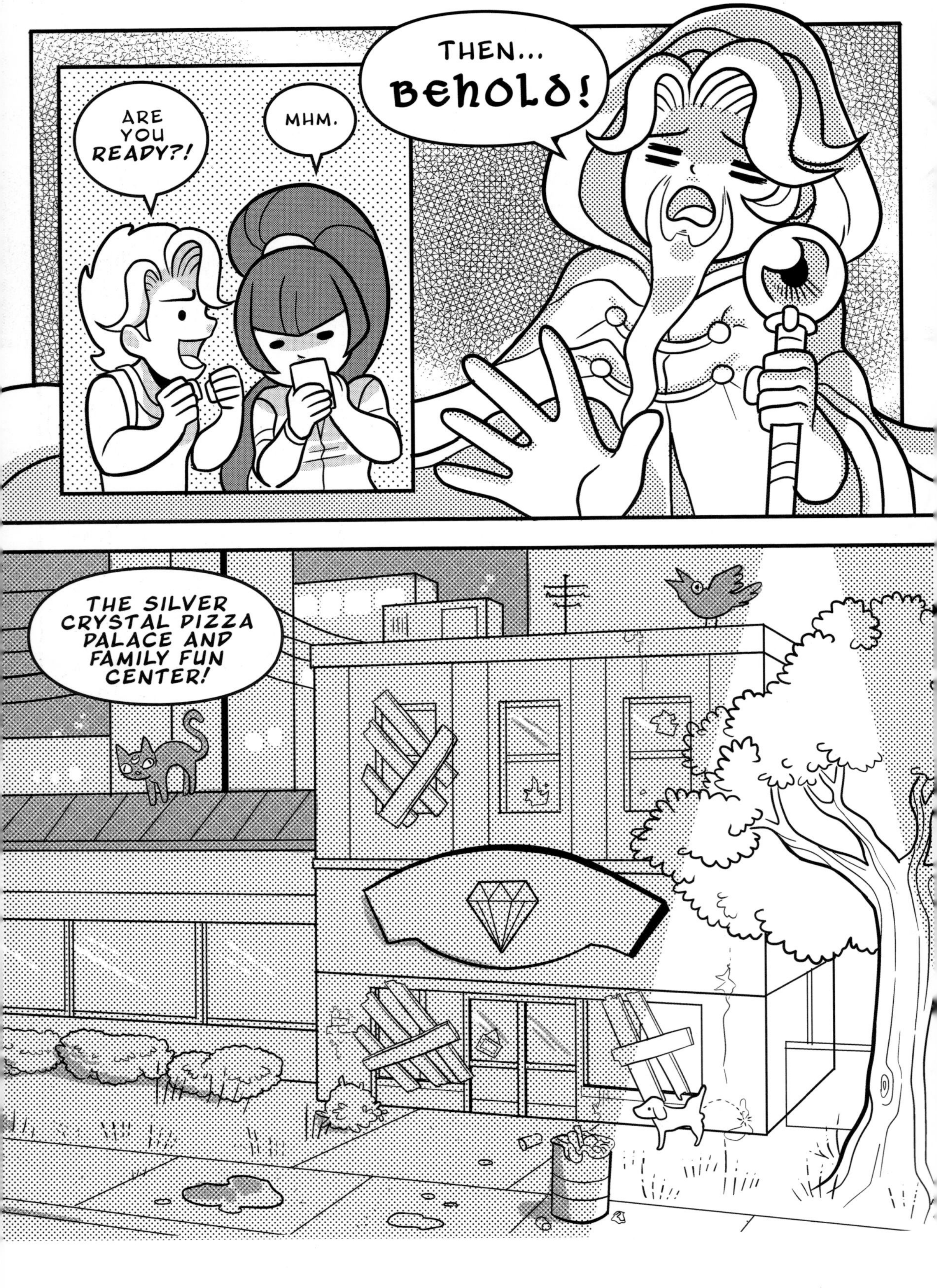
ARE YOU READY?!
MHM.
THEN... BEHOLD!
THE SILVER CRYSTAL PIZZA PALACE AND FAMILY FUN CENTER!

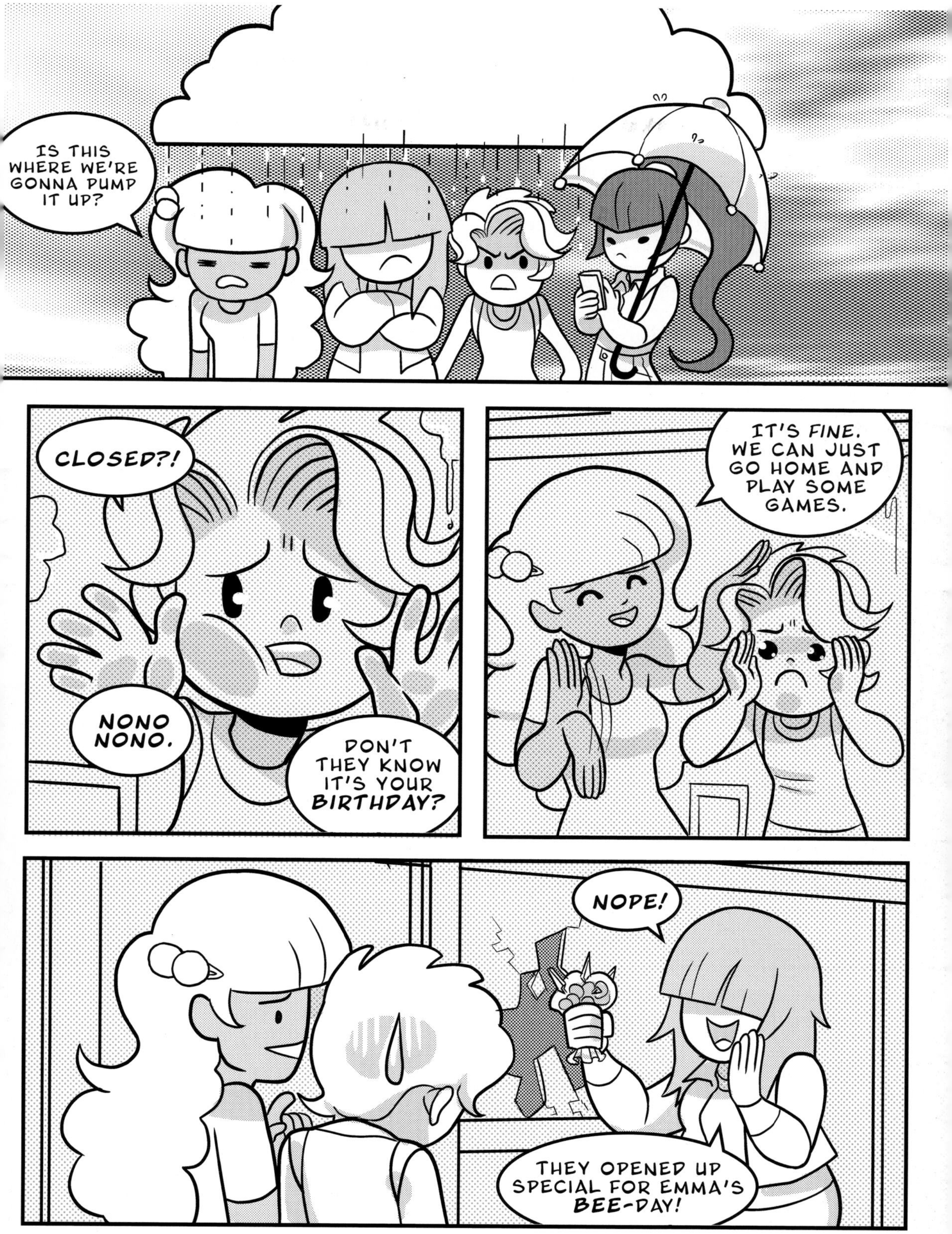
IS THIS WHERE WE'RE GONNA PUMP IT UP?
CLOSED?!
NONO NONO.
DON'T THEY KNOW IT'S YOUR BIRTHDAY?
IT'S FINE. WE CAN JUST GO HOME AND PLAY SOME GAMES.
NOPE!
THEY OPENED UP SPECIAL FOR EMMA'S BEE-DAY!

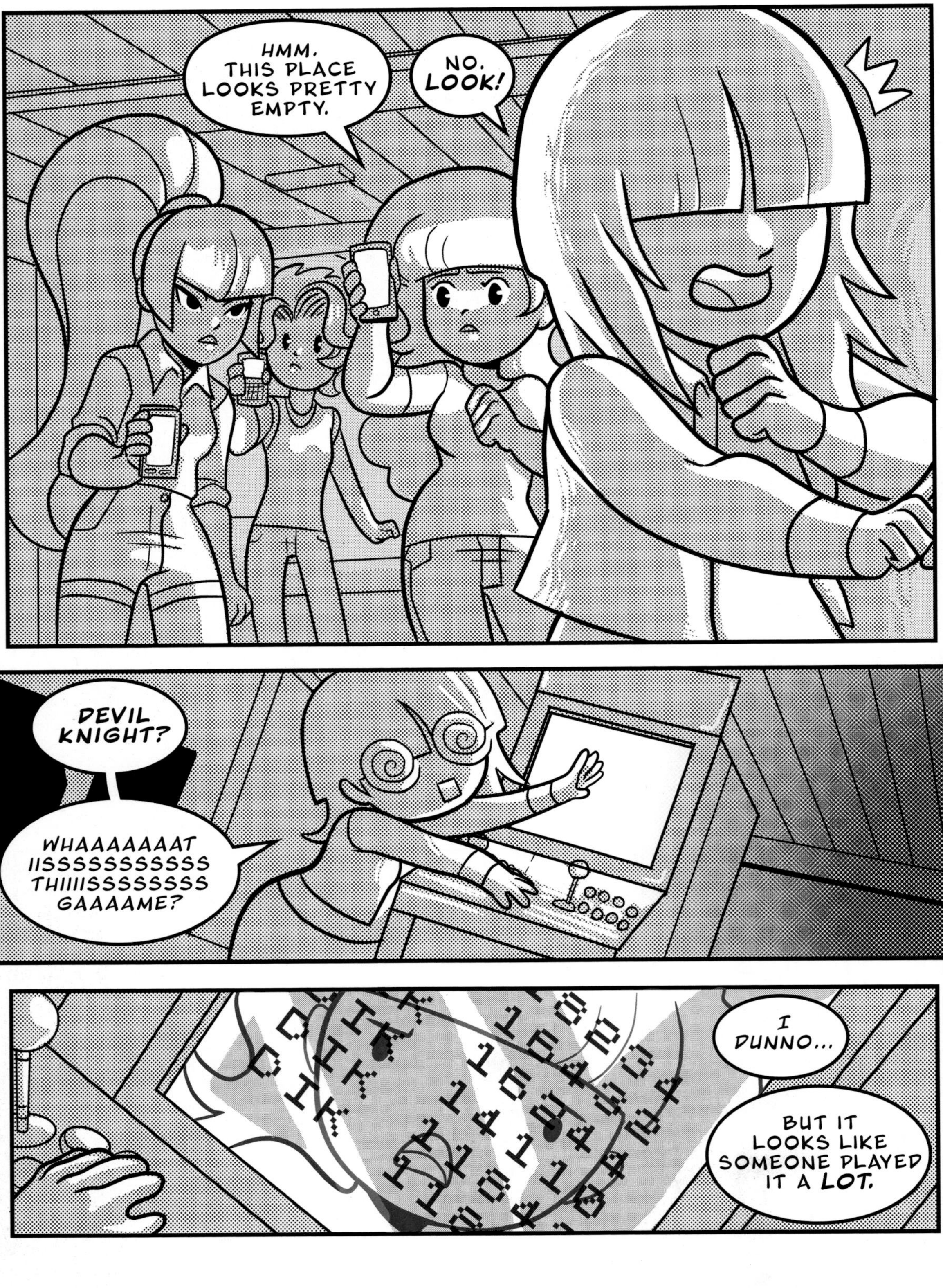
HMM. THIS PLACE LOOKS PRETTY EMPTY.
NO. LOOK!
DEVIL KNIGHT?
WHAAAAAAAT IISSSSSSSSSS THIIIISSSSSSSS GAAAAME?
I DUNNO...
BUT IT LOOKS LIKE SOMEONE PLAYED IT A LOT.

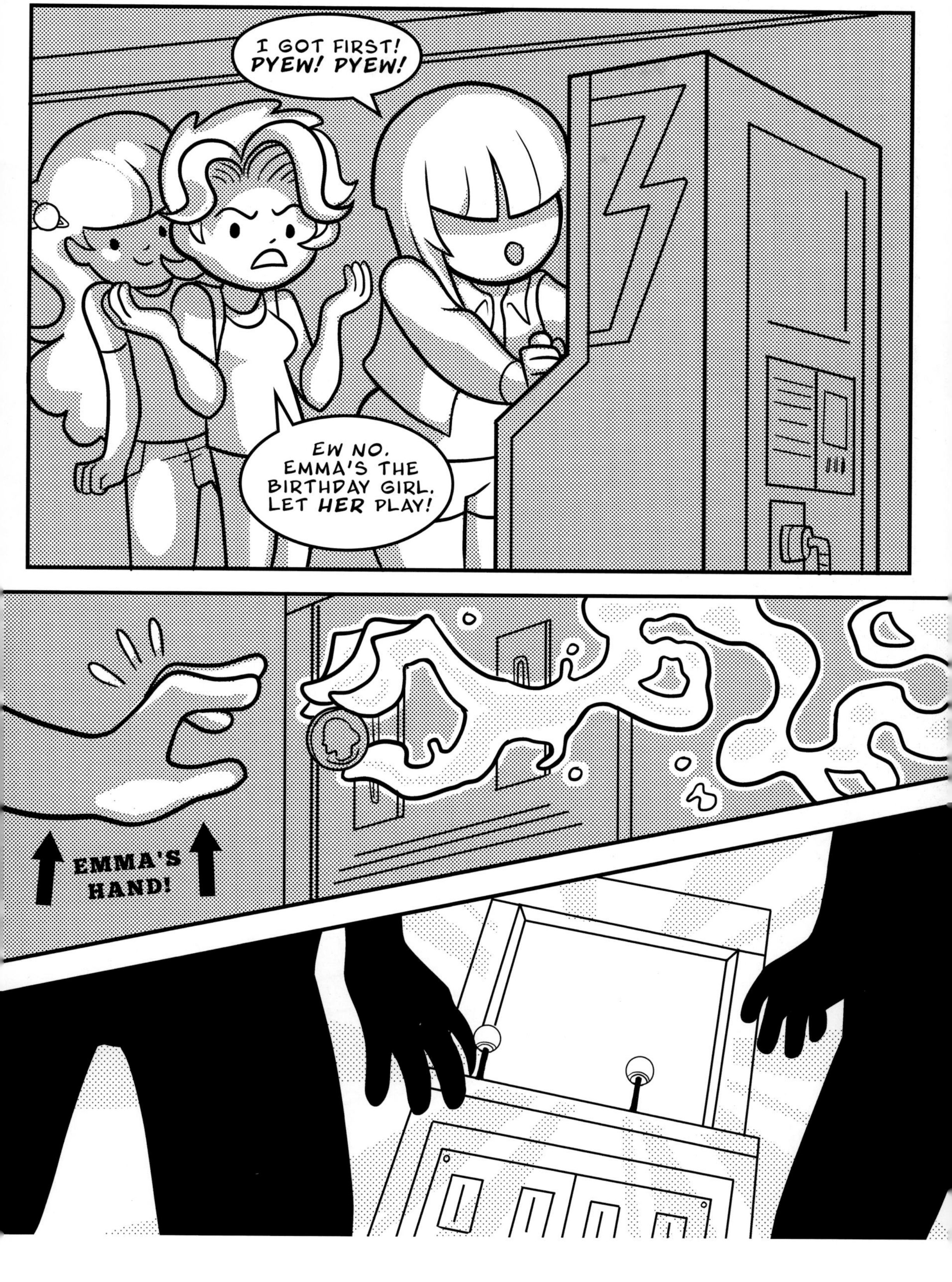
I GOT FIRST! PYEW! PYEW!
EW NO. EMMA'S THE BIRTHDAY GIRL. LET HER PLAY!
EMMA'S HAND!

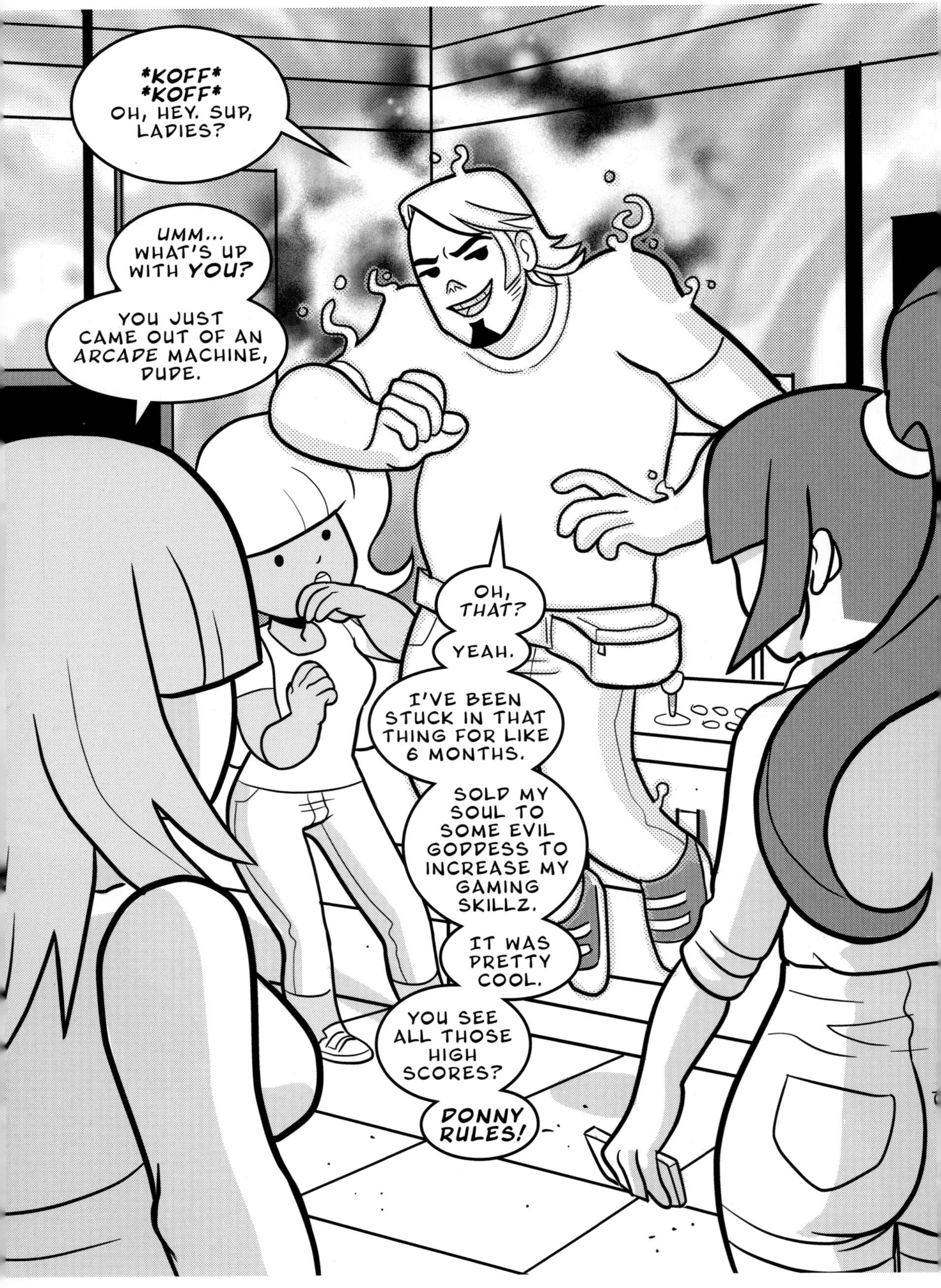
KOFF *KOFF* OH, HEY. SUP, LADIES?
UMM... WHAT'S UP WITH YOU?
YOU JUST CAME OUT OF AN ARCADE MACHINE, DUDE.
OH, THAT?
YEAH.
I'VE BEEN STUCK IN THAT THING FOR LIKE 6 MONTHS.
SOLD MY SOUL TO SOME EVIL GODDESS TO INCREASE MY GAMING SKILLZ.
IT WAS PRETTY COOL.
YOU SEE ALL THOSE HIGH SCORES?
DONNY RULES!

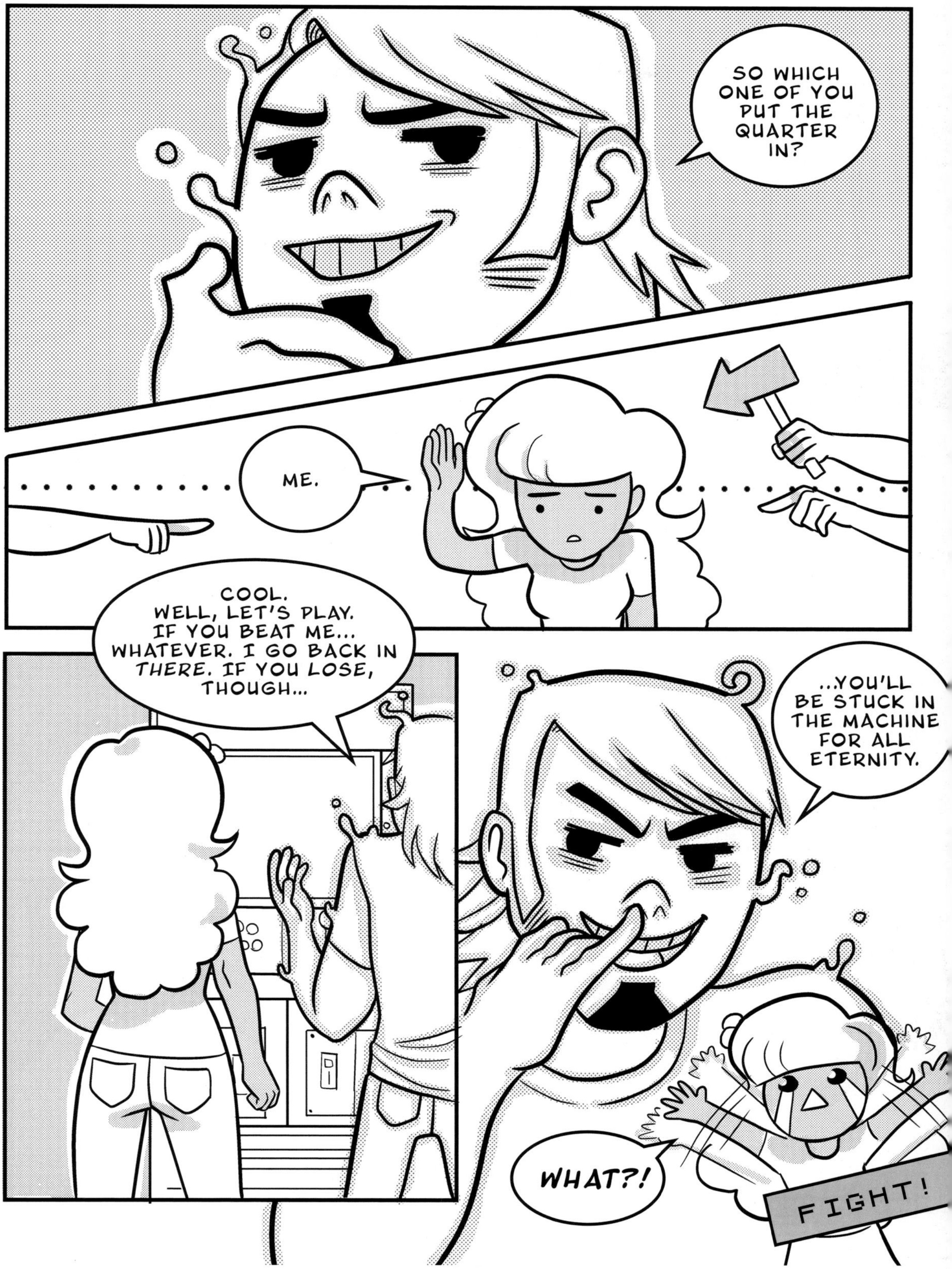
SO WHICH ONE OF YOU PUT THE QUARTER IN?
ME.
COOL. WELL, LET'S PLAY. IF YOU BEAT ME... WHATEVER. I GO BACK IN *THERE*. IF YOU LOSE, THOUGH...
...YOU'LL BE STUCK IN THE MACHINE FOR ALL ETERNITY.
WHAT?!
FIGHT!

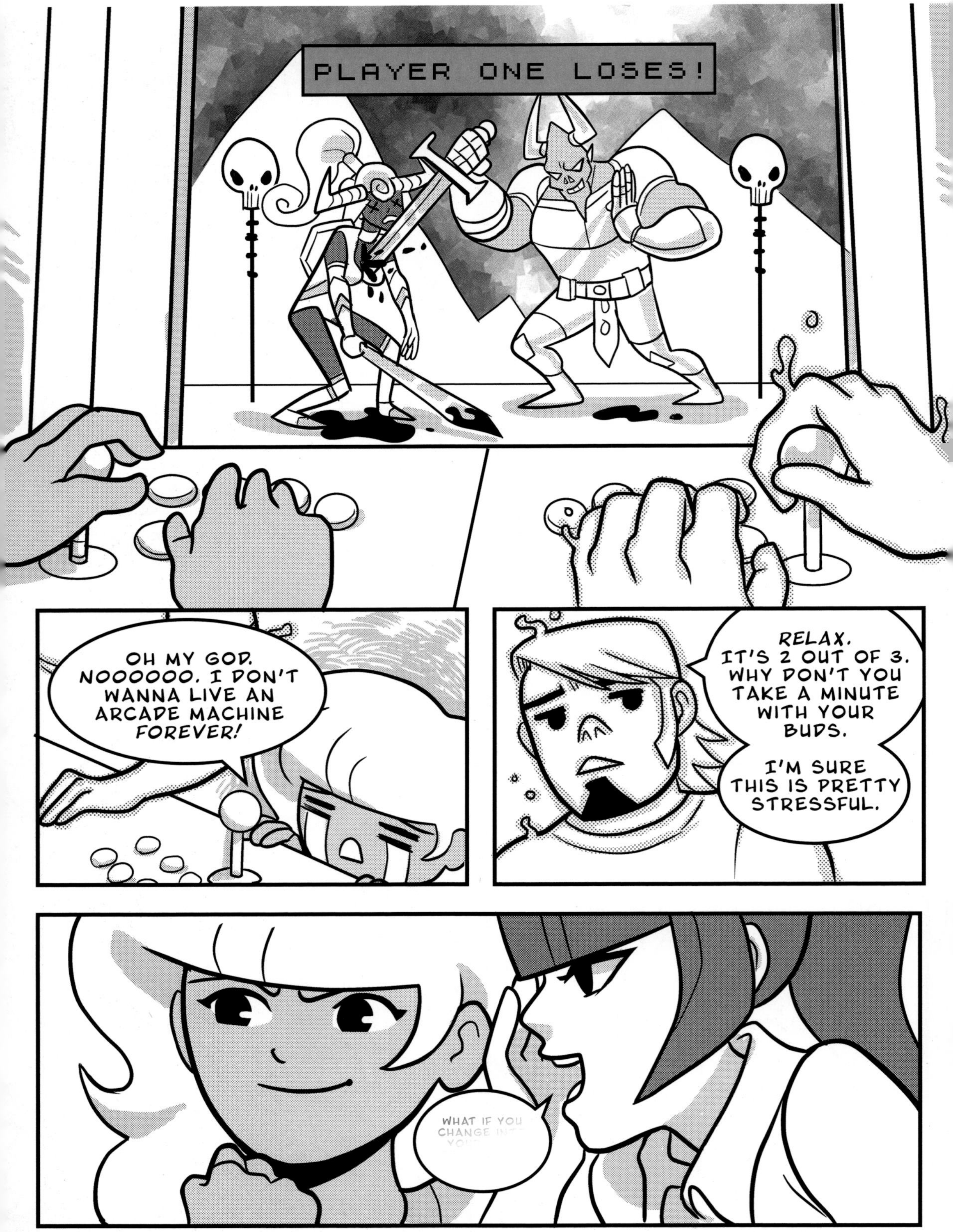
PLAYER ONE LOSES!
OH MY GOD. NOOOOOO. I DON'T WANNA LIVE AN ARCADE MACHINE FOREVER!
RELAX. IT'S 2 OUT OF 3. WHY DON'T YOU TAKE A MINUTE WITH YOUR BUDS.
I'M SURE THIS IS PRETTY STRESSFUL.
WHAT IF YOU

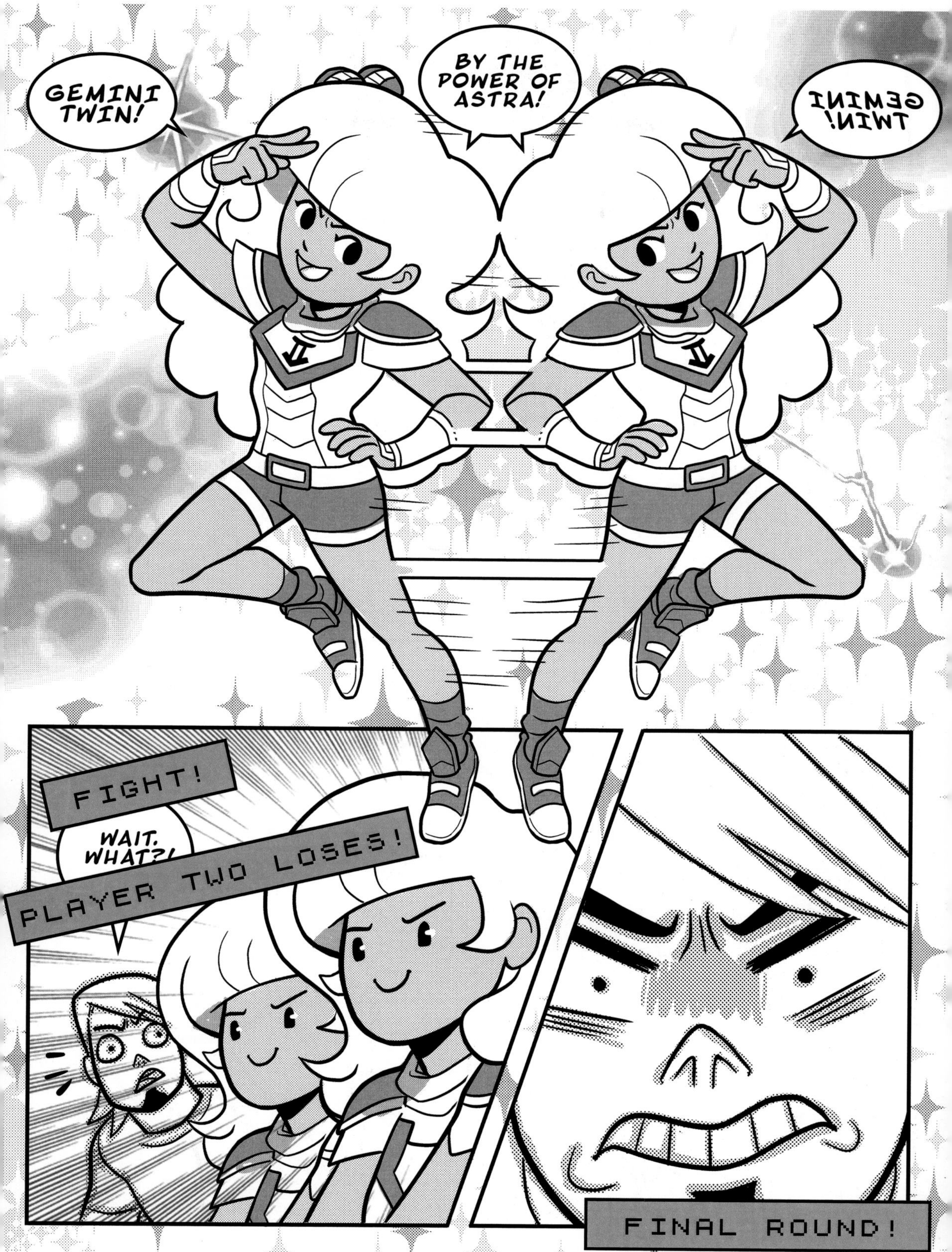
GEMINI TWIN!
BY THE POWER OF ASTRA!
GEMINI TWIN!
FIGHT!
WAIT. WHAT?!
PLAYER TWO LOSES!
FINAL ROUND!

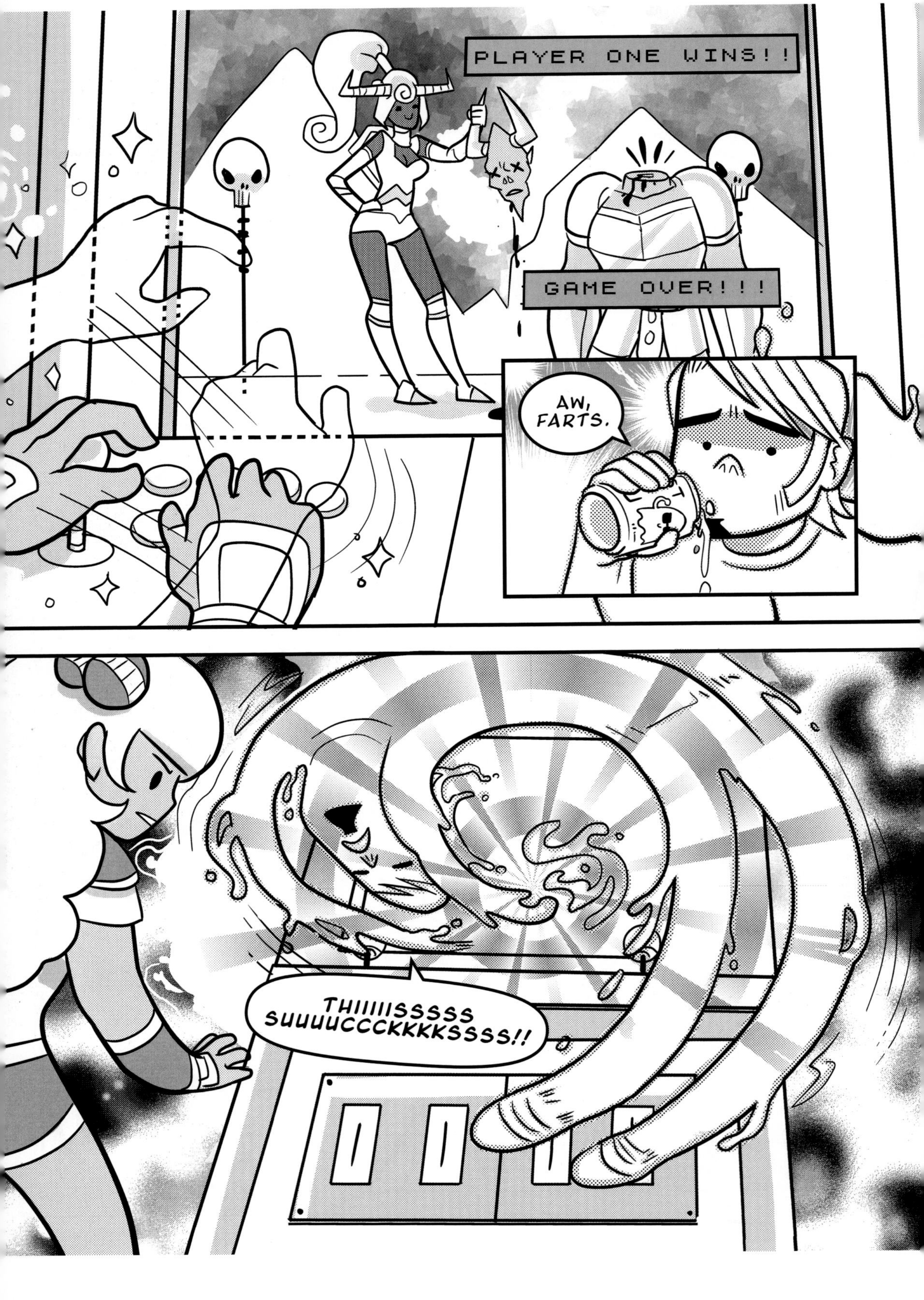
PLAYER ONE WINS!!
GAME OVER!!!
AW, FARTS.
THIIIIISSSSS SUUUUCCCCKKKKSSSS!!

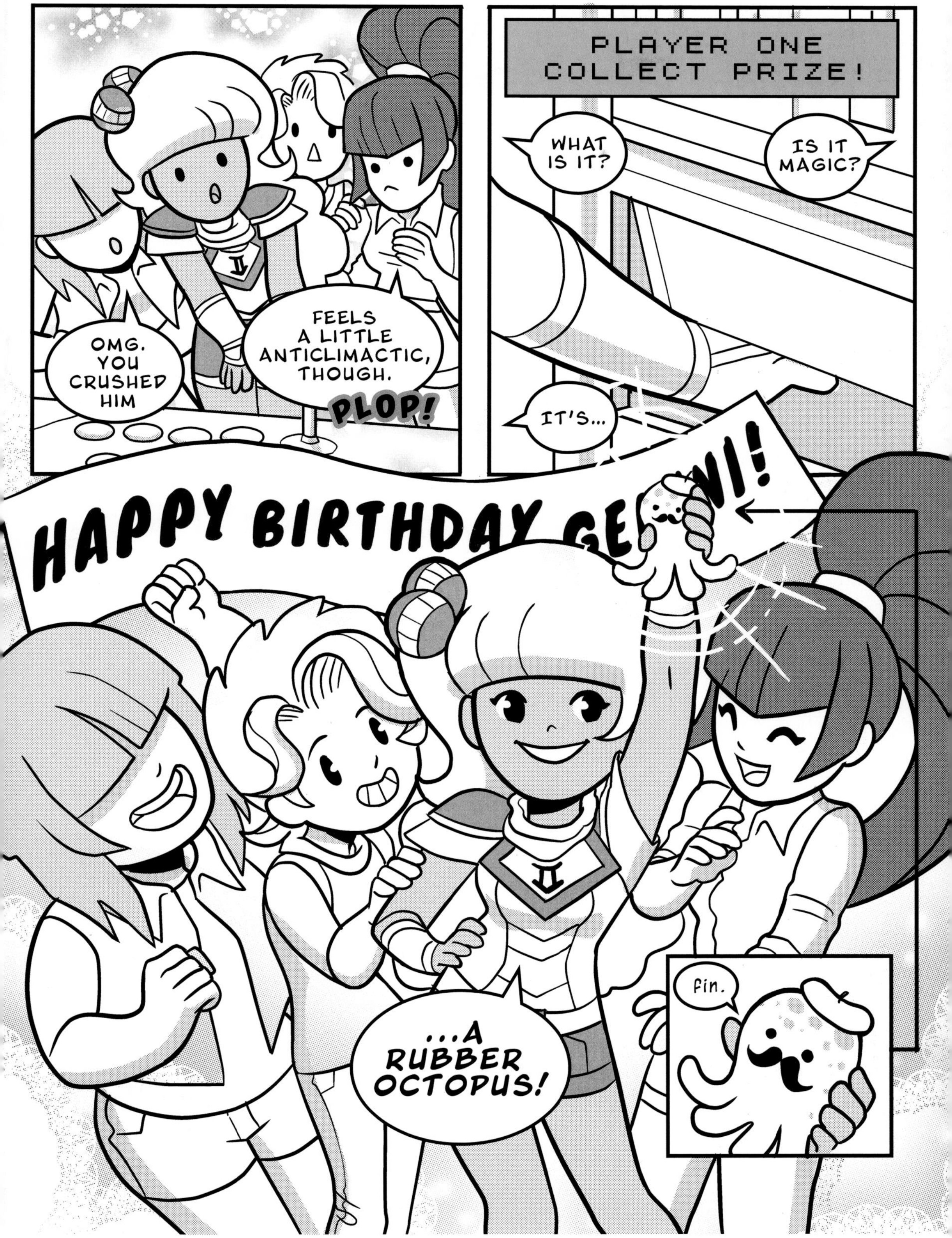
OMG. YOU CRUSHED HIM
FEELS A LITTLE ANTICLIMACTIC, THOUGH.
PLOP!
PLAYER ONE COLLECT PRIZE!
WHAT IS IT?
IS IT MAGIC?
IT'S...
HAPPY BIRTHDAY GE
I!
...A RUBBER OCTOPUS!
fin.

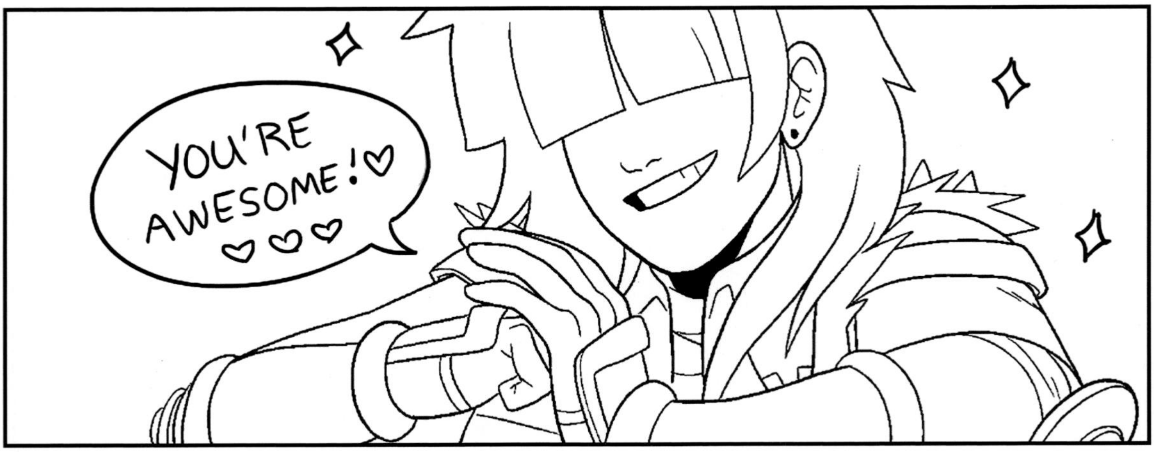
YOU'RE AWESOME!♡ ♡♡♡

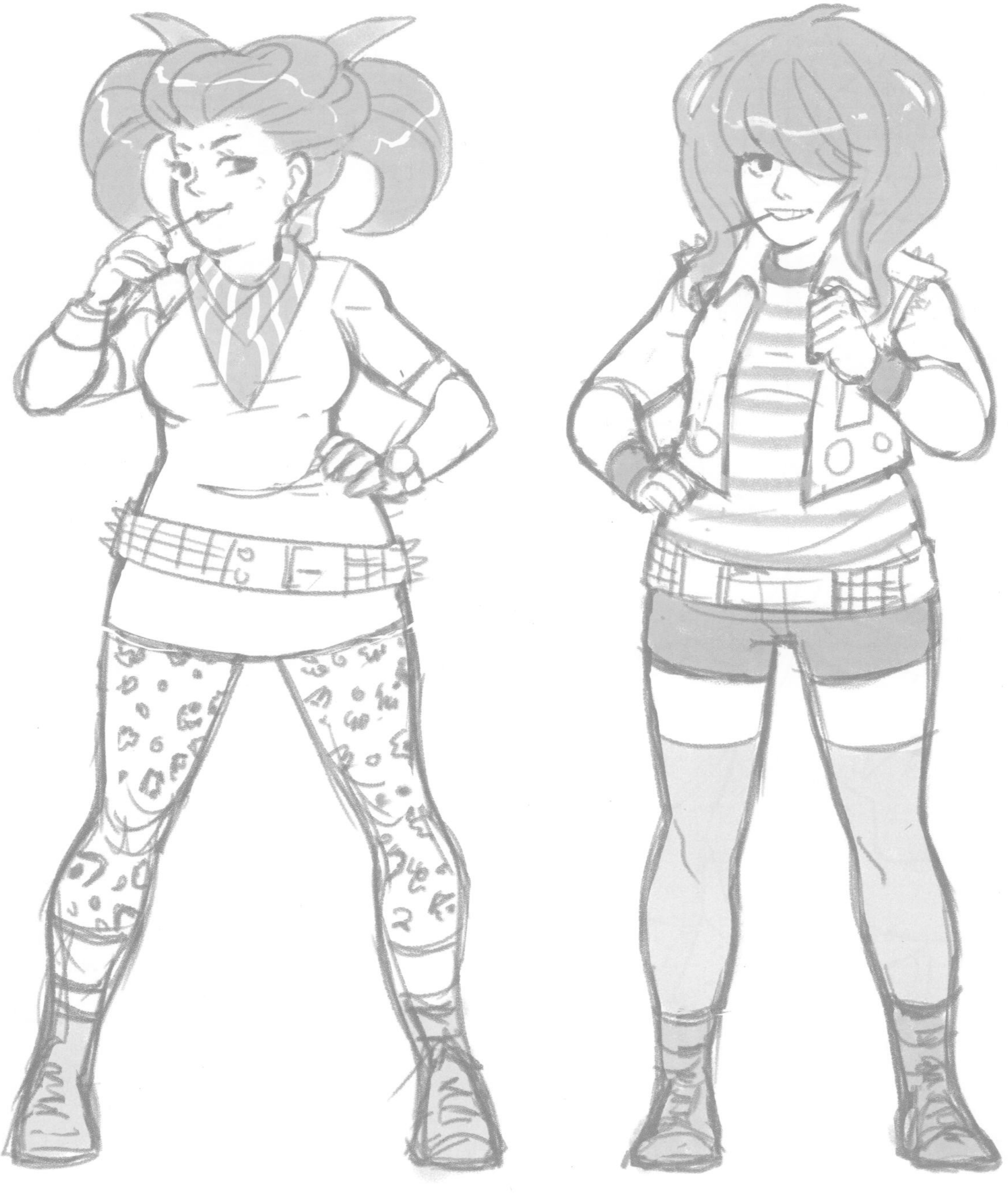

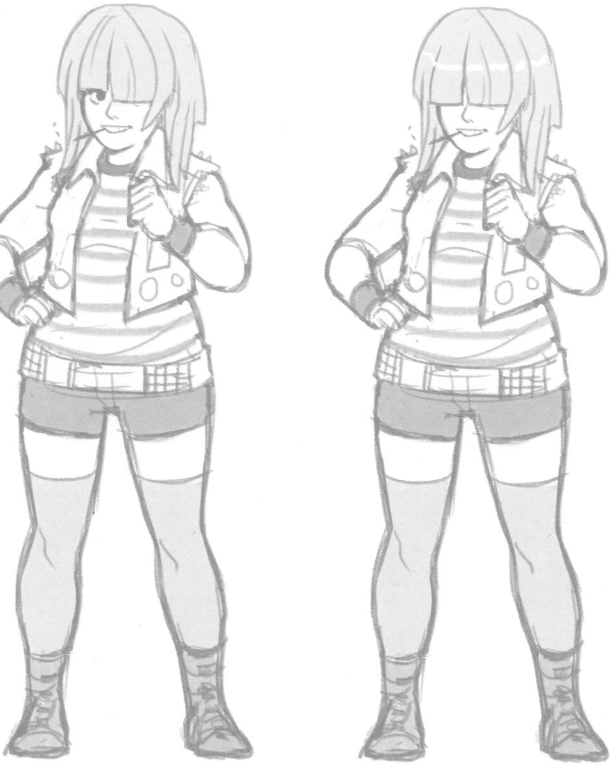

ALL THE KIMS

P: Out of all the characters, I think Kim evolved the most, designwise. Sometimes I can't believe there was ever a time where she actually had eyes! I do still kinda like that one eye peepin' out (*shhh*).

K: For the record, I am anti–Kim eye.

P: We know.

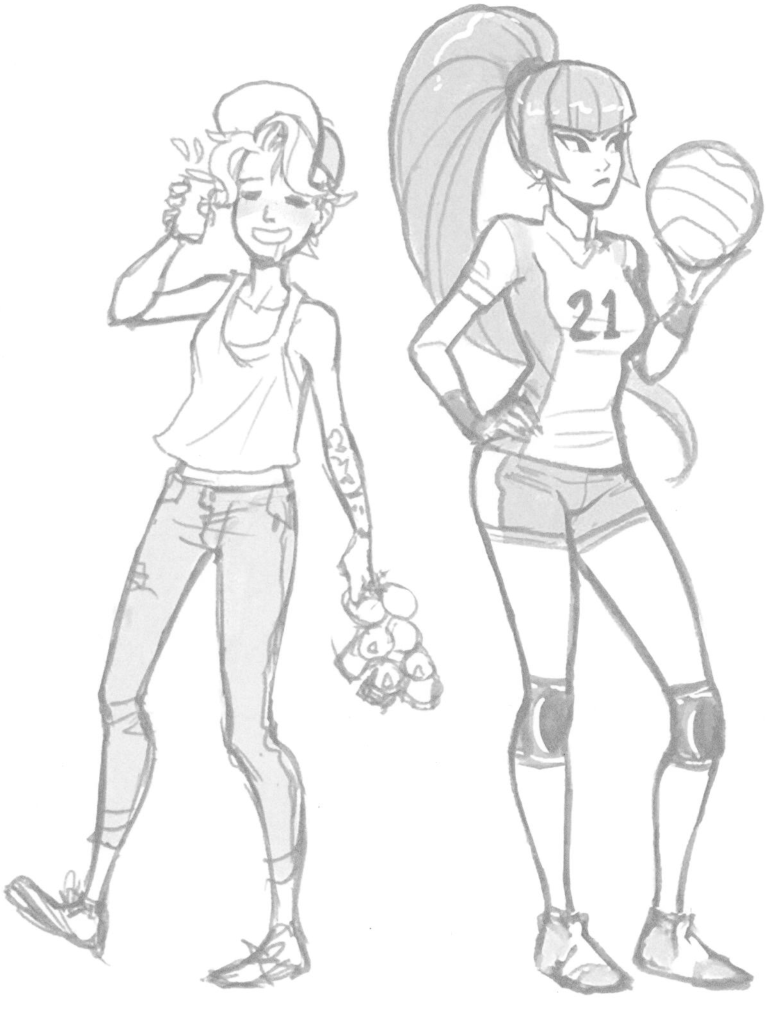
21

BEER AND VOLLEYBALL

P: Drunk Savi and Volley Molly.

K: I almost captioned this "Beer and Molly-ball," to be honest. But, yeah, Savi used to be a little bit of a drunk. That didn't make it into the final comic, haha.

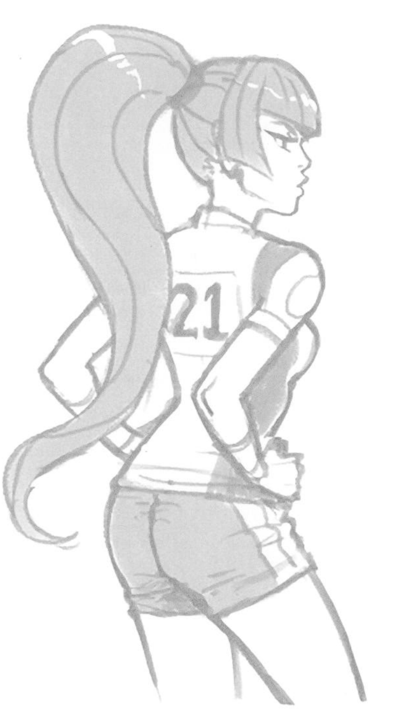
21

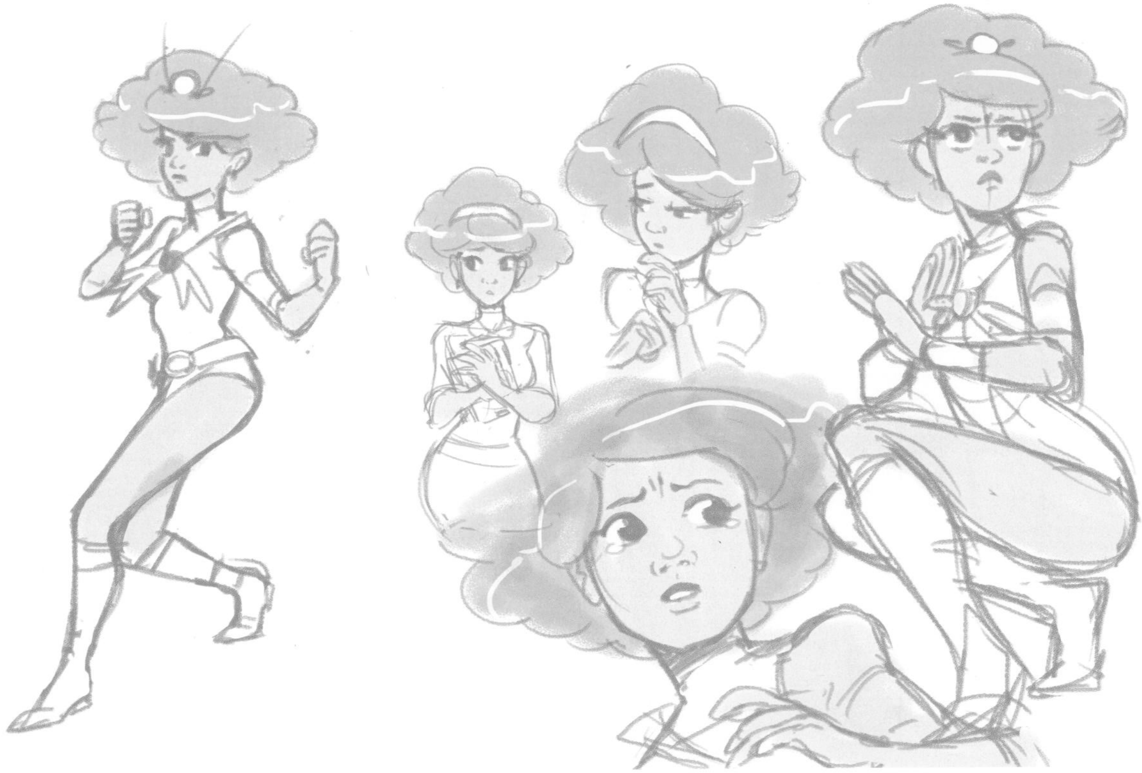

LILY

P: Oh, sweet Lily. Next to Emma she's definitely my favorite character. I drew this picture of Savi and Lily kissing years ago and haven't been able to share it until THIS MOMENT. Happy to be here.

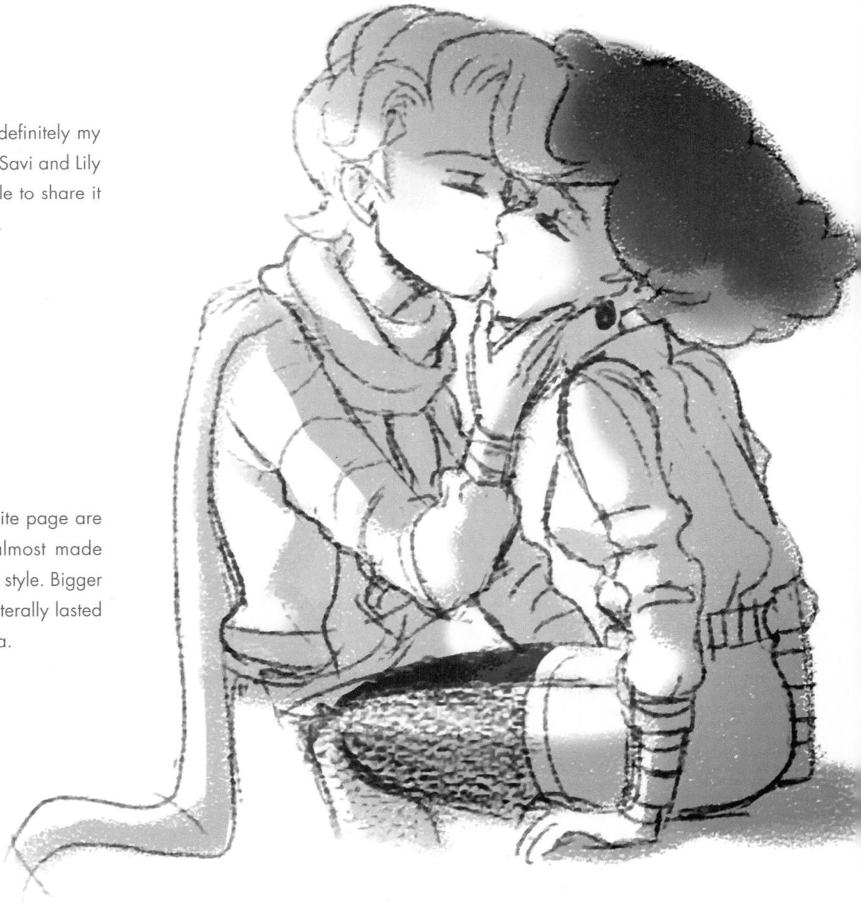

ARTISTIC EXPLORATION

P: The sketches at the top of the opposite page are from a very short moment where I almost made *Zodiac Starforce* much more cartoony in style. Bigger heads, hands, and eyes. That thought literally lasted five minutes because that's not me, haha.

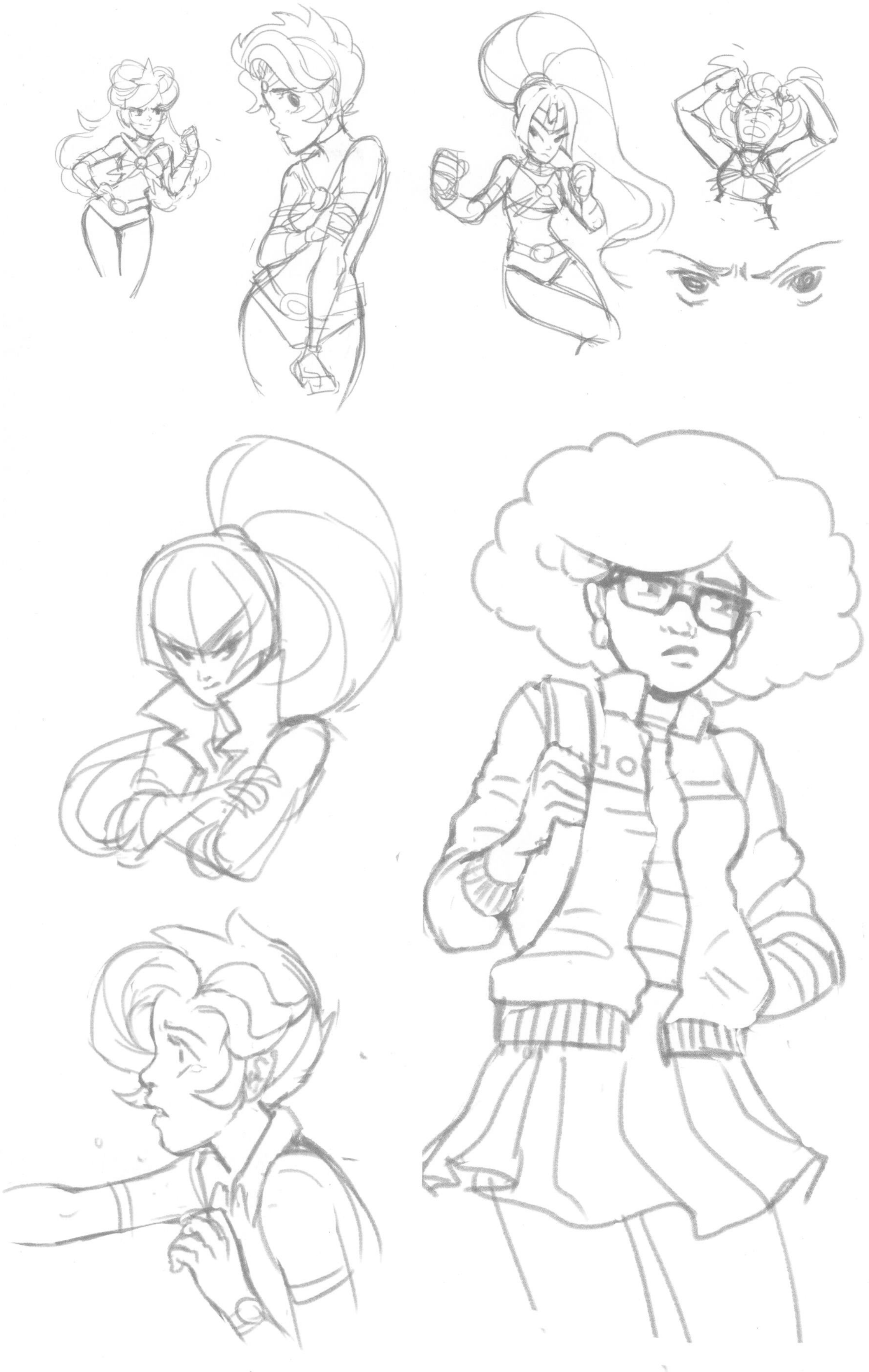

Hand-written labels on the character sketch:

visor

Peterpan collar

weapon: daggers

knee socks

Peridot

LIBRA RISING

K: It was so tough to not spill the beans about Lily becoming Libra. I wanted to put her on all the covers in costume, but we had to keep it under our hats! But now everybody knows, and I can shout it from the rooftops. **LILY IS LIBRA!!!** I HOPE YOU'RE NOT READING THIS COMIC BACKWARD, BECAUSE IF SO, YOU JUST GOT SPOILERED!

BIG HAIR DON'T CARE

P: I'm so glad people enjoy the big hair that I do because I'm never stopping! Emma's cloud hair is by far my favorite to draw. That and Molly's dinosaur-tail pony.

K: I can't wait to see all their new hairstyles in the next series. It's something we talk about a lot!

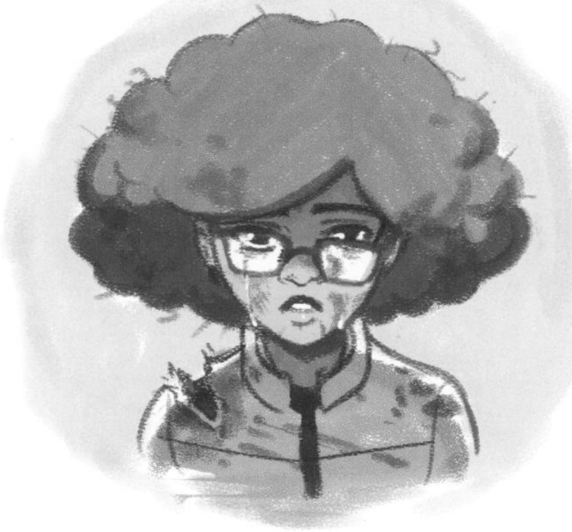

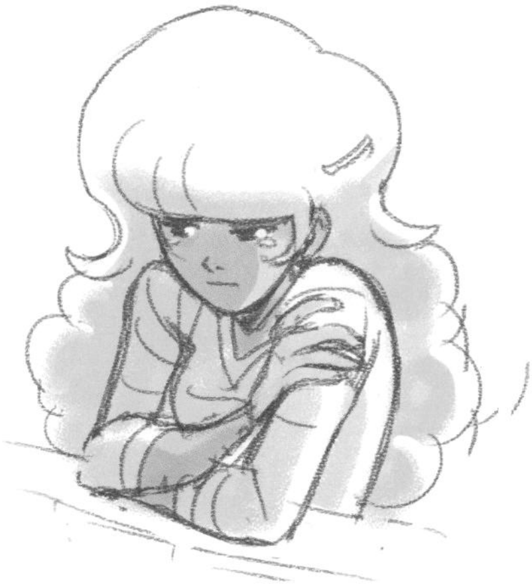

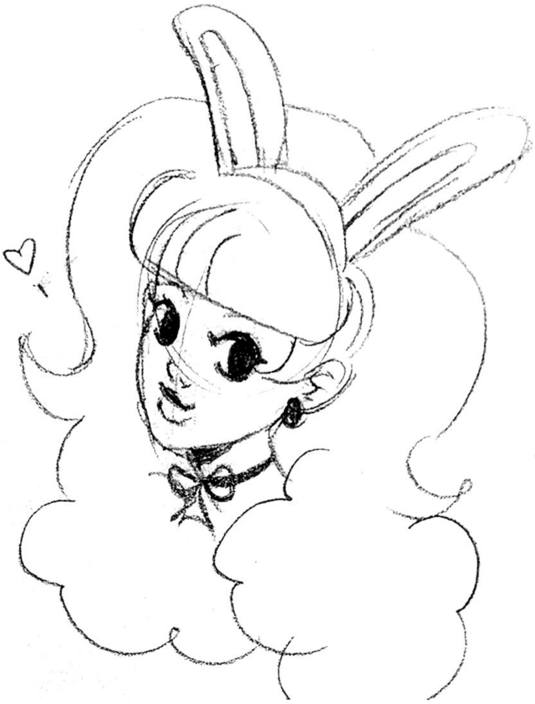

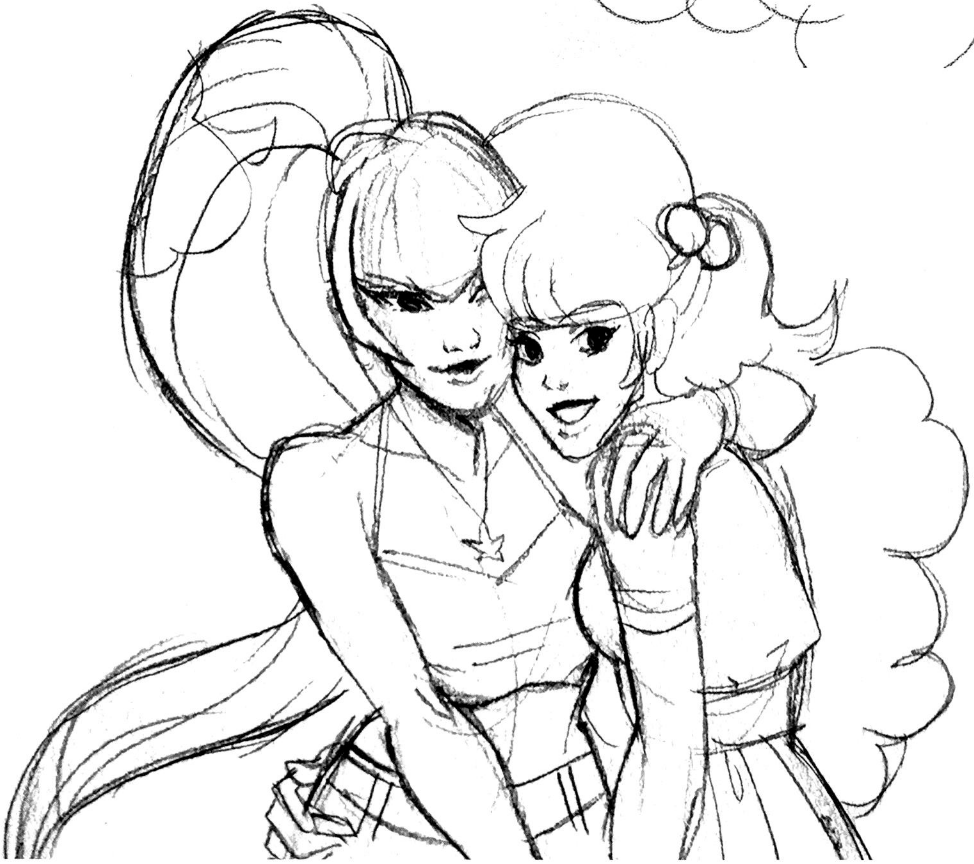

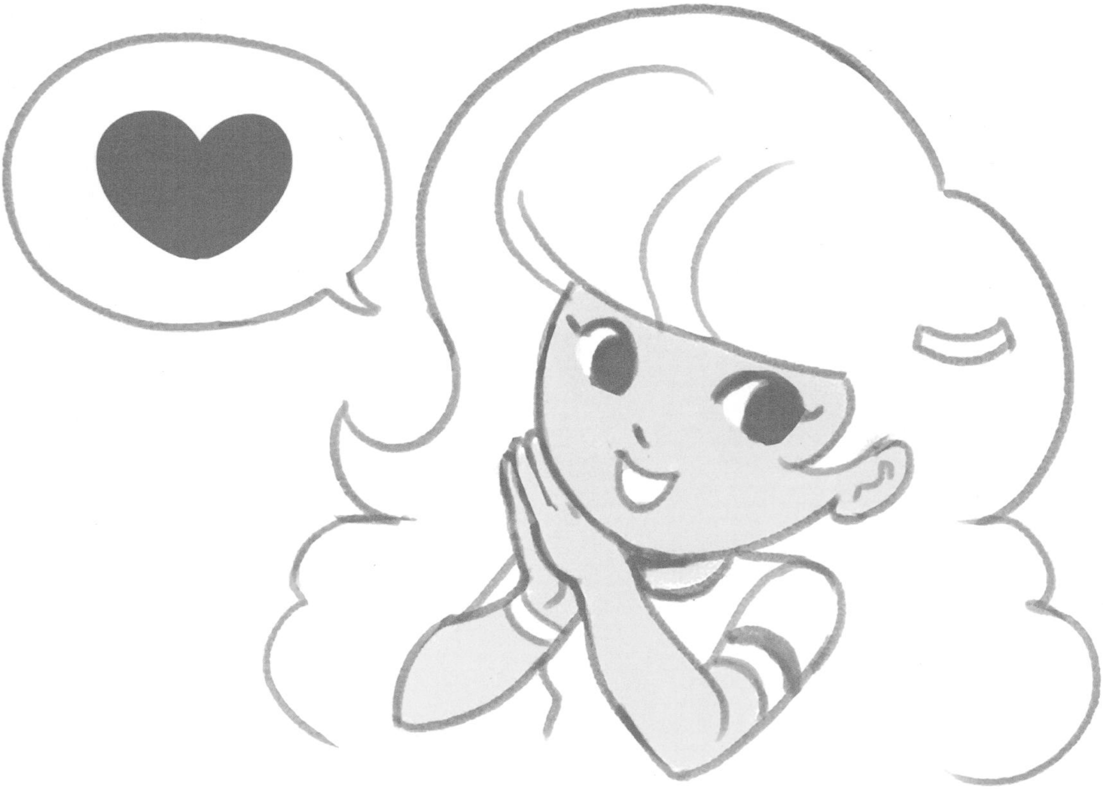

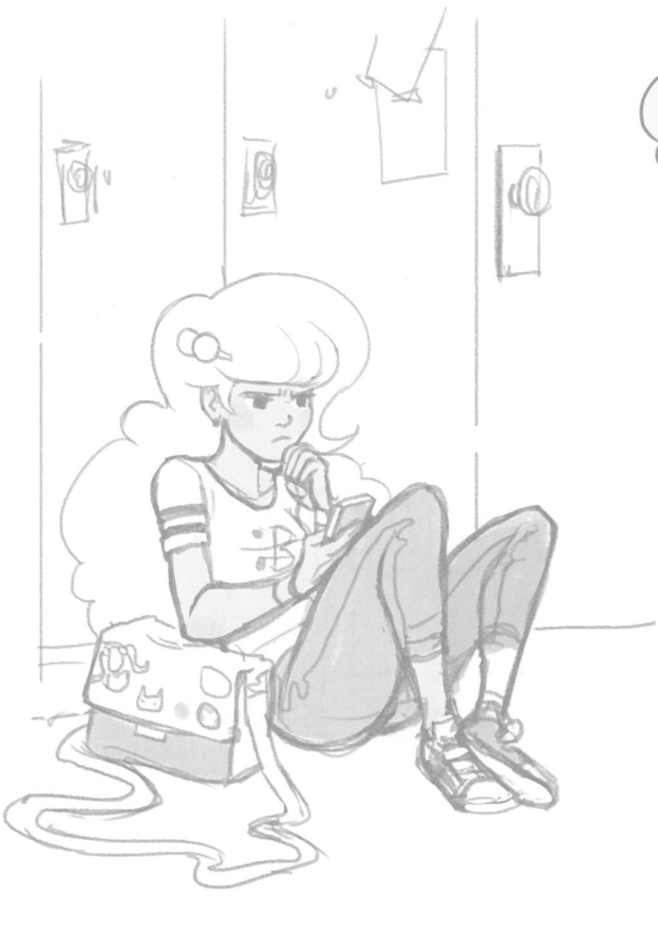

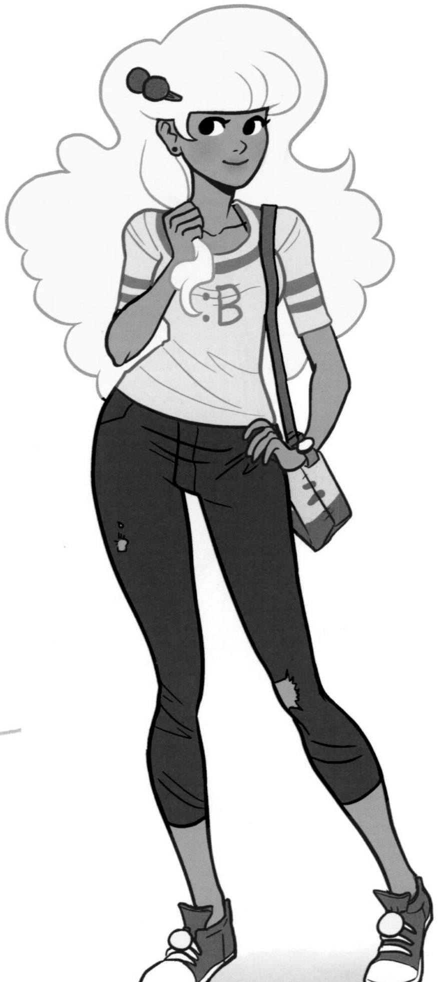

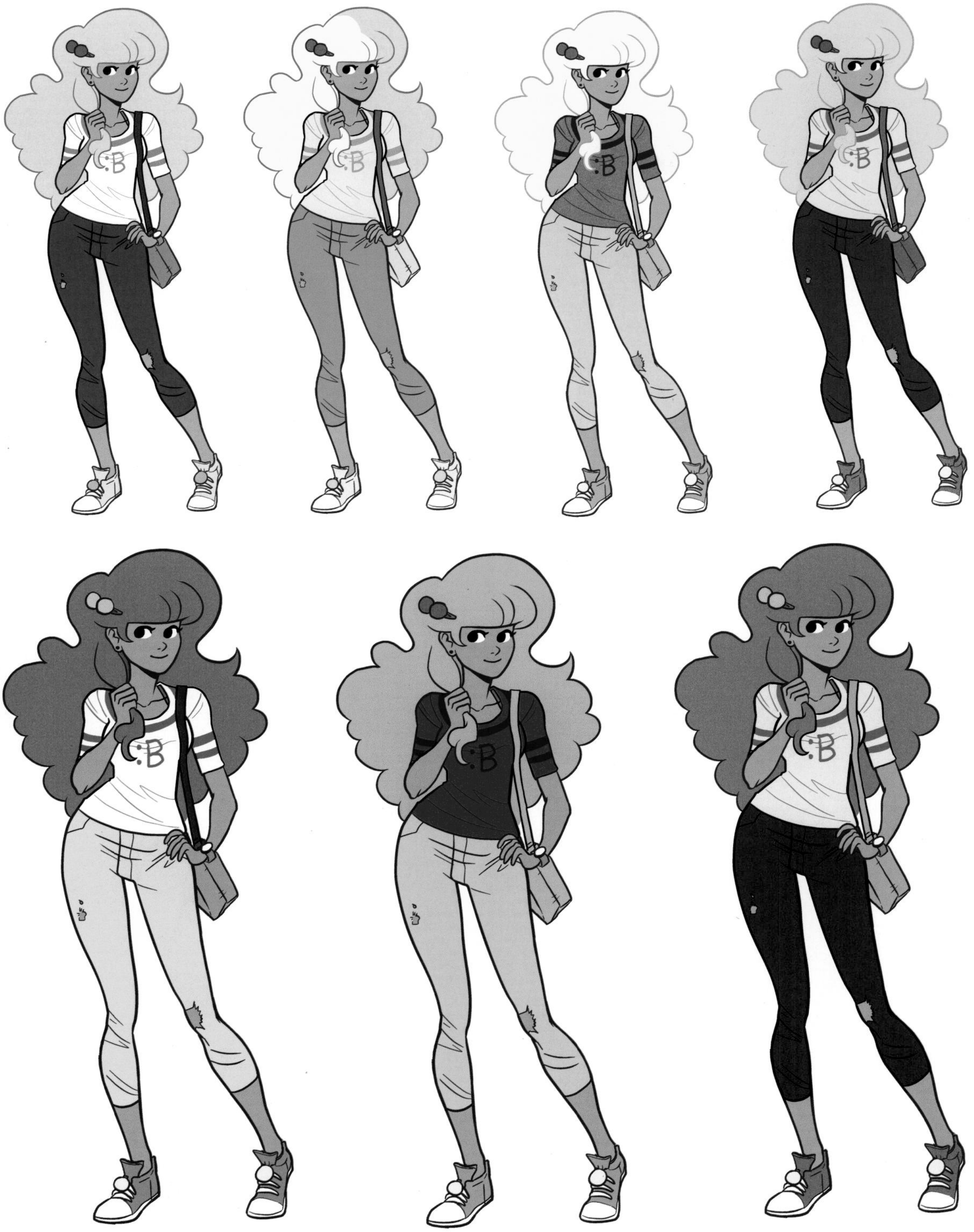

EIGHT SHADES OF EMMA

P: Emma and her many color variations. I remember we ended up liking both the pink and the blond choices. I'm happy we found a way to keep both! The "two-face" hairdo, I thought, would be awesome to show her Gemini duality a little more, but it didn't work with her hair type at all. *C'est la vie.*

K: One thing that never changed about Emma's hair were the hair-bauble-grenade-thingies. (Yes, that's the official name. Hair-Bauble-Grenade-Thingies™.)

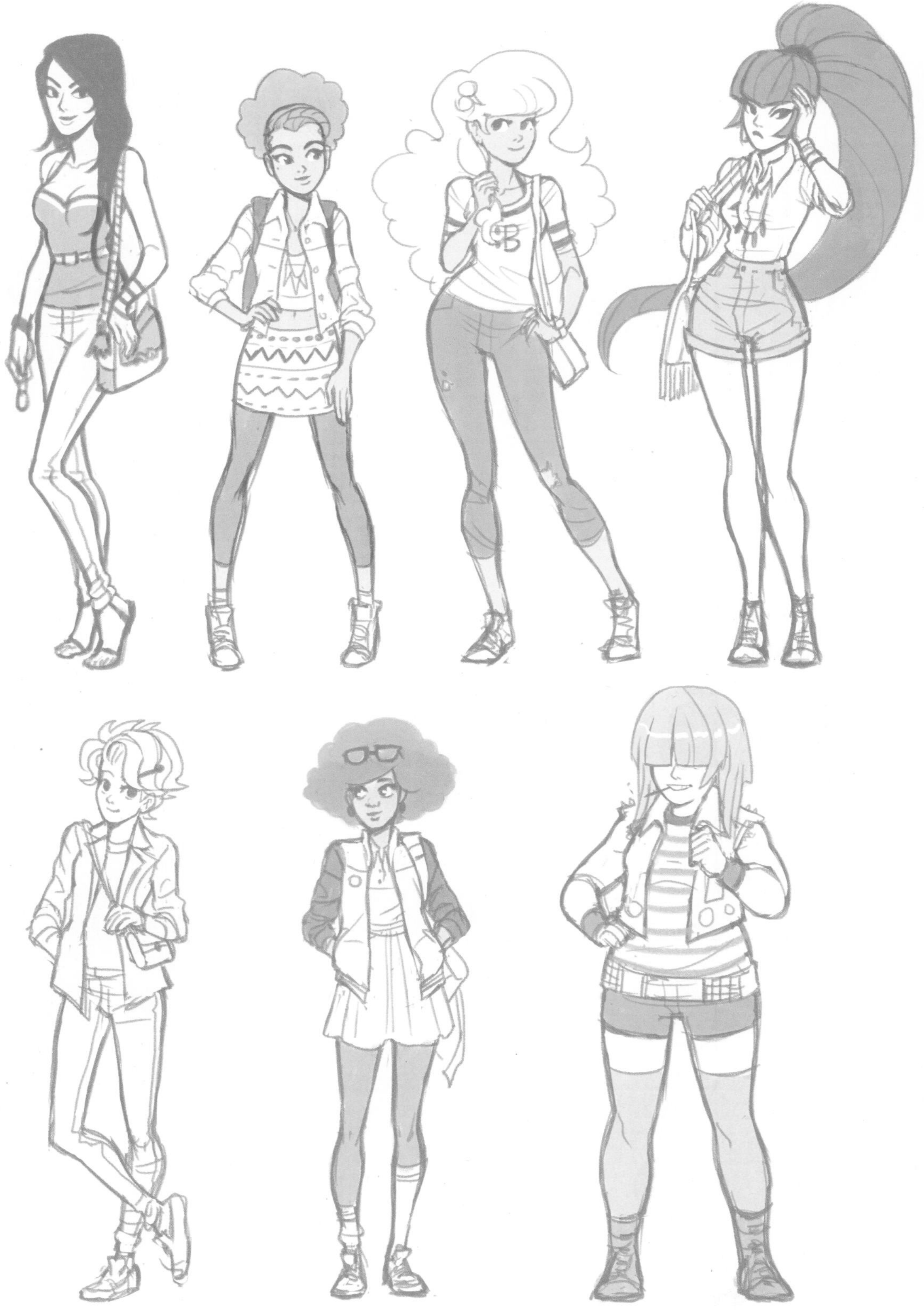

THE GIRLS

P: Old designs (*above*) vs. new designs (*facing*). I'm happy with where they all ended up.

K: I don't have anything to add here. Just . . . Paulina is good at art and clothes.

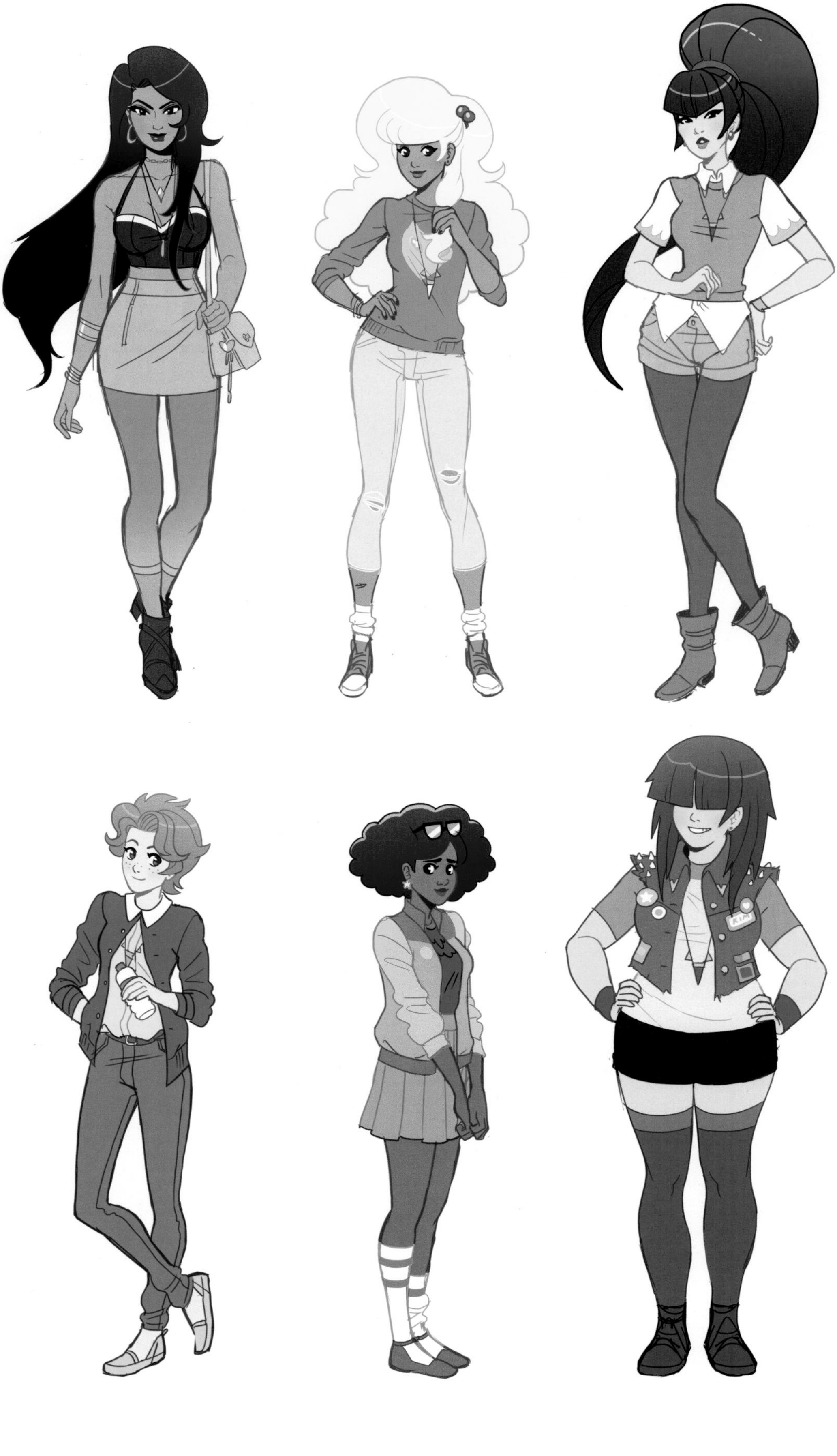

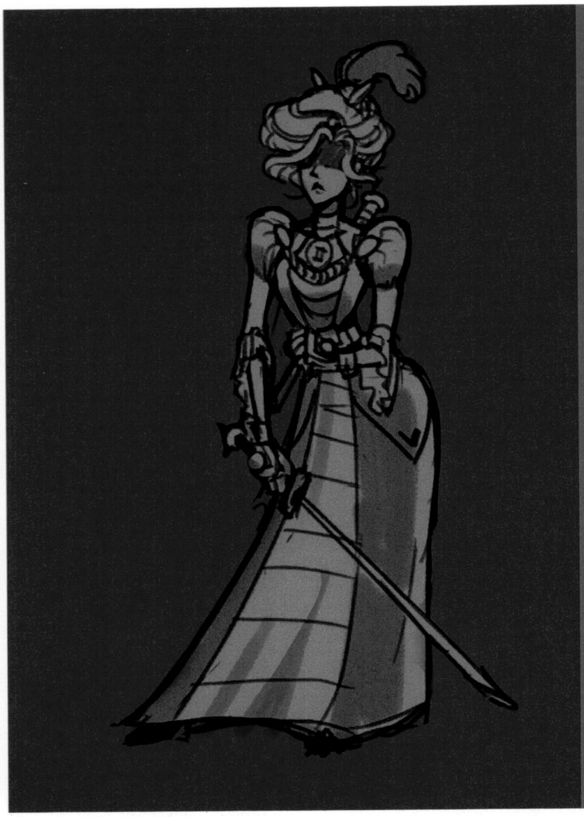

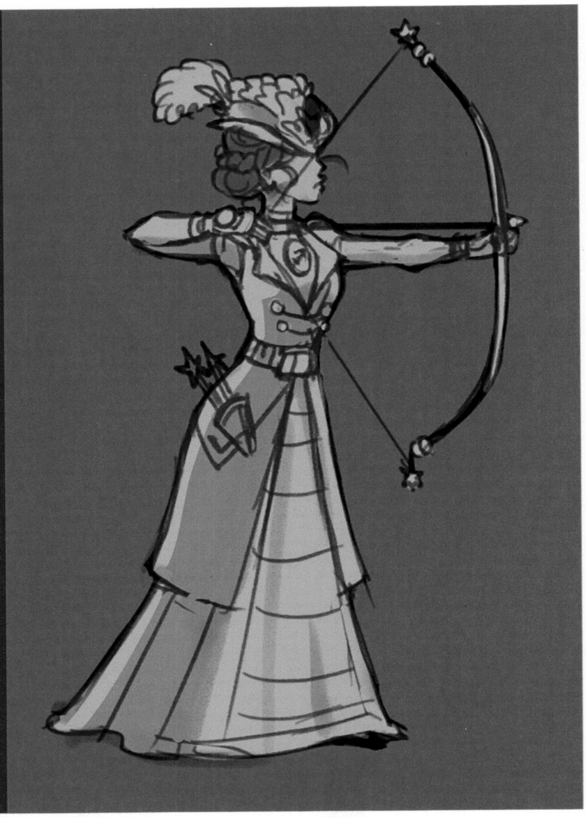

VICTORIAN STARFORCE

P: I. Love. These. I want me or someone else to do a Victorian Starforce one-shot more than anything. It was really awesome collecting reference from historical fashion plates for these. Remember, kids, reference is your friend!

ASTRA

P: Fun fact: I redesigned Astra slightly on the page 'cause I didn't think this design had enough luscious hair. The prompt for her was basically "Disney Princess Goddess." I think she's much more that here than what she ended up being, but I still really like both!

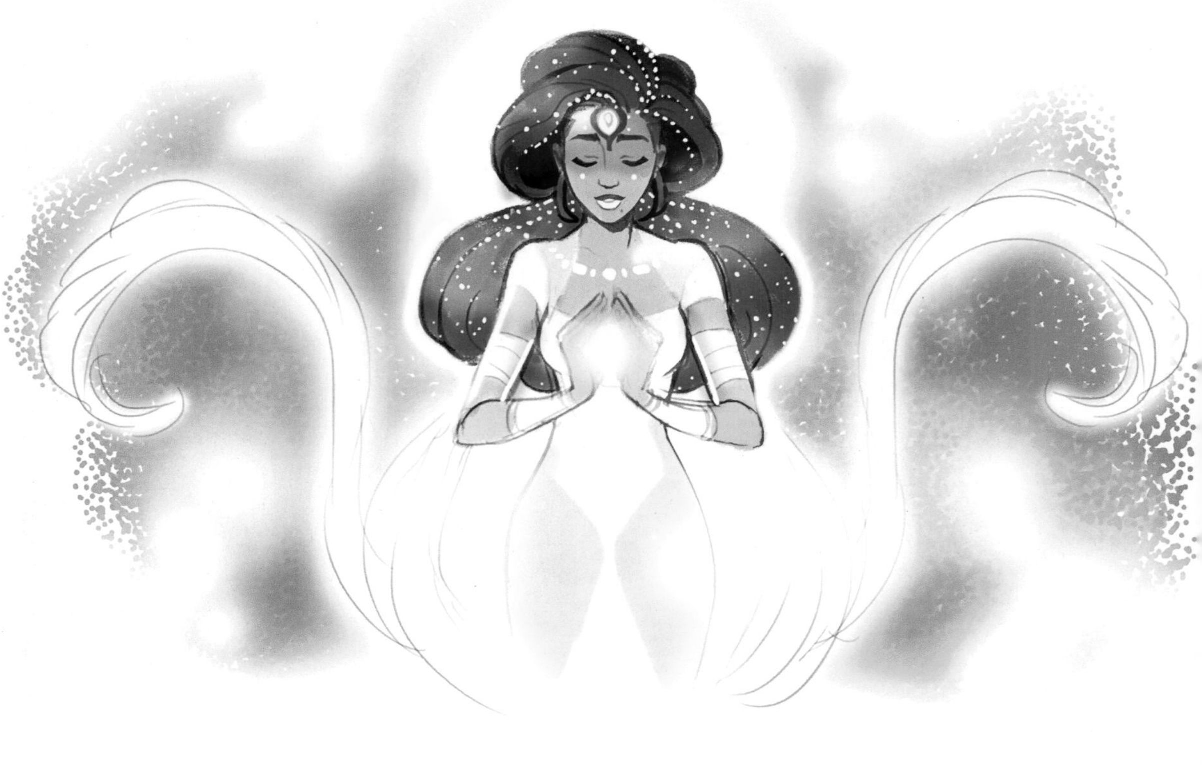

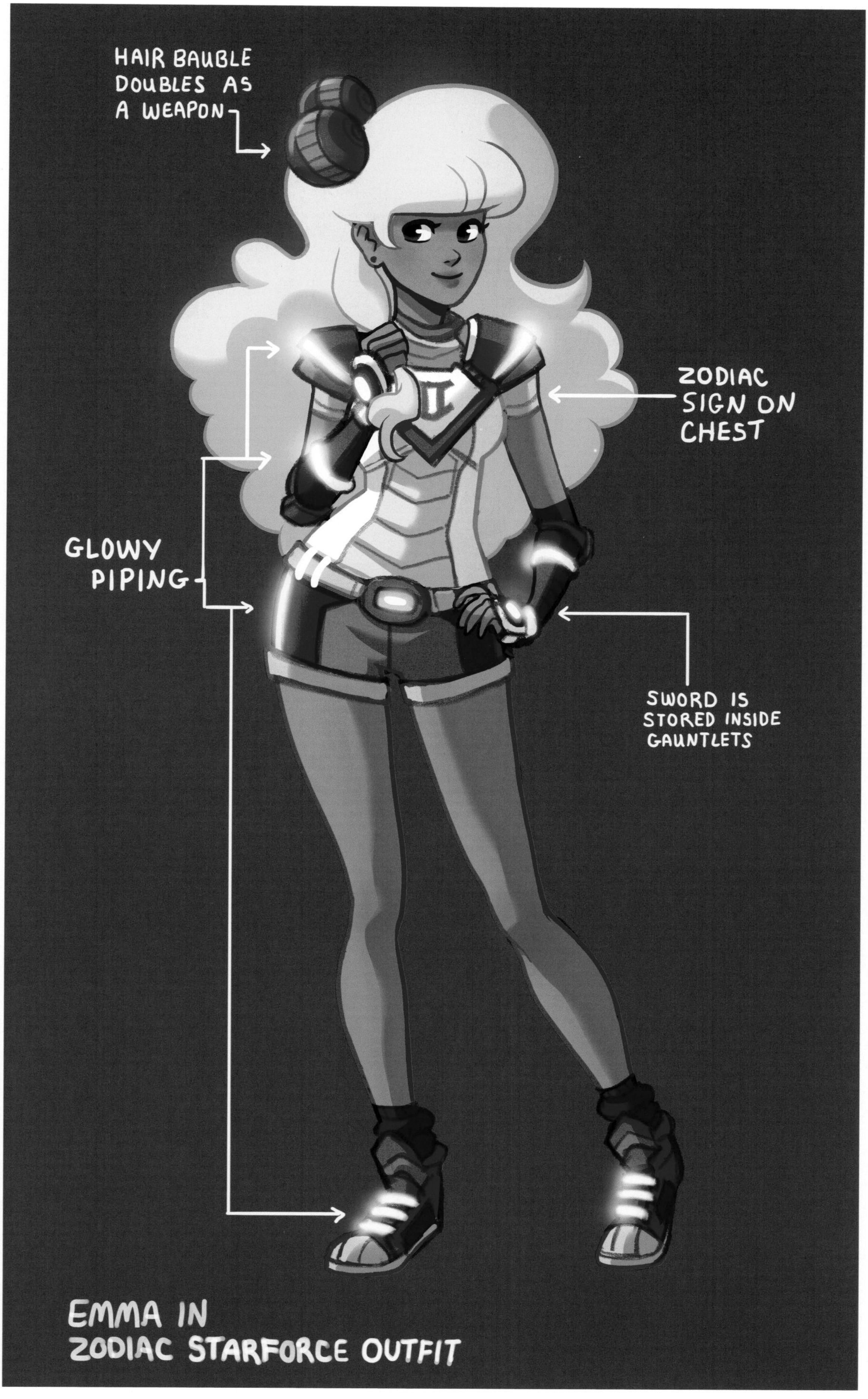
HAIR BAUBLE DOUBLES AS A WEAPON
ZODIAC SIGN ON CHEST
GLOWY PIPING
SWORD IS STORED INSIDE GAUNTLETS
EMMA IN ZODIAC STARFORCE OUTFIT

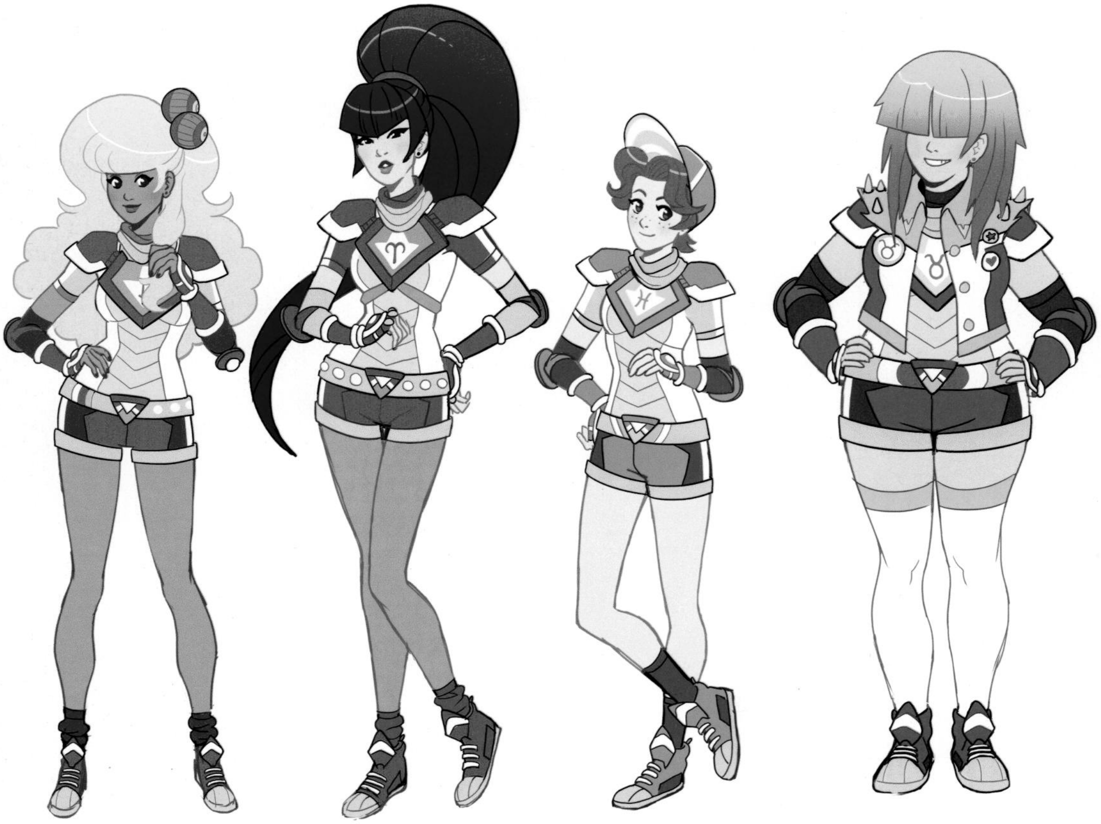

SHORTS AND SNEAKERS

K: We went through a lot of different options for their magical-girl outfits but always kept coming back to shorts and sneakers. It's a cute look that's really practical at the same time!

P: It's my fav-y.

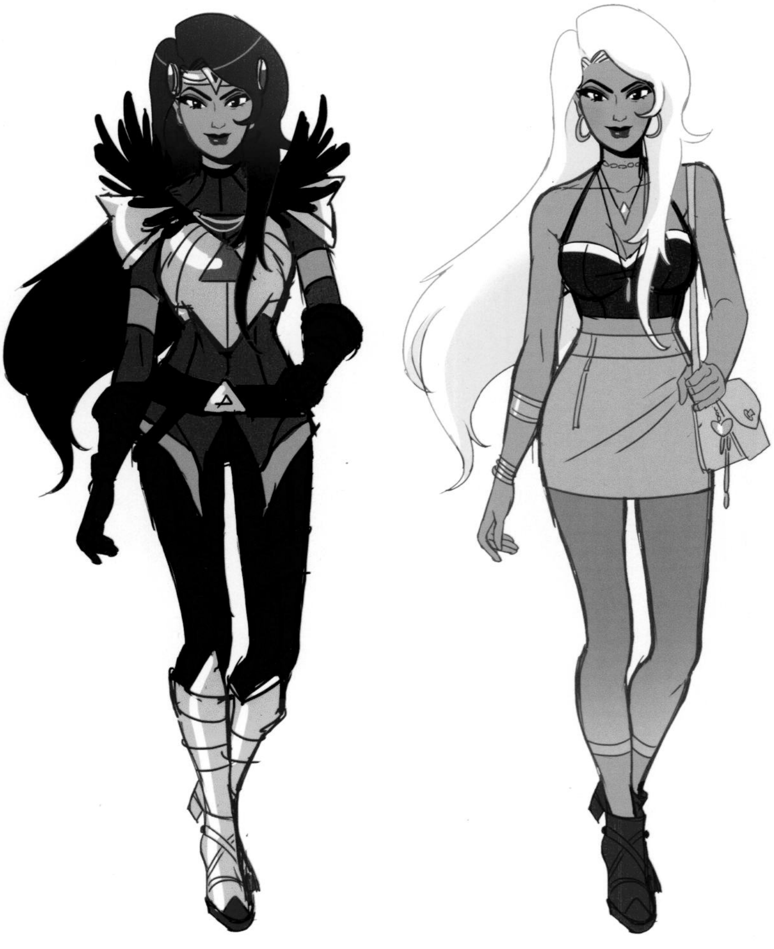

DIANA

P: Diana is that villain you just end up loving even though she's evil. She's conflicted. She's flawed. She's sad. She's human. BTW, I love her with white hair.

K: Diana's "bad-guy speech" in issue three was my favorite thing to write in this whole series.

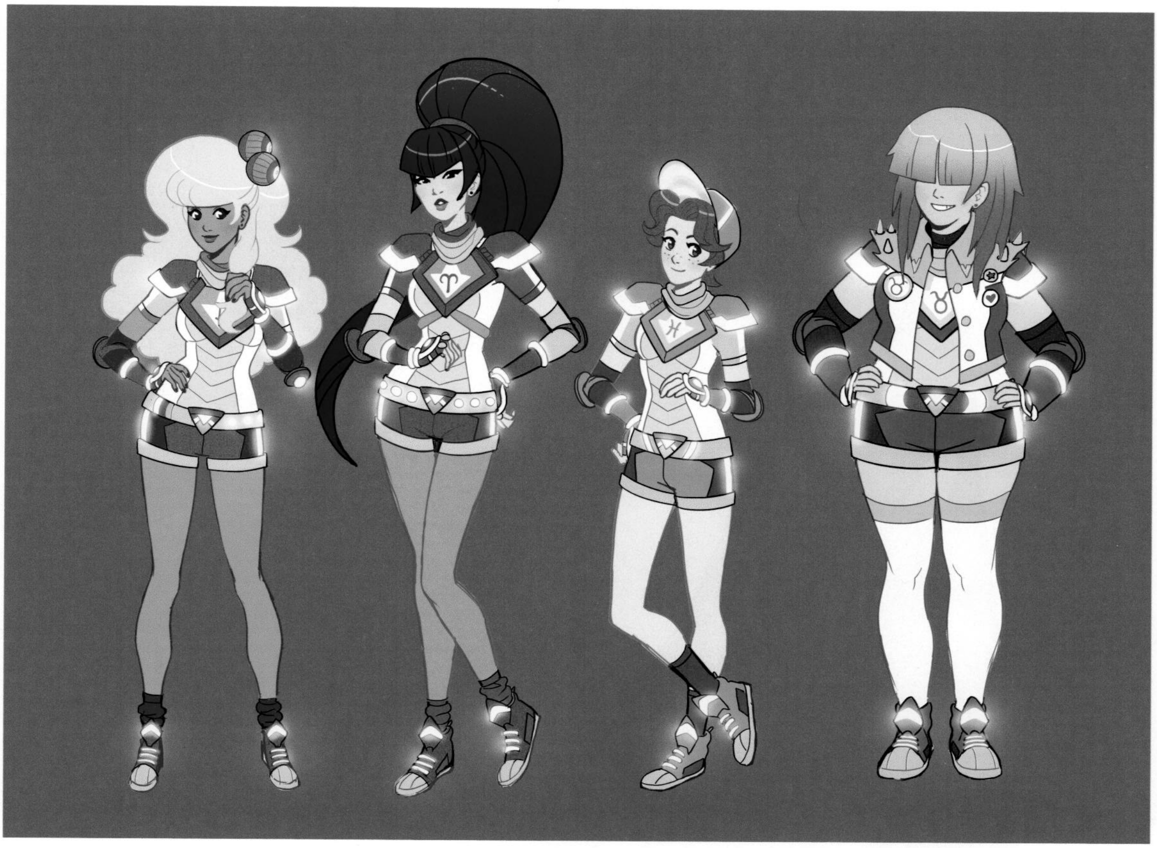

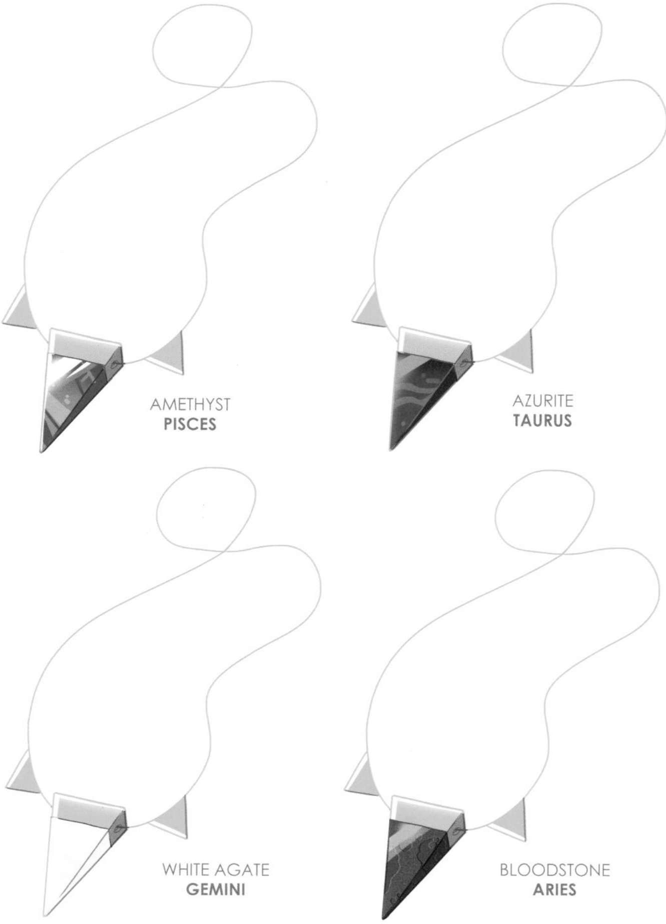
AMETHYST
PISCES
AZURITE
TAURUS
WHITE AGATE
GEMINI
BLOODSTONE
ARIES

THE ASTRAL STONES

P: I was researching stones and crystals when I came across astral stones and I FREAKED out. The lore fit so perfectly with *ZS*, and it opened up options beyond just birthstones for the girls.

K: Astral stone necklaces are the most requested *Zodiac Starforce* merchandise. We should probably make those at some point.

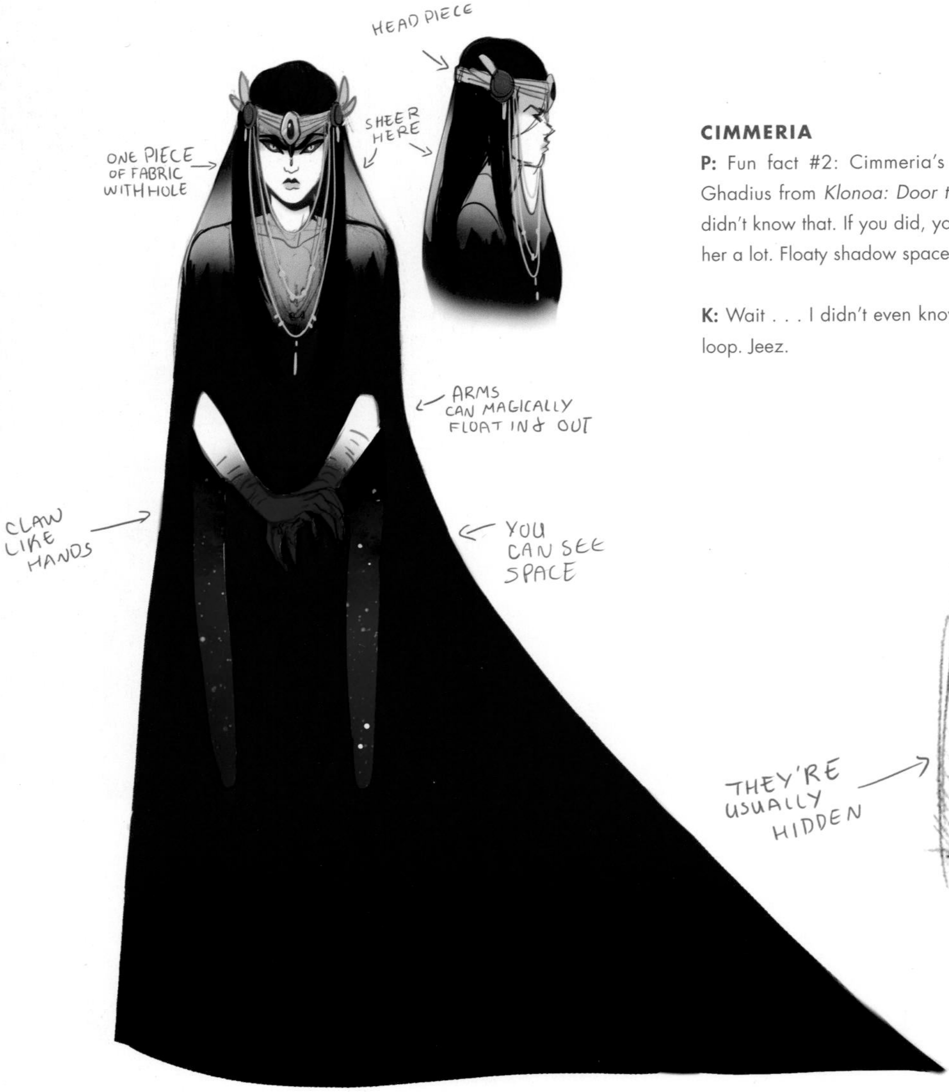
HEAD PIECE
SHEER HERE
ONE PIECE OF FABRIC WITH HOLE
ARMS CAN MAGICALLY FLOAT IN & OUT
CLAW LIKE HANDS
YOU CAN SEE SPACE

CIMMERIA

P: Fun fact #2: Cimmeria's design is inspired by Ghadius from *Klonoa: Door to Phantomile*. I bet you didn't know that. If you did, you're cool. I like drawing her a lot. Floaty shadow space witch.

K: Wait . . . I didn't even know that! I'm so out of the loop. Jeez.

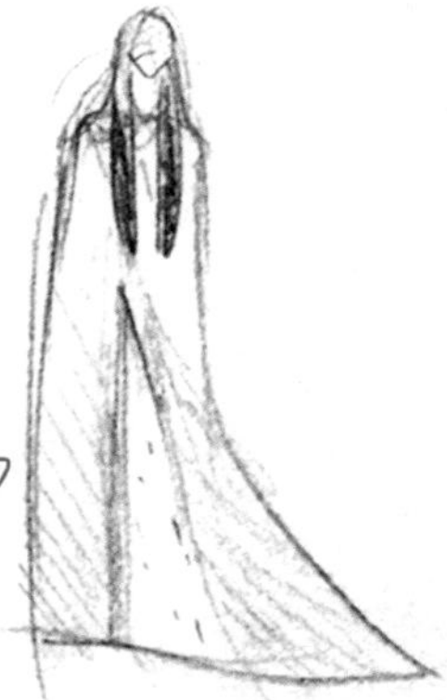
THEY'RE USUALLY HIDDEN

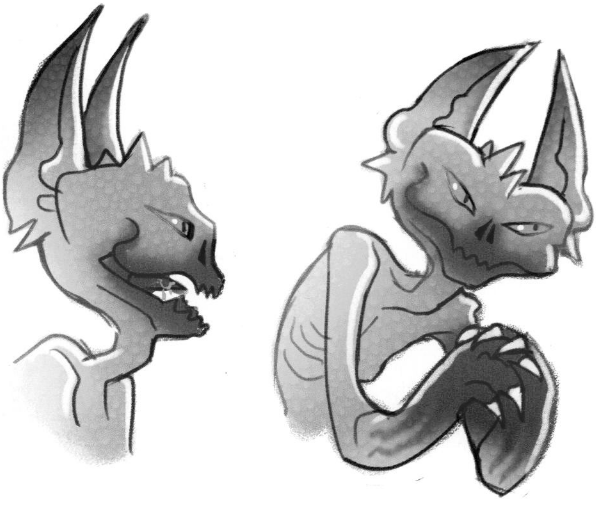

IMP CONCEPT ART

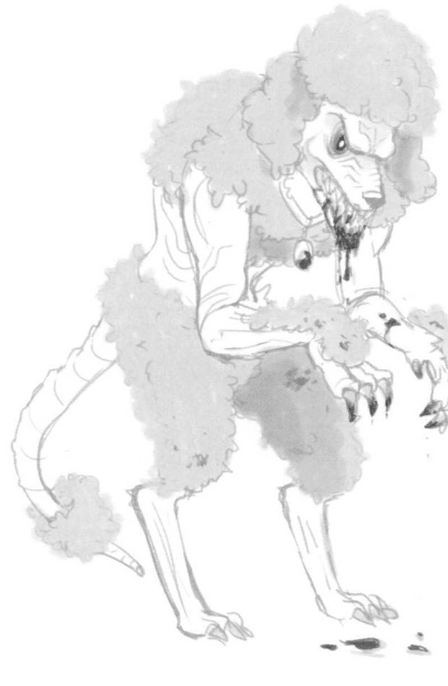

MUTATED POODLE CONCEPT ART

BOOKS-A-MILLION VARIANT COVER BY NOELLE STEVENSON

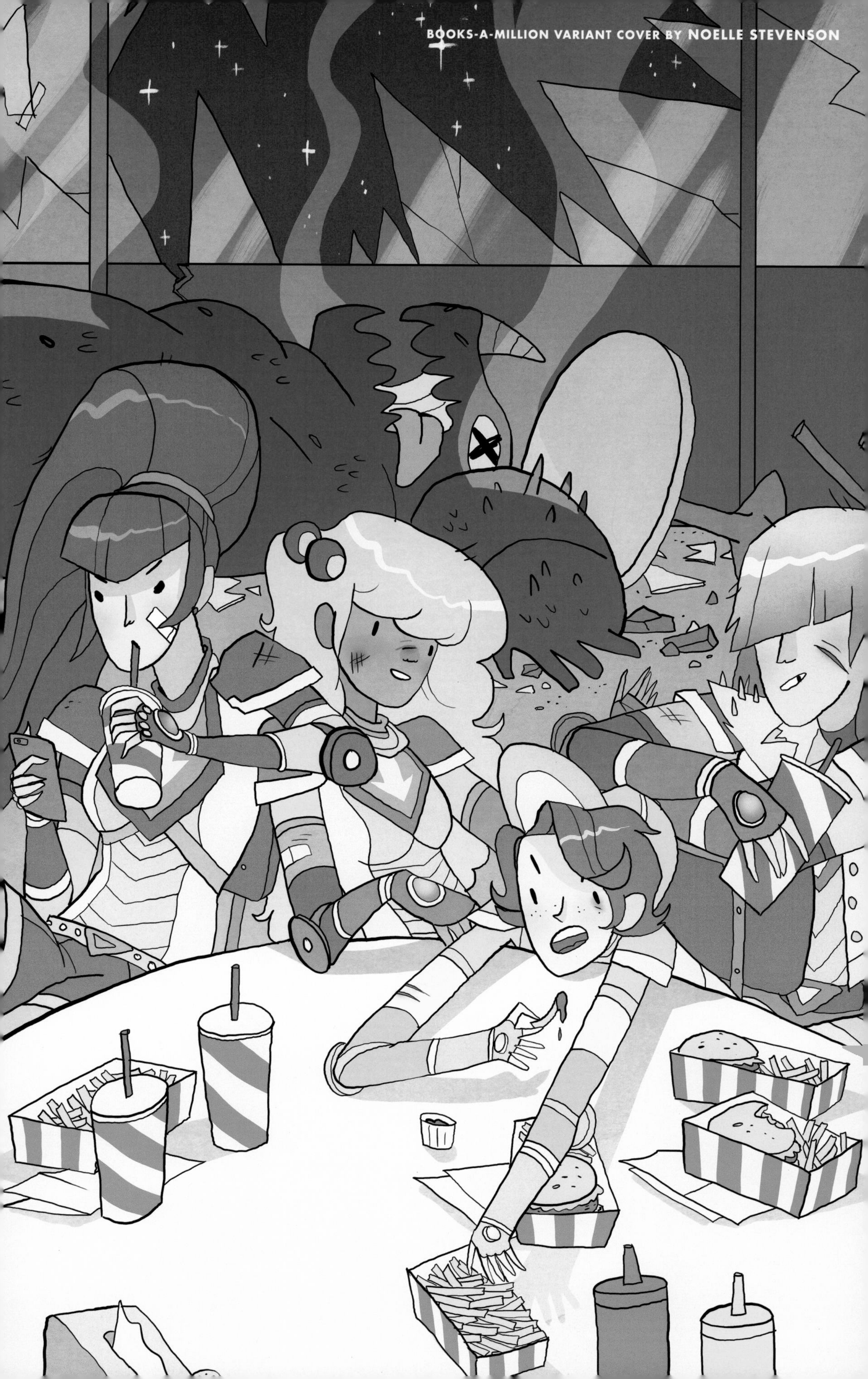

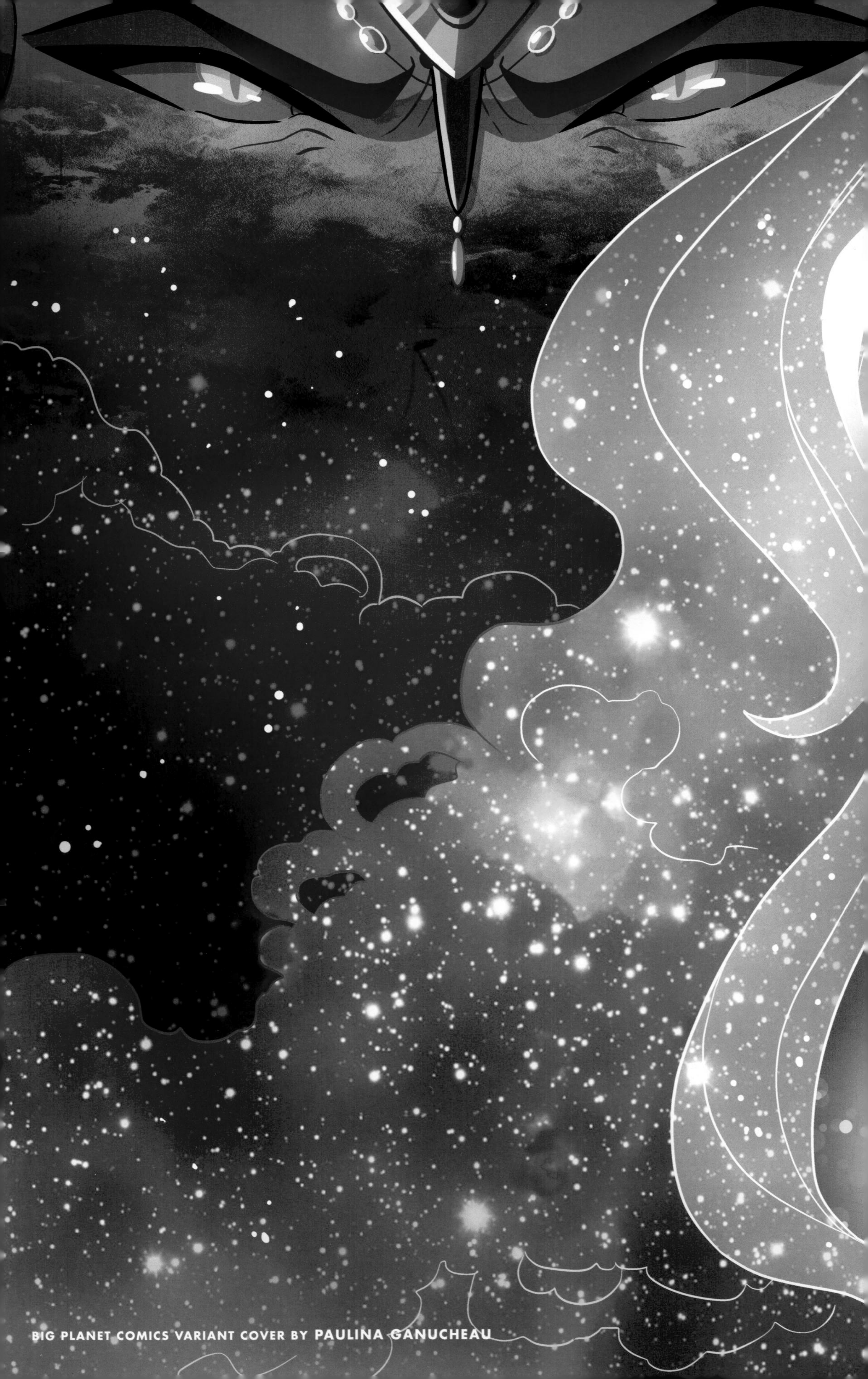

BIG PLANET COMICS VARIANT COVER BY PAULINA GANUCHEAU

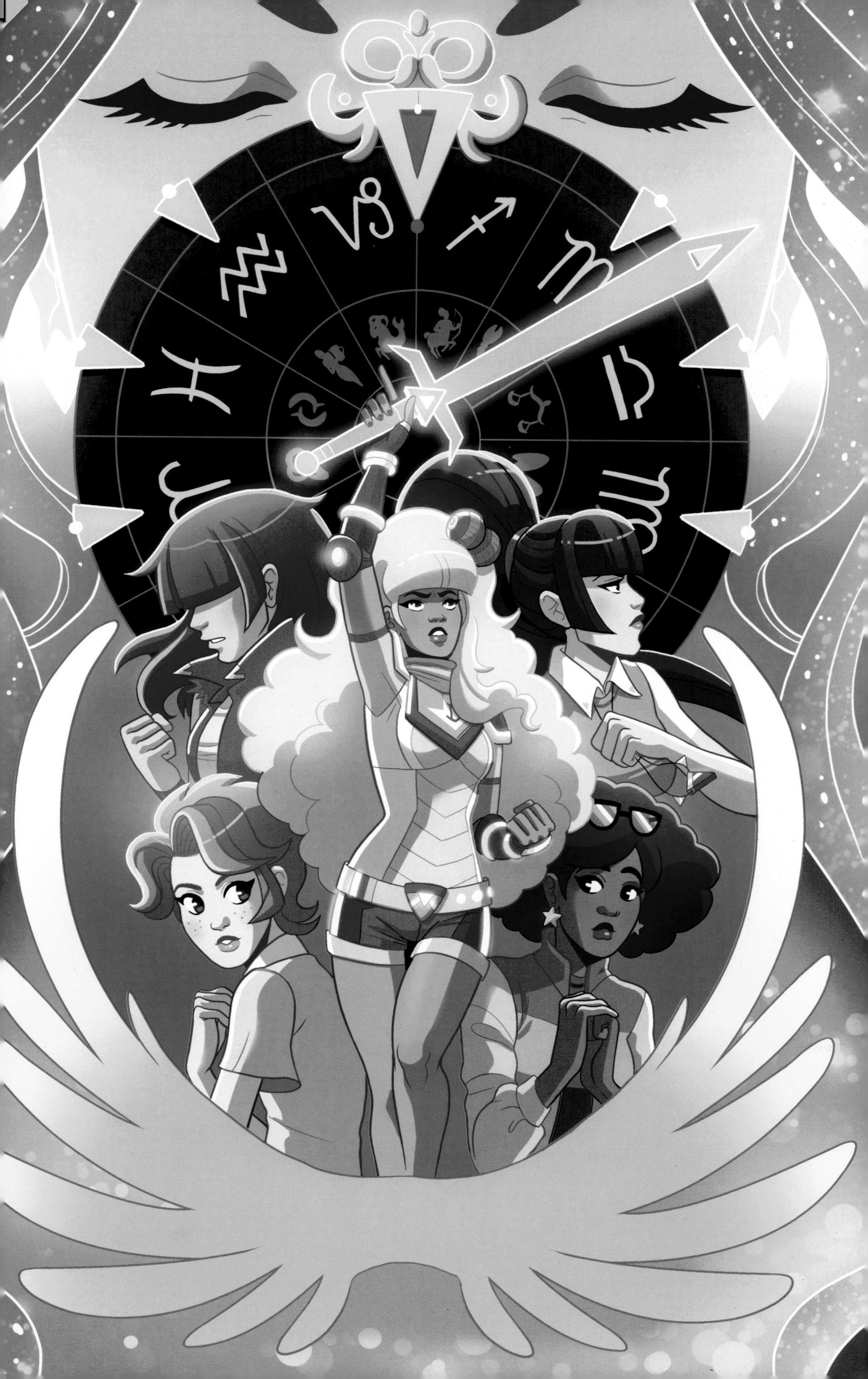

Surviving high school just got a lot tougher.

ZODIAC™
STARFORCE

INDEPENDENT SPIRIT

Original stories that YA readers will love!

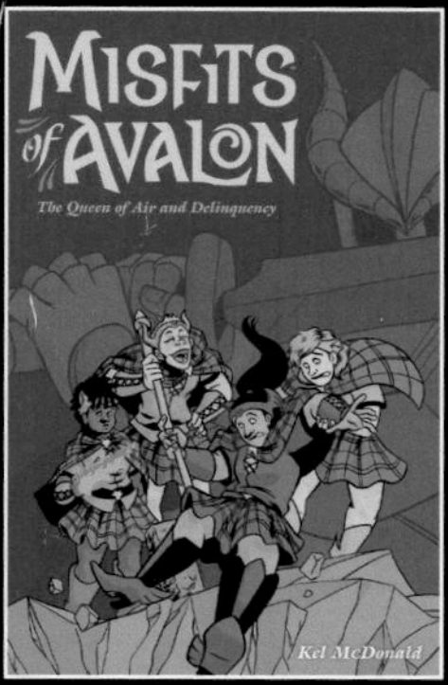
MISFITS of AVALON
The Queen of Air and Delinquency
Kel McDonald

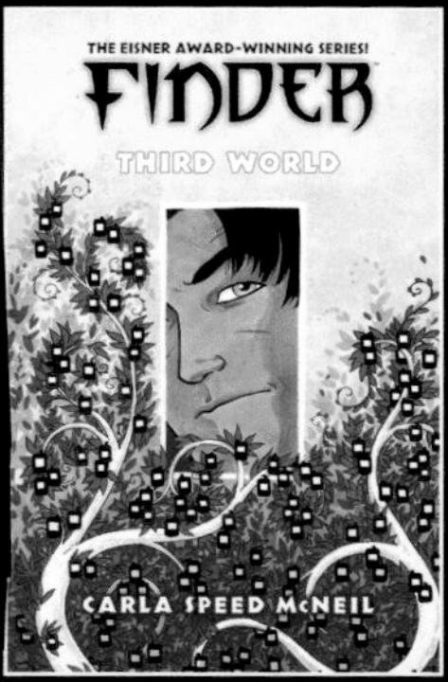
THE EISNER AWARD-WINNING SERIES!
FINDER
THIRD WORLD
CARLA SPEED McNEIL

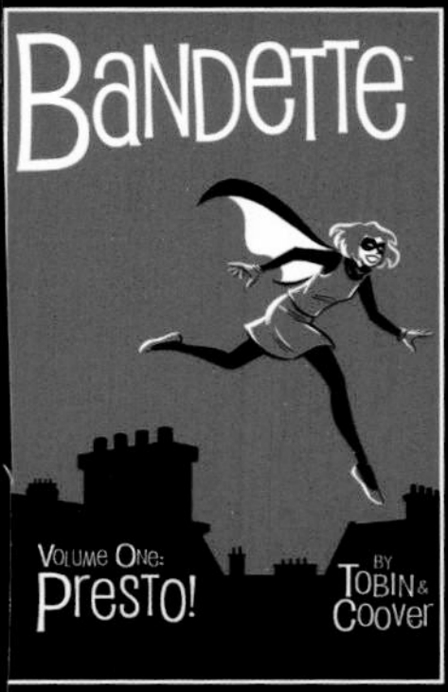
BANDETTE
VOLUME ONE:
PRESTO!
BY
TOBIN &
COOVER

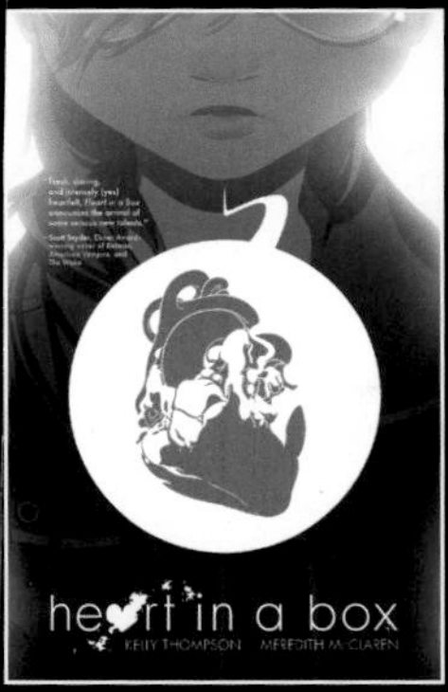
heart in a box

MISFITS OF AVALON

Kel McDonald

Four misfit teens are reluctant recruits to save the mystical isle of Avalon. Magically empowered and directed by a talking dog, they must stop the rise of King Arthur. As they struggle to become a team, they're faced with the discovery that they may not be the good guys . . .

Volume 1: The Queen of Air and Delinquency
ISBN 978-1-61655-538-2 | $14.99

Volume 2: The Ill-Made Guardian
ISBN 978-1-61655-748-5 | $14.99

FINDER: THIRD WORLD

Carla Speed McNeil

Follow enigmatic hero Jaeger through a "glorious, catholic pileup of high-tech SF, fannish fantasy, and street-level culture clash" (*Village Voice*), and discover the lush world and compelling characters that have carved *Finder* a permanent place in the pantheon of independent comics.

ISBN 978-1-61655-467-5 | $19.99

APOCALYPTIGIRL: AN ARIA FOR THE END TIMES

Andrew MacLean

The premiere graphic novel from underground sensation Andrew MacLean! Alone at the end of the world, Aria is a woman with a mission! As she traipses through an overgrown city with a cat named Jelly Beans, Aria seeks an ancient relic with immeasurable power. But when a creepy savage sets her on a path to complete her quest, she'll face death in the hopes of claiming her prize.

ISBN 978-1-61655-566-5 | $9.99

HEART IN A BOX

Kelly Thompson and Meredith McClaren

In a moment of post-heartbreak weakness, Emma wishes her heart away and a mysterious stranger obliges. But emptiness is even worse than grief, and Emma sets out to collect the seven pieces of her heart, in a journey that forces her to face her own history and the cost of recapturing it!

ISBN 978-1-61655-694-5 | $14.99

BANDETTE

Paul Tobin, Colleen Coover, and others

A costumed teen burglar by the *nome d'arte* of Bandette and her group of street urchins find equal fun in both skirting and aiding the law, in Paul Tobin and Colleen Coover's enchanting, Eisner-nominated series!

Volume 1: Presto!
ISBN 978-1-61655-279-4 | $14.99

Volume 2: Stealers, Keepers!
ISBN 978-1-61655-668-6 | $14.99

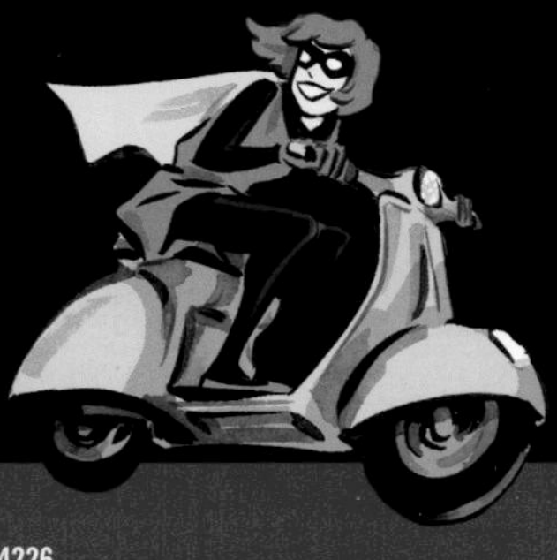

AVAILABLE AT YOUR LOCAL COMICS SHOP OR BOOKSTORE! • To find a comics shop in your area, call 1-888-266-4226.
For more information or to order direct visit DarkHorse.com or call 1-800-862-0052 Mon.–Fri. 9 AM to 5 PM Pacific Time. Prices and availability subject to change without notice.

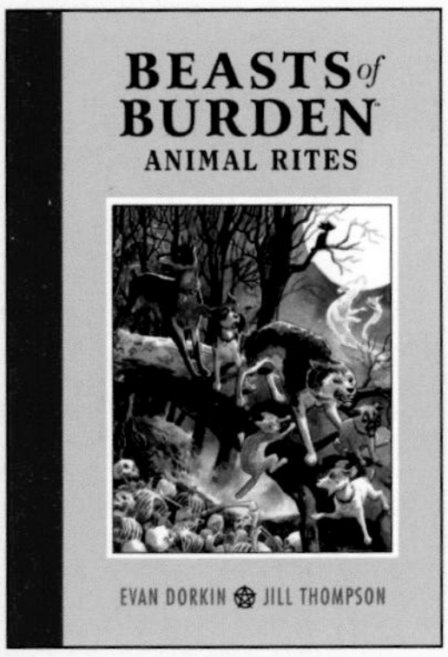
BEASTS of BURDEN
ANIMAL RITES
EVAN DORKIN
JILL THOMPSON

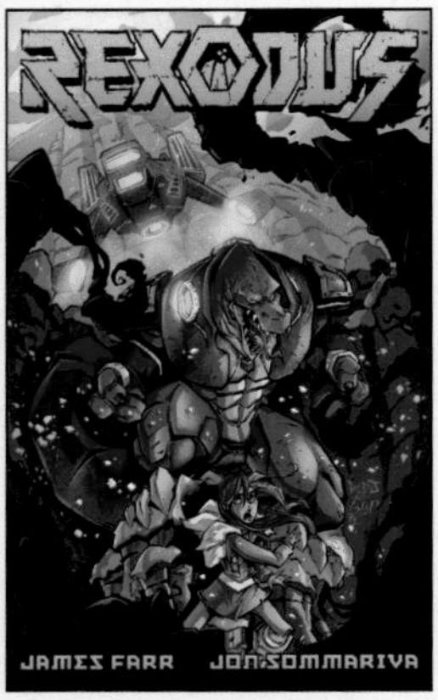
REXODUS
JAMES FARR
JON SOMMARIVA

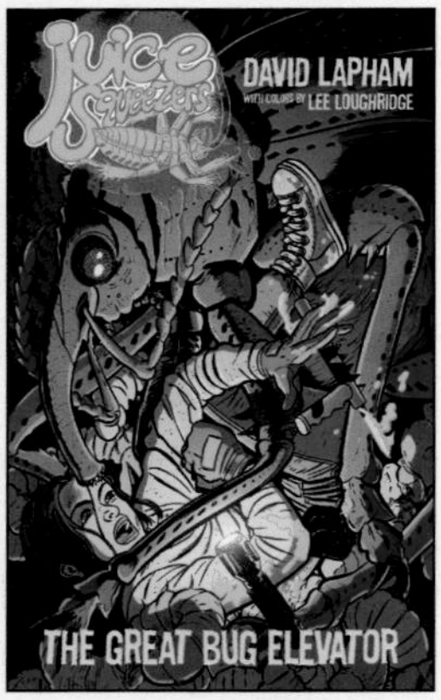
Juice Squeezers
DAVID LAPHAM
THE GREAT BUG ELEVATOR

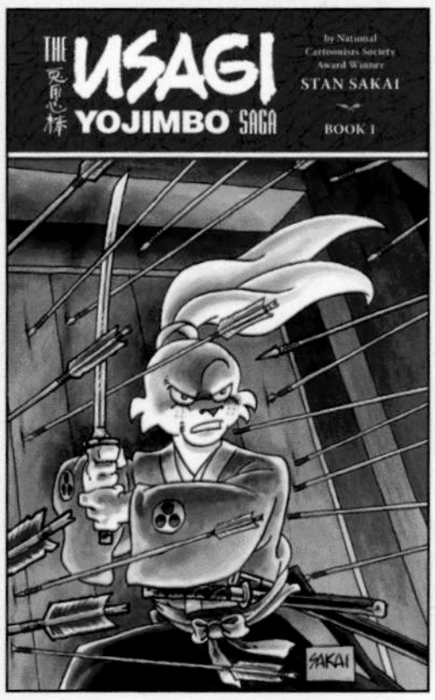
THE USAGI YOJIMBO SAGA
STAN SAKAI
BOOK 1

MORE YOUNG ADULT TITLES FROM

DARK HORSE BOOKS!

BEASTS OF BURDEN: ANIMAL RITES

Written by Evan Dorkin, illustrated by Jill Thompson

Beneath its surface of green lawns and white picket fences, the picturesque little town of Burden Hill harbors dark and sinister secrets. It's up to a heroic gang of dogs—and one cat—to protect the town from the evil forces at work. Adventure, mystery, horror, and humor thrive on every page!

978-1-59582-513-1 | $19.99

REXODUS

Written by James Farr, illustrated by Jon Sommariva

The Black Blood is unleashed upon the earth again, and Amber must save her father—and the world—with the aid of the only other Black Blood survivor, Kelvin Sauridian, a dinosaur from the past. In this high-stakes adventure, can they put aside their differences long enough to save the planet they both called home?

ISBN 978-1-61655-448-4 | $12.99

JUICE SQUEEZERS: THE GREAT BUG ELEVATOR

Written and illustrated by David Lapham

Tunnels made by a legion of giant bugs crisscross the fields below the quaint California town of Weeville, and only one thing can stop them from overrunning the place: the Juice Squeezers. A covert group of scrawny tweens, the Squeezers are the only ones who can fit into the cramped subterranean battlefield and fight the insects on the frontlines!

978-1-61655-438-5 | $12.99

THE USAGI YOJIMBO SAGA

Written and illustrated by Stan Sakai

Dark Horse proudly presents Miyamoto Usagi's epic trek along the warrior's path in a new series of deluxe compilations. The rabbit *ronin*'s adventures have won multiple awards and delighted readers for thirty years!

VOLUME 1: 978-1-61655-609-9 | $24.99
VOLUME 2: 978-1-61655-610-5 | $24.99

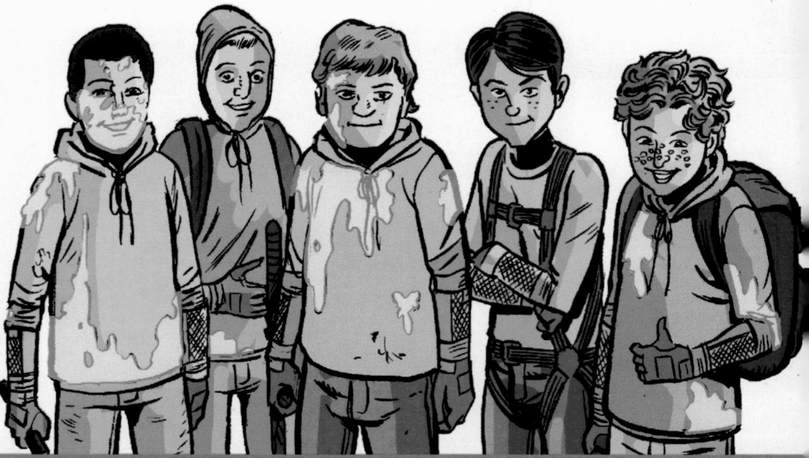